D0910079

## ALSO BY PHILIP FREEMAN

Julius Caesar

The Philosopher and the Druids: A Journey Among the Ancient
Celts

St. Patrick of Ireland: A Biography

War, Women, and Druids: Eyewitness Reports and Early
Accounts of the Ancient Celts

The Galatian Language: A Comprehensive Survey of the
Language of the Ancient Celts in Greco-Roman Asia Minor

Ireland and the Classical World

Lecture Notes: A Professor's Inside Guide to College Success

 Simon & Schuster
1230 Avenue of the Americas
New York, NY 10020

First Simon & Schuster hardcover edition January 2011

SIMON & SCHUSTER and colophon are registered trademarks of Simon & Schuster, Inc.

For information about special discounts for bulk purchases, please contact Simon & Schuster Special Sales at 1-866-506-1949 or business@simonandschuster.com.

The Simon & Schuster Speakers Bureau can bring authors to your live event. For more information or to book an event, contact the Simon & Schuster Speakers Bureau at 1-866-248-3049 or visit our website at www.simonspeakers.com.

Designed by Nancy Singer

Maps by Paul J. Pugliese

Manufactured in the United States of America

10   9   8   7   6   5   4   3   2   1

Library of Congress Cataloging-in-Publication Data

Freeman, Philip, 1961–
    Alexander the Great / Philip Freeman.—1st Simon & Schuster hardcover ed.
        p. cm.
    Includes bibliographical references and index.
    1. Alexander, the Great, 356–323 B.C.   2. Generals—Greece—Biography—Juvenile literature   3. Greece—Kings and rulers—Biography—Juvenile literature.   4. Greece—History—Macedonian Expansion, 359–323 B.C.—Juvenile literature.   I. Title.
    DF234.F74 2011
    938'.07092—dc22
    [B]
    2010027711

ISBN 978-1-4165-9280-8
ISBN 978-1-4391-9328-0 (ebook)

# ALEXANDER THE GREAT

## PHILIP FREEMAN

SIMON & SCHUSTER

NEW YORK   LONDON   TORONTO   SYDNEY

FOR MY STUDENTS

# CONTENTS

# TIMELINE

*All dates in this book are B.C. (B.C.E.) unless otherwise noted*

329    Alexander crosses the Hindu Kush, reaches the Oxus River,
       advances to Samarkand; defeat of Bessus
328    Murder of Cleitus the Black
327    Marriage to Roxane; pages conspiracy; Alexander invades India
326    Battle of the Hydaspes; death of Bucephalas; mutiny on the
       *Hyphasis*
325    Alexander reaches the sea; march through the Gedrosian
       desert; voyage of Nearchus and the fleet
324    Alexander returns to Persia; mass marriages at Susa; death
       of Hephaestion
323    Alexander returns to Babylon; death of Alexander in June

# MACEDONIAN KINGS

| | |
|---|---|
| Amyntas I | ?–c. 498 |
| Alexander I | c. 498–c. 454 |
| Perdiccas II | c. 454–413 |
| Archelaus | 413–399 |
| Orestes | 399–c. 398 |
| Aeropus II | c. 398–c. 395 |
| Amyntas II | 395–394 |
| Amyntas III | 393–c. 370 |
| Alexander II | c. 370–367 |
| Ptolemy | 367–365 |
| Perdiccas III | 365–359 |
| Philip II | 359–336 |
| Alexander the Great | 336–323 |

# PERSIAN KINGS

| | |
|---|---|
| Cyrus the Great | 559–530 |
| Cambyses II | 530–522 |
| Bardiya | 522 |
| Darius I | 522–486 |
| Xerxes I | 486–465 |
| Artaxerxes I | 465–424 |
| Xerxes II | 424 |
| Darius II | 424–404 |
| Artaxerxes II | 404–359 |
| Artaxerxes III | 359–338 |
| Artaxerxes IV | 338–336 |
| Darius III | 336–330 |

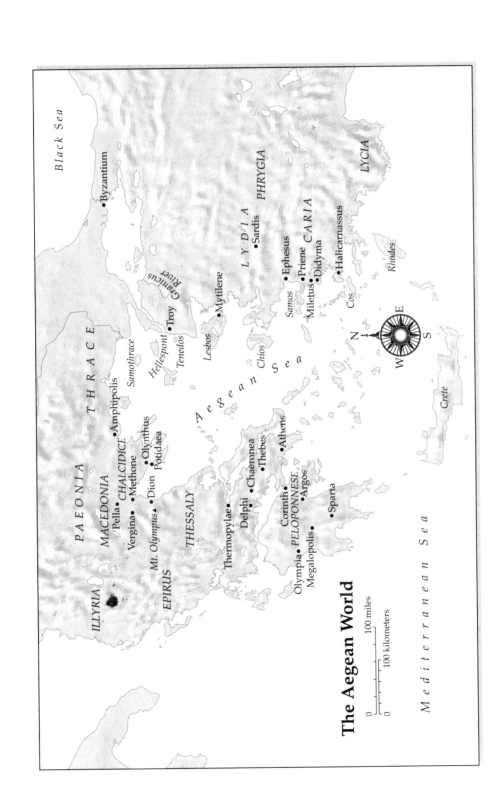

# The Aegean World

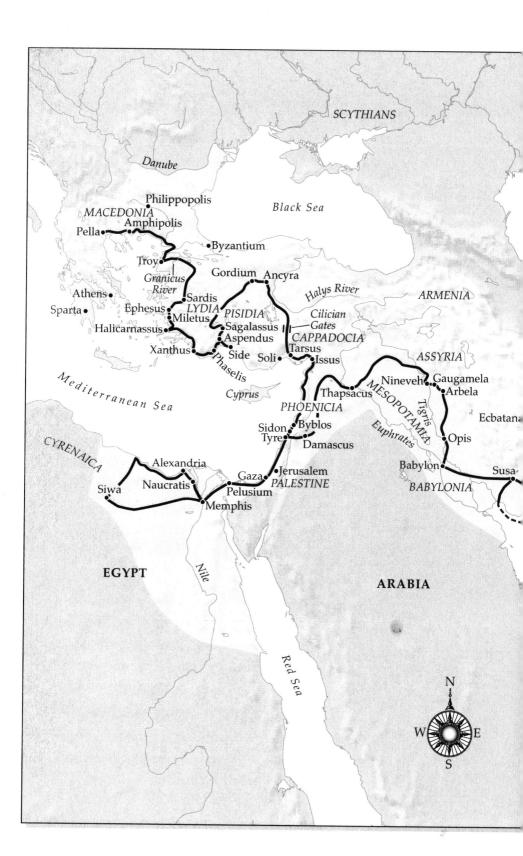

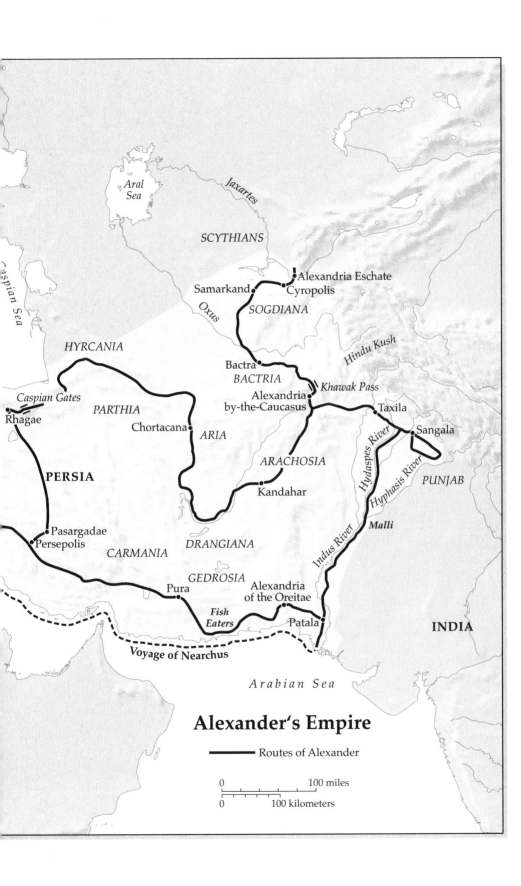

Aral
Sea

Jaxartes

SCYTHIANS

Alexandria Eschate
Samarkand
Cyropolis
SOGDIANA
Oxus

Caspian Sea

HYRCANIA

Hindu Kush

Bactra
BACTRIA
Alexandria
by-the-Caucasus
Khawak Pass
Caspian Gates
Rhagae
PARTHIA
Chortacana
ARIA
Taxila
Sangala

PERSIA

ARACHOSIA
PUNJAB

Hydaspes River
Hyphasis River

Kandahar

Pasargadae
Persepolis
CARMANIA
DRANGIANA

Malli

Indus River

GEDROSIA
Pura
Alexandria
of the Oreitae
Fish
Eaters
Patala

INDIA

Voyage of Nearchus

Arabian Sea

# Alexander's Empire

—— Routes of Alexander

0                    100 miles

0          100 kilometers

# ALEXANDER
## THE GREAT

# Author's Note and Acknowledgments

IF ANYONE IS SURPRISED THAT I HAVE WRITTEN
ON THIS SUBJECT EVEN THOUGH SO MANY
HISTORIANS BEFORE ME HAVE ALREADY DONE SO,
I WOULD ASK THEM TO LOOK AT ALL THE OTHER
BOOKS FIRST AND THEN READ MINE.
—ARRIAN

The ancient Greek historian Arrian believed that his biography of Alexander the Great was unique and surpassed all previous works on the life of the Macedonian king. I make no such claims for my book. There are hundreds of excellent studies available on all aspects of Alexander's life, along with several comprehensive academic biographies in print that surpass mine in detail and technical argument. Why then another book on Alexander? The answer is partially selfish. I grew up fascinated by this man, so I couldn't resist the opportunity to immerse myself in the ancient and modern sources on his life, to visit sites along his journey, and to imagine him racing his horse Bucephalas across the plains of Macedonia or crossing the deserts and mountains of Iran and Afghanistan. But most important, I wanted to write a biography of Alexander that is first and foremost a story. My hope is that this narrative is authoritative and yet accessible to those who love history but may never have read a book about Alexander's life and are not experts on the ancient world.

My search for Alexander was encouraged by many friends and helpers. My colleagues at Luther College have been wonderfully supportive as I researched and wrote the book. The patient counsel of Joëlle Delbourgo guided me through the world of publishing, while my editor Bob Bender, his assistant Johanna Li, and Philip Metcalf at Simon & Schuster saved me from countless mistakes. The libraries at Luther College, Bowdoin College, and Harvard University graciously helped me find the resources I needed. My local guides were most generous in sharing their knowledge as I followed Alexander's footsteps, especially Katikiotes Lazaros in Greece, Osama Iskander in Egypt, and Mine Karahan in Turkey. My wife, Alison, as always was my greatest helper and favorite photographer. Finally, to my students who cheerfully suffered through my ancient history courses and never complained when I made them read just one more book or visit one more museum, my eternal gratitude.

# 1

# MACEDONIA

ALEXANDER WAS BORN ON THE SIXTH DAY OF THE
MONTH CALLED HEKATOMBAION, THOUGH THE
MACEDONIANS CALL IT LOÖS. ON THE SAME DAY
THE TEMPLE OF ARTEMIS AT EPHESUS BURNED TO
THE GROUND.
—PLUTARCH

The solitary messenger rode east from the sanctuary of Zeus at Olympia through the hill country along the Alpheus River. Behind him crowds from all the cities of Greece were pouring out of the stadium after watching the unexpected finish to the horse race at the Olympic games. The rider followed the river until the road split into two paths several miles from town. One branch led south to the land of the Spartans, but his journey lay over the high mountains of Arcadia to the north. Trading for fresh horses and snatching a few hours of sleep whenever he could, the young man flew along steep valleys and beneath lofty peaks. The king awaiting his message would suffer no delays.

Soon the rider descended into the lush valley of Argos, legendary home of Hercules, then north beneath the ancient citadel of Mycenae, where Agamemnon ruled before he led the Greeks to conquer Troy. Onward through the port city of Corinth he raced, then over the narrow isthmus into the land of the Megarians. The road to nearby Athens veered to the east, but his path led ever northward through the city of Thebes, then along the narrow pass at Thermopylae, where over a century earlier three hundred Spartans had stood against the entire Persian army. Mile after mile across the rolling grasslands of Thessaly he rode until at last the towering mass of Mount Olympus rose before him. He skirted the eastern side of the peak through the beautiful Vale of Tempe and then down along the Aegean coast until at last he entered the fertile plains of Macedonia.

The horseman kept the shore to his right as he galloped past the temples at Dion, and into the broad lowlands of Macedonia ringed by mountains on the far horizon. The road to the royal tombs at Vergina lay to the west, but he turned east skirting the capital at Pella and crossed over the Axios River, riding many miles along the coast to the Chalcidice peninsula. Finally he reached the Macedonian army camp beneath the walls of the old Corinthian colony of Potidaea. In recent years the Athenians had taken over the town as part of their long struggle to control the rich timber and mineral resources of Macedonia, but the city was no longer in their hands. Just before the messenger arrived, Philip II, king of Macedonia, had captured the town.

The weary courier dismounted and entered Philip's tent. The triumphant king was only in his late twenties but well on his way to turning a weak and threatened kingdom on the northern edge of civilization into the mightiest state in the Greek world. Philip, in a jovial mood from his conquest of Potidaea and undoubtedly draining copious amounts of wine, according to Macedonian custom, welcomed the rider but ordered him to wait as another messenger had arrived just before him. This first man announced to the king that his favorite general, Parmenion, had defeated the wild Illyrian tribes in a great battle, securing the western borders of Philip's rapidly expanding kingdom. Then the rider from Olympia came forward and saluted Philip, proclaiming that the horse the king had sponsored in the Olympic games had won first prize. It was then that the king noticed a third messenger had entered the tent. This courier bowed and declared that Philip's wife, Olympias, had just given birth to a boy he would name Alexander.

The drunken revelry at the court of the king that night must have been unprecedented even by Macedonian standards. But soon Philip issued a decree to honor the good news he valued above all others—he commanded a special silver coin be struck to celebrate the victory of his horse.

Alexander, son of Philip, was born in the year of the 106th Olympic games, during the leadership of Elpines at Athens, in the third year of the rule of Artaxerxes III, Great King of Persia—or by our reckoning July of the year 356 B.C. Every Greek state had its own calendar based on local festivals. In Athens, the new year had just begun with the rising of the first new moon after the summer solstice and the sacrifice of a hundred animals to the gods. Hundreds of miles north in Macedonia the month bore a different name, but the coastal plains still baked in the summer heat. In winter, when the Athenians enjoyed a mild Mediterranean climate, the Macedonians shivered against the north wind.

The homeland of Alexander lay cut off from Greece by the mountain wall of Olympus and surrounding peaks. Indeed, most Greeks were quite happy with the separation since they considered the Macedonians little more than barbarians. The mountains and plains of the Macedonian north were as foreign to the cultured Greeks of the south as the steppes of Scythia or the dark forests of the Celts.

Viewed from above, the land of Macedonia is a great bowl tipping into the Aegean Sea. On its south, west, and north are towering mountains drained by rivers flowing through plains rich in grains and pasturage. Mount Olympus, almost ten thousand feet in height, dominates the view of the south. To the west and north are mountains almost as high, stretching like a horseshoe from Olympus to beyond the Axios River. To the east the great three-fingered peninsula of Chalcidice reaches into the sea.

But ancient Macedonia was surrounded by more than just difficult mountains. The famed horse warriors of Thessaly to the south cut off Philip's kingdom from Greece, while to the west the powerful tribes of Illyria were a constant threat. From the north the Paeonians and Agrianians staged devastating raids from the highlands they shared with mountain lions, bears, and wild auroch cattle. To the east along the road to Byzantium beyond the Strymon River was the savage land of Thrace, where tattooed warriors crafted intricate gold jewelry and regarded plundering as the only honorable means of living.

Macedonia itself was divided into two vastly different regions. The mountains of the south, west, and north were the traditional home of fiercely independent pastoralists whose lives revolved around the sheep and goats they raised for meat, milk, and wool. During the summer the highland Macedonians grazed their flocks in the mountain pastures high above the plains, but in the cold winter months they were forced to bring their animals down to the coastal lowlands. In this area lived the Macedonian farmers, who raised crops and tended vineyards. Thus the highlanders by necessity had learned to live alongside their lowland cousins for part of the year, giving them a share of their flocks and fertilizing their fields with animal manure in payment.

But it was the mountain Macedonians—from the upland regions of Pelagonia, Lyncestis, Orestis, Elimiotis, and Pieria around Mount Olympus—who for countless generations had fought against the wolves, bears, and human predators that threatened their flocks. Their whole life was a constant war to keep their animals alive in a harsh and rugged land. For the highlanders, the tribe was everything and everything depended in turn on the bravery, cunning, and diplomacy of their chiefs. If Illyrian raiders stole a tribe's best rams by night, the chief immediately led his men in a counterstrike to seize the animals and mercilessly kill the thieves. If lowland farmers threatened to withdraw age-old privileges of winter pasturage, the highland chief would invite them to a splendid feast, flatter them endlessly with tales of their grandfather's generosity, and shamelessly bribe their leaders with promises of fat ewes and warm woolen cloaks. The highland lords were kings of the Macedonian world. The Greeks far to the south might talk of democracy and debate laws in their assemblies, but in the cold northern mountains the Macedonians had for ages lived and died at the word of their chiefs.

The plains of Macedonia were rich in barley and wheat, but the highlands held the resources most coveted by the Greeks. Cities such as Athens had long ago stripped their own hills of timber as their populations grew, but the mountains of Macedonia were still covered with towering forests of pine and oak needed for ships of war and trade. Beneath these forests, especially in the eastern Macedonian mountains, were iron, silver, and gold.

Though the pastoral Macedonians of the mountains differed from the lowland farmers in many ways, they shared a common language that defined them as a single people—and separated them from the Greeks to the south. The Macedonian tongue was so far removed from the Greek of Athens or Sparta that it may as well have been a different language entirely. Years after his birth, when Alexander was in central Asia, he grew so angry at a drinking party one night that he switched from his usual Greek speech to yell at his guards in Macedonian. Later still his soldiers mocked an officer on trial for addressing them in Greek rather than the normal Macedonian of the ranks. Macedonians were known for their odd words and strange pronunciation—they could never quite get Greek sounds right even when they tried. Though their kings bore ancient Greek names, the Macedonian people called Philip *Bilippos* instead of the normal Greek *Philippos*. This only served to make them an object of further scorn to their pretentious critics in the Athenian assembly. Language, as well as politics, culture, and so much else, reinforced the opinion of the Greeks that the Macedonians were a separate people, barbarians from beyond Olympus, no matter how hard their kings might try to behave like Greeks. And to most Macedonians, this was just fine. They saw the Greeks as feeble, effeminate, self-important snobs who had long since squandered whatever manliness and courage they had possessed when they had driven back the Persian invaders more than a century earlier. The Macedonian nobility might study Greek philosophy and recite the poetry of Homer, but the common Macedonian soldier was proud not to be Greek.

Alexander was born into a family that traced its royal roots back to the great hero Hercules—at least that was the story the family told visitors to its court. According to the Greek historian Herodotus, who journeyed to Macedonia a century before Alexander and collected every scrap of gossip he could find on the kingdom, the Macedonian royal family began when a Greek refugee named Perdiccas arrived from Argos in southern Greece. A descendant of Temenus of the family of Hercules, Perdiccas was banished from Argos along with his two older brothers. The brothers eventually made their way north to Macedonia. In the mountains of the west they found refuge with a local chieftain and his kindly wife. Times were hard for everyone, so young Perdiccas and his brothers labored as simple farmhands to earn their keep. One day the wife noticed that the loaves she baked every day for Perdiccas grew to twice the size of the others. When she told her husband, the chieftain feared this was an ill omen and ordered the brothers to depart at once. The brothers demanded their wages, but the flustered chief shouted that all they would receive was the ray of sunlight shining into the room. The two older brothers were ready to fight, but young Perdiccas took his knife and calmly traced the outline of the sunbeam on the dirt floor and said they would accept the chief's offer. He then gathered the sunlight three times onto his tattered garment and left with his brothers. The chief soon realized Perdiccas had performed some sort of magic spell that threatened his own rule and sent warriors to kill the brothers. But a nearby river miraculously rose, cutting off the soldiers and allowing Perdiccas and his brothers to escape to the hills of Pieria north of Mount Olympus. There at a place known as the Gardens of Midas, where young Alexander would one day be tutored by Aristotle, the brothers from Argos established a kingdom that in time spread down from the highlands to the rich farmland along the coast.

This story was told to Herodotus six generations after Perdiccas by King Alexander I, the direct ancestor of Alexander the Great. The elder Alexander began his rule during the Persian Wars against Greece during the early fifth century and, after the victories of Athens and Sparta against Persia, was eager to connect his royal family to the winning side. Thus the foundation story of Macedonia should be taken with a large grain of salt, though it is possible to see a glimmer of history beneath the fairy tale. The divine Greek origins of the Macedonian royal family are fanciful, but the gradual spread of a local highland tribe from the hills near Mount Olympus to the coastal plains beyond the city of Vergina is quite plausible. The takeover of nearby winter grazing lands by a warlike tribe from the highlands would have provided a strong nucleus for a future Macedonian kingdom.

Whatever truth was in the tale, Alexander I was not about to let Herodotus continue on his travels without a few more stories to prove his undying love for the Greeks. According to Alexander, when the Persians invaded nearby Thrace, they sent envoys to the court of his father, Amyntas, requiring him to submit to the Great King by the symbolic act of giving him earth and water. Old Amyntas was terrified and agreed, even inviting them to a feast that evening. During dinner the Persian ambassadors began shamelessly to fondle the wives and daughters of the royal family who were present, but the old king was too afraid to object. Young Alexander was beside himself with anger, though he remained outwardly composed and merely suggested that his father retire for the evening. After the king was gone, his son declared to the Persians that they were most welcome to the company of the Macedonian women for whatever pleasure they might desire. But, with a wink, he suggested the women be allowed to withdraw for a few minutes to freshen up before the orgy began. The eager Persians gladly consented, but while the women were gone Alexander substituted his own warriors, veiled and dressed in women's clothing, to sit beside the visitors. At his signal, just as the Persians were beginning to untie their garments, the disguised warriors pulled out daggers and cut the Persians' throats. Macedonian men might treat their women as chattel, but woe to any foreigner who touched them.

And yet, if this story is true, it is remarkable that just a few years later the elder Alexander, now king, gave his own sister to a high-ranking Persian official in marriage and was considered a loyal ally of the Great King. He was even chosen as Persian ambassador to Athens to plead for the city's submission and fought with his Macedonian troops against the Greeks during the final battle at Plataea in 479—though he claimed secretly to have given the Greeks the

Persian plan of attack on the eve of battle. If the Greeks were later willing to forget about the duplicity of the elder Alexander and even honor him as a friend of the Greeks, it can only be that they needed his timber and mineral resources more than they wanted revenge for his treachery.

Alexander I was a master diplomat who played all sides against one another to expand his kingdom. He was a faithful subject of the Persian Empire when it suited him and a Greek patriot when the Great King turned his back. After Alexander was assassinated—a frequent event in Macedonian royal history—his son Perdiccas II continued his father's policies of international intrigue during the Peloponnesian War between Athens and Sparta. Perdiccas changed sides so many times during the conflict that the Macedonians couldn't keep track of who they were backing during any given year.

Perdiccas was murdered by his illegitimate son Archelaus who—amid the swirl of treachery, violence, and vicious love triangles, heterosexual and homosexual, that were part of everyday life in the Macedonian court—took the throne and began an intensive program of Hellenization. Earlier kings had long encouraged Greek culture among the nobility, but Archelaus made it a top priority. Though the common people scoffed and continued to live as they had for centuries, the Macedonian court under the new king became a center for Greek artists and scholars. Among the many intellectuals wooed to the palace with lavish gifts was the Athenian playwright Euripides, who visited in his waning years and wrote the *Bacchae* there—a wild tale of sex, murder, and insanity that surely owes its inspiration to life among the Macedonian nobility.

In 399, the same year Socrates was forced to drink hemlock in Athens, Archelaus was murdered during a hunting expedition by his friend and lover Craterus. Macedonia was soon plunged into bloody dynastic struggles and debilitating frontier wars. Kings quickly rose and fell, sometimes several in a single year, until at last Amyntas III, grandfather of Alexander the Great, clawed his way to the top and seized the throne in 393. His long reign, however, brought little stability to the kingdom and palace intrigues raged unchecked, including an unsuccessful plot by his wife, Eurydice, and her young paramour to murder him. When Amyntas died, surprisingly of old age, in 370, his son Alexander II succeeded him, only to be murdered by his cousin Ptolemy the following year. Ptolemy in turn was slain by Perdiccas III two years later. Perdiccas himself soon died fighting against the resurgent Illyrians, leaving the last surviving son of Amyntas to take the deeply troubled throne. The untested young man faced an almost hopeless situation. Macedonia was in chaos with the nobility pitted against each other in civil war, barbarians invading on all sides, and the Greeks, especially the Athenians, working tirelessly to weaken, divide, and dominate the beleaguered kingdom. No one believed the new king, Philip, stood any chance of saving Macedonia.

Years later in Asia, Alexander and his men were feasting one night after their hard-won victories. As the wine flowed freely, some of Alexander's dinner companions began to belittle the achievements of his father, Philip. Alexander joined in, boasting that his own victories from the Danube to the borders of India rivaled those of the god Hercules and were not to be compared with the petty conquests of his father. It was then that one of Philip's old generals rose and called the drunken king an ungrateful lout. You would be nothing, he declared, without the achievements of your father—a far greater man than you will ever be.

Alexander personally ran the man through with a spear for his insolence, though he knew there was truth in the soldier's final words. History has been so fascinated with Alexander the Great that it has overlooked the genius of his father. But by his supreme skill at diplomacy, his mastery of intrigue, and his revolutionary innovations in warfare, Philip laid the foundation for everything his son achieved.

Yet when young Philip came to the Macedonian throne after the death of his brother, few would have wagered the new ruler or his kingdom would survive. At first glance Philip was a typical Macedonian nobleman—fiery in temperament, excessive in drink, and exceedingly fond of war, horses, beautiful women, and handsome young boys. But he possessed a keen understanding of the hearts of men and a boundless vision for Macedonia.

Philip also knew exactly how he could change Macedonia's dismal fortunes. When he was only fifteen, he had been sent as a hostage to the Greek city of Thebes by his brother the king. The ancient city of Thebes had lacked the influence of Athens and Sparta, but at the beginning of the fourth century it had taken advantage of the power vacuum created by the end of the Peloponnesian War to build its army into the most powerful force in Greece. In 371, the Thebans crushed Sparta's finest warriors at the battle of Leuctra and ended forever the myth of Spartan invulnerability. The Macedonians immediately negotiated an alliance with Thebes and sent hostages to guarantee their good intentions. If Macedonia behaved itself, the hostages would be treated as honored guests. If not, they would be tortured and killed.

Philip was fortunate to be assigned to the household of the Theban general Pammenes, who was a great friend of Epaminondas, the victor of Leuctra. While the other Macedonian hostages feasted and chased local girls, Philip spent every moment learning the latest techniques in warfare from the Theban generals. The Macedonian army before Philip's time consisted of a peasant infantry led by undisciplined nobles on horseback. Like their counterparts in the Middle Ages, these Macedonian knights saw themselves as the epitome of heroic warfare and treated the lowly farmers and shepherds in the infantry as so much fodder for enemy spears. But Philip discovered a very different kind of army at Thebes.

The Thebans had perfected the art of hoplite warfare. Each hoplite was a proud citizen who could afford to equip himself with a bronze helmet, a thick breastplate, greaves to protect the legs, and an iron-tipped spear eight to ten feet long used for thrusting, not throwing. In addition, each man carried a razor-sharp iron sword and heavy shield (*hoplon*) almost three feet wide on the left arm. As each hoplite was unshielded on his right side, he relied on the man next to him for protection, encouraging by necessity a strong sense of unity in battle. When a hoplite line advanced shoulder to shoulder against the enemy, it was a wall of death.

The Theban hoplites drilled endlessly and, whether common soldier or wealthy cavalryman, were ruled by iron discipline. The very best of the Theban warriors were chosen for membership in the Sacred Band, an elite corps of infantry consisting of 150 pairs of male lovers funded by the state. As lovers, the soldiers fought all the more furiously to protect and impress their partners. They had been crucial in the defeat of the Spartans at Leuctra and were the finest soldiers Greece had ever produced.

Philip also watched and learned from the democratic assembly at Thebes. He saw the grave weakness of a system in which every man could voice his opinion and vote. Debates in the assembly were endless, while political parties worked to destroy the power of their rivals. Philip began to see how an old-fashioned monarchy like Macedonia could act much more decisively than a Greek city and be unstoppable on the battlefield—if it were ruled by the right king.

After three years in Thebes, Philip returned to Macedonia when his brother Perdiccas slew their cousin Ptolemy and took the throne. When Perdiccas marched off to fight the Illyrians a few years later, Philip was left in charge as regent. A few weeks later, Perdiccas and four thousand Macedonian soldiers lay dead on the battlefield. Now Bardylis, king of Illyria, was poised to strike at the Macedonian heartland while the Paeonians on the northern border were already taking advantage of the chaos by raiding deep into Macedonia. In addition to external troubles, at least five other Macedonian nobles were vying for the throne. The Thracians backed one of these candidates, the Athenians another, while each of Philip's three half brothers also plotted to become king.

Philip quickly arrested and executed one brother, forced the other two into exile, then bribed the Thracians to murder their favorite. Finally he struck a secret deal with the Athenians to withdraw support from their candidate, Argaeus, who soon found himself marching against Philip with only the few mercenaries he had hired with his own funds. Philip easily defeated him and made a great show of sending home unharmed the Athenians among the mercenaries. By the autumn of 359, Philip was ensconced as king of Macedonia, but his hold on the throne was tenuous at best. Illyrians, Paeonians, Thracians, Athenians, and especially other Macedonian nobles were waiting for their chance to dispose of this clever young ruler.

Philip began that winter to build the army he had dreamed of in Thebes. Discipline came first. Troops were drilled until they could execute complex battlefield maneuvers in their sleep. Philip marched them countless miles over the mountains with full packs until they were ready to drop from exhaustion. Officers who had previously thought themselves above petty military rules soon learned otherwise. One nobleman lost his command for taking a bath in camp, another was publicly whipped for drinking a cup of water before he had been dismissed. But during that cold winter Philip's reforms slowly began to take hold as the men and officers took pride in their newfound abilities.

Philip knew, however, that discipline and esprit de corps would not be enough against either wild barbarians or Greek hoplites. He needed a radically new kind of army if he was to defeat hordes of screaming Illyrians or the spit-and-polish professionals of the Sacred Band. He knew his troops stood little chance in traditional warfare, especially against hoplites. The hoplites' heavy armor was far too expensive for Macedonian farmers and goatherds—so Philip decided to change the rules. The troops of his new army would wear almost no armor and carry only a small shield, so that even the poorest young man from the hills of Macedonia could qualify for military service. This increased his pool of potential soldiers far above that of any Greek city. But how could such lightly armed peasants hope to stand against the fearsome hoplites? The answer lay in a brilliant innovation developed by Philip—the *sarissa*. Standard hoplite spears were eight to ten feet in length, but the sarissa was almost eighteen feet long. This allowed the Macedonian infantry to march in close formation with overlapping sarissas lowered in front of them to skewer hoplites before the enemy spears could reach them. Of course, the effectiveness of the sarissa depended on the disciplined Macedonians acting as a unit. If even one infantryman swung his sarissa too far to the left or right, the whole line would become hopelessly tangled. But control of the sarissa was made possible by the elimination of heavy armor and weapons so that Macedonian foot soldiers, unlike their Greek or barbarian counterparts, could use both hands to hold and thrust their spears to deadly effect. The Macedonians drilled to such perfection with their long spears that soon they could turn together in any direction, open and close a line in an instant, and charge the enemy with frightening speed. The sarissa was made to destroy hoplites, but the deadly formation would work equally well on barbarian warriors charging the Macedonian lines.

Along with the development of a new kind of infantry, Philip reformed the cavalry to act in coordinated units with his foot soldiers. No longer would Macedonian nobles ride forth on their own in search of glory. In Philip's army, the cavalry worked closely with the infantry, waiting for the sarissas to open a wide enough gap in the enemy line for the cavalry to ride through and strike at the undefended rear. Philip also was one of the first generals in history to create a highly trained corps of engineers. In time these men would be able to span raging rivers, cut roads across soaring mountains, and take any city by siege with awesome new engines of war.

But as impressive as Philip's innovations were on the training field, no one knew whether they could bring victory in battle. The first great test came the next year when the young Macedonian king launched an attack on the Illyrians led by Bardylis, the very man responsible for his brother's death two years before. Details of the battle are sketchy, but we know Philip brought with him at least ten thousand soldiers—almost every man of fighting age in Macedonia. Philip was determined to secure his western border and prove his worth as a general. It was a tremendous gamble, for if he had been defeated not only would his reign have come to an end but Macedonia itself would have been fatally weakened and carved up by its neighbors.

Even though Bardylis brought almost as many men to the field, he was hesitant when he saw the force before him and sent Philip a message offering a truce—but the Macedonian king would have none of it. He personally led his infantry forward against the Illyrians, though instead of striking their front line head-on, he employed

a seemingly odd strategy of hitting the enemy with an angled formation. This meant the Macedonian front line struck the Illyrian troops
on their left, while the right side of the Illyrian line watched. The
Illyrian commanders tried to keep their right side in position, but
the men were naturally drawn to the left to engage the enemy and
protect themselves. It was exactly what Philip was counting on. As
the Illyrians' right slowly bent forward, a gap opened in the center of
their line—and in rode Philip's cavalry. The Macedonian horsemen
successfully concentrated all their effort on breaking through to the
rear of the Illyrian forces and throwing the enemy into chaos. The
battle raged for hours, but eventually the Illyrians were completely
surrounded and thousands were slaughtered on the battlefield. It was
an inspired and innovative strategy that Philip would refine and use
with devastating effect in future battles, as would his son Alexander.

Bardylis sued for peace and Philip, having made his point, graciously accepted. The Illyrian leader agreed to withdraw from all the
territories of western Macedonia that he had previously occupied. To
sweeten the deal, he offered Philip his daughter Audata in marriage.
As was the case elsewhere in the ancient world, marriage was used
in the Balkans to guarantee treaties and seal alliances. Love was ir-
relevant in such political unions. The woman's task was to bind two
kingdoms together, produce children, and serve as a hostage for her
country's good behavior. The wife expected no affection aside from
that needed to sire a child, preferably a son. If her husband took other
wives, concubines, or boys to bed, this was no concern of hers. All that
mattered to the bride in such political marriages was that her status
as a queen was respected and that any son she produced was granted
his proper place in line for the throne.

Philip took to marriage alliances with a gusto unusual even for
a Macedonian king and was notorious in antiquity for adding a new
wife whenever he went to war. By the time of his death, he had married seven brides. After Audata died giving birth to a daughter, he
married Phila from the southern mountain region of Elimeia as part
of his grand strategy to bind the highland tribes of Macedonia more
closely to him. She too died soon after, leaving the twenty-five-year-

old Philip without a queen and, more important, without a male heir. He quickly married two women from Thessaly to strengthen relations with the kingdom on his southern border. The first Thessalian bride eventually bore him a daughter, named Thessalonica, for whom a great city would be named. The second at last gave Philip a son in the year 357. The proud father named him Arrhidaeus—but it soon became clear that the boy was mentally handicapped and unfit to inherit the throne. The eldest son of Philip was quietly put away and rarely appeared in public for the next thirty years.

It was then the king looked to the kingdom of Epirus (roughly modern Albania) on the Adriatic coast just south of Illyria and north of Greece. Epirus had long suffered Illyrian raids, so an alliance with Macedonia to contain their mutual enemy was beneficial to both. The security of Philip's southwest border was also paramount, as was maintaining trade routes between the Adriatic and Macedonia. The head of the royal house of Epirus, Arybbas, had no daughters available and had already married his eldest niece himself, but his younger niece was still unmarried. Her name was Olympias.

As Plutarch tells the story, Philip and Olympias had met several years earlier on the island of Samothrace: "It is said that while still a young man, Philip was initiated into the sacred rites at Samothrace at the same time as Olympias, who was an orphan. They fell in love and pledged to marry, with the consent of her uncle Arybbas."

The occasion and setting of this meeting is so strange it may be true, though Plutarch's seemingly random encounter of two young lovers was likely based more on politics than romance.

Samothrace is a small, mountainous island in the northern Aegean lying between Macedonia and Troy. Its one claim to fame was a religious center on the northern coast dedicated to twin gods known as the Cabiri, who, along with powerful goddesses worshiped at the site, protected travelers, promoted fertility, and promised immortality to initiates. The Macedonians had recently taken an interest in Samothrace and had contributed generously to the temple, perhaps from genuine religious motivation or more likely from a desire to integrate themselves into an ancient Greek cult. That young Philip chose to be initiated into the local religion is no surprise, given his crafty use of diplomacy, spiritual and otherwise, to build alliances and strengthen his ties to the Greek world. But why would an Epiriote princess and her uncle the king just happen to be on a remote island far from home during the same summer festival as a royal Macedonian prince? It seems that Arybbas was very deliberately arranging a meeting between his niece and the young Philip in hopes of laying the groundwork for a future alliance between the kingdoms. Philip himself may well have been in on the plan before he arrived on Samothrace and it is probable that he was more interested in practical discussions with Arybbas about countering the Illyrian threat than gazing into the eyes of the teenage Olympias. Still, he may have liked what he saw in the young woman—beauty, intelligence, passion—all qualities appealing to an up-and-coming prince with hopes of producing a son worthy of his throne. In addition, her family claimed descent from Achilles, the greatest of the Greeks to fight at Troy. To mingle the blood of his own ancestor Hercules with that of Achilles must have been a powerful incentive to the union.

Olympias was no more than eighteen when she married Philip, but she was an experienced hand at palace intrigue and rivalries. In Epirus, however, she had at least been among family and friends, but in the Macedonian capital of Pella she was alone. On her wedding night she was led veiled into the bridal chamber, after which Philip entered and shut the door. As she fulfilled her most important duty as a wife for the first time, a chorus of maidens stood outside the doors and sang hymns to the goddess of fertility.

Later stories say that on the night before the wedding as she lay sleeping a peal of thunder crashed around the palace and a lightning bolt shot into her room, striking her womb without harming her. The legends also say that Philip soon dreamed he was putting a seal with the figure of a lion on his wife's womb, which the prophet Aristander of Telmessus interpreted as a sign that Olympias was already pregnant with a son who would be bold and lionlike. Such stories of miraculous conceptions and divine parentage were common for heroes in the ancient world, but if Philip had any doubts that Olympias was a virgin when he took her to bed that first night, she would have been sent back to her uncle in disgrace.

During those first few weeks of married life together Philip must have devoted himself wholeheartedly to siring a son with Olympias. He would soon be away on campaign for long stretches of time with no opportunity for conjugal visits. Philip was a vigorous young man well known for his sexual appetites, so his young bride from Epirus received his frequent attention. But, according to Plutarch, late one night during those first few weeks of marriage Philip arrived at the bedroom of Olympias fully up to the task before him when he saw his wife sleeping next to an enormous snake. He had known Olympias was particularly devoted to exotic forms of worship common to women from her mountain homeland. He did not object to such sacred activities, many of which involved snakes, as long as they were conducted discreetly, but he was deeply disturbed that she brought serpents into her bed for private ecstatic rituals. Fearful that she might place a spell on him or that he might offend some divinity, he withdrew quietly and thereafter made only rare visits to her bedchamber.

We can be certain that whether the job was done by Philip or one of the gods—as Olympias would later claim—she was soon pregnant. Nine months later, in the hot Macedonian summer of 356, while Philip was conquering the town of Potidaea and awaiting news of his horse at the Olympic games, his wife gave birth to a son. Again, as with many ancient heroes, stories were repeated in later years of extraordinary events surrounding the birth of Alexander. It was said that the great temple of the goddess Artemis at Ephesus on the western coast of Asia Minor burned to the ground while the distracted goddess was busy in Macedonia attending the birth of the new prince. The Persian priests known as Magi who were resident in Ephesus reportedly ran madly about the ruins of the temple beating their faces and declaring that one who would bring calamity on Asia had been born that day. Other writers more soberly pointed out that the highly flammable temple had burned down repeatedly in the past and on this occasion had been set ablaze by a mentally disturbed man.

Alexander's boyhood at Pella was typical of any young Macedonian noble. He lived in his mother's quarters in the palace and, with Philip often fighting on the borders over the years, he seldom saw his father. As was normal in royal households, Olympias turned over the day-to-day affairs of child rearing to a matron from a distinguished family. Alexander's nurse was a woman named Lanice whose brother, known as Black Cleitus, would one day save Alexander's life. But throughout his early years his mother was never far from his side and took a passionate interest in her son's welfare. She was determined that he would keep his rightful place as Philip's heir at all costs and worked tirelessly to that end. Mother and son were close from the beginning and remained so throughout Alexander's life, sometimes to his exasperation.

Alexander did not, however, grow up a spoiled and pampered prince. From almost the day he could walk he began his training in war. Philip's most skilled veterans drilled him in archery, swordplay, and especially horsemanship. Few days passed when Alexander did not mount a favorite horse and tear across the Macedonian plains. His first tutor was a crusty old tyrant named Leonidas, who had all the charm and subtlety of his namesake, the indomitable Spartan king who had fought against the Persians at Thermopylae. Leonidas was a kinsman of Olympias from Epirus, but he showed no favoritism to his young charge. As Alexander said in later years, Leonidas' idea of breakfast was a forced march through the night, and of supper, a light breakfast. His tutor also used to rummage through his chests to make sure his mother hadn't hidden away any luxuries for her son. He was so parsimonious that one day when Alexander took a whole handful of incense to throw on the altar fire, Leonidas rebuked the boy, saying that once he had conquered the spice markets of Asia he could waste good incense but not before. (Years later, when Alexander had taken the entire Near East, he sent his aged tutor an enormous shipment of frankincense and myrrh with a note saying he could now stop being so miserly to the gods.) Yet Alexander loved his cantankerous teacher and thought of him as a second father.

Other tutors taught the precocious Alexander the arts of reading and writing so that from an early age he learned to love Greek literature, especially the poetry of Homer. One of Alexander's earliest childhood games must have been fighting with his friends as Greeks and Trojans beneath the walls of an imagined Troy. The prince also showed an unusual talent for music and became an accomplished lyre player. His other favorite tutor in these early years was a coarse but lighthearted Greek named Lysimachus, who was better known for his sense of humor than personal hygiene. He nicknamed Alexander "Achilles" and called himself Phoenix after the ancient hero's own tutor. Lysimachus would later accompany Alexander to Asia and provoke one of the most dramatic episodes in the young king's life.

One of the earliest stories about Alexander tells how when Philip was away on campaign yet again, the young prince, perhaps seven or eight years old, met ambassadors from the Great King of Persia who had come to the Macedonian court. Alexander was gracious and charming to the guests, winning their respect by not asking after trivial matters but inquiring into the length and conditions of Persian roads, how far it was to the Persian capital, what kind of man the Great King was, and what sort of army he possessed.

We can't be certain, but it is likely that these envoys arrived at Pella to invite three celebrated Persian exiles to return home in safety. One of these men was Artabazus, an important Persian leader who had been involved in a revolt by fellow satraps against the king a few years earlier. His son-in-law, Memnon, a Greek from the island of Rhodes, was another of the exiles, along with an Egyptian named Menapis. They had come to Macedonia seeking a safe haven to weather the turmoil of the Persian court. These men would have been a treasure trove of information about Persia for the young Alexander, and it is not difficult to imagine the boy learning everything possible about the great empire to the east from them during their time at Pella. Even at this early age, he dreamed of kingdoms to vanquish. He often complained to his friends that Philip's success in war weighed heavily on him: "Boys, my father is beating me to everything! He's leaving me no worlds to conquer."

Philip's rapid expansion of the Macedonian kingdom was nothing short of astonishing. In the year before Alexander's birth, he had taken the old Athenian outpost of Amphipolis across the Strymon

River on the border with Thrace. With the city largely undamaged and the grateful inhabitants unharmed, this strategic gateway to the east became a crucial garrison town and commercial center controlling the timber and mineral resources of the whole Strymon valley. The same year Philip took the Athenian fortress at Pydna on the Macedonia coast, just a day's march from Vergina, though the nearby outpost at Methone remained in Athenian hands. The next year his army again struck to the east, capturing the Thracian town of Crenides near Amphipolis. The Thracian king Cetriporis was furious at losing the city, especially as the vast riches from the nearby gold mines fell into Philip's hands. Never modest, Philip now did something unprecedented in the Greek world and named the town after himself. From that day forward until Saint Paul visited in Roman times and founded the first Christian church in Europe on the site, the old Thracian town was known as Philippi.

With the revenues from the mines above Amphipolis and Philippi, the young Macedonian king was able to enlarge his army and equip it with the finest weapons and horses. With these new resources Philip laid siege to Methone in 354 in a final attempt to drive the Athenians from the Macedonian heartland. It was a furious fight, but in the end Philip took the town. The price he paid was the loss of an eye. Whether this was just an unlucky blow or the divine consequences of gazing on Olympias in bed with her serpentine lover, as was later claimed, Philip remained blind in one eye the rest of his life.

Undeterred by his infirmity, Philip began to extend his influence south into Thessaly at first by alliances, then by seizing the key port of Pagasae. His incorporation of large numbers of the renowned Thessalian cavalry into his army became a central component of his military power, as it would be for Alexander. Next, Philip again invaded the Chalcidice peninsula in 349 and attacked the city of Olynthus. This well-protected settlement had long been the center of commercial activity in the area and had served as the capital of the Chalcidic Confederacy against Sparta, then against Athens. The city had been on friendly terms with Macedonia, but when Philip took Amphipolis the citizens had seen the writing on the wall and allied themselves with Athens for protection. The Athenians promised assistance, but somehow the Athenian assembly could never quite agree on what should be done. As the noose tightened on Olynthus, the Athenians debated and delayed until at last Philip had the city surrounded. The king battered the walls and rained arrows down on the defenders, many with bronze tips inscribed with Philip's name. When he at last took the town, Philip was uncharacteristically harsh. He sacked the city, leveled the site, and sold the survivors into slavery. By the devastation of Olynthus, Philip was sending a message to the Greeks—he could be merciful, but if opposed, he could also be ruthless.

The famed Athenian orator Demosthenes—who, according to legend, had overcome a childhood speech impediment by talking loudly with pebbles in his mouth—was one of the first Greeks to realize that Philip posed a deadly threat to the ancient cities of Greece. He saw Philip's conquests in the north as so many stepping-stones to Athens. He tried with all his might to rally his fellow citizens to stand up to the Macedonian king before it was too late:

> Have any of you been paying attention to Philip's progress? Have you seen how he has risen from weakness to strength? First he takes Amphipolis, then Pydna, not to mention Potidaea. After that comes Methone and Thessaly . . . Then he invades Thrace, removing their chieftains and replacing them with his own men . . . Finally he seizes Olynthus—and I won't even mention his campaigns in Illyria and Paeonia!

Although his oratorical skills were unsurpassed, Demosthenes was unable to motivate the apathetic Athenians to offer more than token resistance to Philip and his Macedonian army. Most Greeks were simply unwilling to believe that barbarians from beyond Mount Olympus posed any serious threat to their way of life. The embassy the Athenians sent to Pella was easily charmed by the lyre playing of ten-year-old Alexander, then bribed by Philip to make peace and look the other way while he swallowed up more Greek territory.

But Philip's greatest opportunity for both legitimacy in Greek eyes and the expansion of his influence to the south was yet to come. The sanctuary of Delphi, home to the greatest oracle of the god Apollo, had long been a sacred gathering place for all of Greece. Kings, warriors, shopkeepers, and peasants could freely travel to the temple there and ask the god for advice—should they go to war, open a new business, or marry the girl next door? Delphi lay high on the slopes of Mount Parnassus in the region of Phocis in central Greece. In 356, the same year Alexander was born, a dispute had broken out between the local inhabitants around Delphi and the cities of the Amphictyonic Council, a regional organization of towns dedicated to protecting the oracle. Soon the dispute erupted into a bitter conflict known as the Sacred War between the people of Phocis and their allies from elsewhere in Greece—including Athens—and the council members, most notably Thebes. The war dragged on for years with neither side able to gain the advantage.

In 348 the weary Thebans called on Philip to join them and crush the Phocian rebels once and for all. The Macedonian king hesitated, as he wanted to avoid a direct war with Athens, but the Athenians—constantly harangued by Demosthenes—were finally beginning to take seriously the threat Philip posed. Embassies traveled between Athens and Pella in an attempt to settle the conflict peacefully. Promises were made and oaths were exchanged, but the dark cloud of war loomed over the land. At last, Philip took a bold risk and marched for Thermopylae, the gateway to Greece. There, where the Persians had crushed the Spartans on their way to destroy Athens, Philip, backed by his army, at last forced the Amphictyonic Council to take decisive action against the Phocian rebels and end the impasse. Faced with Macedonian troops on their border, the Phocians capitulated and Philip was granted a place of honor on the council. Athens was not pleased, but it was unwilling to press the matter. Philip, through a skillful combination of diplomacy and military threats, was now the dominant member of the most powerful political alliance in Greece.

One day when Alexander was about twelve years old, he made a friend who would follow him all the way to India. That this friend was a horse named Bucephalas is the most charming quality of a story that has long been one of the most famous and revealing in Alexander's extraordinary life.

Philip himself was present that day, a rare event, when a horse breeder from Thessaly named Philoneicus had arrived at the small town of Dion beneath Mount Olympus and asked if he could show the king his wares. Philip, always keen for a new stallion to ride in battle, gladly agreed and along with Alexander accompanied the trader to the grassy plains just outside town. Philoneicus then led Bucephalas forward to the astonishment of the crowd. He was a truly magnificent animal, tall and powerful, midnight black with a white blaze on his forehead and an ox-head brand from the ranch of his breeder (hence the name *Bu-cephalas*—"ox-head"). Philoneicus knew he had caught the eye of Philip and the rest of the horse-loving Macedonian nobles, so he casually mentioned that he couldn't possibly part with such an animal for less than thirteen talents. This incredible price was enough to support a man for a lifetime, but Philip merely shrugged. As stunning as the horse was, Philip could see at a glance that it was skittish and unmanageable, rearing up against Philip's most experienced groomsmen and allowing no one to mount him. Even a horse as splendid as Bucephalas was useless to the king if he could not be ridden.

Philip ordered the animal taken away, but Alexander confronted his father and proclaimed he was losing a priceless stallion because he lacked the courage and skill to manage him. The king was not used to being chastised before his men, especially by his young son, but Alexander was beside himself with frustration and repeated his charge. Philip was angry now and glared at his son with his eye.

"Are you fool enough to criticize your elders? Do you really think that you know horses better than we do?"

"This horse at least. I can handle him better than any man alive!"

"Oh really? And if you can't, what penalty are you willing to pay for your rashness?"

"I will pay the whole price of the horse."

Even Philip couldn't help but admire the bravado of his son and laughed along with his nobles at such youthful arrogance. But he agreed to the bargain and told his groomsmen to lead the horse to Alexander.

Bold he was, but Alexander was not foolish. While the warriors of the court had seen only the wild nature of Bucephalas, the young boy had noticed something more—the horse became uncontrollable only when the sun was behind him. It was his own shadow on the ground that had frightened Bucephalas. Alexander cleverly took the reins and gently turned the stallion toward the sun so that he cast no shadow before him. He then stroked the horse and spoke to him gently for several minutes until he was calm. To the astonishment of his father and the watching crowd, Alexander then cast aside his cloak and sprang up on the horse's back in a single motion. Bucephalas was ready to fight, but the boy held him on a tight rein as they started trotting across the plain. Little by little, as Alexander got the measure of the animal, he began to loosen the reins and let the mighty stallion gallop across the grasslands at full speed. Everyone was terrified that the prince would be killed, but Alexander and Bucephalas raced far away from the crowd then back at last toward his father. A great cheer went up from all assembled and Philip, bursting with pride, shed tears of joy and kissed his son as he dismounted. He then embraced Alexander and prophetically declared: "My son, you must seek out a kingdom equal to yourself—Macedonia is not big enough for you!"

Philip knew that Alexander had now reached an age when his spirit and intellect had moved beyond the limits of his boyhood tutors. If he was someday to be king and take his place at the head of the rising power in the Greek world, he needed the kind of training that could come from only the greatest mind of the age. To Philip, this could be only one man—Aristotle. He was an unusual choice, since at this time Aristotle was a virtually unknown refugee living in exile, but the man who would one day become one of the most famous philosophers in history had known Philip since they were both boys. Aristotle was from the nearby town of Stagira on the Chalcidice peninsula, but he had been raised at the Macedonian court of Philip's father, Amyntas, where his own father was court physician. Philip was only a year or two younger than Aristotle, so the boys had grown up together. At seventeen, Aristotle had left Macedonia and traveled to Athens, where he spent the next twenty years as a student of Plato at the famous Academy. When Plato died, Aristotle had expected to take over leadership of the school, but instead had been driven out of town by Demosthenes and the anti-Macedonian party because of his connections to Philip. That same year, his rebellious hometown of Stagira was destroyed by Philip's army, so Aristotle fled to a city near Troy where the tyrant Hermias governed in the name of Persia. He remained there three years and even married the adopted daughter of the tyrant, but when Hermias was murdered, he retreated to the nearby island of Lesbos to teach and study the local flora and fauna. Three years later, when Philip invited him to return to Pella as Alexander's tutor, Aristotle jumped at the chance.

Aristotle was an inspired teacher. Just as Socrates had taught Plato and Plato in turn had instructed Aristotle, now the philosopher from Stagira would show Alexander the wonders of the universe. With his skinny legs, small eyes, persistent lisp, outrageous clothing, and gaudy rings, Aristotle must have made a laughable impression on the Macedonian prince, but when the man spoke, Alexander knew he was in the presence of genius. Unlike Plato, who valued theory and speculation above all else, Aristotle was a practical man. He was passionately curious about how things worked and was as likely to be found knee-deep in a swamp collecting tadpoles for dissection as in a library studying the art of poetics. In an age before specialization, Aristotle studied and wrote about everything. He practically invented logic and deduced that the universe must have been created by an all-powerful prime mover who, however, took no interest in his handiwork. Aristotle was the first great experimental scientist, with physics, astronomy, biology, embryology, meteorology, and much more in his realm of expertise. He knew from observation and experimentation that the earth was a sphere and that whales were mammals, not fish. He pioneered the study of ethics and argued that the greatest virtues come from moderation. He declared that man was a political

animal—that is, a creature who finds his true home in the *polis* or
city. No person could lead a meaningful life isolated from others, he
declared, for a life without friends would not be worth living. But
he also believed, as did almost everyone at his time, that slavery was
a natural state of affairs and that men by nature were superior to
women. He also held that people of barbarian nations were inferior
to Greeks and should be treated as such.

Alexander must have studied all these ideas and more under Aristotle, but the subjects that seemed to have interested him the most
were medicine, science, and poetry. Aristotle learned the healing arts
from his own father and passed the knowledge on to Alexander. As a
general on the field of battle in later years, Alexander was known personally to treat wounds and prescribe medicines for his men. He also
collected specimens of plants to send back to his teacher and mapped
out the world with a precision previously unknown. He loved reading, especially Homer's *Iliad*, which he revered as a handbook of war.
Aristotle edited a volume of the poem for him that he carried on his
campaigns in a special box. At night, Alexander placed it reverently
under his pillow—along with a very sharp dagger.

At the site of Mieza west of Pella, where the plains of Macedonia met soaring peaks, Aristotle tutored Alexander and other young
nobles of the court, many of whom became the prince's most loyal
followers. These included his friend Ptolemy, a distant member of the
royal family from the wild Macedonian highlands who would one day
become pharaoh of Egypt. There was also the son of Philip's trusted
companion Antipater, a youth named Cassander, who suffered from
ill health all his life but managed to become a powerful king after Alexander's death. The slightly older Laomedon from the Aegean island
of Lesbos would become invaluable to Alexander as he was fluent
in Persian, while his Macedonian comrade Marsyas would become
one of Alexander's earliest biographers. Alexander also made friends
with Nearchus, originally from the island of Crete, who would use his
seafaring skills to sail the Indian Ocean. But of all the companions
of Alexander who studied with Aristotle, Hephaestion of Pella would
become his closest friend.

Plutarch describes Alexander as fair in complexion with a ruddy face and piercing eyes. He was shorter in height than the average Macedonian, though he never let this hold him back in boyhood games or on the battlefield. His image is preserved in copies of marble busts made while he was still alive by court artists employed by Philip. These follow the conventions of Greek art in many ways, showing a clean-shaven young man with lean cheeks, a square jaw, and a fierce look of determination. A remarkably detailed ivory carving of Alexander just over an inch high from Philip's tomb at Vergina shows similar features along with a muscular neck and deep-set eyes gazing upward to the heavens. Plutarch also says a very pleasant odor rose from his skin. Whether or not this was true, sweet smells were frequently associated with gods in the ancient world, as they were with Christian saints in medieval Europe.

In a court of sexual excess available in a bewildering variety of forms, it might have been expected that the adolescent Alexander would indulge himself shamelessly. But he showed a surprising lack of interest in the pleasures of the flesh, though he was impetuous and bold in every other way. He greatly valued self-control and had about him an air of seriousness well beyond his years. From boyhood, his relationships with women were unusually respectful in a world where slave girls, concubines, and even wives were treated as property. His mother, Olympias, was so worried about Alexander's apparent lack of interest in girls that she procured for him the services of a beautiful Thracian prostitute named Callixeina in hopes of sparking his interest, but to no avail. It seems that the unrestrained passion and subsequent weariness of lovemaking deeply troubled the young man. As Alexander would confess years later, sex and sleep more than anything else reminded him that he was mortal.

One day, when Alexander was asked if he would be willing to compete in the footrace at the upcoming Olympic games, the prince replied that he would, but only if he could compete against kings. If anyone doubted his desire to rule and seek glory on the battlefield, he banished these doubts when he was only sixteen years old. While Philip was busy leading an expedition against his rebellious ally Byzantium, the king left his son at Pella as regent of the Macedonian kingdom. When Philip handed Alexander the royal seal ring granting him power to rule in his stead, there were surely stern words of fatherly warning not to do anything rash. The ring was meant to be a test. If Alexander could successfully resist the temptations of such power for a few months, his position as heir would be secured.

But on the frontiers of a kingdom such as Macedonia, there were always enemies waiting to pounce. The wild Thracian Maedi in the mountains to the north had been kept in check for years by Philip's army. When news reached them that Philip and his troops were in distant Byzantium with only a boy left behind on the throne, they smelled opportunity. The tribesmen left their mountain hideouts and began moving down the Strymon valley above Amphipolis with their hearts set on plunder and revenge.

As soon as word reached Pella, Alexander gathered whatever forces his father had left behind and headed north for his first taste of battle. Details are few, but we know that over the next few weeks Alexander destroyed the Maedi and took over their land. Poorly suited though it was for all but raising goats, the mountains were rich in iron needed for forging weapons. Then in a bold move that foreshadowed future colonization in Asia, Alexander settled a mixed population of Macedonians and foreigners at a Maedi stronghold and renamed the settlement Alexandropolis—city of Alexander. Plutarch says Philip was pleased when he heard the news of Alexander's victory, but any teenager who named a city for himself bore watching.

Alexander soon had an even greater opportunity to prove his worth. Philip had reached the limit of his patience with the Athenians and their endless conspiracies against him. Demosthenes had been warning for years that Macedonia—not Sparta, Thebes, or even Persia—was the greatest threat to their city. With Athenian pirates harassing his coasts and the joint efforts of Athens and Persia to crush his kingdom, Philip decided to strike first. He seized the Athenian grain fleet sailing from the Black Sea as it passed Macedonia, depriving the city of its most important source of food. Then he marched south with his army before anyone knew what was happening and occupied the town of Elatea north of Thebes. Philip was hoping to provoke the Athenians into doing something foolish—and he was not disappointed. Athens was still an important sea power, but it had not fought a significant land battle in decades. Demosthenes, nonetheless, whipped the Athenians into a war frenzy, flattering them that they were the heirs of the victors at Marathon and would certainly crush this upstart barbarian on the field of battle. The Athenians also formed an alliance with Thebes, warning their northern neighbor that Philip would destroy them on his way to attack Athens. Thus on a hot day in early August of 338, the Athenians and their allies, including the elite Sacred Band of Thebes, arrived at Philip's camp in a narrow valley in central Greece near the village of Chaeronea.

The armies that gathered on the swampy plain little more than a mile across were enormous, perhaps sixty thousand men in all, with numbers roughly equal on both sides. But whereas the Athenians were mostly shopkeepers and farmers, the Macedonians were professional soldiers who for years had fought against both Greek hoplites and all manner of savage warriors from the mountains of the north. And yet, it was the three hundred grim-faced lovers of the Theban Sacred Band that worried Philip the most. He had to break them if he was to win the battle. It is surprising, therefore, that Philip placed his now eighteen-year-old son, Alexander, at the crucial point on the end of the Macedonian line opposite the Sacred Band.

Philip's strategy was essentially the same he had first used years earlier against the Illyrians. While the Athenians and their allies formed a straight line across the valley, the Macedonians stood at an angled formation pressing the Athenian line only on the far left. Philip then ordered his men to advance, so that the Athenians on the left felt the full force of the Macedonian attack while those to the right were still untouched. At first, the Athenians held the enemy and even began to force them back. Those farther down the line on the right saw the Macedonians retreating and broke ranks to join in the attack—exactly as Philip knew they would. While the more disciplined Thebans led by the Sacred Band held their line, a gap opened up in the Athenian center and in rushed the cavalry of Alexander. He quickly surrounded the Thebans while his father moved against the Athenians. The sons of Marathon collapsed in shambles and fled, with at least a thousand killed and twice that number captured. Many of Athens's best generals stood their ground and were slain, but among those who ran in terror from the battlefield was the orator Demosthenes. The common soldiers from Thebes fared little better, but the men of the Sacred Band formed a circle and faced Alexander and his Macedonians, prepared to fight to the death. Their corpses soon piled on top of one another until at last there was no one left to fight. Only those few too wounded to resist were taken alive, while the rest fell where they stood. Philip honored the dead of the Sacred Band by burying them on the battlefield and celebrated their courage with the towering statue of a lion that still stands in the quiet valley of Chaeronea.

Philip was gracious in his victory, though he was reluctant to give Alexander the credit he deserved for his decisive role in the battle. The king could have marched south and destroyed both Thebes and Athens, but instead he sent an embassy, led by Alexander, to the Athenian assembly seeking peace. Philip's magnanimity was based on the simple calculation that Athens, especially its navy, was more valuable to him intact. All Athenian property and persons would be respected, while he also returned the Athenian prisoners captured at Chaeronea unharmed and without ransom. He allowed the Athenians to maintain control over the Aegean islands they held and promised not to garrison Macedonian troops in their town. All he asked in return was that Athens become his ally. The assembly was so grateful not to be facing Macedonian troops on the city walls that it granted Philip everything he asked for and conferred Athenian citizenship upon the king and his son. The Athenians even erected a statue of Philip in the marketplace.

For Alexander, the embassy to Athens must have been a grand occasion, the only time he would visit the most famous city in Greece. There he saw the Acropolis soaring above the town, topped by the

Parthenon containing the gilded statue of the virgin goddess Athena. As with all ancient Greek buildings and sculpture, those on the Acropolis were painted in brilliant colors—no Greek would have endured bare white marble. Alexander surely visited the theater of Dionysus on the slopes just below the Parthenon, the very place where Sophocles' *Oedipus Rex* had first been performed. On the hill of the Pnyx across from the Acropolis was the meeting place of the assembly, where Pericles had declared that future generations would marvel at all that Athens had achieved. Nearby was the Academy, where his teacher Aristotle had studied, and the *agora,* where Socrates had cornered hapless citizens, demanding they examine their most cherished beliefs. All of Athens stretched before him that glorious summer, the heart of Greek history and culture whose image he would cherish the rest of his life.

Meanwhile, Philip was wasting no time consolidating his hold on Greece. That winter he called for a general assembly of all the Greek cities at Corinth. In the aftermath of Chaeronea, no one dared to refuse, except for the eternally belligerent state of Sparta. Philip could have wiped the Spartans off the map, but they were no real threat to him and he must have calculated that their absence made the proceedings seem almost voluntary. The terms the king laid out at Corinth were simple—the Greek states were to live in peace with one another, defend each other in case of attack, submit to the decisions of a central representative council (the *synedrion*), and form an alliance with Macedonia, swearing to uphold him and his descendants as leaders of a unified military force. Although this League of Corinth was cast in a democratic mold, there was never any doubt that Philip was now the undisputed ruler of all of Greece.

In his first decision as military leader of the League, Philip proposed a bold plan that he had nurtured for many years—the invasion of the Persian Empire. It was not a quixotic notion, given the political situation in Persia at the time. The Athenian orator Isocrates, now in his nineties, had in fact been advocating such a Panhellenic crusade for decades, though mostly in hope of giving the Greeks someone to fight besides each other. But the aged Isocrates saw at last in Philip a leader with the military might and authority to unite the Greeks in a grand campaign against Persia to avenge the atrocities of the past and liberate the Greek cities on the Aegean coast of Asia from Persian rule. Philip cared no more for the lofty ideals of Panhellenism than he did for democracy, but the respected orator offered him convenient propaganda for his own military ambitions. Not that he entertained foolish dreams of conquering the whole Persian Empire, but its rich Greek cities in nearby Asia Minor were far away from the heartland of Persia. The empire was stretched thin from years of rebellion in Egypt and other provinces, while the palace at Susa was in chaos with the recent assassination of the Great King Artaxerxes III by the eunuch and grand vizier Bagoas. Persian leadership had passed to Arses, the young and untested son of Artaxerxes III, who as Artaxerxes IV was firmly under the thumb of his father's assassin. The timing could not have been better for Philip. With Greece unified under his command and the Persian leadership in crisis, the Greek cities across the Aegean were delightfully vulnerable. The League of Corinth had no choice but to elect Philip leader of the combined Greek and Macedonian crusade against the Persian Empire.

While he was making plans for the invasion, Philip took time to further his own image as patron of all things Greek by commissioning a grand edifice known as the Philippeum in the sanctuary of Zeus at Olympia. This structure was circular in shape, surrounded by columns, and held sumptuous ivory and gold statues of Philip and his family, including Olympias and Alexander. Some believed that Philip was now seeking to establish himself and the Macedonian royal house as semi-divine figures. There had been previous cases of mortal heroes accorded special honor bordering on worship, but to construct a shrine to a living ruler was unprecedented in Greek history. Egyptian pharaohs were seen as divine intermediaries between gods and humans, but not even the Great King of Persia was worshiped as a god. Among Macedonian nobility, the ruling king was seen as the first among equals—blessed by the gods, certainly, but not one of them. Whatever Philip's intentions, whether a proclamation of his power after the victory at Chaeronea or something more, the fact that Olympias and her son were included in the Philippeum made it clear that Philip considered Alexander the undisputed heir to the Macedonian throne.

It was now that one of the strangest events in the turbulent history of the Macedonian court occurred. Philip had no sooner returned to Pella than he announced that he was divorcing Olympias on suspicion of adultery and taking yet another wife, this time from an old Macedonian family of impeccable pedigree. Moreover, he began spreading rumors that Alexander was not his true son. Why would Philip throw the court into turmoil with such baseless charges at this crucial stage of his expansionist plans? Philip was ready to send his generals Attalus, Parmenion, and Amyntas across the Aegean to prepare the way for his invasion of Persia. Thousands of troops and tons of supplies had been requisitioned from his Greek and barbarian allies. It seemed sheer insanity to risk his conquest of the Persian cities of Asia Minor because of a domestic dispute.

And yet, Philip must have had a very good reason for rejecting Olympias and Alexander so suddenly. The answer seems to lie in the political maneuvering among the leading Macedonian families. Olympias had always been an outsider to them, a half-wild foreigner from the mountains of Epirus who worshiped snakes and cared only for securing her son's position as Philip's heir. If the king was to take a bride who was a blue blood Macedonian and if she bore him a son, then that boy would be worthy to inherit the throne. Philip was only in his forties, with plenty of time to sire a son who would come of age before Philip grew old. It just so happened that his general Attalus had a niece and ward named Cleopatra who was young, beautiful, and, he hoped, fertile. Attalus was married to Parmenion's daughter, so that any child of Cleopatra would have ties to almost all the leading families at Pella. In their minds, any future heir of pure Macedonian blood was preferable to a half-Epiriote prince like Alexander.

Philip agreed that rejection of Olympias and her son was in his best interest. He had seldom slept with Olympias in the twenty years since Alexander's birth and had never forgotten the chilling sight of her entwined with a snake on her bed. Her son Alexander was a fine lad, he admitted, handy as could be in battle, but too talented and ambitious for his own good. It would be a shame to lose him, but Philip was confident he could father other sons to take his place.

Philip wanted to show there were no hard feelings and so invited Alexander to the wedding banquet. As with all Macedonian parties, the wine flowed without ceasing, with Philip drinking more than anyone. It was late into the night when Attalus rose and proposed a toast to his niece the bride and a very drunk Philip. He called on all Macedonians to offer a prayer to the gods that they would soon grant the couple a legitimate successor to the throne. Alexander was furious at the none-too-subtle insult and threw his cup at Attalus, demanding to know if he was calling him a bastard. Philip then jumped up and drew his sword, intending to strike down his son, but stumbled and fell flat on the floor. Alexander glared down at him in disgust and proclaimed: "Look, everyone! The man who wants to cross from Europe to Asia can't even make it from one couch to the next." Alexander then stormed out of the room. By dawn he and his mother had fled to her family in the mountains of Epirus.

Months passed while Philip fumed in Pella and Alexander brooded in Epirus, then moved on to stay with friends in Illyria. The next summer Cleopatra gave birth to a daughter named Europa, not the son Philip and the Macedonian nobility had hoped for. But time was now short before the planned invasion of Persia would have to begin. Troops and supplies were ready. The Persian court was more chaotic than ever with the timely murder of Artaxerxes IV—again by the eunuch Bagoas—and his replacement with the new Great King, Darius III (Darayavaush, in the Persian language). Philip had even sent to Apollo's oracle at Delphi for the god's approval of his upcoming expedition. After appropriate offerings were made, the priestess replied in verse: "The bull is ready for slaughter, the end is near, the sacrificer is present."

It was a typically ambiguous response from Delphi, but Philip chose to interpret it favorably, seeing the bull as Persia and himself as the sacrificer. Soon others would see it differently.

For a king to begin a long and distant war without an heir at the ready was a risky proposition. Even some of the old Macedonian families began to worry that the kingdom would descend into chaos if Philip were killed in Asia. Finally it was the arrival of an old friend, Demaratus of Corinth, that brought the king to his senses. When he met Philip, they exchanged the usual pleasantries, then Philip asked if the Greek cities were still quarreling. Demaratus shook his head and then, as only a longtime companion could, told Philip he was a fine one to ask about affairs in Greece when he couldn't even manage his own family. He admonished Philip, saying that he had brought the recent bitterness and dissension on himself. It was time to end the feud with his son and establish him again as heir before sailing to Asia. Philip was taken aback, but he saw the wisdom of Demaratus and reluctantly agreed. Soon messengers were on their way over the mountains of Illyria to bring Alexander home.

Philip welcomed his son back to Pella, but before long he began to regret his clemency. No sooner had Alexander returned than an ambassador arrived in Macedonia from Pixodarus, the Persian satrap of Caria in southwestern Asia Minor. The satrap had recently seized the Carian throne from his sister, Ada, and now wanted to make sure his position was secure if Philip made it as far as Halicarnassus. His message to Pella proposed marriage between his daughter and Philip's eldest son and Alexander's half brother, the mentally handicapped Arrhidaeus. Philip would gain the favor of a key Greek city on the Aegean coast and Pixodarus would benefit from ties to the Macedonian royal family, though never breaking officially with Persia. Philip was unimpressed with the proposal, but drew out negotiations while he finalized his campaign plans. However, when Alexander and his closest friends heard of these dealings, the prince immediately sent his own ambassador to Caria, Thessalus, an actor famed for his role in tragedies. Thessalus asked Pixodarus why he would want a half-wit for a son-in-law when he could instead have Alexander? Pixodarus jumped at the chance to marry his daughter to Philip's heir and readily agreed.

When news reached Pella of Alexander's behind-the-scenes talks, Philip was livid. He burst into Alexander's bedroom and demanded to know why he was working behind his father's back to marry into the family of a Carian schemer who was nothing more than a pitiful slave of the Great King. Philip declared that Alexander showed little hope for being a worthy king someday if he behaved so foolishly. How dare he listen to the traitorous advice of his friends and usurp the royal prerogative! Alexander, caught in the act and unwilling to challenge his father so soon after his return from exile, admitted he had behaved imprudently. Philip was still furious, but instead of forcing his son out of Macedonia again, he ordered the actor Thessalus sent home in chains and banished four of Alexander's closest friends—Ptolemy, Nearchus, Harpalus, and Erigyius.

The time for the invasion was now at hand, but there was one final task to complete before Philip left Macedonia. The recent unpleasantness with Olympias and Alexander had outraged Philip's allies in Epirus. The king of that country, also named Alexander, was the brother of Olympias and a man who could cause trouble for Philip once he had crossed the Aegean if his indignation at the treatment of his sister was not mollified. Philip therefore decided to give his own daughter to Alexander of Epirus in marriage. This daughter, also named Cleopatra, like Philip's latest wife, was the child of Olympias and therefore young Alexander's full-blooded sister. To an outsider the confusion of similar names and overlapping family relationships must have seemed a perfect muddle, but to Macedonians it was clear that Philip was bestowing a great honor on Alexander of Epirus by allowing him to marry his own niece.

Philip realized that this wedding could be much more than just a cementing of ties between Macedonia and Epirus. As he was soon leaving for Asia, this would be his last opportunity in perhaps many years to entertain visitors in the grand Macedonian style. He therefore decided to invite friends, dignitaries, and ambassadors from all of Greece and beyond to attend the lavish festivities at Vergina. Pella was the administrative capital of the kingdom, but ancient Vergina was the heartland of Macedonia and the burial place of its kings.

Philip ordered athletic games, sacrifices to the gods, and lavish banquets to be readied. Greek visitors renewed their pledges of loyalty to him as leader of the League of Corinth. The Athenian ambassador even brought a golden crown for the king and declared that if anyone dared to plot against Philip and fled to Athens for refuge, he would be delivered to Macedonia for justice. The famed actor Neoptolemus offered a song for the king at a state banquet and proclaimed:

Your dreams soar higher than the sky,
 of greater fields to sow,
 of palaces grander than men have ever known . . .
But death is coming, sudden, unseen,
 that robs us of our distant hopes.

Philip was enchanted by the verses, which spoke, of course, of the upcoming demise of the Persian king.

The games were set to begin at sunrise the next day with opening ceremonies at the hillside theater of Vergina. Crowds flocked to claim a seat while it was still dark, so that as rosy-fingered dawn appeared in the eastern sky that summer morning, a multitude was waiting for the king. Philip had constructed a splendid entry to the theater flanked by superbly crafted statues of the twelve Olympian gods decorated with gold. Only the most distracted guest would fail to notice one additional image among the gods, a statue of Philip himself, enthroned as if he were the thirteenth member of the divine pantheon.

At last the king entered the theater clothed in a shining white robe. He had dismissed his bodyguards that morning, trusting in the benevolence of his adoring subjects. The crowds rose from their seats and cheered the king with all their might. On one side of Philip was his new son-in-law, Alexander of Epirus, and on the other was his son and heir, Alexander. It must have been a glorious moment for Philip. After all the years of struggle and fighting to secure his throne and expand his Macedonian empire, the greatest men of Greece were gathered around him shouting his name. The riches of Persia were just waiting to be seized by the best army the world had ever known. And there was his son, Alexander, a headstrong but promising young man who would someday continue his legacy as ruler of his kingdom.

It was then that another young man approached the king. He was a royal bodyguard and familiar to the members of the court, so no one thought anything of his presence at the entrance to the theater. No one noticed the beautifully inlaid Celtic dagger he pulled from beneath his cloak as he rushed at the king and plunged the knife into Philip's heart.

The young assassin fled as screams filled the air. The king collapsed, his blood pouring onto the ground around him. As he drew his final breath, his last glimpse of the world of mortal men were the eyes of his son, Alexander, staring down at him.

# 2

# GREECE

THUS AT THE AGE OF TWENTY ALEXANDER
INHERITED THE KINGDOM OF MACEDONIA, BESET
AS IT WAS BY GREAT JEALOUSY, BITTER HATRED,
AND DANGERS ON EVERY SIDE.
—PLUTARCH

The man who murdered Philip was named Pausanias, from a noble family in the Macedonian mountain district of Orestis. He had been welcomed to the court of Philip as a royal page and soon found favor in the king's eyes because of his beauty. But as adolescence gave way to full manhood, Philip lost interest in his young lover and turned his attention to another youthful courtier, also named Pausanias. The first Pausanias was beside himself with jealousy and launched a smear campaign against his rival, whispering to everyone who would listen that the king's new bedmate was a womanly hermaphrodite and shameless slut who would give his body to anyone. The second Pausanias, however, was a brave soldier and a man of honor who could not bear such slander. Soon afterward, when he and Philip were fighting on the front lines in one of the countless battles against the Illyrians, young Pausanias deliberately threw himself into the thick of the bloody fight to prove his courage and manliness at the cost of his own life.

Unfortunately for the first Pausanias, his dead competitor was a friend of Attalus, one of Philip's best generals and a leader of the advance force assigned to cross into Asia Minor to prepare the way for the king's invasion of Persia. Attalus, as mentioned, was also the uncle of Philip's recent bride, Cleopatra, and a powerful supporter of the king among the Macedonian nobility. When Attalus heard that his young friend Pausanias had sacrificed his life to prove his honor because of the rumors spread by the first Pausanias, he devised a suitably Macedonian revenge to punish the slanderer.

Attalus invited the surviving Pausanias to dinner, entertaining the young man royally with food and drink. Macedonians normally added water to their wine at banquets, but Attalus kept refilling Pausanias' goblet with unmixed wine until he passed out on the dinner couch. Attalus then sodomized the young man and invited all the dinner guests to do likewise. When they were finished, he handed Pausanias over to his mule drivers to be gang-raped in the stables by the lowliest servants in his household.

When Pausanias recovered his senses the next day, he found that he was now an object of ridicule at the court. He rushed to Philip demanding justice against Attalus, but the king hesitated. He was genuinely disgusted by his general's shameless behavior, but he had to consider the larger picture. Attalus was crucial to his plans for the Persian invasion and a key supporter whose family and friends in Macedonia might turn on the king if he punished the general. Therefore Philip put off the irate Pausanias with promises of future justice. In the meantime, he tried to soothe the young man's anger with splendid gifts and a post of honor among his bodyguard.

But Pausanias was not so easily mollified. He went about his duties and tried to ignore the laughter behind his back, all the while watching as Attalus received the king's favor and was sent across the Aegean. The new bodyguard sought solace by attending lectures of the visiting Greek sophist Hermocrates. One day, when Hermocrates was discussing fame, Pausanias asked the philosopher how one might best achieve undying glory. Hermocrates replied that the surest way was to kill a famous man. That was all that Pausanias needed. His tormentor Attalus was beyond reach in Asia, but Philip, his former lover and the man who denied him justice, was close at hand.

On the morning of the royal wedding of Alexander of Epirus and Philip's daughter Cleopatra, Pausanias was ready. He had planned his escape with three sympathetic friends who were also members of the king's bodyguard. A horse would be waiting in the trees just outside the theater. Thus when Pausanias slipped his dagger between Philip's ribs and watched the king fall to the ground, he had every reason to expect he could flee to safety. The Athenians, in spite of their promises, would surely welcome the man who had slain their hated enemy. All of Greece would rise and proclaim his name, shrines would be built, and perhaps a golden statue would be dedicated at Delphi in his honor. He would truly live forever in the memory of all who loved freedom and justice.

Pausanias was therefore surprised when things immediately began to go horribly wrong. His three friends, instead of helping him escape, lunged after him with swords drawn as he fled the theater. He had almost made it to his waiting horse when his foot became tangled in a vine and he fell to the ground. His pursuers were on him in an instant and quickly slew the bewildered Pausanias. He died beneath the trees at Vergina before he could speak a word. His body was hung on a cross like that of a slave so that all might gaze on him in shame.

It is no surprise that historians from ancient times to the present have looked at the assassination of Philip and imagined various conspiracies that reach far beyond the simple vengeance of a wronged lover. Suspicion has centered primarily on Olympias, the mother of Alexander, rather than on Alexander himself, though many would grant that the king's son had ample motive and opportunity. Philip was soon leaving for his campaign against Persia and had no plans to include his son in the glory the expedition would surely win. Alexander would serve at home as regent, perhaps for years, while Philip increased in power and won the riches of Asia by his sword.

The reported actions of Olympias before and after the murder lend credence to the idea that she was involved in Philip's death. She had been urging her brother to declare war on Philip ever since her divorce, only to see her disgrace overlooked when Philip offered the king of Epirus a royal princess as his bride. Some say she then lent young Pausanias a sympathetic ear as he complained of his gross mistreatment at the hands of Attalus. It was absolutely unthinkable, she assured him, that such injustice could go unpunished. When Pausanias revealed his plans to her, the story goes, she encouraged him and even provided the horse for his escape. After his death, stories circulated that she placed a golden crown on his head while he still hung on the cross. When his body was taken down a few days later, she allegedly cremated it over the remains of her husband and later erected a tomb for Pausanias next to that of Philip.

Which, if any, of these reports are true is unknown, but we can be certain that in the months after Philip's death Olympias struck against her enemies like a viper. When Alexander was away, she forced Philip's young bride, Cleopatra, to commit suicide after forcing her to watch as her infant daughter was roasted alive. Alexander was reportedly shocked by his mother's behavior, but he did not punish her.

As for Alexander, we will never know if he was involved in Philip's assassination or if he had knowledge of the plot and did nothing to stop it. Plutarch records a story that Pausanias came to him after his vile abuse at the hands of Attalus seeking sympathy and advice. Alexander listened to his complaints, but instead of offering assistance he merely quoted a passage from Euripides: "The giver of the bride, the groom, and the bride."

This cryptic line from the *Medea* in which a wronged wife plots revenge against her husband, his new bride, and the bride's father would have been taken by Pausanias as a suggestion to do away with Attalus, Philip, and Cleopatra. However, this episode, as so many in the aftermath of Philip's death, may well have been invented after the fact. What we can be certain of is that, guilty or not, Alexander had everything to gain from his father's murder.

Alexander performed the duties of a faithful son and buried Philip with all royal honors in a grand tomb at Vergina. Philip's body was first placed on a pyre then cremated according to custom in front of the whole Macedonian army. When the fire had died down, attendants gathered Philip's bones, washed them in wine, then wrapped them in a royal purple robe. The remains were placed in a stunning golden chest decorated on top with a sixteen-point star, along the sides with intricate blue glass rosettes, and on the bottom with the carved feet of a lion. This chest in turn was placed inside a stone sarcophagus in a magnificent tomb along with silver drinking vessels, armor, weapons, a golden wreath fit for Zeus himself, and many other priceless objects worthy of a Macedonian king. Above the entrance to the tomb was a colorful painting of a hunting scene, one of Philip's favorite activities. Finally, in front of the tomb Alexander ordered the construction of a small shrine for the worship of his father as a divine hero. In death Philip had at last achieved what he had sought in life—a place among the gods.

No sooner was Philip buried than Alexander began the fight to secure his throne. One of his first supporters was another Alexander, from Lyncestis in the western mountains of Macedonia. He enthusiastically hailed Alexander as king even before Philip's body was cold and accompanied the prince into the palace, though this deed may have been motivated by self-preservation more than genuine affection. The two brothers of Alexander of Lyncestis were soon executed for suspicion of involvement in Philip's murder and it is quite possible that their sibling wanted to distance himself from their actions in a very public way.

But the new king's most important early ally was wily old Antipater, one of Philip's top generals. He had faithfully served Philip's brother Perdiccas, then Philip, and now he saw his future dependent on securing the kingship for Alexander. He knew the key to Macedonian power was the army, so he accompanied the young man to an assembly of the troops. If Alexander could win their backing the throne would be his, but it would not be easy. Many of the soldiers were weary from serving in Philip's endless wars far from their homes and families. Quite a few saw the murder of Philip as a convenient excuse to cancel the Persian campaign and return to their farms. All the men knew that Alexander would soon be challenged by the Greeks to the south and barbarians to the north, meaning months if not years of fighting if they gave him their loyalty. But in this crucial moment Alexander rose to the occasion. His years of rhetorical study under the best Greek masters and his almost supernatural ability to inspire men shone forth as he wept with them over the death of their matchless general, his beloved father. He called on them to put fear aside and remember who they were—the greatest army the world had ever seen. Nothing was impossible for them. If they would but follow him he would lead them to riches and glory beyond their dreams. It must have been an incredible speech. These hardened veterans who longed for nothing more than home and hearth cheered their young king with all their hearts and promised to follow him wherever he might lead. Of course, it didn't hurt that Alexander also promised to repeal all taxes for Macedonians.

Now that he had the backing of the army, his next step was to win over or eliminate any potential rivals among the Macedonian nobility. Chief among these was Attalus, who along with Parmenion was still in Asia Minor preparing the way for the invasion of Persia. The two generals had crossed to Asia in the spring, just a few months before Philip's murder, and had advanced with ten thousand troops along the coast as far as Ephesus before being driven back by Memnon, the Persian general who had once been a refugee in the Macedonian court. When they heard the news of Philip's death, the two old warriors realized that young Alexander could not hope to hold the throne without their support. Attalus, who had recently married Parmenion's daughter, held the loyalty of many Macedonian noble families, second only to Parmenion. Though Parmenion was cautious, Attalus immediately began making plans to overthrow Alexander. He even contacted Demosthenes and his party at Athens to gauge their loyalty to the new king and was not surprised to find they were eager to throw off the Macedonian yoke.

But Alexander was no novice at politics. Having been raised in the rough and tumble world of the Macedonian palace, he knew how to forge unexpected alliances and quietly do away with his enemies.

Alexander realized that he needed the support and experience of most of Philip's old generals if he was to rule his father's empire and move against Persia. It was simply a matter of discerning who was willing to betray whom and at what price. Since Attalus had publicly insulted Alexander just a few months before at Philip's wedding banquet and as he was the uncle of the bride who had replaced his mother and forced him into exile, there was never any question about which general's head would be on the chopping block. Alexander sent his loyal friend Hecataeus to the Macedonian camp across the Aegean with orders to reach an understanding with Parmenion and see that Attalus never returned home.

Parmenion, never anyone's fool, realized that advancement for himself and his extensive family lay with supporting Alexander. If that meant Attalus would have to be sacrificed, a son-in-law could always be replaced. Soon Attalus was dead, but the price Parmenion had extracted was high. In return for his backing, he would be second only to Alexander himself in the upcoming campaign against Persia. Moreover, his kinsmen would fill almost every key post in Alexander's army. It was a bitter pill to swallow for a young man who yearned to purge the Macedonian forces of his father's old cronies. He desperately wanted to come out from under the shadow of Philip and be his own man. But Alexander was a realist and recognized that, at least for now, he needed Parmenion.

Alexander did not forget his boyhood friends who had been exiled by Philip after the Pixodarus affair. He sent for Ptolemy, Nearchus, Harpalus, and Erigyius to join him as he faced the struggles ahead. He knew he would need them in the days and years to come. And with one glaring exception, they would serve him loyally in his war against Persia.

Alexander's next task was to subdue the rising rebellion among the Greek cities. Although they had sworn to support Philip and his heirs, the Greeks jumped at the chance to regain their independence. Macedonian garrisons were driven away, alliances forged, and secret messages sent to the Persians seeking gold to fund the uprising. No one was willing to recognize Alexander as the leader of the Hellenic league his father had founded. The Thessalians and Thebans turned on Alexander, the Spartans saw their chance to regain hegemony in southern Greece, and the Athenians, led by Demosthenes, declared a day of public thanksgiving and awarded a posthumous crown to Philip's assassin. Demosthenes even stopped mourning for his beloved daughter who had died just a few days earlier. He wasted no time in portraying Alexander to the assembly as a young fool playing the king on his father's throne.

With affairs still unsettled in Macedonia, most new leaders would have stayed home and consolidated their hold on their native land instead of striking out against powerful enemies beyond their borders. But Alexander was not a typical king. He immediately left Pella with his army and headed south toward Thessaly. The Thessalian rebels had blocked the only road through the Vale of Tempe just south of Mount Olympus and forced the Macedonians to a halt. Instead of a suicidal charge against this well-protected position, Alexander set his engineer corps to work building a winding path on the far side of Mount Ossa overlooking the sea. Before the Thessalians knew what was happening, Alexander and his troops had outflanked them. With Macedonian swords at their throats, the towns of Thessaly swiftly recognized Alexander as their leader in his father's place. They also agreed to pay taxes to the king and, most important, to join their superb cavalry to his army as auxiliaries.

Before the ink was dry on the treaty with Thessaly, Alexander was moving south to Thermopylae, where he convened the Amphictyonic Council and accepted the loyalty of the cities of central Greece. Thebes was next, surrounded by walls that had repelled invaders for centuries. The Thebans had chafed under Philip's rule and more than any other Greek city had both the will and the manpower to stop his impudent son from taking on his father's mantle. The men of the town had been preparing for the battle they knew lay months ahead after Alexander had secured his position to the north—but they were shocked a few days later when they awoke to find thousands of Macedonian troops in full battle gear surrounding their town. The

Thebans now realized this boy king was no pampered prince but an ambitious warlord and clever strategist who marched his troops faster and harder than anyone had believed possible. Alexander stared at them from across his lines and the Thebans blinked. They knew they were not ready—at least not yet—to stand up to the Macedonians and so they surrendered and accepted Alexander as their sovereign. The Macedonian garrison was restored to the fortress on the edge of town, while Alexander continued his march south.

When a horseman rode into Attica the next day proclaiming the submission of Thebes, the Athenians fell into a panic. Citizens in the countryside rushed into town seeking protection away from their isolated farms. No one had expected a Macedonian assault so soon and therefore the Athenians had neglected to repair the city walls. As the men tried to shore up the ramparts, they dispatched an embassy to Alexander to buy time. Among the envoys was a sheepish Demosthenes, who had every reason to believe the young king would not think well of his recent harsh words or his secret dealings with the Persian king. He was in such a panic that he turned back at the outskirts of Athens and went home to hide. But, like his father, Alexander wanted the Athenian navy intact for his invasion of Persia more than he wanted to see the Acropolis in flames. He therefore received the envoys kindly and assured them the Athenians had nothing to fear.

Athens breathed a sigh of relief when Alexander and his army bypassed their city and instead headed south across the isthmus to the Peloponnesian peninsula. There Alexander summoned the League of Corinth to meet with him under the watchful eye of the Macedonian army. The nervous delegates quickly affirmed him as leader for life of all the Greeks. Next, in a colorful ploy worthy of the Athenian stage, Alexander brought before the delegates a messenger claiming to be from the Greek city of Ephesus on the western coast of Asia Minor. This impassioned actor pleaded with the representatives of free Greece to liberate his beleaguered city from the rule of the tyrannical Persian king. On cue, the league members rose in applause and vowed to help their oppressed countrymen across the sea. They then appointed Alexander as general plenipotentiary in command of the renewed Panhellenic expedition against Persia.

Alexander immediately presented the delegates a complete list of men, money, and supplies they were to contribute to the upcoming campaign. The Athenians were obligated to make their fleet available to Alexander along with sailors and provisions. Other cities were required to provide soldiers and goods as the king saw fit. Conspicuous in their absence were the Spartans, who as usual had stayed home and refused to participate in the war. But Alexander, with a sufferance he would later regret, contented himself with appointing pro-Macedonian regimes in the cities around Sparta's mountainous borders. Like his father, he found the stubborn Spartans useful as proof of the voluntary nature of his alliance. If they caused trouble, he believed he could easily deal with them.

With the formalities of the meeting complete, statesmen and scholars crowded around Alexander competing with one another to offer their congratulations to the young king. He accepted their enthusiastic if insincere praise with the good grace of a born politician, but he searched the crowd in vain for the one man he had most hoped to meet. This was Diogenes the Cynic, a philosopher in exile from the Greek colony of Sinope on the shores of the Black Sea. He had been banished from his home for defacing currency and had spent most of his life abroad in Athens and Corinth. Diogenes believed in living out his philosophical beliefs, usually to the amusement and disgust of others. He and his scruffy band of followers held that life should be conducted in accordance with nature to the point of performing bodily functions in public like dogs (hence the term *cynic*, from the Greek word for dog). His asceticism was sincere, however, and he actively worked to entice others to reject the conventions of society. At the time, he was living in a large jar on the outskirts of Corinth. Alexander went looking for him and found him there enjoying the beautiful day wearing only a loincloth. The king stood by waiting for recognition, but the philosopher only gazed at him with mild contempt. Alexander, in some discomfort, at last asked if there was anything he could do for him. Diogenes replied that yes, indeed, he could move out of the way since he was blocking the sun. Alexander's friends mocked the old philosopher as a fool and madman, but the young king wistfully responded: "If I were not Alexander, I would be Diogenes."

On the way home, Alexander made a detour through the mountains of central Greece to the sacred site of Delphi beneath Mount Parnassus. Like so many kings before him, he wished to consult the oracle regarding his upcoming military campaign. Unfortunately, he was informed that the priestess who spoke for Apollo was in seclusion and as a matter of religious principle was not available that day, even for the ruler of all Greece. Alexander promptly marched into her lodgings and began dragging her forcibly into the shrine. This grossly sacrilegious act had its intended effect, however, when the priestess cried out: "You are invincible!" This was all Alexander wanted to hear. He donated a modest amount for the upkeep of the temple, then gathered his troops and marched north to Macedonia.

There was no time for Alexander to rest when he reached Pella. It was already late spring and the barbarians on his borders were raiding deep into Macedonian territory. The Greeks to the south were subdued for the moment, but the tribes to the north of his homeland threatened to destroy his kingdom as well as his dreams of a Persian invasion. If he did not establish control over the Balkans he could never hope to cross into Asia. He would have to teach the rebellious tribes a singular lesson. His father Philip had fought many skirmishes to the north, but Alexander planned a full-scale invasion of the lands along the Danube River.

The young king undertook such a bold campaign for two reasons. First and foremost, his borders had to be secured before he could move against Persia. He had no idea how long the fighting in the east might last—years, perhaps—and he would not be able to return to Macedonia before he was finished. Alexander had to make such an impression on the Balkan tribes that they would not trouble his kingdom even if he was far away. The second reason for the northern campaign was that it would be excellent training for the Persian war. He and his army would climb mountains, cross rivers, face unknown perils, and overcome all manner of fearsome enemies together. His men would learn that they could trust him with their lives.

Alexander and his troops left Amphipolis and marched east into Thrace along the Aegean coast. He crossed the river Nestos just west of the Greek city of Abdera, once home to the philosopher Democritus, who had first proposed that all matter was composed of indestructible particles called atoms. Alexander knew his theories well, but there was no time to visit the city as he turned his army north into the high mountains and made his way through alpine valleys to the garrison town of Philippopolis at the head of the Hebros River valley. His father had established the outpost several years earlier as a frontier post to defend the northern approaches to his kingdom. It was inhabited by two thousand Greek, Macedonian, and Thracian settlers who were as rough and wild as the land around them. Visitors had given it the nickname Poneropolis ("Crook Town") and counted themselves lucky to escape with their lives.

Alexander almost certainly recruited some of these outlaws into his ranks as he headed toward the great wall of Mount Haemus stretching across the northern horizon. As hazardous as Philippopolis might be, it was still Macedonian territory. But among the peaks of Mount Haemus were the Triballi, some of the fiercest warriors in Europe. Somewhere in a narrow defile through these peaks, perhaps at the modern Shipka Pass, Alexander's scouts came upon the Triballi warriors. They had occupied the only crossing point of the mountains for a hundred miles and blockaded it with carts. Alexander came forward and studied the situation. The approach to the pass was steep and wide enough for only a few dozen men abreast. The Triballi had a tremendous advantage as they held the high ground, but Alexander saw an even greater danger. The mountain tribesmen had positioned the carts so that they could be sent crashing down the path into his soldiers to crush the men and break his line. It was Alexander's first great test of command—and he faced it with an ingenious daring that would become the hallmark of his generalship.

He ordered his men to advance up the trail in standard formation, but to be ready at a moment's notice to open the line to let through any carts that came crashing toward them. If that was not possible, they were to fall to the ground and link shields in front to form a ramp so that the speeding carts would roll onto the shields at full speed and fly up over them. The men were terrified they would be ground to a pulp beneath the carts, but they advanced nonetheless. As soon as the first vehicles came hurtling down the path, some of the well-trained Macedonians moved to the side to allow them through while others locked shields and braced themselves for impact. The carts reached the line and hit the shield wall with tremendous force, but they sailed over the men and crashed to pieces on impact. Alexander meanwhile moved to the left with his best men and advanced up the pass while his archers launched a volley at the astonished but undeterred Triballi. The tribesmen were brave, but they were poorly armed and badly organized. As Alexander and his men reached the head of the pass, the Triballi cast aside their weapons and ran down the northern side of the mountain as fast as they could. Over a thousand warriors were slain and large amounts of treasure seized, while many of their women and children were captured for the slave markets. They, along with the booty, were sent back to the Aegean coast as a sign to all that this was a king who could lead his army to victory.

From the top of the pass, Alexander gazed over forests and rolling hills into the Danube valley below. His army marched down from the mountains and soon arrived at a small river called the Lyginus, three days away from the Danube. The Triballi king Syrmus had heard of Alexander's advance and sent many of the women and children of his tribe to safety on a large island called Peuce ("pine tree") in the middle of the Danube. Allied tribes had already gathered there and were soon joined by Syrmus himself, reasoning that his person was too valuable to risk in battle. But the mass of the Triballi warriors cleverly moved around behind Alexander as he left the Lyginus River and took up a defensive position in a thickly wooded grove. In such a location, they were safe from massed assault by Alexander's infantry or cavalry. They intended to make the Macedonian king abandon his military advantage of a disciplined line of troops and fight them man-to-man amid the rocks and trees in true barbarian style.

When Alexander's scouts reported that most of the Triballi were now behind him, he did not hesitate to turn his army around and return to the Lyginus. When he arrived, he saw immediately what the Triballi wanted but had no intention of falling into their trap. He lined up his infantry in deep formation with their long sarissa spears aimed square at the woods in front of them. Then he ordered Parmenion's son Philotas to lead the cavalry wing on the right while the rest of the horsemen formed up on the left. Alexander himself took position in the front ranks at the center of the infantry. The Triballi expected a charge, but instead the king sent his archers and slingers forward to provoke the Triballi into leaving their wooded shelter. Soon the Triballi warriors were so indignant that they were being picked off by auxiliaries that their tempers got the better of them and they rushed out onto the open ground in front of Alexander's lines screaming for blood. It was then that the king put his plan into action and sent both his infantry and cavalry forward. The spearmen skewered the Triballi at close quarters while the horsemen moved in from the sides. The Triballi, like so many sheep, were herded into such a tight mass that the Macedonian cavalry used their horses as weapons as much as their javelins, pushing the tribesmen down and trampling them beneath their hooves. The brave but foolish Triballi at last broke and ran back into the woods, but only a handful escaped in the approaching darkness. Three thousand barbarian warriors perished defending their homeland that day, while Ptolemy reports that only about fifty Macedonians died in the battle.

Three days later Alexander was standing beside the Danube River. Since the Greek poet Hesiod in the eighth century B.C., the Mediterranean world had known that the distant Danube—which the Greeks called by the Thracian name Ister—was one of the great rivers of the world. To the Greeks, it was a mysterious waterway arising somewhere in the Alps and descending through dark forests and the lands of savage tribes to the Black Sea. Among those nations who lived along its banks were Celts, Germans, Dacians, Scythians, and Thracians, including the Getae on the northern bank opposite Alexander. As a keen student of the Greek historian Herodotus, Alexander knew that the Getae were unusual in the ancient world for their belief in a single god and the happy immortality of the soul. To these tribesmen, a slain warrior did not descend into a dismal Greek underworld as a pale shade but went to live with the divine Salmoxis, master of thunder and lightning. Every five years they would toss a victim chosen by lot onto the spear points of their soldiers to take messages to their god. If the man died quickly, the sacrifice was considered a success—but if he did not perish in a timely manner they would chose another victim in his place.

The Greeks had long traded with the tribes of the Danube valley for grain, fur, and slaves. Over a century earlier, the barbarians of these northern lands had even seen a mighty southern army on their borders. Darius, the Great King of Persia, had led his forces to the Danube and crossed the river on a lengthy pontoon bridge to fight the Scythians above the Black Sea. Now young Alexander stood by the same river and considered the scene before him. The Triballi and their allies occupied a fortified island with steep banks in the middle of the wide river. On the northern banks were the warriors of the Getae, many thousands strong, taunting the Macedonian soldiers they knew could never reach them. Some of Alexander's supply ships had arrived at his camp having sailed up from the Black Sea coast, but they were not enough to carry an army. It seemed as if Alexander could go no farther.

It was then that Alexander was seized with a longing, a *pothos*, in Greek, to cross the river into lands no Macedonian had ever trod. Darius had led a Persian army north of the Danube—why not Alexander? To cross the river was something even his father, Philip, had never dreamed of. Such a daring adventure would inspire his army for the campaign against Persia and make a suitable impression on the troublesome Greeks. But how could he move his army to the other side? There were not enough boats to transport them or time to build a bridge, and it was much too far to swim.

Fortunately for the king, he had read the story of Xenophon and the ten thousand Greek mercenaries who had fought in Mesopotamia seventy years earlier. Faced with a similar predicament on the Euphrates River, Xenophon devised an ingenious solution: "The soldiers took their tent covers and filled them with hay, then folded the edges together and sewed them so that the water could not dampen the stuffing. On these they crossed the river."

Alexander's men were dubious, but they trusted their king and began to sew. With the addition of the few ships from Macedonia and the confiscation of every dugout canoe they could find, over five thousand infantry and cavalry set off across the river that night.

The Macedonian army reached the northern bank of the river safely and rested in a tall wheat field until daybreak. Alexander then ordered his men to advance silently toward the Getae camp. He placed his infantry in front with their spears turned sideways to smooth down the grain for those following behind. When they emerged onto untilled ground in front of the Getae camp, Alexander led the cavalry on the right wing while Nicanor, another son of Parmenion, commanded the infantry. The Getae were caught completely off guard. They were amazed that Alexander had crossed the Danube in one night without even building a bridge, as their ancestors said the Great King of Persia had once done. They now faced a solid wall of Macedonian spears advancing toward them while the enemy cavalry struck them from the side. They soon broke and ran to their nearest town, a short way up the river, but Alexander was on their heels all the way. The Getae then packed as many of their women and children as they could carry on horses and rode for the endless grasslands to the north. Alexander reached the settlement and looted everything of value—surely including much fine Thracian gold work—and burned the town to the ground.

After sending the booty back across the river, Alexander conducted what would become a regular ritual on his Persian expedition. He sacrificed to Zeus the *Soter* ("savior"—the same Greek word Christians would later use for Christ), to his ancestor Hercules, and to the local god personifying the Danube, who had allowed him safe passage across his waters. He had no desire to chase the Getae refugees farther because his point had been made. Word would quickly spread from the Alps to the Crimea that the new Macedonian king was not to be trifled with. His northern border secure, Alexander returned the same day to his camp on the southern bank of the Danube.

Once Alexander was back at his camp, Syrmus, king of the Triballi, sent ambassadors to him to sue for peace. We don't know the exact terms, but they must have included a contingent of soldiers for Alexander's army because ancient sources tell us that the Triballi troops marched with Alexander into Asia. Records show at least one of these Thracian warriors from the Danube settled permanently in a town the Macedonian king would establish on the banks of the Oxus River in central Asia. Other embassies arrived at this time from local tribes seeking peace, but the most memorable visit was from a tribe of Celts. Over the years Alexander would receive many notable delegations, but this early encounter on the Danube proved to be one of the most remarkable in the king's career.

The Celts had long lived in Gaul and Germany near the Alps, where they herded cattle, collected heads from fallen enemies, and gained an impressive reputation as some of the toughest warriors in the world. Just a few generations before Alexander they had begun to move out of their forest homeland into Britain, Ireland, northern Italy, and the upper valley of the Danube. Alexander's friend Ptolemy, who was present at the meeting, records that this group of Celts arrived after a long journey from a settlement near the Adriatic Sea. He was most impressed by their height, as they stood at least a head above the Macedonians, but he also says they swaggered into camp as if Alexander should be the one honored by their visit. They came seeking friendship with the king and to exchange pledges of peace. The Macedonian king received them warmly and with great curiosity as his teacher Aristotle had frequently mentioned them in his lectures on virtue. Aristotle had taught that bravery in a man was an admirable quality, but that an excess of boldness was undesirable. As an example of such behavior, he had put forward the Celts, who would allegedly attack the waves of the ocean itself. As Alexander shared a drink with his visitors, he asked them what they most feared, hoping they would say him. But the leader of the Celtic embassy looked squarely into the eyes of the king and replied that they feared *nothing*—except, he said with a laugh, that the sky might fall on their heads. But for the sake of diplomacy he did add that they valued the friendship of a man like Alexander more than anything. After the Celts had left his camp to begin their long march home, Alexander turned to Ptolemy and declared that the Celts were unbelievable braggarts.

From the Danube, Alexander struck southwest over the mountains toward the highlands ruled by Langarus, king of the Agrianians. Alexander had known Langarus for years and planned to let his men rest in the territory of his old friend before returning to Macedonia. His army had marched hundreds of miles and fought several difficult battles in just a few weeks, so their proud general was pleased to grant his soldiers a respite. He spent the first few days renewing ties with Langarus and recruiting some of his best warriors into his army, tough mountain troops who would become a key element of his forces in Asia. It was one of the earliest instances of Alexander integrating non-Greek or non-Macedonian soldiers into his ranks— a farsighted policy that would nonetheless cause endless troubles between the king and his officers during the Persian campaign.

But there was to be no rest for the weary. A messenger soon rode into camp bearing the news that the Illyrians were in revolt, led by Cleitus, son of Bardylis, the old adversary of Philip. Glaucias, king of the Taulantians on the Adriatic coast, had joined Cleitus as had the Autariatae tribe to the north. This was devastating news for Alexander since an alliance of hostile Illyrian tribes could delay his invasion of Asia and even threaten the survival of his kingdom. The Illyrians were not as well organized as the Macedonians, but they were brave and numerous.

Alexander knew he had to act at once even though his men were exhausted. He quickly gathered intelligence about the uprising and discovered that the Autariatae, who were previously unknown to him, were the least of his threats. Langarus dismissed them as a minor tribe and offered to lead some of his own Agrianians against them while Alexander handled Cleitus. The Macedonian king was so grateful that he promised Langarus his half sister Cyna in marriage when he returned. This popular daughter of Philip and his early wife Audata had been married to one of the alleged conspirators against Philip, but with this first husband now exterminated Cyna was once again a pawn in the endless game of royal marriage alliances.

Langarus would die before he could claim his bride, but at the time he was so grateful at the prospect of joining the Macedonian royal family that he followed Alexander's orders with enthusiasm and devastated the Autariatae. By then Alexander was already deep into Illyrian territory near the walled town of Pellium, headquarters of Cleitus. Alexander had raced to the town to prevent Glaucias and his Taulantians from joining up with Cleitus. The Macedonians arrived so suddenly that they interrupted a gruesome sacrifice in progress outside the walls. Alexander's men were no strangers to blood and gore, but they were sickened to see the remains of three black rams, three young boys, and three girls on the altars of the local god. Human sacrifice was rare in the Mediterranean world, but it was still practiced in the mountains and forests of Europe.

More disturbing to Alexander was the perilous situation in which he now found himself. Pellium was heavily fortified and could be taken only by a lengthy siege, while the hills around the town were held by the Illyrians. To make matters worse, he received news that the army of Glaucias had just arrived in the valley. The Macedonians had managed to pen Cleitus inside the walls of the town, but if they made any move against the soldiers in the valley surrounding them, the men in the town would surely rush out and attack them from behind. On the other hand, if they stormed the walls of Pellium, Glaucias would pounce on them. Alexander had already sent Philotas with a cavalry contingent to forage for supplies at nearby farms, but he had been forced to rescue them personally when they were caught by nightfall. It was an impossible situation for Alexander. He couldn't take the town nor could he attack the surrounding enemy. His escape was now cut off and his food was running low. Cleitus and Glaucias must have been delighted to trap the young Macedonian king in such a dangerous position. All they had to do was close the vise to crush Alexander once and for all.

But now Alexander once again showed his genius for unconventional warfare. The king knew he was outnumbered and had no chance of escape or taking the city. Faced by this hopeless predicament, he decided to put on a parade.

Early in the morning the Illyrians in the surrounding hills saw the king draw up his infantry into tight formation over a hundred lines deep. Each Macedonian foot soldier held his eighteen-foot sarissa before him. They had been ordered to move in complete silence, so that on signal each raised his spear to the sky without a sound. To those watching it was as if a forest had suddenly sprung from the field in front of the town. With incredible precision borne from endless practice, the infantry swung their sarissas to the front as one, then to the right, then the left. At Alexander's command they marched straight ahead without a word, then wheeled to each side in perfect formation.

The Illyrians were fascinated by this display. They themselves fought in the old way, with reckless bravery their only rule. But these Macedonians moved together like a machine, with such beauty it was a wonder to behold. The enemy practically cheered as Alexander's men moved briskly toward their lines, then practiced intricate patterns, concluding with a wedge-shaped phalanx aimed straight ahead. It was then that the Macedonians, at Alexander's signal, struck their shields against their spears and raised a battle cry that would have woken the dead. The Illyrians were so completely caught off guard by this brilliant piece of psychological warfare that they ran away in terror, clearing the way for Alexander's army to escape.

It was, nonetheless, a hard-fought march out of the valley. The Illyrians quickly recovered their senses and struck back against the Macedonians. They blocked their escape on a small hill along the road until Alexander sent his cavalry to drive them away. The Macedonians had no sooner arrived at the river crossing at the end of the valley when they saw thousands of Illyrian warriors heading down from the hills toward the ford. Alexander lined up his archers in midriver to cover his retreating men as best they could, then ordered his artillery to set up quickly on the far side of the river and aim their catapults at the approaching horsemen from maximum range. The missiles hit the first of the horsemen from such a distance that Glaucias and his cavalry ground to a halt. They had heard of catapults in siege warfare, but few before Alexander had used them against the enemy on the field of battle. This unconventional maneuver, sprung from the young king's imagination at a desperate moment, bought enough time for the rest of the Macedonian army to make it across the river to safety without losing a single man.

If Alexander had been any other general, he would have thanked the gods for his miraculous escape and retreated back to Macedonia as swiftly as possible. But the king was not one to withdraw from a fight without victory. Three days later, when Cleitus and Glaucias were confident that the Macedonians were far away, Alexander quietly moved back across the river under cover of darkness. A scout had told him the enemy were deployed just as he suspected—no defensive walls, no trenches, and no sentries—believing they had seen the last of the Macedonians. Alexander and his men moved into the Illyrian camp and killed the first of the enemy as they slept, then attacked the panic-stricken barbarians with such swiftness that they threw aside their weapons and ran from the city, the survivors escaping into the mountains. Cleitus set fire to the town and fled with Glaucias and his Taulantians, never to be heard from again.

Just when Alexander dared to hope that he could at last begin his invasion of Asia, news arrived from the south that the Greek states had once again risen against him. Since he had been campaigning for weeks beyond the borders of civilization, it seemed the perfect opportunity for the disgruntled cities of Greece to rebel. As they reasoned, an inexperienced boy just short of his twenty-first birthday could not prevail against the barbaric tribes of the north. Even if Alexander was still alive, his long absence had given the Greeks plenty of time to seethe in discontent. And as usual, the Persians were on hand with plenty of gold to pay off the Greeks and thwart any Macedonian plans for an Asian campaign.

The Athenian orator Demosthenes was once again at the fore in stirring up trouble for Alexander. That summer he climbed to the speaker's platform at the Athenian assembly and declared that Alexander and the entire Macedonian army had been annihilated by the Triballi on the Danube. He even produced a supposed veteran of the battle wrapped in bloody bandages who declared that he himself had seen Alexander fall. The Athenians rose to cheer the rebirth of Greek independence. News spread quickly throughout the land that the young tyrant was dead, for as Arrian wisely observes, "As often happens in such cases when there are no certain facts, people believe the truth to be whatever it is they most desire."

No Greek city was more anxious to rebel than Thebes. Only three years earlier the Thebans had watched in horror as their army had been crushed by Philip and Alexander at Chaeronea. Then they had twice endured the humiliation of surrender and the posting of a Macedonian garrison on the Cadmeia citadel overlooking their town. Thebes, the fabled city of Oedipus and conqueror of Sparta, had been reduced to a provincial outpost of the Macedonian empire. It was too much for the citizens to bear. Although they had lost many of their best men at Chaeronea, they were still a proud people with an ancient military tradition. According to myths passed down from their ancestors, they had sprung from dragon's teeth sown in the earth. They were now determined to prove they could still bite.

The spark that lit the flames of rebellion came when a small group of Theban exiles driven out several years earlier by Philip snuck back into town with the aim of inciting an uprising. The Macedonian garrison at Thebes had become so confident in its invulnerability that the men had taken regularly to wandering the streets of Thebes beyond the protected walls of the Cadmeia, no doubt in search of wine and women. One night the exiles ambushed two of these soldiers, Amyntas and Timolaus, and brazenly killed them. The murderers then came before the Theban assembly and boasted of their deed, urging the citizens of their town to join them by evoking that most cherished of Greek ideals: *eleutheria*—freedom.

The Thebans enthusiastically took up the call and rushed to the

Cadmeia. The stronghold was an oval-shaped hill on the southern end of the town fast against the city wall. There was no way for the citizens to storm the fortress, but they could isolate the Macedonian defenders. They quickly dug trenches and built palisades to deny the occupiers supplies and reinforcements, then the assembly sent messages to friendly Greek cities asking for help. Horsemen sped to Arcadia, Argos, and Elis, all in the distant Peloponnese. Unfortunately for the Thebans, their history of belligerence had made bitter enemies of their neighboring states. Even the Peloponnesians were not eager to lend a hand. Only the Arcadians sent reinforcements, but these made camp thirty miles away near Corinth to wait on events. The messengers had no better luck at Athens, where Demosthenes—in typical fashion—led a rousing vote in support of the brave Theban rebels, then did nothing.

Meanwhile at Thebes, the commander of the Macedonian garrison watched from the Cadmeia as the townspeople built double siege walls completely around him. They even constructed palisades beyond the southern walls of the town to prevent escape. The commander ordered his soldiers to make what preparations they could, but without reinforcements there was little they could do except wait.

Alexander, however, had not been idle. As soon as he had heard of the uprising at Thebes, he struck camp in Illyria and began racing south. By themselves the Thebans were a powerful force, but if they were allowed to join with the Peloponnesian infantry and the Athenian navy—all backed by Persia—they could create a formidable alliance. So, with no time to waste, he marched his men from Pellium day and night with little rest along the impossible mountain trails of central Greece until at last they emerged onto the plains of western Thessaly. From there they advanced south through the pass at Thermopylae and across Boeotia to the outskirts of Thebes. At almost twenty miles a day through some of the most grueling terrain in Europe, it was a singular achievement. And since in ancient times a rapid army could outpace the news of its approach, the Macedonians arrived at the gates of Thebes before the rebels even knew they were on the way.

What happened next depends on which Greek historian you believe. Our two primary sources for the assault on Thebes—Arrian and Diodorus—paint two equally compelling pictures of Alexander's actions at the town. They agree on the basic facts, but the motives that drove the king and the degree to which he sanctioned what would become a watershed event in Greek history couldn't be more different in their accounts.

Both authors describe how Alexander made camp near the northern end of the city walls to give the Thebans time to reconsider their revolt. The king did not want a war if it could be prevented—not because he loved Thebes, but because every day he spent in Greece only diminished his chances for success in Asia. If possible, Alexander would have preferred the Thebans surrender and be forgiven. If they had done so, he probably would have been content with the execution or exile of a few ringleaders and promises of better behavior in the future from the rest. But the Thebans would have none of it. Their assembly approved a unanimous resolution declaring they would fight.

Alexander had thousands of Macedonian and allied soldiers surrounding Thebes including, as Arrian emphasizes, contingents from Plataea, Orchomenus, and Thespiae—three nearby cities that had suffered severely at the hands of the Theban army in the past. These soldiers had grown up with stories of their towns burned, their territory confiscated, and their mothers violated by vicious Theban soldiers. Alexander may have wanted peace, but many who joined him at Thebes yearned for revenge.

As the hours passed, Alexander waited for a sign of submission from Thebes. Instead the citizens rushed out of the gates with their cavalry and a sizeable force of light-armed troops to surprise the Macedonians. The move succeeded because Alexander was not expecting the outnumbered Thebans to attack him first. They managed to kill a few of his advance guards before fleeing back behind the city walls. With his frustration mounting, the next day Alexander moved his camp south of the city near the road to Athens. This location was also closer to his troops blockaded within the Cadmeia. He sent another herald to the walls to announce that he was still willing to forgive the Thebans even though they had killed some of his men. No doubt hoping to divide the citizens, he proclaimed that any citizen of the town who wished could surrender to him and join in the peace that was his gift to all Greeks. Instead the Thebans began to shout from their towers that anyone in Alexander's army who wished to join them and the Great King in fleeing from the tyranny of Alexander was welcome inside the city.

Arrian omits this episode and blames what happened next on one of Alexander's officers, but Diodorus records a version that in many ways is more believable. He says that something inside Alexander snapped when he heard the Thebans call him a tyrant, especially as they invoked the Great King of Persia as a liberator of Greece. Alexander knew from reading Plato's *Republic* that tyranny was the basest form of government, even more disreputable in the eyes of that aristocratic philosopher than democracy. The king flew into a towering rage and declared he would make an example of Thebes. As Diodorus says, "He decided to utterly destroy the city. By this deliberate act of terror, he hoped to take the heart out of anyone who might rise against him in the future." With this goal firmly in mind, Alexander called in his engineers to prepare siege engines and laid his plans to wipe Thebes off the map of Greece.

But according to Arrian, what happened was the fault of a captain of the guard named Perdiccas. This officer was one of Alexander's most loyal followers and hailed from a noble family in the Macedonian highlands of Orestis. He had fought bravely with Alexander in Illyria and in the future would become one of the most important Macedonian leaders, but now he was simply an eager young soldier who wanted to impress his king. Perdiccas was camped close to the enemy palisades on the southeast of the city. He saw an opportunity to rush the gate with his troops and did so without consulting Alexander. Before anyone knew what was happening, Perdiccas and his men were inside the walls with another Macedonian battalion close behind them. At that point Alexander had no choice but to commit his army to an assault that had already begun.

Whichever version of the story is true, the fight for Thebes was brutal. The king ordered the Agrianians and the archers from Crete inside the palisade, but kept his infantry in reserve. The impetuous Perdiccas meanwhile had rushed deep into the city and had been grievously wounded. His troops dragged him to safety and the doctors saved his life with difficulty, but his men continued the attack near the temple of Hercules just below the Cadmeia. There they surrounded a large contingent of Thebans, believing they had the citizens trapped, but with a shout the soldiers of Thebes turned on the invaders. Alexander's men were caught off guard and panicked in the unfamiliar streets, so that almost seventy of his archers were slain within minutes.

Alexander watched as the frightened auxiliaries rushed out of the city. He knew he had to do something fast. He lined up his veteran Macedonians and with their deadly sarissa formation attacked the pursuing Thebans. It was now the turn of the Thebans to panic as they faced those fearsome spears. They ran back to the gates of the city in such a disorganized mob that the last ones through forgot to bar the gates. Alexander burst into Thebes and his men spread throughout the town.

Like the fall of any city in war, the result was uncommon bravery mixed with butchery and horror. In the narrow streets of Thebes, the sounds of screams and clashing metal filled the air. Some of Alexander's men made it to the Cadmeia and freed the Macedonian soldiers trapped inside, but most fought house by house through the town. The Thebans urged one another to resist with all their might, remembering the fate that awaited their families if they failed. Alexander marveled at the spirit of the citizens as they stood their ground, but he was still determined to make them pay dearly for their betrayal. Arrian says it was the fellow Greeks from cities near Thebes who slaughtered the women and children without mercy, but the Macedonians surely killed their share. Houses were plundered, wives and daughters raped, old men were slain in their beds, and even citizens who had sought refuge in the temples were cut down as they clasped the altars of the gods.

Over six thousand Thebans perished that day, while at least thirty thousand captives were taken. It was a holocaust unlike anything the Greek world had ever seen. Other cities had been sacked in war, but never before had one of the great towns of Greece fallen so suddenly and so completely. It was as if the old stories of the sack of Troy had come to life.

Alexander made a pretext of letting the League of Corinth decide what was to be done with the ruins of Thebes, but it was only a show. The declaration that the city would be razed, the lands surrounding the town distributed to allies, and the Theban survivors sold into slavery was a foregone conclusion. The vast amount of money generated at the slave auctions went directly to the Macedonian treasury. The only citizens Alexander spared were the priests and priestesses, those who had shown unwavering friendship to Macedonia, and—since Alexander had a particular appreciation for Greek verse—the descendants of the Theban poet Pindar.

One story of Alexander's mercy in the midst of such horror may have a basis in fact, given as he was to acts of kindness to women. According to Plutarch, when a band of Thracian marauders broke into a large Theban house during the battle, they met a young widow named Timocleia, known throughout the town for her piety. While his soldiers plundered her property, their leader raped her, then asked if she had any hidden treasure. She confessed that, yes, she did have riches hidden in her garden. The Thracian captain followed her to a well in which she told him she had cast her valuables at the beginning of the siege. As the greedy man bent over the open well, Timocleia came up behind him and pushed him in. She then threw heavy stones on the trapped man until he was crushed. When the rest of the Thracians discovered what had happened, they bound her and led her to Alexander to be punished. The captive woman appeared before the king with a calm demeanor and surprising dignity. Alexander asked her who she was and she boldly replied that she was the wife of the Theban commander who had fought his father at the battle of Chaeronea. Alexander was so impressed by Timocleia that he let her depart the town in freedom along with her children.

When the news of the destruction of Thebes spread throughout Greece, the cities that had risen against Alexander rushed to explain that they had always, in fact, been on his side. The Arcadians who had sent a contingent of soldiers as far as Corinth voted to execute the leaders who had instigated the action. Other towns sent embassies to Alexander begging his forgiveness and assuring him of their undying loyalty to Macedonia. All of Greece suddenly remembered that they had never really cared for Thebes. Indeed, hadn't the Thebans supported the hated Persians during the great war for Greek survival in the previous century? Certainly they deserved whatever evils had befallen them.

Like Philip, Alexander had heard it all before and knew how to play his part in this tiresome drama. He graciously forgave the Greeks and promised he would take no vengeance on them—with the exception of Athens. When the first messengers from Thebes arrived in Attica, the Athenians were celebrating the mysteries of the goddess Demeter at the nearby town of Eleusis. The goddess guaranteed that the warm sun and fruits of the earth would return again after the coming winter, but to the Athenians it must have seemed as if darkness were about to descend forever. They had not actually sent troops in support of Thebes, but how many times could they expect Alexander to forgive them for plotting against him? They abandoned the religious festival at once and streamed back into the walls of Athens with all the possessions they could carry. This time surely the king would unleash his Macedonians on them and destroy their city once and for all.

The aged Athenian statesmen Demades proposed that the Athenians send an embassy to Alexander congratulating him on his safe return from the barbarian lands of the north and his magnificent victory over Thebes. This the assembly did immediately, but Alexander sent them back to Athens with a message that he was willing to overlook their disloyalty only if they would send to his camp ten of his longtime enemies, including the chief troublemaker Demosthenes. To the conservative party leader Phocion, this seemed perfectly reasonable. He was a respected military veteran who had once been a student of Plato's. He also detested Demosthenes and would be thrilled to see his longtime adversary crucified by the Macedonians. He rose before the assembly and called on his fellow citizens to remember the story of the Athenian heroes Leos and Hyacinthus, who had sacrificed their own willing daughters to save the state when it faced destruction. Turning to Demosthenes, he declared that these mere girls had gladly gone to their deaths to save their city—wouldn't any true Athenian patriot do likewise?

In spite of Phocion, the supporters of Demosthenes still controlled the assembly and threw the old general off the platform. Demosthenes then climbed the stone steps and addressed his fellow citizens in a carefully prepared speech. It was not without reason that he was considered the best orator of the age. By the end of his address, he had won the crowd to his side. Demades, heavily bribed by Demosthenes' party, then proposed that they send a second embassy to Alexander begging him to reconsider and spare the Athenian leaders. Since the king still needed the Athenian navy for his Persian invasion, this time Alexander relented with the condition that they surrender only the general Charidemus to him. This was a clever ploy, since he was not a native-born Athenian and could be safely sacrificed by all parties. Charidemus knew which way the wind was blowing and immediately sailed off to join the Persians. Honor satisfied, Alexander agreed to leave the Athenians in peace.

From Thebes, Alexander and his men marched home to Macedonia. It was now late autumn and there was much to be done before his army could cross to Asia in the spring. The king reluctantly recalled Parmenion from Asia Minor to be his second in command on the expedition as the price of the old general's support. Philip's other elder statesman, Antipater, was made regent in Macedonia to rule in the king's place and keep the Greeks in line while he was at war across the Aegean. Both men advised Alexander to marry and produce an heir before he departed for what could be a very long and dangerous campaign. It was sound advice and in accord with Macedonian tradition, but the king had no interest in domestic life. He was only twenty-one and, with the confidence of youth, believed he had more than enough time to worry about family matters in the future. He also had no patience to wait for a wife to become pregnant and bear a son. Marriage would mean delaying the Asian expedition for at least another year, which was unthinkable to Alexander.

To entertain his troops and ready them for the upcoming war, the king held athletic contests and festivals at Dion beneath the snows of Mount Olympus. A decade earlier Alexander had tamed Bucephalas at this holy site. Now, the mighty stallion still at his side, he hosted games of every kind for his men and presented splendid prizes to the winners. For nine days he sacrificed lavishly to Zeus, father of the gods, and to the nine muses who would inspire bards to sing of great deeds to come. An enormous tent was erected to hold a hundred dining couches for Alexander's guests. The whole army dined like kings for days and drank wine every night like true Macedonian warriors on the eve of battle. They would need all the courage they could muster—before them lay the awesome power of the Persian Empire.

# 3

# ASIA

THUS SAYS THE LORD TO HIS ANOINTED, TO
CYRUS, WHOSE RIGHT HAND I HAVE GRASPED,
TO SUBDUE THE NATIONS BEFORE HIM AND STRIP
KINGS OF THEIR ROBES, TO OPEN CITY DOORS
BEFORE HIM—AND THE GATES SHALL NOT BE SHUT.
—THE PROPHET ISAIAH

There was once a king named Astyages who ruled over the Medes in the mountains east of Mesopotamia. One night he had a dream that his daughter Mandane would someday give birth to a son who would rule all of Asia. Fearing he would lose his throne, he gave her in marriage to a man from the insignificant province of Persia to the south. But after Mandane had been married for a year and was pregnant, Astyages had another dream in which he saw vines spreading from her womb to cover all the lands of his empire and beyond. He consulted the wise Magi, who interpreted the dream and told him the baby would one day become a mighty king in his place. Thus Astyages decided to slay the child as soon as it was born. When the baby, named Cyrus, was delivered, the king gave him to a servant with orders to take the child away and kill it. This servant in turn gave the baby to a kindly cowherd, who secretly raised him as his own. Although his surroundings were humble, young Cyrus showed the qualities of royalty from an early age and was in time brought before the suspicious king. After discovering the truth, Astyages again consulted the Magi, who now told him he had nothing to fear from Cyrus. Nevertheless, when the prince had grown to manhood, he led a revolt of his father's people against his Median grandfather and became the first Great King of the Persian Empire.

This is the heroic legend told by Herodotus, but the true story of Cyrus and the creation of the Persian Empire is even more remarkable. Starting from the Persian highlands near Persepolis in what is now southern Iran, Cyrus conquered Media by 549, then the kingdom of the Lydians in Asia Minor three years later when their wealthy king, Croesus, underestimated the Persian ruler. The empire of Babylon was next in 539, followed by much of central Asia.

Cambyses, the eldest son of Cyrus, ascended to the throne in 530 at the death of his father and soon added Egypt to the empire. After the untimely death of Cambyses in 522, Darius I seized the throne in a bloody struggle. He gained the Indus Valley for Persia, but his adventures in Europe were less successful. His crossing of the Danube and invasion of Scythia were only nominal victories, while the rout of his army at Marathon near Athens in 490 was a clear defeat. Though the Greeks looked back on Marathon as the greatest battle the world had ever known, to the Persians it was at worst a minor setback. Xerxes, the son of Darius and grandson of Cyrus, invaded Greece again in 480. The celebrated Spartan defense at Thermopylae is not worthy of mention in surviving Persian records, nor is the destruction of Athens the same year. However, the Persians' defeat at Plataea near Thebes the next year put an end to Persian dreams of conquering Greece. After the death of Xerxes in 465, the borders of the Persian Empire remained largely unchanged, though there were frequent internal revolts put down by every Great King until Darius III took the throne in 336, the same year Alexander became king of Macedonia.

The policies of the Persian Empire begun under Cyrus continued for almost two centuries. Local inhabitants were left in peace to live and worship as they pleased so long as they paid their taxes and caused no trouble. However, if there was rebellion against the Great

King's rule, retribution was swift and harsh. Egypt and Babylon in particular suffered after their people rose up against Persia. Cities were burned, rebels massacred, and onerous tribute imposed. And although the Persians had no interest in spreading their religious beliefs to the provinces, most of their rulers had little genuine respect for or understanding of the spiritual practices of their subject people. Time and again the Great Kings punished uprisings by destroying local temples and profaning sacred symbols, only increasing the bitter resentment of the natives.

The Persians themselves were polytheists who believed in many gods, as did almost every culture in the ancient world aside from the Jews. Like the Greeks, Celts, and peoples of northern India—to whom the Persians were particularly close in culture and language—the countrymen of the Great King saw the world as ruled by many divine powers. But the Persians also viewed the cosmos as a battleground between the forces of light and darkness. At the head of their pantheon was Ahuramazda, known as the Wise Lord, who created the world and embodied all goodness. Opposing him was Ahriman, a powerful spirit bent on evil and leading humans astray. The great Persian religious teacher Zoroaster, who lived centuries before Alexander, taught that all must choose whom they would follow, but that at the end of time Ahriman would be defeated by the Wise Lord. There were other deities as well, such as Anahita, the mother goddess, Mithra, protector of justice, and Atar, son of Ahuramazda and guardian of his sacred fire. The worship of all these gods and many others was carried out by the ancient priestly caste known as the Magi. They sacrificed and chanted hymns to the gods, as well as foretold the future and read in the stars the signs of things yet to be. Wherever the Persians went in their conquests, the Magi followed, not as missionaries but as religious practitioners for the Persian elite. Let the Egyptians worship jackal-headed deities and the Greeks pray to Athena—it was Ahuramazda and his fellow gods who had granted the Persians dominion over the earth.

This vast empire of the Persians—over two thousand miles from end to end—was divided into provinces, each ruled by a satrap, a

governor directly responsible to the Great King. Communications
were maintained by an efficient road system crossed by royal couriers,
who, according to Herodotus, "Neither snow nor rain nor heat nor
dark of night hinder from the swift completion of their appointed
course." Like the Macedonians, the Persians were a warrior race from
the mountains who learned the arts of civilization from the ancient
kingdoms they conquered. Although they prided themselves on their
simple education—"to ride horses, to shoot the bow, to speak the
truth"—they were in fact quite receptive to outside influences and
adapted many cultural elements from their subjects. While written
Persian was used primarily for monumental carvings, beginning in
the time of Darius I, everyday court records were documented by
scribes in Elamite, Babylonian, or Aramaic. From the earlier empires
of Mesopotamia, the Persians learned art, engineering, and the magnificent architecture of their palaces. But their own unique contribution to history was the gathering of dozens of nations into the first
truly international empire. From the cataracts of the Nile and the
shores of the Aegean to the steppes of central Asia and the valley of
the Indus, the Great King ruled the largest and mightiest kingdom
the world had ever known.

In the early spring of 334, Alexander at last began his war against
Persia. He left General Antipater behind as regent in charge of
Macedonia and Greece. His mother Olympias was surely at Pella
that day to bid her son farewell. She had schemed and sacrificed for
years so that he could pursue his destiny. Now, as he rode across the
plains of Macedonia with snow still covering Mount Olympus to the
south, Alexander could not have known that he would never see his
mother or home again.

Alexander had precious little money to pay his troops. The Macedonian treasury was almost bare and the Greeks, parsimonious in the
best of times, had been reluctant to contribute financially to what
they believed was Alexander's folly. The only good the citizens of
Athens and the rest of Greece saw arising from the invasion was the
imminent destruction of the Macedonian army at the hands of the

Persians. They worried little about their fellow countrymen as there were few Greek troops among Alexander's army. In fact, there were far more Greek soldiers serving as mercenaries in the Persian army than marching under Alexander's banner. But Greek or Macedonian, the king would not be able to feed his soldiers for long unless he could quickly make the expedition profitable.

Ancient sources say the Macedonian army numbered almost fifty thousand men, including the few thousand soldiers Parmenion already had in Asia waiting for Alexander. Whatever the number, the Macedonian forces were vastly outnumbered by the men available to the Persians. At the core of Alexander's army were the hardened Macedonian foot soldiers who had fought for years with Philip and followed his son to the Danube and back. In addition, there were key auxiliary troops from allied tribes in the Balkans, especially the fearless warriors of Thrace. The rest were cavalry from Macedonia and Thessaly, mounted scouts and archers from Thrace, and the few professional soldiers from Greece that Alexander could afford to hire. A support squad of reluctant Greek sailors followed the army along the coast. In addition, there were Philip's superb corps of engineers, a staff of secretaries to handle the king's correspondence, physicians, mapmakers, scientists, and the official campaign historian, Callisthenes, nephew of Aristotle and chief propaganda officer for the expedition.

Alexander's march from Pella took his army past Amphipolis and over the Strymon River along the north Aegean coast. It was the same road Alexander had followed the previous year on the way to the Danube. But now, instead of turning north, Alexander pressed eastward over the marshes along the mouth of the Hebros River and down to the Gallipoli peninsula across the narrow strait of the Hellespont from Asia. At the town of Elaeus opposite Troy, Alexander offered sacrifice for the last time in Europe at the tomb of the hero Protesilaus, the first Greek to reach Asian soil—and the first to die—at the start of the Trojan War. Beneath the elms of the sacred grove, Alexander prayed that the gods would show him favor. He had good reason to worry. A large Persian fleet was active in the Aegean and knew of the young king's plans. If they had wished, they could have easily prevented Alexander's crossing. But the Persians decided to let the king and his Macedonians land freely in Asia before they made their move. Rather than blocking his advance across the strait with their navy, they intended to draw him into the interior, where they could destroy his army with their superior forces.

When the Great King Xerxes had crossed the Hellespont on his way to invade Greece in the previous century, he had ordered the construction of pontoon bridges across the strait to speed the passage of his enormous army—but a storm arose and destroyed the bridges before he could cross. The Persian king therefore ordered the Hellespont to be whipped with three hundred lashes and a pair of shackles thrown into its waters before he began construction of new bridges. Alexander knew this story and was determined that his own crossing would be more propitious. While Parmenion supervised the ferrying of the Macedonian army using warships and cargo boats, Alexander decided to leave the main body of the army and cross from Elaeus, steering the vessel himself to the middle of the Hellespont. There he sacrificed a bull to the sea god Poseidon and poured a drink offering from a golden bowl into the water. Then he guided the ship toward Troy to the place Homer said the Greeks had come ashore a thousand years earlier. As the coast drew near, Alexander took his spear and cast it with all his might onto the beach, claiming Asia for himself as spear-won from the gods. Then he leapt ashore before the boat had even reached land and waded through the surf onto Persian territory.

Alexander's first act in Asia was to sacrifice to Zeus, the patron of safe arrivals, as well as Athena and his own ancestor Hercules. He was always scrupulous in religious ceremonies, but even more so now that he was surrounded by a mythological landscape straight from his childhood stories. Here was the very beach where the Greeks had made camp. Just beyond was the wide battlefield where Hector and his Trojans had stood against the invaders in the ten-year war for the honor of Helen, whose beauty had launched a thousand ships to bring her home. And there, rising above the plain, was the citadel of Troy itself—not the town it was in former days, to be sure, but still looming large in Alexander's imagination. His hero Achilles, great-est warrior of the Greeks, had fought and.died beneath those walls, preferring a short life of undying glory to peaceful old age surrounded by family and friends.

The Troy Alexander visited was only the latest in a series of towns at the site stretching back almost three thousand years. Over the cen-turies, the settlement had been sacked and burned several times, only to be rebuilt ever higher on top of the ruins. The town that Alexan-der entered was nothing more than a small village with a temple to Athena attended by a few local priests eager for the occasional tourist. The Spartan admiral Mindarus had visited there many years before, as had the Great King Xerxes on his way to Greece, but the arrival of the Macedonian leader and his entourage was the most memorable event at Troy for decades.

Alexander first sacrificed at the temple of Athena, dedicating his own armor at her altar. In place of his breastplate and shield, he took from the temple arms said to have been left there since the Trojan War. His favorite soldiers would proudly bear these weapons before him in battles across Asia, including a shield that would one day save his life in India. Alexander next visited the tombs of the warriors who had died fighting to capture or save the town. Most moving was the moment when he poured libations at the tomb of his boyhood hero and ancestor Achilles. Then, along with his companions, including Hephaestion, Alexander stripped off his clothes and oiled his naked body like an athlete. In honor of Achilles, Alexander and his friends then raced around the tomb and crowned it with garlands. Finally, he sacrificed to the spirit of the Trojan king Priam, who had been slain seeking sanctuary at the altar of Zeus, contrary to all sacred cus-tom. Achilles' son, Neoptolemus, had carried out this shameful deed, prompting the young king to beseech the shade of the Trojan leader not to vent his anger on his Macedonian descendant.

As the priests led him on a final tour of the broken remains of the city, they asked if he wished to see the lyre of Paris before he de-parted. The young king, however, disdained Paris the Trojan prince as a coward drawn more to beautiful women than fame in battle: "I care little for that harp," he said, "but would gladly see the lyre of Achilles on which he sang the glorious deeds of famous men." Alexander's greatest regret, he lamented, was that he had no Homer to celebrate his own glory.

From Troy, Alexander moved north twenty miles along the Hellespont to the small town of Arisbe, where his main force was waiting for him after crossing the strait. The next day they marched a short distance to the village of Percote, just a few miles from the large and prosperous city of Lampsacus guarding the northern entrance to the Hellespont. Lampsacus had been a wealthy ally of Athens during the Peloponnesian War in the previous century and was well known for its gold coinage. Being desperately short of money, Alexander needed the riches of the town and the prestige of freeing it from Persian control. Unfortunately for the Macedonian leader, the citizens of Lampsacus had no desire to be liberated. Like many Greek towns under Persian rule, they enjoyed relative freedom and prosperity with a minimum of interference from the Great King. The good people of Lampsacus had certainly heard of Alexander's dealings with cities in Greece and especially his destruction of Thebes. They had little reason to trust him and even less motivation to trade the easy yoke of Persia for the potentially heavy burden of Macedonian rule. Alexander fumed, but he had no time to waste besieging a city. Even more than money, Alexander needed victory. He had to defeat the Persians in battle soon to establish his credibility as a general. Once he did, the Greek cities of Asia Minor would begin to open their gates to him, as well as their treasuries, out of fear and self-interest. Stories say that the philosopher Anaximenes, a scholar in Alexander's entourage who happened to be from Lampsacus, begged the general to spare his hometown even though it favored the Persians. This served to enhance Alexander's reputation for mercy, but he surely would have burned the city to the ground if he had had the time.

Alexander was a master of propaganda in war. He ordered his soldiers not to loot nearby farms and villages since it would be foolish to destroy what would soon be their own. This was a proven policy to build goodwill among the inhabitants of hostile territory, but Alexander cleverly added that they should take special care not to damage the estates belonging to the Greek-born Persian general Memnon of Rhodes. The king knew that word would quickly spread back to the Persian satraps that Memnon's property was being treated with respect—as if the general were secretly supporting the Macedonians. It was an inspired stroke of psychological warfare that would soon bear fruit.

From near Lampsacus, Alexander moved his forces two days' march east to the town of Hermoton, then on to the small town of Priapus, named for an unusually lustful son of the god Dionysus. Scouts reported to Alexander that the citizens of Priapus were willing to surrender the town to him, allowing the grateful king his first opportunity to liberate a Greek city, however insignificant it might be.

But as pleased as Alexander was finally to portray himself in dispatches back across the Aegean as a liberator of the Greeks, his overriding concern was more practical—where were the Persians? At that moment, they were much closer than he realized. The Persian governors and generals of Asia Minor were encamped only twenty miles away across the Granicus River at the town of Zeleia. With them were thousands of troops, including cavalry from distant Bactria and thousands of Greek mercenaries. While the Macedonian army moved toward the Granicus, the Persians were holding a council of war to decide what to do about Alexander.

Arsites, the satrap of the Hellespont region, presided at the meeting along with Spithridates, who ruled over nearby Lydia and the Greek cities of the Aegean coast. The satrap Arsames was there as well from Cilicia on the southern seaboard of Asia Minor. These leaders and their generals were all pledged to defend the realm of the Great King with their lives. And if honor were not enough motivation, they knew their wealth was derived from the land they held in the areas under their governance. If Alexander won, they would lose everything.

Also present was Memnon of Rhodes, perhaps the best general in the Persian army. He had defeated the advance forces under Parmenion the year before and driven them back to the Hellespont to wait for their king. When it was at last his turn to voice his opinion at the council, he rose and declared that the best way to defeat the Macedonians was to destroy all the crops in the region, empty the towns, and launch an expedition to take the war to Macedonia itself. With no fodder for his horses or food for his men, Alexander would be forced to withdraw from Asia in defeat to defend his own home. In addition, Memnon warned, the Macedonian infantry was far superior in skill if not numbers to its Persian counterparts. If the foot soldiers of Macedonia with their long sarissa spears came up against the Persians, the troops of the Great King would lose. As the Greek general surely reminded them, he had spent time in exile at the court of Philip and knew firsthand the power of the Macedonian army.

Memnon's advice was sound and, if taken, would have almost guaranteed that the world would never have heard of Alexander the Great—but the Persian leaders would have none of it. Who did Memnon think he was to advise the noblemen of the Persian Empire to turn and run from an untried boy-king who had invaded their land? They would never allow their own fields and houses to be burned before the Macedonian army as if they were peasants shaking in their boots. They suspected that Memnon wanted to delay the war so that the Great King, who favored him, would appoint him as commander in their place. There must have been questions as well about why Alexander had ordered his men not to harm Memnon's estates. But in the end it was their sense of honor and dignity that would not allow them to take Memnon's counsel seriously. They were warriors from the highlands of Persia, the heirs of Cyrus, conquerors of the world—and they would fight.

The Granicus River rises in the mountains beyond Troy and flows north across the coastal plain into the sea. It is a small river fed by spring rains, but its banks are steep and difficult to climb. Here at this ancient crossroads on a late afternoon in May, Alexander finally saw the Persians. His scouts reported their cavalry was drawn up on the far bank with their infantry behind, an unusual positioning of forces but effective given the situation. If Alexander's men engaged the Persian

army here, they would have to cross the river unprotected, then struggle up the far banks as the mounted soldiers of the enemy struck at
them from higher ground. The deadly sarissa formation of the Macedonians would be useless as they tried to climb from the riverbed to
the open ground beyond. The Persians had deliberately chosen a field
of battle that would yield nothing to the strength of the Macedonian
infantry but would instead give themselves every advantage. They had
set a trap for Alexander and were daring him to walk into it.

Alexander surveyed the situation with his keen eye for terrain
and could not help but appreciate the Persian plan. A more cautious
general might have sought a better location to cross the river or with-
drawn south along the Aegean coast. But Alexander prided himself
on his swiftness and daring—which was, of course, exactly what the
Persians were counting on. They were betting the brash young king
could not resist the bait.

As with the siege at Thebes, we have two versions of what happened
next. One tradition from the historian Diodorus says that Alexander
made camp for the night and prepared for an assault the next morning.
But the other, from Arrian, says that he drew up his troops facing the
river even though there were only a few hours of daylight left. In the
latter version, old general Parmenion urged Alexander to remain on the
near side of the river until the next day, when the army could be organized more effectively for what would be a grueling fight. A military setback at this point of the campaign, he warned, would be a disaster. In this
account Alexander dismissed the general's hesitation and said he would
be ashamed if, after crossing the wide Hellespont, he were stopped by a
petty stream. A delay, he declared, would only make the Persians think
he was afraid of them. Arrian describes a similar dialogue between Parmenion and Alexander four other times during the expedition, always
on the eve of battle, so that the reader begins to suspect that the veteran
commander is being used as a foil to highlight Alexander's boldness. But
whether the Macedonians made camp or began the attack that evening
makes little difference. Alexander had decided to fight the Persians there
at the Granicus and risk everything on a single roll of the dice.

Facing thousands of Persian cavalry and at least an equal number of infantry across the river, Alexander arranged his troops in a standard battlefield formation with horsemen on the wings and foot soldiers in the center. He placed Parmenion in command of the Thracian and Thessalian cavalry on the left, while he himself mounted one of his battle horses and rode to the right. Philotas and his cavalry units were stationed near him with the archers and wild Agrianian spearmen from Thrace. Among the many other officers in the line were Nicanor, another son of Parmenion; Craterus, who would become one of Alexander's most trusted commanders; and Black Cleitus, friend of his father, Philip, and brother of his childhood nurse. The king of Macedonia himself was unmistakable in his splendid armor as he walked beside his horse among the men, cajoling and encouraging them. The Persians had spotted Alexander as well and moved their best cavalry squadrons opposite to strike him down.

After both sides were set, they stood facing each other unmoving and in silence for several long minutes as if taking a deep breath before the battle began. Neither side wanted to be the first to move, but finally Alexander jumped up on his horse and moved the right wing forward into the river with the sounding of trumpets and a mighty cry to Ares, god of war.

Alexander flew across the river and up the banks so fast that the Persian horsemen couldn't hit him, but many of his companions were pinned down in the water as arrows rained on them from above. Parmenion moved in from the left and the infantry pushed forward into the Granicus, holding their long spears as best they could. The Macedonian strategy was to outflank the Persian cavalry using its two wings, but plans soon gave way to bloody chaos as horses and men on both sides became so tightly packed they were barely able to move. The first Macedonians to reach the Persians on the far side of the river were badly outnumbered and cut down. Memnon and his grown sons were at the forefront of the Persian lines slaughtering as many of Alexander's men as they could reach. As more men climbed over bodies to the opposite side, they put up a ferocious fight surrounded by Persian cavalry, who stabbed them with javelins. Alexander saw what was happening and in a frenzy led his closest men into the thick of battle. Gradually the Macedonians gained a foothold on the far side of the river as Alexander's cavalry used their lances from horseback against the shorter javelins of the Persians.

A fierce struggle raged around Alexander as the Persians tried to kill him and end the war with one blow. The king's lance was broken in the fight, but when he called on his groomsman for another he was told the young man's lance had snapped in two. Surrounded and unarmed, his old companion Demaratus of Corinth, veteran of wars in distant Sicily and the man who some say years earlier had bought Bucephalas for the brash prince, rushed forward and gave him his own weapon. Alexander took courage from his friend and rushed back into the fray, charging a Persian noble named Mithridates and stabbing him in the face. The death of this son-in-law of the Great King distracted Alexander from the approach of another Persian nobleman, Rhoesaces, who rode at the king and struck him so hard on his head with his sword that his helmet split in two. The king was stunned by the blow, but managed to knock Rhoesaces onto the ground and skewer him with his lance. Even as he struck, the satrap Spithridates now charged Alexander from behind and raised his sword to strike a death blow when suddenly Black Cleitus threw himself at the Persian lord and cut off his arm cleanly at the shoulder. Alexander may have been frustrated at the number of Philip's old officers in his ranks, but he owed his life that day to the courage and skill of Cleitus.

In every battle there is a turning point when both sides realize by unspoken consent that one will be the victor and the other lucky to escape with their lives. It was now that the Persians knew they could not hold back the Macedonians and so began to retreat. Their center then collapsed and they began to flee in panic from the Granicus. Over a thousand Persian horsemen were slain, among them nobles, satraps, and relatives of the Great King.

But Alexander was not yet finished as he quickly surrounded the Greek mercenaries who had been held in reserve by the Persians at the rear of the battle. These men knew they had lost, but as professional soldiers and by the accepted practice of the day they expected to pay a ransom and be allowed to depart. Alexander instead ordered his men to slaughter them, sparing only a few to work for the rest of their short lives as slaves in the mines of Macedonia. They would be a lesson to other Greeks who might side with the Persians against him.

Alexander visited his wounded and examined their injuries himself, offering advice to the camp doctors based on his studies with Aristotle. For the dozens of Macedonians who had fallen, he ordered burials with honor at the battle site while their families back in Macedonia were granted special privileges. For the noblemen among his dead he ordered bronze statues erected at Dion beneath Mount Olympus to be carved by Lysippus, the greatest sculptor of the day. He was generous to the enemy dead as well, allowing the Greek mercenaries to be buried so that they might journey with the boatman Charon across the river of the dead. He shipped all the fine drinking cups, purple robes, and other luxury goods he had captured from the Persians to his mother. Finally he sent three hundred sets of Persian armor to Athens to be set up as trophies on the Acropolis. He ordered an inscription carved beside them for all visitors to read:

Alexander son of Philip and all the Greeks—
except the Spartans—sent these spoils from
the barbarians in Asia.

Alexander was not without a biting sense of humor. He wanted everyone in Greece to know that his Panhellenic crusade against the Persians was proceeding splendidly with the support of all the Greeks—except the Spartans.

The elation that Alexander felt after his first victory was soon replaced with the mundane necessity of governing his newly acquired territory. He appointed his cavalry commander Calas as satrap of the Hellespont region in place of the Persian Arsites, who in shame had committed suicide after the battle at the Granicus. This apparently minor administrative decision on Alexander's part in fact had monumental consequences for the future. In appointing Calas as satrap, the king was making use of a Persian title and keeping in place the Persian structure of government. This continuity became even more clear when Alexander announced that the cities of northwest Asia Minor would continue to pay taxes in the same manner and at the same rates as they had under the Great King.

Local nobles who had fled to the hills at Alexander's approach now returned to their estates and were pardoned. Charges were apparently brought against the town of Zeleia, which had hosted the ill-fated Persian conference a few days earlier and served as the military headquarters against the Macedonians. However, Alexander forgave the town in an act of calculated mercy. His campaign was still young and he wanted the cities ahead of him to know he was a generous man—a prudent move since it would encourage citizens to surrender knowing they would not be condemned for their previous Persian sympathies. Alexander then sent Parmenion to take over Dascylion, the Persian capital of the area. It was a prosperous Greek town long accustomed to serving the resident Persians. With the Macedonians now in charge, the mechanisms of rule—and presumably the numerous scribes, tax collectors, and other civil servants—would remain in place under Alexander. The new king knew better than to disrupt a smoothly functioning administration. He needed money to fund his campaign, be it through taxes or tribute payments, and the longtime employees at the satrapal palace were highly skilled at fleecing the local sheep.

Life on the campaign, in spite of the brutalities of war, must have been enjoyable for the young king. He would rise every morning and begin the day by sacrificing to the gods. This was his religious duty as king of Macedonia, but Alexander seems to have been quite sincere in his devotion, especially to Athena and his distant ancestors Zeus and Hercules. After his duties at the altar, he would sit down to breakfast. If the army was not breaking camp, he would spend the day organizing military affairs, answering correspondence, administering justice, or, if there was time, hunting with his friends. He loved to read and would snatch spare moments from the day to read from Greek works by the historians Herodotus and Xenophon, the dramatists Sophocles and Euripides, or poets, especially his beloved Homer.

On the march he would often stop and practice archery or mounting and dismounting from a moving chariot. Whether on the move or based in a town, he would finish the day with a bath or an anointing with oil and scraping in the Greek manner. While he was removing the day's dirt, he would inquire what the cooks and bakers had prepared for the evening meal. He loved unusual fruits and fresh fish, so that travel along the sea coast was a special treat. His suppers were always magnificent, with Alexander and his friends reclining on couches to dine as any civilized person would. He always made sure his companions received enough to eat and personally dished out delicacies to everyone else at the table first so that often he was left with nothing.

He was fond of drinking wine in abundant quantities, in the Macedonian fashion, but at least at this stage of his life he was not given to drunken binges. He had many virtues, but like most rulers he loved flattery and would often boast of his own deeds like a common soldier. His companions would sometimes compete with one another to compliment the king, causing the more reticent among them to grow uncomfortable lest they fall behind the others in praise. It was for Alexander a tragic flaw, or *hamartia*, a Greek word meaning to miss the mark when shooting an arrow (Christians would later use the same word to mean "sin"). Love of praise was a pardonable fault of Alexander's that in time would grow to be a serious problem.

From the Granicus, Alexander marched south along ancient pathways through the mountains to the city of Sardis. This inland capital of the prosperous land of Lydia was a key city of the Persian Empire and the end point of the royal road that stretched well over a thousand miles to Susa in Mesopotamia. The fortified citadel of the town towered hundreds of feet above the valley of the Hermus River, which ran just north of the city down to the Aegean Sea. The fortress was considered unbreachable by all who had visited the site and was surely a major cause of concern to Alexander as he approached the town.

The Lydians were not Greeks but descendants of early settlers in Asia Minor. They still spoke a language related to that of the Hittites, who had ruled the land a thousand years earlier, but the people of Sardis were accustomed to Greek visitors and ways. Their territory was rich in gold and horses, a powerful kingdom long desired by many conquerors. The Lydians were so wealthy and creative that they were the first nation to mint coins. In the sixth century the last native king, Croesus, had amassed such power that he longed to spread Lydian rule beyond his borders. He was a great supporter of Greek oracles, so that when he contemplated attacking the rising kingdom of Persia under Cyrus, he sent messengers to Delphi to seek the advice of Apollo. After making lavish donations to the oracle, he asked if he should invade Persia. The priestess, possessed by the god, uttered a typically cryptic response: "If Croesus sends a great army against Persia, a mighty empire will fall."

Croesus was elated at this proclamation and prepared for war. What he didn't realize was that it was his own empire that would fall. Through the creative use of camels to terrify the Lydian cavalry, Cyrus took Sardis and became ruler of Asia Minor. After a close brush with being burned alive on a giant pyre as a sacrifice to the gods, Croesus became a trusted advisor to Cyrus, and Sardis became the most important Persian city in the west.

Alexander had no camels and no clear idea how to take Sardis other than a long siege he could ill afford. Every day he spent starving the city into submission was a drain on his still limited resources and also gave Darius more time to raise a powerful army against him. It was therefore a tremendous relief to Alexander when Mithrenes, the Persian commander of the city's citadel, met him several miles outside of Sardis and surrendered the town to him without a fight. Why Mithrenes would do this is something of a puzzle. He may not have been able to hold the surrounding countryside against Alexander's army, but he could have resisted the Macedonians from the safety of the fortress for months. Whatever the reason, Alexander warmly welcomed Mithrenes and allowed him to retain his previous rank. The Persian commander was to follow the king's retinue throughout the campaign in Asia Minor, but rather than an honor, this may have been a sign of Alexander's mistrust of a man who would betray his lord so easily.

The city of Sardis now belonged to Alexander, including, to his delight, a treasury full of Lydian gold. The money would not last forever, but it allowed the king to proceed with the war knowing he could finally pay his men. The rank and file soldiers were equally thrilled since after weeks of marching and fighting they at last had a few coins in their pockets. From his camp outside of town Alexander declared that all the Lydians were now free and would be allowed to follow their ancient customs. This was a pleasant but meaningless gesture since the Persians had always allowed the inhabitants of their empire to follow ancestral customs. As for freedom, it was true only in the sense that the Lydians were now liberated from the Persian into the Macedonian Empire. As long as the citizens of Sardis paid their taxes and did as they were told, they could consider themselves as free as they liked. Alexander then entered the city as a conqueror and climbed to the top of the citadel, where the view across the wide valley of the Hermus was magnificent. The king examined the defenses of the hill and thanked the gods yet again that he didn't have to lay siege to such a towering fortress. Then a summer storm suddenly broke loose from the heavens with peals of thunder and sheets of rain. The king had been contemplating the construction of a temple to his ancestor Zeus at the top of the citadel, but now he was certain he should do so.

Alexander appointed a Macedonian named Pausanias as the new commander of the citadel and charged Nicias, a Greek, with the assessment and collection of taxes for the region. Asander, who may have been Parmenion's brother, was chosen as satrap of Lydia and was left enough cavalry and light infantry to maintain order. The king sent most of the Greek troops who had followed him from Macedonia back to garrison the region around Troy while he stationed the Greeks from the allied town of Argos on the citadel of Sardis with Pausanias.

These seemingly minor dispositions open an important window into Alexander's mind at this stage of the campaign. He had successfully won his first battle and had now taken a key city of the Persian Empire. He felt he could dispense with most of the Greek troops in his army and cast aside the facade that this was a campaign of Panhellenic liberation. From now on, it was a Macedonian war of conquest. The Greeks would still have their uses, of course, but Alexander no longer wanted to share his glory with them. He was also anxious to begin paring away as many kinsmen and supporters of Parmenion as possible from his command staff, beginning with Asander. He continued to need Parmenion's support, but little by little he would begin to wear away the old man's power as his own grew. Finally, the number of different officials Alexander left behind to govern his growing empire shows a keen recognition of the dangers of concentrated power. As the Persians had before him, the king knew that competition between officials was the surest check on unfettered ambition. Asander would be satrap, but Nicias would control the purse strings while Pausanias commanded the high ground. None of these men had reason to trust each other—which was exactly the point. Alexander could continue his march knowing that no one man would dominate the rich and powerful province of Lydia.

Alexander's next stop was the coastal city of Ephesus, a four-day journey from Sardis. The town had been founded by Ionian Greeks centuries earlier, but had fallen under the rule of Croesus of Lydia and then to Persian control. The Ionians were the same branch of Greeks as the Athenians, though the Ephesians did not always support their kindred in war. To the Persians, who saw little difference between the various Hellenic tribes and dialects, all Greeks were lumped together as Ionians, or *Yauna*, in the Persian language. The city of Ephesus was best known for its famous temple of Artemis, the virgin goddess of hunting, which had reportedly burned down the night Alexander was born and was still being rebuilt. "Great is Artemis of the Ephesians," later generations would chant, and the citizens of Alexander's time could not have agreed more.

The backers of democracy at Ephesus had opened the gates to Parmenion two years earlier, even setting up a statue of Philip at the temple. But Memnon had retaken the city and restored the ruling aristocracy that supported Persia. Now the democrats returned from

exile seeking vengeance. They launched a pogrom against the aristocrats and murdered anyone they could find who didn't share their political convictions, including those who had torn down Philip's statue.
One oligarch named Syrphax was dragged from the temple along
with his nephews and publicly stoned to death. Alexander had little
sympathy with the aristocracy and allowed the bloodshed to continue
for a few days, but eventually even he felt things were going too far.
He knew that soon the violence would descend into general mayhem
and personal grudges that had nothing to do with politics. He halted
the vendetta and, to help distract the Ephesians from infighting, he
offered to donate his own money to help rebuild the temple of Artemis and restore the lucrative tourist trade. Surprisingly, the citizens
declined, though this refusal may have been orchestrated by Alexander to spare himself an enormous expense. Still, the king ordered
that all city taxes previously paid to the Persians would henceforth be
directed to rebuilding the great temple. To entertain and intimidate
the restive citizens, Alexander then staged a grand parade and battle
drill through the streets of the city with his troops in full battle dress.

Representatives from the nearby towns of Magnesia and Tralles
soon arrived to surrender their cities to Alexander. The king graciously
accepted and sent Parmenion with a large force of cavalry and infantry to make sure they meant it. He also dispatched troops to other
Greek towns on the coast to drive out Persian garrisons, overthrow
aristocratic rulers, and proclaim democracy and freedom for all. Now
that they were free cities, they would not be subject to distasteful tax
payments to the Great King in distant Persepolis. Instead, as liberated Greeks, they would be permitted to make hefty contributions to
the Macedonian cause.

The famous painter Apelles was resident in Ephesus when Alexander arrived and the king could not resist commissioning a portrait
of himself astride Bucephalas. The king had seen Apelles' work before,
including the painting of his own father, Philip, and had great expectations for a matchless work. However, when the painting was finished,
Alexander was not impressed. Apelles then brought it over to show Bucephalas, who neighed in apparent approval. The bold artist then told

Alexander that his horse had better taste than he did. But the king, who had studied artistic theory with Aristotle and fancied himself a connoisseur of fine paintings, demanded that Apelles try again. This time Apelles played to Alexander's vanity and showed him as Zeus wielding a thunderbolt. He even used a secret varnish formula to give the portrait a striking tone. The king was pleased with this very un-Greek style of portraiture and gave Apelles a large bag of gold as payment.

While Parmenion was away, Alexander took the rest of the army and left Ephesus for the key city of Miletus thirty miles to the south. On the way he stopped at the small Ionian Greek town of Priene at the mouth of the Meander River. The river was notable for its wandering course (hence our modern term *meander*) and in time it would silt up the entire bay between Priene and Miletus. Alexander wanted to visit the newly completed temple to Athena in Priene, designed by Pythius himself, architect of the Mausoleum at Halicarnassus, one of the seven wonders of the ancient world. At Priene, Alexander donated enough money so that, unlike at Ephesus, he was named patron of the new temple. The dedicatory inscription in Greek, which survives to this day, is one of the few pieces of contemporary evidence we possess naming the Macedonian king:

ΒΑΣΙΛΕΥΣ ΑΛΕΞΑΝΔΡΟΣ ΑΝΕϑΗΚΕ ΤΟΝ
ΝΑΟΝ ΑϑΗΝΑΙΗΙ ΠΟΛΙΑΔΙ
*King Alexander dedicated this temple to Athena,*
*Protector of the City*

Alexander rarely missed a chance to combine his genuine devotion to the gods with useful propaganda.

Parmenion and his forces rejoined Alexander at Miletus. It was an ancient settlement dating back to the days of the Trojan War and had been a major naval center for centuries. It was now the city's ability to shelter the Persian fleet that most concerned Alexander. The Great King had four hundred ships, primarily from Cyprus and Egypt, operating in the eastern Mediterranean, as opposed to his own, untried fleet, less than half that size, drawn from various Greek cities of questionable loyalty. If the Persians were allowed to use Miletus as a naval base, they could hamper his advance and strike against him anywhere in the Aegean.

The commander of the garrison at Miletus had sent a message to Alexander offering surrender, but when he heard the Persian fleet was near at hand he reneged on his offer and barred the city gates to the Macedonians. Alexander then ordered his small fleet to race for Miletus to prevent the Persians from seizing the harbor and nearby islands. The Greek navy arrived in time to set up base on the island of Lade just offshore while the tardy Persians were forced to anchor in an unfavorable location ten miles to the north. Alexander ferried several thousand Thracians and other mercenaries to Lade to help hold the island against any Persian attack.

It was now Parmenion who urged boldness against the Persian fleet. He advised the king that a naval attack by the Greek ships could succeed, especially as he had seen an eagle, a favored bird of Zeus, perching on the stern of one of the ships. It would be a great victory if they could win, the general claimed, but only a minor defeat if they lost. Alexander, however, was uncharacteristically cautious. He had little experience with naval warfare and less trust in Greek sailors. He countered that it was foolish to engage a much larger fleet with his inexperienced navy. He would have to place Macedonian marines on each ship to fight the Persians at sea, a frightening prospect to men from the mountains of his homeland. Moreover, a defeat would indeed be serious and give the Greek cities courage to rise up against him. Finally, the eagle Parmenion saw was facing the land, not the sea, so that Zeus clearly wanted him to wage war on solid ground.

When Alexander's engineering corps arrived at Miletus, the king put them to work knocking down the city walls. It was the first opportunity his engineers had during the campaign to prove they could work miracles. Soon there was a hole wide enough in the defenses to send the Macedonian army through into the city. Alexander's men swarmed through the town, killing all the defenders they could find, and headed for the harbor. There the Greek fleet had moved in to blockade the Persians from landing reinforcements. The Persian soldiers in the city, made up largely of several hundred Greek mercenaries hired by Memnon, were pushed to the sea, where many climbed onto their concave shields and paddled to a small island in the harbor to make a final stand. They had heard of the fate of their comrades at the Granicus and were determined to sell their lives dearly. But Alexander sailed to the island himself and told the mercenaries that he admired their bravery and loyalty. He offered them mercy on the condition that they join his army. Given the circumstances, they had little choice but to accept. The citizens of the city who had survived the assault were likewise spared the horrors of enslavement and allowed to remain in the town, undoubtedly after paying a large indemnity for their resistance.

The Persian navy continued to harass the Macedonians even after the fall of Miletus. Each day they would sail from their base and draw up before the harbor, trying to tempt Alexander into a fight at sea. But fume as he might, the king remained firm in his plan to avoid a naval battle. Instead he sent Parmenion's son Philotas to the coast near the Persian anchorage to prevent them from collecting fresh water. In frustration, they sailed to the nearby island of Samos for supplies and then struck at Miletus again. Five Persian ships managed to slip into the inner harbor, hoping to catch Alexander unprepared, but the king quickly gathered whatever troops were at hand and launched ten ships to strike back. The Persians had convinced themselves that the Macedonians were afraid to face them on the water, so they were surprised to see Alexander at the helm of a force twice their size sailing toward them in the harbor. They turned and rowed for their lives, but not before Alexander captured one of their ships.

In spite of his modest naval victory, Alexander now made a momentous decision that was to determine his course for the rest of the war—he ordered his fleet to disband. Ancient and modern historians have long argued about why he did this, but the reasons given by the historian Arrian seem plausible, namely that he did not have enough money to support a navy and even if he did, his fleet was no match for the Persians. One might add that he found the Greek sailors untrustworthy and far more trouble than they were worth. But decommissioning his navy meant that he had no choice but to defeat the Persian fleet by land. The only way he could do this was to deny them a safe harbor anywhere in the Mediterranean. In effect, Alexander was committing himself and the Macedonian army to seizing the entire coast from Troy to Egypt. Until he could accomplish this, he was leaving himself vulnerable to Persian naval strikes against Asia Minor, Greece, and even Macedonia. But to conquer the entire eastern Mediterranean was an astonishingly ambitious plan. Most of Alexander's officers and soldiers had probably assumed they would limit their campaign to the shores of the Aegean Sea, but one suspects that the young king had planned from the beginning to drive his army all the way to the pyramids if not to the heart of Persia and beyond.

Word soon reached Alexander that the Great King had overruled the objections of his nobles and at last appointed Memnon as commander of the Persian army and fleet in the war against the Macedonians. The price of this appointment was that Memnon had to send his wife, Barsine, and his children to the court of Darius as hostages. The new commander then moved his forces to the coastal city of Halicarnassus, south of Miletus. It was an astute decision on Memnon's part as this southernmost of the major Greek towns in Asia Minor had one of the finest harbors on the Aegean coast and was surrounded by formidable walls.

Halicarnassus was in the mountainous land of Caria, inhabited by a people of non-Greek origin related in language to the Lydians. The Dorian Greeks, relatives of the Spartans, had settled along the coast centuries earlier and founded outposts such as Halicarnassus. In later times, the Greek towns of Caria became Ionian in culture and produced such famous figures as the historian Herodotus, a native of Halicarnassus. Greeks and Carians lived amicably side by side, but the rulers were a native dynasty known as the Hecatomnids. As in Macedonia, the nobles embraced Greek culture while the vast majority of the people carried on the ways of their ancestors, even in the Hellenized cities. To the proud Carians, a father was *ted* and a mother *en*, not *patēr* and *mētēr* as among the Greeks. Ancient pastoralism was the foundation of the economy and it was practiced largely from isolated hilltop villages scattered throughout the land. But in spite of royal initiatives to promote Hellenic culture, the Carians remained loyal to their kings and queens even while they ignored their attempts to spread Greek ways.

Caria had fallen under Persian control in the late sixth century as had the rest of Asia Minor, but the royal family continued to rule in the name of the Great King. Most famous of these monarchs was Mausolus, who, following a custom Carian royalty shared with Egyptian pharaohs and Persian kings, had married his sister. He then moved the Carian capital from the inland town of Mylasa to Halicarnassus. He had briefly joined a revolt of the satraps of Asia Minor in the 360s, but was soon forgiven and spent the remainder of his reign increasing Carian power in the region while remaining loyal to Persia. His crowning achievement was the construction of the famous Mausoleum, named after himself, that was to serve as his tomb and a monument to his rule. It was indeed a wonder of the world, soaring almost 150 feet and topped by a pyramid. It was elaborately decorated with splendid Ionic columns and sculptures of lions, Amazons, and centaurs.

When Mausolus died and was buried as a cult hero in his magnificent tomb, royal power passed in time to Pixodarus, with whom the impulsive Alexander had tried to arrange a marriage alliance several years earlier. Pixodarus had seized power from his sister, Ada, and soon married his daughter to a Persian nobleman named Orontobates, who took over rule of Caria at the recent death of Pixodarus. The resourceful Ada, however, still held the mountain fortress of Alinda just fifty miles away. The Carians chafed under the rule of a foreign overlord and longed to see Ada on the throne once again. It was a situation that Alexander could exploit to his own advantage.

On the march from Miletus to Halicarnassus, the Macedonians captured several smaller towns along the way, presumably including the sacred oracle of Apollo at Didyma. It seems unlikely that Alexander could have resisted the opportunity to visit this hilltop site overlooking the sea, as it had been one of the greatest prophetic centers in the Greek world before the Persian king Darius I destroyed it at the beginning of the fifth century. Darius deported the ruling priesthood, known as the Branchidae, to central Asia even though they had collaborated with the Persians, to protect them from retribution by their Greek neighbors. Alexander would have known of their fate and the rituals once conducted at the temple. As at Delphi, a consecrated prophetess conveyed the will of the god to mortals. At Didyma she first bathed, then entered the shrine to hear the questions put forth by petitioners. She sat on an axle suspended over a sacred spring, dipping her foot into the water before she answered. It must have saddened the king that the voice of Apollo had grown silent at this holy place, and he may have given orders to reestablish the oracle.

At the seaside town of Iasus, Alexander met a delegation of officials who welcomed him and anxiously petitioned him to restore the fishing rights they had lost under the Persians. Such prosaic matters may have seemed to some beneath the concern of the king, but Alexander knew that the support of local leaders was crucial to his enterprise and gladly granted their request. There he also met a young boy who had tamed a friendly dolphin. The king was so impressed by the lad and his talent with sea creatures that he afterward named him as chief priest of the god Poseidon at Babylon.

As he approached the border of Caria, Alexander was met on the road by the former queen, Ada. The Macedonian ruler had never shown much interest in members of the opposite sex his own age, but had always gotten on well with older women. Ada welcomed Alexander to Caria and proceeded to work out a deal with him. Alexander needed someone he could trust to rule the land once he had taken Halicarnassus and moved on. Ada was loved and respected by her people, who saw her as the legitimate ruler of Caria rather than the Persian usurper Orontobates. She would throw her support behind Alexander in return for the throne. In addition, she would formally adopt Alexander as her own son, thus giving him legitimacy as overlord in the eyes of the Carians. He would not be invading their country as just another foreigner bent on conquest, but as a liberator restoring his mother, their beloved queen, to her rightful place. Alexander was charmed by Ada, but also saw the practical benefits to her proposal and readily agreed. The Carian reaction was indeed favorable as delegations from towns throughout the land began to arrive at Alexander's camp bearing golden crowns and promises of cooperation. Ada herself was soon sending her new son delicacies from her own kitchen.

But as sympathetic as Ada and the Carian country people might be to Alexander's cause, Halicarnassus was going to be very hard to conquer. When the Macedonians arrived at the city, Alexander looked down in dismay from the surrounding hills at the Persian for-tifications. The fleet headquarters at the entrance to the harbor was cut off from land attack, while heavy walls encircled the entire city, including two fortresses on opposite sides of the town. Since he had dismissed his fleet, Alexander could not prevent supplies or reinforce-ments from reaching Halicarnassus by sea. The only way to take the town was to find a way through the walls.

On the first day of the siege, some of Memnon's troops burst through the northeast gate and struck at Alexander's surprised troops. They were easily driven back within the walls, but it was just the start of what would be a long series of hit-and-run forays by the Persian forces to throw the Macedonians off balance. Alexander then ordered his troops to begin filling in the trenches the defenders had dug around the city. Days went by as the Macedonians tried to secure the moats, but were repeatedly driven back by troops on the walls. Alexander tried sheltering his men with movable sheds to keep off rocks and arrows, but the rain of projectiles from above was still too much. In frustra-tion, he led a diversionary attack on the Persian-held city of Myndus ten miles to the west, hoping to draw away some of Memnon's troops from Halicarnassus. Here he faced the same difficulties even after his engineers dug a tunnel under the wall to collapse it from below. When Memnon's reinforcements arrived, they were able to link up with the defenders of Myndus and drive the Macedonians away in defeat.

Returning to Halicarnassus, Alexander redoubled his efforts at taking the wall and brought up a huge tower on wheels to shower the defenders with missiles while a battering ram pounded the stones beneath them. In response, the Persian troops made a night raid to burn down the tower, but were caught just in time by Macedonian guards, who roused their comrades to action. The Persians lost almost two hundred men that night while only sixteen of Alexander's men fell, but three hundred Macedonians were badly wounded during a chaotic battle in darkness.

The stalemate dragged on as summer turned to autumn and the fierce heat of the Carian coast began to wane. Still Alexander was no closer to taking Halicarnassus than he had been when he first arrived. His men were frustrated as well. One night two drunken Macedonian soldiers on guard duty decided they had had enough. With wine to give them courage and insults to each other's manhood, they armed themselves and rushed one of the city gates in a foolhardy bid for glory. A few defenders met them and were slain by the Macedonians. This brought out more troops from both sides until there was a full-fledged battle outside the gates. Dozens were killed on both sides as the Macedonians almost stormed the walls, but by dawn defenders and attackers alike were forced to retreat.

Alexander decided he had to take the city soon or withdraw before winter set in. Over the next few days the king himself led a series of attacks against the walls, causing a great deal of damage, only to be met by defenders equally determined to drive the Macedonians back. Alexander was losing too many officers and men with each assault, but the Persians were losing more. At last Memnon decided that his troops could no longer hold the entire city. He ordered his men to set fire to the town. Leaving garrisons at the city's fortresses, Memnon and the fleet then sailed that night to the nearby island of Cos, out of Alexander's reach.

The Macedonian king was at last victorious in his most grueling battle yet. Now he controlled the entire Aegean coast of Asia Minor from the Hellespont to Caria. He spared the lives of the people of Halicarnassus, but finished what the Persians began and burned their city to the ground. Concerning the fate of the thousands of men, women, and children left homeless as winter was descending, our sources are silent. Alexander placed Ada on the throne of Caria as his satrap in the smoldering ruins of the city and stationed enough troops nearby to drive out the last of the Persians from their citadels. But even in the midst of celebrating, the king knew that just across the narrow strait on the island of Cos, the Persians were waiting. Their navy was intact and they had thousands of troops at their disposal. Memnon had lost Halicarnassus, but Alexander's most capable foe was far from defeated.

Many of Alexander's soldiers were newly married and had left their young brides behind when they departed Macedonia the previous spring. Now that the campaign season was over and all the Greek coast of Asia Minor was in Alexander's hands, the king sent these recent grooms home to spend the winter with their wives and sow the seeds for a new generation of Macedonian warriors. In the spring, they would rejoin the army to continue the war against Persia. It was a popular decision with the men and a great boost for morale. The furloughs were also a clever propaganda ploy since the men could give eyewitness accounts of Alexander's victories against the Persians and build support back home. To lead the men, Alexander sent Coenus and Meleager, both newlyweds themselves. Meleager was a loyal officer from the Macedonian highlands who had served Alexander on the Danube and at the Granicus. Coenus had also fought bravely for the king, but his new bride was a sister of Philotas, making him the son-in-law of Parmenion. It is no surprise that Alexander wanted to be rid of as many of Parmenion's family as possible, at least for the winter. At the same time he sent Cleander, brother of Coenus, to the Peloponnese in southern Greece to recruit mercenaries from the neighbors of Sparta. Apart from their marital duties, Meleager and Coenus were ordered to recruit new soldiers in Macedonia during their short stay and bring them back to Asia in the spring. Parmenion himself was dispatched with most of the cavalry north to Sardis with orders to rendezvous at Gordium in the Phrygian highlands of central Asia Minor in a few months. Splitting the army not only freed Alexander from Parmenion's unwanted advice but reduced the amount of food and fodder needed from any one region.

Conventional wisdom in the ancient world said that wars were never fought in winter. Alexander, however, was not one to follow tradition. With his lean and hardened army, he set off from Halicarnassus into the wild highlands of Lycia along the southern coast of Asia Minor just as the leaves were falling from the trees. It was a bold move, but without Parmenion around to tell him why he was being a fool, Alexander was at last free to do as he pleased. His objective was to conquer the region, especially key naval bases on the coast, while the Persians were unprepared. But aside from military objectives, Alexander was seeking the glory that comes from taking an unexpected risk—and winning.

Bundled against the increasing cold, Alexander's army marched through the mountains and along the coast almost a hundred miles to the port of Telmessus, home of the king's favorite soothsayer, Aristander. According to one story, Nearchus, the childhood companion of Alexander, had a friend in the Persian-controlled town who suggested a ruse to take the citadel without a fight. With his friend's help, Nearchus smuggled a troop of dancing girls into a dinner party for the Great King's soldiers. After dinner and entertainment, when all the soldiers had drunk far more wine than was wise, the girls pulled daggers from their baskets and massacred the garrison. Whether or not the story is true, Alexander was able to take the citadel of Telmessus without a fight and gain control over a key port on the southern coast.

From Telmessus the army marched over the rugged mountains to the Xanthus River and down to the city of the same name on the coast. There representatives from over thirty Lycian towns, including the key port of Phaselis, met the king and offered their submission. Near the Xanthus, Alexander found a sacred spring that conveniently spewed forth a bronze tablet engraved with ancient letters. It was probably the seer Aristander who read the inscription and claimed it said that one day the empire of the Persians would be destroyed by the Greeks. Alexander was encouraged by this prophecy as he struggled over snow-covered passes to eastern Lycia.

Alexander and his men finally arrived at the port of Phaselis, founded by Greeks three centuries before. The path north from the

town was more fit for goatherds than an army of thousands, so the
king sent his Thracian soldiers to carve a road over the pass and down
into the plain of Pamphylia. He allowed the remainder of the army
a few days' rest and enjoyed the local wine himself. One night, after
a typically raucous Macedonian drinking party, he led his friends
into the town square, where they found a statue to the late local poet
Theodectes, a friend of Aristotle's during the philosopher's years in
Athens. Alexander must have heard his teacher speak favorably of
the man, for the king and his companions crowned his statue with
many garlands.

While at Phaselis, Alexander received a disturbing report from
Parmenion. The general's message said that the leader of the Thessalian cavalry on his staff, Alexander of Lyncestis, was conspiring
with the Great King to murder Alexander. Parmenion had captured
a Persian agent, Sisines, on the way to Phrygia who under torture
had confessed that Darius was offering the supposed conspirator a
king's ransom in gold and his full support in seizing the Macedonian
throne in return for his cooperation. Alexander of Lyncestis was already a suspect character to some as his brothers had been executed
for plotting the murder of Philip. Only the fact that he had been the
first to hail Alexander as king and accompany him as a guard into
the palace had saved his life. In addition, Alexander's mother, Olympias, had been warning her son to beware of Alexander of Lyncestis
for months, whether because she had been receiving her own reports
questioning his loyalty or because she simply didn't like the man. Her
son, however, was accustomed to frequent, unsolicited advice from his
mother. He would later complain that she charged a very high rent
for nine months in her womb.

The charges placed the king in a difficult position. He knew the
other Alexander as a brave and capable officer, having appointed him
commander of the important Thessalian cavalry after he had made
the former leader, Calas, satrap of the Hellespont region. Alexander
of Lyncestis was also the son-in-law of Antipater, whom the king had
left as regent of Macedonia during the campaign. He immediately
called a council of his closest friends to seek their advice, but they

agreed with Parmenion that such a man should be eliminated. They also reminded Alexander that while he was still besieging Halicarnassus, a swallow had flitted about his head during a nap and chattered until he awoke. Aristander the seer had interpreted this as an omen that someone close to the king would soon plot against his life. But Alexander was deeply suspicious of the charges. Parmenion would love to remove the king's appointee from his staff and replace him with his own choice. What better way than to accuse a man from a traitorous family of conspiracy? In addition, Alexander had met Sisines a few years before, when he had arrived at Pella as a secret messenger from Egypt trying to persuade his father to support a rebellion against Persia. He was a shady character of dubious integrity, moving between kings and kingdoms, serving whoever paid him the most. As for Aristander and the bird, even Alexander didn't believe everything the old soothsayer prophesied.

Still, it would not be prudent to risk a knife in the back when he arrived in Phrygia, so Alexander sent a trusted envoy undercover to Parmenion dressed as a mountain tribesman. The mission was so delicate that the king did not commit his orders to writing but instructed the herald to memorize them—a precaution against his capture by Persian agents. The herald instructed Parmenion to detain Alexander of Lyncestis, but not to execute him. The king himself would investigate the charges of conspiracy quietly in due time. Alexander then appointed his old friend Erigyius to fill the vacant position as head of the Thessalian cavalry to forestall Parmenion from selecting one of his relatives for the post.

When the Thracian road builders had finished their work, Alexander gathered the rest of his army and marched north from Phaselis over the pass at Mount Climax, then down to the narrow trail along the sea. It was a tricky path during the storms of winter as the south wind would frequently send waves surging over the shore. The historian Arrian, drawing on the official account of Callisthenes, reports that the north wind began to drive the water back just as Alexander arrived. It was thereafter claimed that the gods had miraculously vanquished the waves to allow the Macedonians safe passage. Diodorus, however, using a more sober account perhaps written by a weary soldier in the ranks, says that the army marched all day long in freezing water up to their waists.

Somewhere in this region, while his men were strung out in a long column, Alexander was attacked by a local tribe known as the Marmares. They killed many of his rear guard and captured others, seizing as well many of the pack animals with their crucial supplies. The Marmares retreated to a mountaintop fortress called the Rock, confident that they were safe from attack. The natives failed to realize that Alexander was unlike any foe they had ever faced and was especially dangerous when he was angry. In a prelude to assaults the king would make against towering citadels in the Hindu Kush, Alexander launched a full-scale assault on the mountain. Within two days it became clear to the natives that they had no hope of resisting the Macedonians, but neither would they surrender their families and their freedom to the invaders. The elders of the tribe urged the warriors to kill their wives and children themselves rather than allow them to fall into slavery and abuse at the hands of the enemy. The young men agreed and so retired to their homes for a final feast before the slaughter began. When the time came, however, a few could not carry out the deed with their own hands and so set fire to their houses instead, burning their families alive. Unencumbered by women and children, the warriors of the Marmares then slipped through the Macedonian lines that night and fled into the mountains.

With this gruesome scene behind them, Alexander and his army at last marched into Pamphylia, a beautiful plain stretching some fifty miles along the shore and surrounded by mountains. The largest city in the area was Perge, famous for its temple to Artemis centered around a cult object that was probably a large meteorite. The citizens spoke an archaic form of Greek that sounded quite odd to Alexander's ears, but they surrendered peacefully. Down the road a day's march was the hilltop town of Aspendus, supposedly settled by colonists from Argos in Greece but loyal to the Persians, who had long used it as a base. The town was famous for the wealth it had built on the salt and olive oil trades. A delegation of city elders met the king and offered to submit to his authority if only he would not station a garrison of his troops in their town. Alexander agreed on the condition that they give him all the horses they bred for the Great King in their lush meadows and donate an outrageous sum to pay his army. This was blackmail, but the citizens of Aspendus had little choice but to consent.

Alexander then moved on to Side, the easternmost town in Pamphylia, posting a garrison before he doubled back to Aspendus to collect his money and horses. But in the short time he had been away, the people of Aspendus had found their courage and now shut the gates of the city in his face, fleeing to their acropolis. The lower town was surrounded by a short wall that the Macedonians easily stormed, but the fortified upper city was on a steep hill bordered on one side by a river. The army made themselves at home in the houses of the lower town and waited since Alexander badly needed both the money and horses. A shrewd judge of human nature, he was betting the people of Aspendus would crack when they saw their homes occupied and their city cut off. He was soon proven right when a deputation appeared begging the king to accept their surrender on the terms to which they had previously agreed. Alexander must have smiled as he shook his head and replied that they now must not only give him the horses, but double the amount of gold agreed on before. In addition, he would be posting a large garrison in their town, taking their leading citizens as hostages, collecting an additional yearly tax, and—by the way—he would be looking closely into complaints that they had unjustly annexed land from their more cooperative neighbors along the coast. The citizens of Aspendus had learned the hard way that no one double-crossed Alexander.

With his cavalry mounted on fresh horses and gold from Aspendus loaded on his pack animals, Alexander set out toward Gordium to rendezvous with the rest of his army. The only problem was that he had little idea how to get there. He started in the wrong direction, heading west until he arrived at the fortress of Termessus commanding the pass into the mountains. The citadel, surrounded by gorges and cliffs, was occupied by highlanders who had never submitted to the Persians. For a few days the Macedonians skirmished with these brigands, but to little avail. Given enough time, Alexander could have taken Termessus, but the king did not want to get bogged down in a protracted siege. It was at this point that messengers from the nearby town of Selge arrived at his camp to make a treaty of friendship. They also pointed out that Alexander was going the wrong way. There was a much easier road that ran near their village directly through the mountains to Gordium. Swallowing his pride, the king left Termessus untouched and marched his army north into the heart of Asia Minor.

Alexander's first stop on the road to Gordium was the town of Sagalassus in the mountainous land of Pisidia. The people were warlike and their town well fortified, but this was one location the king could not leave unconquered as it commanded an important passage to the south. On the other hand, it was the worst possible setting for a battle. The Macedonians would have to fight uphill the whole distance without cavalry support because the ground was too rough for horses.

The army spread out and charged the enemy with infantry, archers, and Thracian spearmen. It was a fierce battle in the winter cold, but at last the Pisidians began to give way as they had no armor and were suffering grievous injuries. Most of the warriors from Sagalassus escaped since the Macedonian army was too exhausted to pursue them, but at least five hundred died defending their home.

The ice was beginning to break up on the streams of the Anatolian plateau when the Macedonans at last arrived at Celaenae midway on the march to Gordium. The inhabitants of the area were known for their trade in the salt that crystallized naturally from the briny lakes of the regions. They also sat astride the main road linking Persia to the Aegean coast. It was a city Alexander absolutely had to take if he was to control his line of communication between Macedonia and all points east. The citadel of the town was formidable, especially as it was occupied by more than a thousand Carian and Greek mercenaries—but soldiers of fortune are nothing if not practical. They sent a delegation to the king offering to surrender to the Macedonians if no help arrived in two months. Alexander hated to make deals like this, but he did not want to waste weeks besieging the city. He agreed to their terms, leaving fifteen hundred troops behind to guard the city under the command of the one-eyed general Antigonus, whom the king appointed as satrap of the region. Selecting this ambitious and capable soldier to oversee a key piece of the growing Macedonian empire would in time have profound consequences.

Alexander reached Gordium in the ancient kingdom of Phrygia just as spring was beginning in the highlands of central Asia Minor. King Midas of the golden touch had once ruled this rich land, but for almost two hundred years it had been a key outpost of the Persians. Alexander hoped to meet Parmenion and the reinforcements from Macedonia at the town and was not disappointed. The crusty old general was waiting for him, as were the returning newlywed troops along with three thousand additional Macedonian infantry, three hundred cavalry, and two hundred mounted warriors from Thessaly. Trailing behind was a delegation from Athens that had journeyed all the way from Greece to ask the king for clemency on behalf of the Athenian mercenaries captured months earlier at the battle on the Granicus River. These unfortunate men had been sent to the mines of Macedonia to labor and die underground as punishment for siding with the Persians. Alexander was polite, but he informed the Athenians that regretfully he could not grant their request at this time. However, he did consent to free their countrymen when the war against Persia was complete. Since the life expectancy of mine slaves was exceedingly short, this was in fact a confirmation of their death sentence.

But the king had much more to worry about that spring than disgruntled Athenians. News arrived at Gordium that the Persian general Memnon had been busy in the Aegean while Alexander was campaigning in Asia. Memnon had taken the fleet north from Cos after his defeat at Halicarnassus and seized the island of Chios, then sailed to Lesbos, which he captured except for the chief town of Mytilene. At the same time, he was making overtures to disgruntled Greeks on the mainland, especially the Athenians and Spartans. If they would support the Great King, he would launch an invasion of Greece and Macedonia that would drive out the hated Macedonians.

Most of the Greeks were enthusiastic at the prospect of Persian intervention and many sent delegations to welcome Memnon and his army. It was a scene that would have astonished their ancestors, who had laid down their lives to drive back the Persians at Marathon and Thermopylae in the previous century.

The reports from Greece were a devastating blow to Alexander. He was winning the war in Asia only to risk losing Greece and Macedonia. With the Greeks in revolt and his homeland threatened, how could Alexander continue his campaign in Asia? He would surely have to return to the west—and yet, if he did, the victories he had won against Persia would be for nothing. His dreams of conquest would vanish and he would be remembered as just another small king who had dared great deeds only to fail.

It was now that one of those fortuitous events in history occurred that changed everything. While he was besieging the town of Mytilene on Lesbos, Memnon suddenly fell ill and died. Alexander could not believe his luck when he received the news. Memnon had handed over command of the Aegean to his Persian nephew Pharnabazus on his deathbed, but the young man, though a skillful soldier, was not his uncle. He continued the war and took Mytilene, then captured the small but crucial island of Tenedos at the mouth of the Hellespont. Pharnabazus continued to plan the invasion of Greece and Macedonia, but things had changed because of the death of Memnon. The Greeks began to have second thoughts about the rebellion. More important, the Great King doubted that he could win the war in the west without his favorite general. He sent one of Memnon's other nephews, a Greek named Thymondas, to relieve Pharnabazus of most of his army and bring the soldiers to Babylon. The campaign in the Aegean continued, but it was a halfhearted effort, biding time until Darius decided his next move.

The Great King called a meeting of his closest advisors to discuss the matter. Should he send his generals west to carry on the war with a mercenary army or should he take command himself and face Alexander in a decisive battle in Asia? Most of his advisors argued that he should lead the army in person and defeat this upstart Macedonian king once and for all with the full might of the Persian army. It would be an inspiring victory with the Great King leading his men from his war chariot on the glorious field of battle. But the experienced mercenary leader from Athens named Charidemus, who had earlier been exiled on Alexander's orders, strongly disagreed and urged Darius not to risk everything on a single battle with the Macedonians. He advised the Great King to keep his army in reserve in Babylon while a skilled general led an army composed largely of Greek mercenaries to fight Alexander. He also strongly hinted that he himself would be willing to take on this commission.

Darius was impressed by his arguments, but his Persian councilors began to rail against Charidemus, arguing that he wanted an army only so that he could gain glory for himself and probably betray the Great King as well. Charidemus grew livid and began to berate the advisors of Darius and Persians in general as effeminate cowards who couldn't face real men on the battlefield. Darius was so offended at this outburst that he rushed down off the throne, grabbed Charidemus by the belt, and ordered his immediate execution. As he was led away to his death, the defiant Charidemus shouted back to the Great King that he would soon see his empire fall to pieces around him. After the execution, Darius regretted that he had been so hasty in killing one of his best generals. He was haunted by dreams of Alexander and his Macedonian soldiers ever before his eyes. He sought in vain for a worthy replacement for Memnon to lead his army against the invaders, but soon decided that he would take command himself. He would gather a mighty host from the far corners of his empire and personally lead them against Alexander. It would take many months of preparation, but when the army was ready it would grind the Macedonians into dust.

# 4

# ISSUS

The story of the Gordian knot begins with an old man, a plow, and an eagle. There was a poor farmer named Gordius who was tilling his field one day when an eagle came and settled on the yoke of his plow. The holy bird of Zeus was an astonishing sight to Gordius and he went at once to a local family of prophets to have the omen interpreted. As he neared their village, he saw a girl drawing water at a well and asked if she was one of the soothsayers. She was and when he told her what had happened to him, she said he must return to the same spot and offer a sacrifice to Zeus. Gordius was only a simple farmer and knew nothing of religious rites, so he asked the girl to return with him and conduct the sacrifice. She did and decided to stay to become his wife. In time they had a son named Midas, who grew into a handsome man. The land of Phrygia in those days was torn by strife, but an ancient prophesy foretold that a man with a wagon would arrive who would become king and bring peace. When the people of Phrygia saw young Midas arriving one day with his father's wagon, they made him king. He soon brought an end to discord in the land and dedicated the family wagon at the temple of Zeus as a thanks offering for the god's favor. A legend grew up that whoever could undo the knot of the wagon's yoke would rule all of Asia.

Alexander had heard this story since he was a boy sitting at the feet of Aristotle in the Gardens of Midas in Macedonia. There was an alternate tradition that Midas had originally ruled in Macedonia before leading his people to Asia—a tale supported by the fact that Phrygian was more similar to Greek than to the ancient languages of Asia Minor. In any case, the king could not have resisted the chance to see the famous wagon and try his hand at untying the knot. It was made of rough bark wound so that no ends were visible no matter how carefully Alexander examined the knot. A crowd had grown and the king's friends began to worry. It would look bad if Alexander left the temple with the task undone, but it was clearly impossible for anyone to untie the Gordian knot.

There are two stories about what happened next. One comes from a biographer and military officer named Aristobulus who accompanied Alexander on his campaign. He says that the king, after carefully considering the knot, pulled out the lynchpin around which the knot was tied and was then able to loosen it. But another tradition, more likely given Alexander's nature, says that the king promptly pulled out his sword and cut the knot in two. After all, he said, it doesn't really matter *how* the knot is undone. Whichever story is true, the king of the gods was clearly pleased with Alexander's ingenuity because that night there was a great storm of thunder and lightning in the heavens.

The second year of Alexander's campaign against Persia began with a march through the highlands of central Asia Minor. He left Gordium and traveled several days east to Ancyra, where he was met by an embassy from neighboring Paphlagonia on the southern shores of the Black Sea. They submitted to him, but asked him not to lead his army into their land. Since Paphlagonia was a mountainous country of small villages with few riches besides timber, the king agreed and told them they were now subject to Calas, satrap of the Hellespont region.

From Ancyra, the Macedonians turned south back toward the Mediterranean. Alexander crossed the Halys River and after many days came to the highlands of Cappadocia. Our sources say little of this part of the campaign—it must have been brutally hot—except that the invaders were victorious. Then several weeks after leaving Gordium, the Macedonian army arrived at the Taurus Mountains separating the uplands of Asia Minor from the Mediterranean coast. The only way through this barrier was an infamous pass known as the Cilician Gates, a narrow defile barely wide enough for a handful of men to march side by side. Alexander ordered his soldiers to make camp in a large field on the north side of the pass. Xenophon's army had also camped here a few decades before, as the king would have known from his reading. This was the entrance to the fertile land of Cilicia and the gateway to Syria. If the Macedonians could force their way through, the eastern Mediterranean coast would be open to them.

The Persian satrap of Cilicia was Arsames, who had been present at the conference before the battle of the Granicus, at which Memnon had advised a scorched-earth policy to hinder the Macedonians. Arsames now took this advice to heart and began to burn everything in Alexander's path. In his eagerness to set fire to the countryside, he posted only a small guard to hold the Cilician Gates. Never one to miss an opportunity, the king left Parmenion with the main body of the army and led a small force himself by night to the pass. The defenders panicked at the sight of Alexander and fled south as fast as they could in the darkness. By morning, the Macedonians commanded the most strategic position in Asia Minor.

The satrap was now in a panic himself and rushed to burn his seaside capital of Tarsus before Alexander could arrive. The king heard of this from scouts and would have none of it. He pushed his advance force at full speed down the valley of the Cydnus River to Tarsus and was at the gates of the city just in time to see Arsames running for his life toward Persia. To make sure that he controlled the road to the east, the king immediately sent Parmenion to guard the passes from Syria into Cilicia. Now, at last, the Macedonians could rest from their travels. In the weeks since Alexander had left Gordium, he and his weary army had marched hundreds of miles over deserts, mountains, and volcanic wastelands, but they were finally back on the Mediterranean coast. The king was now ruler not only of Macedonia and Greece, but all of Asia Minor as well.

The plains of Cilicia were like an oven when Alexander reached Tarsus. The king was so hot that the first thing he did when he arrived in town was strip off his clothes in full view of the army and plunge naked into the Cydnus River. Although the seaside plain was broiling, the river was fed by melting snow from the mountains and was ice cold. The king must have known that the Cydnus was famed for its healing properties, especially for swollen muscles and gout. But as soon as Alexander was immersed in the water, his limbs began to cramp, the blood drained from his face, and the cold penetrated into his bones. He had probably been sick before this, perhaps with a bronchial infection or even malaria, but the sudden shock to his body left him paralyzed as his friends carried him from the water. To his watching army, he must have seemed like a dead man as they rushed him to his tent.

The next few days he hovered between life and death. His body burned with a fever that threatened to kill him as he drifted in and out of consciousness. For his soldiers, this was a fearful turn of events. They were far from home in a hostile land with the Great King marching toward them at the head of an enormous army. Now more than ever, they needed Alexander. If he died, how would they get home alive? How could they return across Asia Minor with the Persians in pursuit? They were torn with pity both for their king and themselves as they stood waiting outside his tent.

The physicians that accompanied the expedition had no idea how to treat Alexander and were afraid even to try. If the king died under their care, they would surely be blamed for his death and suffer the consequences. The only doctor who dared to offer a cure was

Philip from the land of Acarnania in northwest Greece. He had been a trusted physician at the Macedonian court since Alexander was a boy and had treated the young king for any number of ailments over the years. In one of his lucid moments, Alexander listened as Philip explained the treatment he was proposing. It was a strong purge that would make the king even sicker before it worked, so there was great danger in the procedure. But, in the end, if the potion was successful, his health would be restored.

Greek medicine was based on the concept of balance. Hippocrates of Cos had taught that the different fluids or humors of the body—namely blood, yellow bile, black bile, and phlegm—maintained a natural equilibrium in a healthy person. When one or more of these humors was in excess, it was the task of the skilled physician to restore balance to the body. This could be done in many ways, but the most frequent was therapy by opposites, such as dosing the sufferer of a cold with peppers or applying cooling oils to hot rashes. The opium poppy was also a frequent ingredient in Greek pharmacology for its soothing effect.

Alexander listened to Philip's proposed therapy with the ear of a student who had been trained by Aristotle and practiced some medicine himself. He knew the purge was dangerous, but he also knew that his army was in grave danger every day he lay helpless in bed. Darius had surely heard of his infirmity through his network of spies and was hastening his plans for attack. The king knew he had to get well quickly or die trying. He ordered Philip to prepare the potion and bring it to him as soon as it was ready.

At this moment, a note arrived from Parmenion bearing a brief message: *Beware of Philip! I have word that Darius has bribed him to poison you.* As with the earlier affair involving Alexander of Lyncestis, a warning from Parmenion of treachery among his friends put the king in a difficult position. He had known Philip his whole life, but any man could be corrupted, especially with a kingly bribe. He also remembered that Philip's people in Acarnania had been rebels and fought against the Macedonians at Chaeronea. Was the physician now planning to kill Alexander and escape across the Persian lines to collect his reward? On the other hand, this could be a trick by Parmenion to discourage Alexander from treatment and hasten his death. The old general would be the natural choice as the next army leader and even as king. With Alexander out of the way, he could perhaps strike a deal with Darius and withdraw back to Macedonia, keeping the rich provinces of Asia Minor as part of the bargain. It was also possible that Darius was encouraging false suspicions by Alexander of his friends. All the Macedonians knew that the Great King had offered a huge reward to anyone who would kill Alexander. Who would be in a better position to do the deed than a trusted doctor?

Philip, unaware of the message from Parmenion, now returned to Alexander's tent bearing the potion in a cup. What happened next provides a marvelous insight into Alexander's character. He took the cup and began to drink the medicine while at the same moment handing Philip the note from Parmenion. As he drained the cup to the last drop, he watched the physician read the message. The expression on Philip's face did not change, he merely shrugged and told the king that the medicine would quickly take effect. Alexander lay back on his bed and was soon unconscious as his breathing became more and more labored. Philip remained by his bed, massaging the king with oils and waiting as the medicine spread through his body. After many hours, Alexander began to stir. His fever slowly eased while the king grew stronger in both mind and body. After three days he walked out of his tent to the deafening cheers of the entire Macedonian army.

There was little time to spare before he faced Darius on the battlefield, but Alexander spent the next two weeks securing his hold on Cilicia. One of his first actions was to take over the imperial Persian mint in Tarsus and order the engravers to strike a new silver coin. On its front was the head of young Hercules, the king's ancestor, wearing his customary lion's skin. On the reverse was Zeus seated like the Semitic god Baal—a blending of Greek and Oriental themes that was to become a hallmark of Alexander's new empire. The silver currency was most useful to the king as payment for his troops. Coinage was also important propaganda since the money would quickly find its way to markets and brothels throughout the eastern Mediterranean. If anyone wondered who had issued it, all he had to do was read Alexander's name imprinted next to the image of Zeus.

The king then marched for a day southwest along the coast to Anchiale, once a great city in an outlying kingdom of the Assyrian Empire. There local guides showed him a monument left by the Assyrian king Sardanapalus four hundred years earlier. On it was the carved relief of the eastern king snapping his fingers along with an inscription in cuneiform letters. The guides were quick to translate it for Alexander: "Sardanapalus, son of Anakyndaraxes, built Anchiale and Tarsus in a single day. But you, stranger, eat, drink, and make love—for the lives of other men compared to mine are not worth even this."

The *this* referred to was the snapping of the Assyrian king's fingers. Although Alexander suffered from no lack of self-confidence, he had to admire the cheek of Sardanapalus. He sent a copy of the translation back to Aristotle, who said the epitaph belonged on the tomb of a bull.

Just a few hours farther down the coast was the wealthy city of Soli, where Alexander extorted a huge ransom from the citizens in exchange for the privilege of remaining alive. He used the city as his headquarters for the next week while he and his men scoured the nearby mountains for rebellious Cilician highlanders. When he returned to Soli, a dispatch was waiting from the west informing the king that his troops had finally taken the remaining fortresses inside Halicarnassus, along with the nearby town of Myndus, the island of Cos, and a number of other settlements in Caria. His adopted mother Queen Ada could now rule as satrap throughout her native land. The good news from the Aegean would not last, but for the moment the king was happy to celebrate his victories with sacrifices to the gods, along with athletic and musical contests for his army.

Alexander had already ordered Parmenion ahead, but now he sent Philotas forward to the town of Mallus while he himself made a short detour to the coastal settlement of Magarsa to sacrifice at the local temple of Athena. The next day he caught up with Philotas at Mallus and offered more sacrifices, this time to Amphilochus, a celebrated veteran of the Trojan War. The king knew a decisive battle was coming and so prayed at the shrine of every god and hero on his march toward Darius.

However, not every Macedonian believed that heaven would favor them in the approaching fight. Alexander's childhood friend and campaign treasurer Harpalus suddenly fled to Greece along with a rascal named Tauriscus. The ancient sources never give his motive explicitly, but it is reasonable to think that Harpalus absconded with as much money as he could carry.

The plains of Cilicia are separated from Syria by a narrow but rugged range of mountains. Alexander knew from reading Xenophon that there was a pass called the Gates at the southern end of these mountains that served as the main entry into Syria. Accordingly, he moved his army rapidly down the coast past the town of Issus and over the Pinarus River to the small city of Myriandrus near the pass. He heard from his scouts that Darius and his army were on the other side of the mountains waiting for him. He also learned that the Great King had carefully chosen a broad plain there for the upcoming battle. It was near the Orontes River, just north of the future site of Antioch, and was the perfect location for war from the Persian point of view—open grasslands where the Great King could use his superior numbers, matchless cavalry, and terrifying battle chariots to his greatest advantage.

The only problem for Darius was that Alexander was not walking into the trap. Darius knew his enemy had been delayed in Cilicia by illness, but his scouts reported that the Macedonians had headed west toward Soli when their king recovered, then spent a week hunting mountain tribesmen and playing athletic games. Darius began to worry that Alexander, in spite of his reputation, was afraid to face him in battle. His Persian advisors urged the Great King to carry the war into Cilicia and crush the Macedonians there. However, a refugee from the Macedonian court named Amyntas warned Darius against such a change in plans, urging him to wait for Alexander at the chosen battle site.

Darius was no fool and was a far better general than many ancient historians claim, but he was in a difficult position. He could not afford to linger in Syria with his army while Alexander waited just over the mountains. His power ultimately depended on his ability to project military force anywhere in his empire at any time. If he seemed afraid to face Alexander, his control over his vast kingdom could collapse. He therefore ordered his army to march into Cilicia, but not by the southern pass. He believed the Macedonians were still near Tarsus and so moved through a northern pass into the plains above the town of Issus.

Alexander, meanwhile, too devoted to Xenophon's memoirs for his own good, had already moved beyond Issus in ignorance of other entries into Syria. He was not, in fact, afraid to face Darius there even if the Persians had chosen the site of battle. The Macedonian king had complete confidence in himself and his men to win, no matter the circumstances. He was at the southern pass preparing to cross the mountains when his scouts reported that the Persians were now *behind* him on the narrow coastal plain near Issus. Alexander thought the scouts surely must be mistaken and sent men back to verify the report. Meanwhile Darius had arrived in Cilicia only to hear that the Macedonian army was now behind *him*. It was a perfect muddle for both kings and not at all what either had planned. Darius was in such a bad mood that he rounded up some injured Macedonians left behind at Issus to recuperate and tortured them, cutting off both their hands for good measure. He had good reason to be upset. He had needlessly exchanged the broad plains of Syria for a confining strip of land between the mountains and sea.

Like Darius, Alexander immediately recognized that the new situation seriously compromised the Persians. As with the great sea battle at Salamis in the previous century in which a smaller Athenian navy drew a larger Persian fleet into a narrow strait, the fight on the plain of Issus would diminish any advantage in numbers. Even so, it would be a very tough fight. The Persian lines might not be broad, but they would be deep and filled with proven soldiers the Great King had summoned from the many nations of his empire.

Darius had begun gathering his army soon after the battle of Granicus over a year earlier. The recruitment of troops did not move swiftly in the Persian Empire, but once an army was assembled it was an awesome sight to behold. The Great King ordered troops from his whole realm to gather at Babylon in Mesopotamia. Although the entire army was not at his disposal, the force was considered sufficient to deal with the Macedonians. Some ancient sources say the Persian army numbered six hundred thousand men. This is surely an exaggeration typical of Greek historians on the winning side, but the army was large enough so that the muster of nations at Babylon took a whole day to pass before the Great King's eyes.

The native Persians who gathered were brave troops who proudly pledged their lives to defend the honor and life of the Great King. Besides his countrymen, Darius also summoned infantry and cavalry from the Medes and Tapurians to the north, as well as Armenians from the Caucasus mountains. The wild Hyrcani from the southern shore of the Caspian Sea supplied a host of cavalry, as did the Barcani from central Asia, who fought with double-edged axes. The Derbices, from the same lands as the Barcani, fought with bronze and iron-tipped spears, though some preferred to use wooden pikes hardened by fire. Also present were thousands of Greek mercenaries—tough, experienced troops who were not at all afraid of the Macedonians. These professional soldiers, along with the native Persians, would form the heart of the Great King's battle formation. Many other nations from throughout the empire were also present, though their names are not recorded.

Aside from Persian soldiers there were countless attendants, slaves, cooks, physicians, wagon drivers, scribes, priests, and eunuchs on hand as support staff for the Great King. According to Persian custom, Darius was also accompanied by his family on the march, including his mother, wife, and three children. They traveled in grand style and camped in lavishly decorated tents full of magnificent treasures. The opulence of the Great King's surroundings on campaign was scarcely less extravagant than if he were in his palace at Persepolis.

It began to rain on Alexander and his men that night. Soon the entire army was soaked to the skin and shivering in the November wind. They were wet, cold, and trapped on a narrow plain with the strongest army in the world only a few miles away waiting to destroy them. The sole path of retreat was behind them, through the Gates into Syria, but this would take them only deeper into enemy territory. Like their king, the Macedonian army recognized that they had to fight at Issus and win or they would all perish.

When the storm lifted, the Macedonians could see thousands of Persian campfires in the distance like stars in the sky. Alexander ordered his men to eat a hearty dinner and prepare to leave before dawn. While his soldiers tried to sleep, the king climbed a nearby hill and looked out at the vast Persian army. This was what he had dreamed of all his life, but now that the moment was here at last, he did know fear. Not for his life or for his brave men, but fear that something would go wrong. He spent the night sacrificing to the local gods, praying that they would be kind to him.

While it was still dark, Alexander led the army toward Issus. He stopped his men periodically on the march to rest and accustom themselves to the sight of the enemy spread out across the plain from the mountains to the sea. As they neared the Pinarus River, he drew them up in final battle order. On his far right against the foothills he placed Parmenion's son Nicanor with a unit of foot soldiers. Next to them were Macedonian cavalry, then thousands of infantry stretching almost a mile across the center of the battlefield, and finally the elite Thessalian cavalry next to the sea. Parmenion was in overall command of the left side of the line, while Alexander positioned himself on the right toward the center. It was a classic formation that he had used at the Granicus—swift-moving cavalry on the wings to encircle the enemy, and the mass of the infantry in the center to stab and slash their way through the Persian lines.

Across the river tens of thousands of Persians were drawn up in deep formation with archers in front and the rest of the infantry extending across the whole line to the sea, where Darius had placed all his cavalry to sweep behind the Macedonians. He also stationed some foot soldiers on the heights above Alexander's right wing to descend at an opportune moment. The Great King himself was in the center of the army with Greek mercenaries and his best Persian troops at his side.

As the Macedonians advanced the final mile, the Persians remained in position on the far side of the river. The banks of the Pinarus were smooth on the side where Alexander's men were approaching, but steep once they crossed the river. It was the same plan the Great King's generals had used at the battle of the Granicus—force the Macedonians to attack across the river and up a high embankment. But even though the strategy had failed before, the Persians, while superior in numbers, were again taking a defensive stand against an aggressive enemy.

Just before they were in range of enemy arrows, Alexander halted his army and rode down the entire Macedonian line encouraging his men. He not only cheered on his generals and officers, but the common soldiers as well. He called these by name and reminded them of their bravery in past battles. A mighty shout rose up from the Macedonian army that echoed across the plain. Alexander then ordered them to advance at a run as he turned his horse toward the river and led them into battle.

Alexander and his companions charged at such speed that they were underneath the Persian arrows before the archers could take aim. They hit the river at a gallop and broke through the enemy formation, striking panic into the front-line troops. The Persians near Alexander began to pull back in terror as the Macedonians cut through their defenses. But suddenly the Greek mercenaries fighting for Darius struck hard against the Macedonian center and opened a gap in Alexander's lines, tearing into his infantry. They pushed the Macedonians back into the river and killed many, all while the two sides shouted the vilest insults at each other in Greek.

While the center of the Persian line was holding, the Great

King's cavalry near the sea rushed across the river and pushed back the horsemen from Thessaly. The fight on horseback along the coast was unrelenting as neither side gave way. Meanwhile Alexander's right wing, the one part of his line that was actually advancing against the Persians, managed to break through and circle around behind the Greek mercenaries. This was the moment when the battle turned. Unable to fight both in front and behind, the mercenaries fell back. The Persian center then began to collapse and the cavalry, seeing their infantry lines crumble, turned and fled back across the river, riding over their own men to escape.

Darius watched in horror as the unthinkable unfolded all around him. But even though he realized the Macedonians would win the battle, he refused to withdraw. He stood atop his war chariot ready to strike down any enemy who approached. Alexander could not resist such a perfect target. If he could slay Darius with his own hand, not only would the war be over but his glory, like that of Achilles, would never die. As Alexander rushed toward Darius, one of the Great King's brothers led his horsemen between the two kings. But he was cut down. Atizyes, former satrap of Phrygia, died defending his lord, as did Rheomithres, who had fought bravely at the Granicus, along with Sabaces, satrap of Egypt. As the Macedonians closed in, it may have been Darius himself who slashed at Alexander, wounding him in the thigh with his sword. Even so, the Great King was now cut off from his army and about to die.

What happened next is frozen in time, preserved in an exquisitely detailed mosaic found buried beneath the ashes of Mount Vesuvius in the Roman town of Pompeii. On it we see Alexander charging from the left, bare-headed but wearing a breastplate with a Gorgon's head staring out to turn his enemies to stone. With his spear he skewers a Persian guard standing between him and Darius. The ground is littered with the dead and dying of both sides. A lone, barren tree stands in the background. A dark brown horse bleeds to death in the center. A Persian soldier taking his final breath as he lies on the ground sees his own reflection in a polished shield. A forest of Persian spears rises as men rush forward to save their king, who at last has turned to flee the battlefield in his chariot. But the most haunting image of all is the face of Darius, who has locked eyes with Alexander and stares at him, not in fear or anger, but in astonishment.

Our written sources paint much the same picture, with Darius retreating at the last minute before the irresistible force of Alexander. Darius then broke through the chaos of battle and fled with the remains of his army eastward across the mountains. Alexander and his troops vainly pursued Darius for miles, riding out of the battlefield over gullies filled with the bodies of dead Persians. In all, many thousands of Persians were slain, while the Macedonian losses, though heavy, were far fewer. Alexander was bitterly disappointed that Darius had escaped, but as his companions surrounded him to offer their congratulations, he could rejoice that at twenty-three years of age, he had just defeated the Great King of Persia.

When Alexander arrived at the camp of Darius, it was already late at night. He was exhausted from the battle and pursuit, in addition to not having slept for two days. He could see his soldiers looting the camp and portioning out the Persian women they captured. His men had reserved the royal tent of the Great King himself for Alexander. He entered this magnificent enclosure and was struck immediately by the superb furniture and treasures scattered throughout. "So this is what it means to be a king," he marveled. The plates, basins, and even the bathtub were all made of gold, while the fragrance of rich perfumes and spices filled the air. The royal Macedonian pages had prepared a banquet for him with captured Persian food and had readied a hot bath. Alexander removed his dusty armor and went to the tub, remarking to one of his friends that he would like to wash off the sweat of battle in the bath of Darius. "No," his companion corrected, "rather it is the property of Alexander."

After bathing, the king and his companions were settling down to eat when they heard wailing from a nearby section of the tent. Inquiring who was making such a horrible noise, Alexander was told that it was the mother of Darius, along with the Great King's wife, two virgin daughters, and young son. They had torn their garments and were weeping for Darius, whom they believed to be dead. Alexander sent one of his companions, Leonnatus, to calm them. He arrived at the entrance to their quarters, but was unsure if he should enter without being announced. Finally, he pulled back the flaps and came before the women, who cried out in fear thinking that he had come to kill them. They begged him to allow them at least to prepare the body of Darius properly for burial before they were slain. Leonnatus assured them that the Great King was still alive and that Alexander meant them no harm. He was, in fact, insistent that they be treated with the utmost respect as royal ladies. The women finally calmed down and expressed their gratitude for the king's kindness.

The next morning, Alexander, accompanied by his closest friend Hephaestion, paid a visit to the Persian women personally to reassure them of their safety. When the two entered their quarters, the women fell on their faces before Hephaestion, thinking he was king as he was the taller of the pair, much to the amusement of Alexander. The Great King's mother, Sisyngambris, was profuse in her apologies once the translator had explained the mistake, but Alexander was reassuring. He raised the elderly woman from the ground, addressing her as "mother," and remarked that Hephaestion too was an Alexander—a reflection of the teaching both had received from Aristotle as boys that the truest friend was another self.

Ancient writers made much of the treatment of Darius' women as an illustration of Alexander's kindly nature. While this may well be true, his benevolence was also eminently practical. By protecting the women of the Great King's household, Alexander took on the symbolic role of son, husband, and father in the eyes of his new subjects. As with his adoption by Queen Ada in Caria, the Macedonian king was using family ties to build power. He decked the queen mother with jewelry and assured her that her dignity would in no way be lessened under his rule. To the wife of Darius, who was also the Great King's sister, he promised that she would enjoy all former benefits of her station as queen and would be touched by no one, least of all him. He assured her that her two maiden daughters would be inviolate and would be granted dowries from his own treasury when the time came for them to wed. He then called the young son of Darius to him and kissed the boy, who was not frightened at all. Alexander admired the young lad's courage and swore that he would raise him as his own son. It was all very moving, but from this day forward the family of Darius knew they were hostages of Alexander.

The following day, after he had visited the wounded, Alexander called a formation of his entire army arrayed in their finest armor. He conducted a funeral for those who had fallen in battle, then honored the worthiest of the survivors with special citations and prizes equal to their bravery. The king appointed one of his bodyguards, Balacrus, as satrap of Cilicia and promoted other of his companions to new offices. Alexander was in such a forgiving mood after his victory that he even reduced the fine he had previously levied on the city of Soli. He also erected altars of thanksgiving to Zeus, Athena, and Hercules, offering grand sacrifices to these, his favorite gods. As a lasting monument to his victory, he now founded the first city of his campaign—Alexandria, near Issus. While still a teenager, he had renamed a Thracian city for himself following his first military success, but this first of many Alexandrias was a new kind of city—a Macedonian settlement of Greek culture in a foreign land. Founded in a strategic location near the entry to Syria, it was an important first step in spreading Hellenic civilization, which the king would repeat all the way to India.

Alexander had won glory and honor at Issus, but not the vast amounts of gold he had hoped for since Darius had left the bulk of his treasury at the Syrian city of Damascus, several days' travel from the battlefield. The cache from Darius' tent was all fine and good, but Alexander needed a great deal more if he was to pay for the rest of his campaign. He therefore sent Parmenion with a squadron of more than a thousand Thessalian cavalry at a fast gallop to Damascus to seize the treasury of the Great King before the Persians could get there. He may not have liked the old man, but Alexander knew Parmenion could accomplish this dangerous mission deep into enemy territory.

The Persian satrap at Damascus was meanwhile considering his future very carefully. When he heard that Alexander had been victorious at Issus, he knew the Macedonians would be coming for the treasure. He therefore decided it was in his best interest to surrender the riches of Darius to Alexander in hope of preferred treatment. He sent a messenger to the Macedonians stating his intentions, but Parmenion immediately suspected a trap and headed into Syria with great caution. He crossed the Gates and moved south with his cavalry in spite of the winter cold through mountains and deserts until he at last arrived at the oasis town of Damascus.

The Syrian city was the center of Persian government in this arid region. It was also a wealthy town in its own right, known for its figs and for its caravan trade east to Mesopotamia and south to Arabia. The crafty satrap had planned not only to surrender the Great King's riches to Alexander, but also the many Persian guests and hostages who had been entrusted to him by Darius. To facilitate this exchange, he told the resident Persians that they would be fleeing with him to Babylon along with the treasure of Darius. Thousands of mules were hastily loaded with all they could carry, then the enormous caravan set out through the gates of the city.

Snow had fallen that night. It was so cold that the attendants for the pack animals pulled out military uniforms from the baggage to cover themselves on the journey, while the crowd of frightened refugees shivered and hoped they could escape before the Macedonians arrived. It was at that moment that Parmenion and his cavalry troop appeared on the horizon. The general saw a column of men dressed as Persian soldiers and hastily arranged his men for battle, assuming they were in for a tough fight. The mule drivers and refugees saw the line of horsemen charging them and ran for their lives. Countless riches soon lay scattered in the snow and brambles along the trail. When Parmenion discovered that it was not an army he had attacked, he ordered his men to round up the treasure and refugees. He offered the mule drivers the choice of guiding the baggage animals back to Alexander or being killed on the spot.

After many days under the watchful eye of Parmenion, the treasure caravan reached the Macedonian camp. Alexander was thrilled as the riches were unloaded—decorated vases, war chariots, royal tents, five hundred pounds of silver, a beautifully decorated box that the king henceforth used to hold his favorite edition of Homer's poetry, and enough gold to pay his army for many months to come. But also among the precious cargo were the Persian refugees, who now became pawns of the Macedonian king. These included the wife and three maiden daughters of the previous Great King, Artaxerxes IV, as well as a brother of Darius himself. There were also two terrified envoys from Athens who had been dealing secretly with Darius in spite of their city's official support for Alexander's campaign. Four stoic Spartans were also captured, though their city had made no pledges to the Macedonians.

The chief prize in the eyes of Alexander was Barsine, widow of his rival Memnon of Rhodes. She, along with her children, were presented to the king, expecting little mercy from Alexander. To her surprise, Alexander treated her with great kindness. Barsine had been a young refugee in the court of Philip years earlier when her father and Memnon had sought sanctuary there. She had probably known Alexander in Macedonia and the two may have been friends. There was certainly something unusual about Barsine, as she was the first woman Alexander fell in love with. He did not marry her, but the two began a long affair. She was by all accounts a brilliant, beautiful, and charming woman. She was Persian by birth, but had received an excellent Greek education and spoke the language well. In time, she would give birth to Alexander's first child, a son named Hercules. The traitorous satrap of Damascus, however, had no such happy ending. One of the Persian refugees cut off his head in the night and escaped with it as a gift for Darius.

While Alexander had been preparing to meet the Persians on the battlefield, the agents of the Great King in the Aegean had been busy. Memnon's nephew Pharnabazus had captured several important islands and retaken Halicarnassus. He then sailed to the island of Siphnus for a clandestine meeting with an old enemy of Alexander—Agis, king of Sparta. Agis had arrived in a single trireme to meet with the Persians and seal a pact that would strengthen the second front against Alexander. The Spartan king received plentiful funds from Pharnabazus along with ten ships to conduct naval operations against the Macedonians.

But just as the two were celebrating their new alliance, news arrived that Alexander had defeated the Great King at Issus. Pharnabazus was dumbfounded at the report and immediately set sail for Chios off the Asia Minor coast to secure this important Greek island against rebellion. Agis was grimly undeterred by Alexander's victory and continued with his plan. He hired sailors for his new ships and sent his brother to Crete to establish a new naval base there. Meanwhile Agis laid the groundwork for an uprising in Greece.

Events in the Aegean did not escape Alexander, but he was faced with a difficult decision at this point in the campaign. Darius had been humiliated at Issus, but was not defeated. The army he had gathered in Syria represented only a small portion of the forces available to him. Given enough time, the Great King could summon a much larger force to defeat the Macedonians on the battlefield. Alexander knew his only chance of stopping Darius from building a new army was to chase him relentlessly into the heart of his empire. But this was a dangerous proposition given that the Greeks were rebellious and the Persians still controlled most of the Mediterranean. If he pursued Darius at this point, he might lose everything he had conquered in the west.

As Alexander weighed his options, it seemed best to continue his plan to seize the Mediterranean coast of Lebanon, Palestine, and Egypt while his generals in Macedonia and Asia Minor tried to contain the Persian threat closer to home. He knew he would have to face Darius at some point as the Great King could not allow him to ravage his empire unpunished. Darius would need at least a year to gather his army from the four corners of his realm to face Alexander, but when that day came it would be the greatest battle the world had ever known.

Alexander broke camp at Issus and marched over the Gates into Syria, then south toward the coast of Lebanon. He passed the ancient Greek trading colony at al-Mina near the mouth of the Orontes River, then traveled along the narrow plain between the sea and mountains until he arrived at the Phoenician town of Marathus. But the Phoenician ships of the Great King's fleet were not there to oppose him because they were busy in the Aegean. The local king of Marathus had in fact left his son in charge of the town while he served Darius in the west. The prince knew it was pointless to stand against Alexander, so he met the king before the city gates and bestowed upon him a golden crown, the traditional token of submission. The young man also surrendered the nearby island of Aradus and the city's inland possessions.

Alexander was pleased with the reception he received and stayed at Marathus several days. While he was there two envoys from Darius arrived with a letter from the Great King. Alexander took the document into his private quarters and read it to himself. The contents of the letter vary according to different ancient historians, but it is clear that Darius was willing to make a deal. He began by chastising Alexander for invading his empire under no provocation. He pointed out that the Persians and Macedonians were old friends, though Philip had shown a notable lack of respect toward Persia now continued by his son. The outcome of the recent battle in Alexander's favor was the unfortunate result of some god's mysterious intervention, though the Macedonians could not count on heaven's blessing in the future. Even so, the Great King was merciful and invited Alexander to conclude a peace treaty with Persia. If he withdrew, he would grant him sovereignty over all the territory of Asia Minor from the Aegean to the Halys River near Gordium. In addition, he would pay Alexander a generous ransom for the return of his captive family. All this could be Alexander's if he would cease his invasion of the Great King's realm. If he were to reject this generous offer, it was understood that Darius would unleash his army against the Macedonians at a time and place of his own choosing and destroy them.

Alexander knew that if he presented this letter to Parmenion or any of his officers, they would surely rejoice. Darius was offering them everything they had ever dreamed of. They would hold the richest parts of Asia Minor including all the Greek cities of the Aegean. The

Persians would recognize their conquests and withdraw their navy. Macedonia would have grown in their lifetimes from a beleaguered minor kingdom to an empire ruling all the lands from the Adriatic to the highlands of Anatolia. They would all be rich men and could return home as heroes.

But Alexander had to find a way to convince his men to continue the war. He had tasted victory and would not settle for less than the entire Persian Empire as his own. He saw himself and his army marching along the Nile, dining among the gardens of Babylon, covering themselves with gold at Persepolis, and marveling at the wonders of distant India. But how to convince the Macedonians? The plan he devised was a favorite tactic of politicians throughout the ages—he lied. The king composed a forgery of Darius' letter full of unreasonable demands, insults toward the Macedonians, and no mention at all of territorial concessions. When he presented it to his council of advisors, they took the bait and angrily rejected the Great King's terms out of hand.

Alexander then composed his own letter to Darius, skillfully crafted to provoke the Great King in every possible way. He began with the condescending heading "King Alexander to Darius—Greetings," omitting the Persian ruler's titles as a very deliberate insult. He then went on to blame Darius for the current war since his ancestors had started it when they invaded Greece at Marathon in the previous century. He then implicated the Persians in the murder of his father and even accused Darius of collusion in the assassination of the previous Persian king. Alexander declared himself Lord of Asia, saying he would gladly return the Great King's family to him without ransom only if Darius would appear before him as a lowly suppliant. Finally, he warned Darius to surrender immediately or he would pursue him to the ends of the earth.

Two days of marching along the coast brought Alexander to the important Phoenician trading center of Byblos. This ancient port had enjoyed commercial relations with Greece since the time of the Trojan War. Byblos had long been a shipping center for Egyptian goods, including papyrus, so that the Greeks who first used this material for scrolls called their books *biblia* after the town (thus our word *Bible*).

South of Byblos was Berytus (Beirut) on a prominent headland, then the famous Phoenician port of Sidon halfway down the coast of Lebanon. The people of Sidon despised the Persians, especially after their rebellious town had been sacked by the Great King's armies just a few years earlier. The Persian puppet ruler was forced by the populace to open the gates to Alexander, who promptly deposed the hated ruler and appointed his best friend Hephaestion to find a replacement. Hephaestion was staying in the town at the home of two distinguished young men to whom he offered the crown in turn. They politely declined, explaining that it was the custom of their city only to be ruled by a king of noble blood. Alexander's friend then commissioned them to find a suitable candidate.

Living on the edge of town was a poor man named Abdalonymus (or in Phoenician, Abd-elonim, "servant of the gods") who was distantly related to the royal family of Sidon. His honesty in business dealings among his crafty Phoenician neighbors had left him only his tiny hut with a struggling garden. He was so busy that day clearing the weeds from his vegetables that he didn't hear the two young men approach until they hailed him, calling him king. Abdalonymus had no time for jokes and dismissed the pair, but they explained that he needed to change his dirty clothes if he was going to rule Sidon. The gardener thought they were crazy and turned back to his weeds, but the young men finally convinced him by fearful oaths that their message was true. Abdalonymus hadn't even heard of Alexander and had no idea the town was occupied by Macedonian troops, but he put on his best clothes and went to the palace to meet the man who had driven off the Persians. Alexander liked the man at once and saw in him the paradigm of a just ruler in spite of—or perhaps because of—his dirty fingernails and sun-scorched brow. He happily anointed Abdalonymus the new king of Sidon.

A day's march south along the Lebanese coast was Tyre, the most powerful and important of all the Phoenician cities. It was an ancient rival of Sidon and one of the richest trading centers in the whole Mediterranean. The main part of the city was located on an island well offshore and surrounded by walls more than a hundred feet high, making it virtually untouchable by any invading army. It was also the most vital naval base for the Persians in the western part of their empire.

As Alexander approached the city, he was met by Tyrian envoys who welcomed him to their city with provisions for his army and a golden crown of submission. They regretted that their king, Azemilcus, was not there to greet him personally, but he was indisposed while serving with the Persian fleet in the Aegean—all a regrettable misunderstanding, of course. Alexander thanked them courteously for the supplies and the crown, then casually mentioned that he would like to offer sacrifice to his ancestor Hercules at his famous temple on their island. He had arrived at Tyre just at the start of the celebrated festival of Melqart—the Phoenician equivalent of Hercules—along with religious pilgrims from as far away as Carthage. The Tyrian envoys took council together, then informed the Macedonian king that it was unfortunately impossible to allow him into the city at the moment as this might seem a provocation to the Persians. However, there was a very nice temple of Hercules on the mainland opposite their city that he was most welcome to visit.

Both parties in this discussion knew they were not really talking about a simple act of sacrifice. The Tyrian envoys realized that if they allowed Alexander inside their walls, he would take over the city and post a garrison there. Alexander knew that Tyre was not really submitting to him but merely buying time to see if the naval offensive of Darius in the Aegean would force him to return to the west. The merchant rulers of Tyre did not particularly care if Alexander or Darius won the war. They wanted only to maintain their very profitable trading dominance in the Mediterranean as they had for over a thousand years, with as little outside interference as possible.

Alexander was normally able to control his fierce temper, but he did not handle rejection well. He leapt up from his chair and vented the full measure of his wrath on the Tyrian envoys: "Do you really think you are safe from me because you live on an island? Do you despise this army of foot soldiers so much? I am going to show you that you do not live on an island at all! You will either welcome me into your city or I will besiege it!"

The envoys were terrified and returned to their city with his message. The Tyrian elders discussed the situation and concluded that they were safe from Alexander. Their city was half a mile from the coast, separated by deep water and protected by powerful currents and violent winds. They were far out of range of catapults and other artillery on the mainland. The walls surrounding their town had never been breached, not even by invaders who had besieged the city for years. The Macedonians had no navy to prevent the Tyrians from coming and going in their own ships as they pleased. Their visitors from Carthage also promised they would provide any supplies or help Tyre might need. Let Alexander try to take their city—they would laugh at him from the walls as they watched.

The citizens of Tyre had seen invaders come and go for centuries with little effect on their vast commercial network. The Phoenicians were a Canaanite people who spoke a language closely related to Hebrew. Squeezed into a narrow coastal plain along the arid eastern Mediterranean shore, they naturally looked to the sea for their livelihood. Beginning in the eleventh century b.c., cities such as Tyre and Sidon began establishing trading posts at ever more distant locations to the west. Cyprus, Sicily, northern Africa, and Spain were all the sites of early Phoenician colonies in the Mediterranean. Carthage on the African coast across from Sicily was the most famous and successful of these outposts, maintaining close ties to its mother city, Tyre, throughout the centuries. But the Phoenicians did not stop at the Straits of Gibraltar. They sailed out into the Atlantic, perhaps as far as Britain to the north and Senegal to the south. Herodotus relates that they even circumnavigated Africa. Along their way they traded with many peoples and developed a reputation as shrewd businessmen—and as thieves and pirates. Greek literature from the time of Homer is replete with stories of wicked Phoenician traders who steal children and sell them into slavery. Whatever the truth of this, they certainly spread their crafts and culture throughout the ancient world. The Greek alphabet was borrowed and adapted from the Phoenicians by the eighth century B.C., so that the *aleph, bet,* and *gimel* of Phoenician became the alpha, beta, and gamma of Greek. These wide-ranging traders were especially known for trafficking in the cedars of Lebanon from the coastal mountains of their homeland and a rare purple dye derived from the murex shells of the Lebanese coast. Their Hebrew neighbors admired the skill of the Phoenicians and employed them in the building of King Solomon's temple, but they also condemned their religious practices, such as the alleged sacrifice of children to their gods.

The siege of Tyre began with the demolition of older parts of the town on the mainland for construction materials for a causeway to the island. Alexander then sent parties deep into the mountains to cut cedar trees for the many poles his engineers would need to drive into the seabed. He also sent messengers to the high priest in Jerusalem requesting supplies and reinforcements for him at Tyre. He informed the Jews that the tribute they had previously paid to Darius would now go to him. If he had any hesitation, Alexander counseled, he should rest assured that choosing the friendship of the Macedonians over that of the Persians would be to his benefit.

At first the construction of the causeway went well. The water near the shore was shallow and it was not difficult to drive the piles into the soft mud. The space in between the timbers was filled with abundant rubble, providing a firm foundation for a wide road into the sea. The causeway would have to bear the weight of thousands of men and heavy machinery, so great care was taken in its construction. Alexander was present every day, conferring with the engineers, encouraging his men, and carrying stone after stone into the sea himself.

The Tyrians found all this terribly amusing. When the weather was fair, they would row small boats up to the Macedonians just out of arrow range and mock the soldiers. They shouted out that such famous soldiers had now become mules bearing loads on their backs like donkeys. They asked if Alexander thought he was Poseidon, god of the seas. But as the mole progressed steadily seaward week after week, the laughter of the Tyrians ceased. They still didn't believe that the Macedonians could ever reach their island, as they had now come to the deepest part of the channel and their work had dramatically slowed, but the Tyrians began to worry that the causeway might get close enough for Alexander to reach their walls with his artillery. In response, they evacuated some of their women and children to Carthage. They then began a concerted effort to hinder the construction project by every possible means. The Macedonians were now within arrow range of the high walls of the city, so the Tyrians showered them from above without ceasing. Because the Macedonians were stripped of their armor for work, they were vulnerable. Some of the arrows were dipped in pitch and set afire any equipment they hit. At the same time, triremes from the city would sail up to the causeway and pummel the builders with missiles. In response, Alexander ordered towers wheeled onto the causeway manned by archers to strike back against the ships. He covered these towers with hides to block arrows from the city walls and allow his men to work in safety.

In response, the ingenious Tyrians constructed an incendiary juggernaut. They found an old cavalry transport ship and filled it with all the dry timber they could cram into its hold. Then they raised the sides of the ship and added wood chips, sawdust, and anything else at hand that was flammable, stuffing sulfur into the cracks and pouring pitch on top. They rigged a double yardarm onto the masts to which they attached cauldrons full of flammable liquid. Then they added extra ballast to the stern to raise the bow high into the air to allow the speeding ship to ride high onto the causeway when it hit.

They waited until a strong wind was blowing toward the mole and then launched the ship towed by several triremes pulling it with all their might. When the Macedonians saw this very strange vessel approaching, they could not understand why the Tyrians would bother to attack them with a large horse boat. Then they started to worry as the vessel drew closer with flames beginning to shoot from its deck. The skeleton crew on the fire ship then jumped overboard and swam toward the waiting triremes, which had just cut their lines and pulled away. With the blazing ship rushing toward them, all the terrified Macedonians could do was run for their lives. Just as the ship flew onto the causeway and into the towers, the yardarms on the masts burned through and dropped the cauldrons onto the fire below. When the liquid hit the flames, it exploded into a raging inferno unlike anything the Macedonians had ever seen. The causeway was engulfed in fire and the towers burned like matchsticks. Any unfortunate builders still alive on the mole were picked off by archers in the Tyrian triremes or by raiding parties that dashed onto the mole. As the gods would have it, there was a terrific storm that night that pounded the remains of the damaged causeway with towering waves, loosening the piles and sending tons of rock and rubble into the water. By the next morning, months of hard work had disappeared beneath the sea.

As Alexander surveyed the ruins of all his efforts, he debated with himself what he should do next. Every day he delayed at Tyre meant more time for Darius to collect a larger army. But if he left Tyre unconquered, it would continue to serve as a base for the Persian navy and, even worse, as a glaring emblem of his failure. He therefore decided to begin again on an even grander scale with a wider causeway and more protection for his men. However, he now knew he was not going to take the city with engineers and infantry alone. He had to have ships to conquer Tyre.

After resuming construction on top of the broken remains of the old causeway, he led some of his men back to Sidon to collect whatever boats he could find. It was there his luck began to change. The Phoenician kings of Sidon and Marathus, having heard that Alexander now held their cities, deserted from the fleet of Darius in the Aegean and sailed home to join the Macedonian forces. This added eighty superb triremes and their crews to his navy. Over the next few days, other ships arrived from the Greek island of Rhodes, the Cilician cities of Soli and Mallus, the towns of the Lycian coast, and even a fifty-oared ship from Macedonia commanded by Proteas, the son of Alexander's childhood nurse Lanice. Just as the king was welcoming these vessels, he saw a fleet of ships from Cyprus sailing into the har-

bor of Sidon. The Cypriot kings had decided that the Persians were
on the losing side of the war and begged Alexander to accept their
service. He was glad to forgive any past transgressions, especially as
he now had more than two hundred warships at his disposal.

First, Alexander decided to make a quick strike against the Arab
natives in the nearby mountains who had been leading a guerrilla
campaign against his woodcutting teams. He needed those trees for
causeway piles and siege engines, and was not about to let highland
brigands ruin his plans. He personally led a tough squadron of Thracian warriors and archers up through the beautiful Beqa'a valley to
put an end to the raiding. It was just the sort of mountain fighting
both he and the Thracians relished. For some unknown reason, Alexander's old tutor Lysimachus, who had accompanied the expedition
into Asia, asked if he could come along, assuring the king that he
was no weaker than Phoenix, the elderly teacher of Achilles who had
traveled with his pupil to Troy. Alexander must have laughed, but he
had a soft spot in his heart for the old man and agreed.

The troops rode swiftly into the mountains, but were forced to
leave their horses behind when the terrain became too steep. They
marched up into the highlands, but Lysimachus was having a difficult
time keeping up. Alexander sent the rest of the men ahead the first
day to make camp but remained behind with a handful of friends
to walk beside his tutor. The king encouraged Lysimachus and half
carried him up the trails, but by nightfall they were far behind the
main party and lost in the mountains. It was already spring, but when
darkness fell the temperature plunged. Alexander had not planned to
bivouac and so had no shelter or fire. The small band of Macedonians
huddled together as the king tried desperately to keep his elderly
teacher from freezing to death. Then in the distance Alexander saw
the light of a campfire. He left Lysimachus and worked his way by
himself through the trees toward the glow ahead. As he approached,
he saw that there were two men keeping watch over a cluster of sleeping Arab raiders. With utmost care, Alexander crept up alone behind
the guards and silently slit their throats. He then stole a flaming stick
from the campfire without waking any of the men who slept around

it. Moving as fast as he could through the darkness, he reached his own camp and kindled a roaring fire for his companions. The Arabs awoke and saw the nearby blaze, but ran off thinking a large force had suddenly descended on them. Alexander spent the rest of the night next to Lysimachus, warming his old friend and perhaps suggesting that next time he should remain in town.

When Alexander returned to Sidon after defeating the Arab hill tribes, he found four thousand Greek mercenaries awaiting his commands. He had sent Cleander to recruit them over a year earlier, but the Macedonian had little luck until the defeat of Darius at Issus. Now, with a major victory under his belt and plenty of gold in his treasury, Alexander had no trouble recruiting professional soldiers from Greece. The king packed everyone on board his new fleet and set sail for Tyre in battle formation. Naval warfare was a novelty to Alexander, but he took to it like a born sailor. He placed the Cypriot and Phoenician squadrons on the left nearest the land and took command on the right, with the newly arrived Macedonian galley serving as his flagship.

The Tyrians had heard reports that Alexander had recruited a fleet in Sidon, but they had no doubt they could overcome any pathetic armada the Macedonians were able to scrape together. They positioned their fleet on the north side of the island to strike hard against the ships Alexander sent their way. What they didn't expect that spring morning was more than two hundred warships bearing down on their city. Alexander was hungry for a battle at sea, but the Tyrian admiral in charge signaled his fleet to retreat quickly into the protected harbor on the north side of their town. The Macedonians saw their Tyrian counterparts turn toward home and so began a race to see who could reach the harbor first. It was a close contest, but the Tyrians sacrificed three of their triremes to block Alexander's advance and allow the remainder of their fleet to enter the city safely. They then blocked the narrow mouth of the northern port with triremes facing outward, forming a daunting wall across the harbor's entrance. Try as he might, Alexander could not break through and seize the city from within as he had hoped, so he decided on the next best thing and blockaded both the northern harbor of the city and its southern counterpart facing toward Egypt. Unless they could find a way out, the grand battle fleet of Tyre was trapped.

Alexander's engineers had been working around the clock while he was away and now redoubled their efforts to repair and expand the causeway. There were setbacks, such as a powerful storm that struck the mole, tearing into the new construction. The tempest also drove onto the causeway what one ancient historian called a giant sea monster. It rested part of its body against the rubble for a long time, then swam off into the sea. This was probably a whale, not uncommon in the Mediterranean, but certainly a creature unfamiliar to the mountain-born men of Alexander's army. Superstitious and hopeful as always, both the Macedonians and Tyrians took the appearance of the beast as a sign that Poseidon was on their side.

After weeks of continuous labor under the shelter of improved protective towers, the Macedonian causeway at last drew close enough for Alexander to reach the walls of Tyre with his artillery. He rolled powerful stone-throwing catapults down the mole until they were in position, then launched a nonstop volley against the city. At the same time, he placed improvised battering rams on the ships of his fleet and covered the vessels with sturdy shields above. They pounded the sea-facing walls of the city even as the defenders facing the causeway were showered with enormous boulders.

The Tyrians, however, knew how to fight back. The people of the city shot flaming arrows on the Macedonians to keep them away from the walls. They heated great shields full of sand until the contents were glowing red, then rained them down on the soldiers. This hot sand worked its way into the breastplates of Alexander's men in a torturous manner. The men stopped wearing armor in response, but then they were vulnerable to archers on the walls above. The Tyrians also set up rotating wheels on the walls with rapidly turning spokes to deflect arrows and missiles launched at them. Blacksmiths of the city forged barbed tridents tied to ropes that the defenders launched against the shields of the Macedonians, pulling the shields away and exposing the attackers. Some threw down fishing nets to engulf and disable Alexander's men. The people of the city also arranged large screens of animal skin to blunt the force of rocks launched from catapults. Divers were sent to cut the ropes of the Macedonian ships until Alexander ordered the ropes replaced by chains. Swinging scythes were placed on the seaward side to eviscerate any Macedonians who approached. The workshops of Tyre were kept busy night and day producing these and other ingenious instruments of war to use against Alexander's men.

Week after week the assault and defense continued with neither side able to make any headway. The Tyrians, to ensure the gods would remain on their side, tied down their statues in the island's temples with golden chains. The ships of the city made a valiant effort in the early summer to break loose and attack the Macedonian fleet, but were driven back into harbor. The people of Tyre finally pinned their hopes on a relief force from their daughter city of Carthage. But an embassy of thirty ambassadors from that city somehow made their way inside the walls to inform the elders that they were, most regrettably, involved in a demanding war in the west against the Sicilian city of Syracuse and were unable to help their ancestral home.

Almost a year had passed since the battle of Issus and more than six months had wasted away without victory over Tyre. Alexander now celebrated his twenty-fourth birthday with a new determination to take the stronghold at any cost. Then, as the scorching month of July came to a close, the Macedonian causeway finally reached the island.

Alexander gave his men two days to rest, then launched a massive assault on the city from all sides. Towers were rolled down the mole to stand ready with bridges to reach over the walls, but the initial breakthrough was to come by sea, not land. The king boarded the lead ship and ordered his fleet to attack the seaward walls around the city at every spot so the Tyrians would not know where to concentrate their defense. One of his armored ships with a battering ram at last broke a hole in the wall, then backwatered to allow a trireme with crack Macedonian marines to anchor at the gap. The assault squad was led by a brave officer named Admetus, who led his men into the breach. This captain was soon cut down, but men continued to pour into the hole, including Alexander himself, who was the first on top of the city walls. The Tyrians countered with everything they had against the invaders, but other ships took advantage of their distraction to push through the triremes blocking the two harbors into the heart of the city. The mass of the army then moved down the causeway and up the towers to cross over into Tyre.

The ferocity of the slaughter was staggering. The Macedonians had spent seven long months laboring to take the stubborn town. They had seen many of their friends crushed by stones hurled from the walls or burned to death by fire bombs. They were angry, exhausted, and passionately hated the people of Tyre for putting them through hell. Alexander didn't even try to hold them back as they killed every man, woman, and child they could lay their hands on. The Tyrians fought back street by street with the desperation of those who have no hope of mercy. Thousands died within the first few hours of the attack. Some made a last stand at a shrine dedicated to Agenor, the legendary founder of Tyre. Alexander himself led the charge against them and killed all the defenders. But by then the Macedonian bloodlust was cooling and the citizens still alive were rounded up to be sold into slavery, some thirty thousand souls in all. Those few who made it into the temple of Hercules seeking sanctuary were spared by the king, including the Carthaginian envoys. But two thousand men of fighting age captured in the attack were taken to a mainland beach across from the city and crucified—the most agonizing form of death known in the ancient world. Now, at last, with the city taken and funerals conducted for the many Macedonians who fell there, Alexander walked to the center of the ruined town and offered his long-delayed sacrifice at the temple of Hercules.

Alexander and his army were glad to leave the smoking ruins of Tyre behind as they continued their march down the Mediterranean coast. The causeway they had worked so hard to build soon began to gather silt and sand, so that in time it would be covered and grow to become a stretch of land permanently connecting the former island of Tyre to the shore.

The coast of Palestine was baking under the summer sun as the Macedonians made their way south. The ancient records do not mention Alexander taking the less direct but more hospitable road inland through Galilee and down the Jordan River valley. The Jewish historian Josephus alone asserts that Alexander journeyed to the temple at Jerusalem to pay his respect to the high priest, but this is almost certainly pious fiction. Instead the Macedonians took the shorter path down the coast past Mount Carmel, then on to Joppa, where Jonah reportedly took ship before being swallowed by a great fish.

Somewhere along this arid road, envoys from the Great King met Alexander with a new offer of peace. The Persian campaign in the Aegean had all but collapsed with the defection of the Phoenicians, so that the hoped-for uprising in Greece now seemed most unlikely. Even as the Persian ambassadors were arriving in camp, envoys from the Greek cities—except the Spartans, of course—were present, offering congratulations to Alexander on his victories. It was taking Darius much longer than he had anticipated to collect an army from the distant provinces of his empire. He needed at least another year to prepare for war, so it seemed best to buy time by striking a deal with Alexander. The Great King therefore was willing to increase the ransom he would pay for his family, allow Alexander to marry his eldest daughter, and grant him all the lands west of the Euphrates River if he would end his campaign. Darius reminded the young king that the Persian Empire was vast and filled with warlike people. If he was foolish enough to try to conquer it, he would grow old in the attempt, even in the unlikely event that he was to defeat the Persian army in battle. Better to accept the lands of the eastern Mediterranean as a gift than throw away his life on some battlefield in Persia or in the wastelands of Bactria.

When Alexander read the letter to his council, Parmenion said that if he were Alexander, he would accept the terms of Darius. The king shot back that he would accept them as well—if he were Parmenion. Instead, Alexander wrote back to Darius saying that he had

all the money he needed without the Great King's ransom and that
he could marry his captive daughter any time he chose without her
father's permission. As for the lands Darius offered, they were nothing compared to the empire he was going to conquer. Lydia, Cilicia,
and Phoenicia were just the beginning. Media, Persia, and even India
were all going to be his. He dismissed the envoys with a final word for
Darius that they would soon meet again in battle.

The only obstacle left for Alexander on his journey to Egypt was the
fortress town of Gaza on the coastal plain at the edge of the Negev
desert. Like Troy, it was an ancient hilltop town near the sea built
on the layers of its own past. Since the days of the Philistines, it had
dominated caravan traffic deep into Arabia. Gold, frankincense, and
myrrh all passed through its markets, which Herodotus considered
one of the largest in Asia. It was once ruled by the pharaohs, but had
passed in turn to the Assyrians, Babylonians, and finally the Persians.
The Great King's governor at Gaza, a eunuch named Batis, was confident the Macedonians could not take his city. Behind his high walls
he had ample water and grain to sustain a long siege. Moreover, he
had hired Arab mercenaries hardened to desert fighting. In spite of
Alexander's success at Tyre and the terrible consequences to its inhabitants, Batis dared Alexander to try to take Gaza.

As the king and his engineers rode around the city the first day,
they had to admit that it would be very difficult to capture. The town
sat so far above the plain that the Macedonian siege engines could
not reach the walls. Therefore Alexander commanded his men to
build a mound completely around the city equal to it in height. When
complete, he would place towers on this rampart and storm the city.
It was a monumental task for his soldiers, who had just spent months
building a causeway across the sea to Tyre, but they followed orders.

One morning during construction when Alexander was sacrificing below the city, a bird of prey swooped down on him and dropped
a stone it was carrying in its talons. The king turned to his soothsayer
Aristander to interpret this omen. The old prophet said that Alexander would take the city in time, but he must not fight that day.

The king reluctantly obeyed the will of the gods, but when the Arab mercenaries made an unexpected foray against the Macedonians that afternoon, Alexander could not help but rush to the front lines of the fight. He was almost immediately hit by an arrow fired from a catapult that pierced his shield and went straight through his armor into his shoulder. The king cursed his luck but ordered the wound dressed and continued the fight, at least until he collapsed unconscious from loss of blood. Batis and the people of Gaza rejoiced, thinking he had been killed.

Alexander was not dead, but he was very angry. When the siege towers he used at Tyre at last arrived by ship, the king ordered his engineers to put them in place on the ramparts they had constructed. The Macedonians then launched a massive assault on the city that was driven back three times by the defenders. Then Alexander, in spite of his bandaged shoulder, led his troops in a fourth assault that finally breached the walls. The people of Gaza fought as bravely against the invaders as had the citizens of Tyre, but they could not stand against the fury of the Macedonians. All the men of Gaza died at their posts defending their city, but the women and children were captured and sold into slavery. A badly wounded but still defiant Batis was brought before Alexander, who threatened him with cruel punishments if he would not bow down before him. The eunuch merely gazed at the king in contempt. Then Alexander in his anger did something so horrific that most ancient historians omit the episode altogether. In the *Iliad,* Achilles took the body of his slain Trojan opponent Hector and dragged it around the Greek camp behind a chariot. Alexander now took Batis, still alive, lashed his ankles with leather thongs, tied him to his own chariot, and pulled him through the rocky desert around the city of Gaza until long after he was dead.

Alexander summoned local Bedouin tribes to rebuild and repopulate Gaza as a fortress, this time under Macedonian control. He sent his fleet ahead, then advanced with his army into the coastal deserts of the northern Sinai. It was November, so the days were cool and pleasant, but there were still difficulties. Water was scarce along the way and the paths around brackish Lake Serbonis on the final stretch were notorious for quicksand. But six days after leaving Gaza, Alexander came to the frontier town of Pelusium. Here almost two centuries earlier, the Persian king Cambyses, son of Cyrus the Great, had defeated the army of the pharaoh. Herodotus saw the bones of both sides still bleaching in the sun when he visited many years later. Here at Pelusium, the easternmost branch of the Nile flowed into the Mediterranean. And it was here that Alexander entered Egypt, a land that would change his life forever.

# 5

# EGYPT

IN MY ACCOUNT OF EGYPT, I WILL GIVE A
LONGER DESCRIPTION WITH MANY MORE
FACTS THAN USUAL BECAUSE THIS COUNTRY
HAS MORE MONUMENTS AND WONDERS
THAN ANY OTHER LAND.
—HERODOTUS

Almost everything Alexander knew about Egypt came from the writings of Herodotus, the Greek historian of the previous century who wrote of things he saw along the Nile during his travels, as well as recording quite a few facts and secondhand stories of a more dubious nature. Herodotus knew that the Nile valley flooded every year, depositing rich alluvial soil on the fertile fields on either side of the river, but he did not know why this happened. He reports that an earlier pharaoh discovered the original language of humanity by secluding two newborn children among mutes until they uttered their first word, which presumably would be in the tongue of our earliest ancestors (it was *bekos,* the Phrygian word for "bread"). Herodotus also records that the Egyptians venerated cats and frequently mummified them. He overstates the size of Nile crocodiles, but relates they can be caught by using a small pig as bait. He was fascinated by the pyramids and passes on the tale he heard from

Egyptian priests on how they were built. He had a particular interest in Egyptian religion, claiming that the Greeks learned many of their sacred rituals from Egypt. He also writes of the divine origins of the great oracle of Zeus-Ammon in the distant western oasis of Siwa. Alexander had grown up hearing stories of this sacred site that the Persian king Cambyses had once tried to destroy, only to lose fifty thousand men to a sandstorm. For Alexander, Egypt must have been a land of wonder and mystery.

Egypt was such an ancient kingdom that the great pyramids of Giza were almost as old to Alexander as he is to us. Farmers had already lived on the banks of the Nile for several thousand years when, according to tradition, Menes united the kingdoms of upper (southern) and lower (northern) Egypt at the end of the fourth millennium B.C. The Old Kingdom began a few centuries later with a highly centralized government under the pharaohs. Soon the rulers of Egypt were commissioning grand monuments and establishing diplomatic ties with kingdoms in Mesopotamia and beyond. After the collapse of the Old Kingdom, there was a period of localized rule until the pharaohs of the Middle Kingdom reestablished authority over the whole country. A people known as the Hyksos later seized control of the northern Nile valley, but the New Kingdom arose in the middle of the second millennium B.C. and extended its power all the way to the Euphrates River. Hatshepsut, a woman of royal blood, ruled as pharaoh during this period, as did Tutankhamun and the long-lived Rameses the Great, famous for the colossal rock-cut statues he built at Abu Simbel as well as his war against the Hittites of Asia Minor. But during the age of the Trojan War, the mysterious Sea People attacked Egypt from the north, ushering in a long period of decline and foreign incursions from Nubians, Assyrians, Babylonians, and finally the Persians.

The Great King Cambyses conquered Egypt in the late sixth century B.C. and initiated a century of ill will when he burned temples throughout the country and killed the sacred Apis bull at Memphis in a fit of anger. The Persians were thereafter seen as impious oppressors who mocked Egyptian religious traditions and bled the country dry through high taxes and grain levies. Finally, after decades of Persian rule, the Egyptians revolted and drove out the Great King's troops. For sixty years Egypt was independent until Artaxerxes III led the Persian army into the land once more. The last native pharaoh of Egypt, Nectanebo, fled south to Nubia and a satrap was appointed to once again impose the will of the Great King.

Two years had passed since the Macedonians crossed into Asia. Alexander's fleet had followed him down the coast of the Sinai to Pelusium, where the king found the ships anchored in the Nile. Also waiting for him was Mazaces, the recently appointed Persian ruler of Egypt. His predecessor, Sabaces, had taken most of the Great King's army from the province to Issus a year earlier. Since Sabaces and many of his soldiers had died in battle there, Mazaces decided that discretion was the better part of valor and surrendered the entire province to Alexander without a fight. To win the favor of Alexander and, he surely hoped, save his own life, Mazaces also brought along the entire treasury and all the royal furniture he could load into carts. In one day, the Macedonian king had added a province larger and far wealthier than all of Greece to his growing empire.

But even though the Persian garrison in Egypt had surrendered to him, Alexander realized that truly possessing the land would require the utmost in tact and diplomacy. The Egyptians could well seize this moment to stage another of their revolts against the new foreign overlord. Alexander had to proceed very carefully in order to have the Egyptians accept him willingly as their ruler, but to do this he had to have the priests on his side. Alexander therefore dedicated the next few months to showing the people of the Nile valley that he not only respected their religion but was an enthusiastic supporter of the Egyptian gods.

Sending his fleet up the Nile, Alexander and his army marched through the endlessly flat plains of the Nile delta. The army moved along with the Nile on their right and the barren desert on their left. They passed fields of wheat and barley, date and fig trees, cattle and fishermen, and vast stands of papyrus used for making the most prized writing material in the ancient world. Along the way villages of farmers and local nobility welcomed the new king, although with his army beside him they had little choice. Alexander passed through the land of Goshen, where stories said the Hebrews had once settled after a famine in their homeland. He also passed the site of Avaris, where almost a thousand years earlier Rameses had built a glorious city only to have it swallowed up in time by desert sands.

After a week of traveling along the river, Alexander came to the ancient city of Heliopolis, a center for learning and priestly activities in Egypt for millennia. Here on a raised mound where the eastern-most branch of the Nile met the main channel of the river was the celebrated temple of Ra, known to the Greeks as the sun god Helios. The king surely treated the priests at Heliopolis with great respect—in pointed contrast to the Persian king Cambyses, who had tried to destroy the holy site and tear down the nearby obelisks.

Across the Nile just a day's journey south of Heliopolis was Memphis. Ever since the earliest days of the Old Kingdom, the city had been the most important religious center in lower Egypt. Even when the capital was elsewhere, pharaohs still maintained palaces at Memphis and lavishly supported the city's priesthood and temples. In the western part of the town was the step pyramid of Saqqara, the first of these great structures built in Egypt. Just beyond Saqqara on the edge of the floodplain were miles of elaborate tombs. The city proper was also a commercial center well known to the Greek world, but it was most famous for its temple of the creator god Ptah. His earthly mani-festation was the sacred Apis bull, a carefully chosen animal cared for in the courtyard of the temple. Pilgrims would come from all over Egypt to seek the blessing of the bull at Memphis. When each Apis died, it was embalmed and carried to a special burial chamber at Saqqara.

For the Great King to have killed the Apis bull in the previous century was a sacrilege beyond belief and a deed the Egyptians would never forget. It was therefore with great reverence that Alexander approached the temple of Ptah and offered copious sacrifices to the god, in deliberate contrast with the Persian ruler. The priests could not have been more pleased. And although the best ancient sources do not confirm it, it is likely that Alexander was now crowned pharaoh of Egypt. Statues of the king in Egypt soon show him dressed as lord of Upper and Lower Egypt, while inscriptions name him as beloved of Ra, son of Amun. Then, to celebrate his new status and to entertain the local population as well as his own troops, Alexander had previously arranged for the most famous athletes and musicians from Greece to meet him at Memphis. There Egyptians and Macedonians alike feasted and drank, cheered on races and wrestling contests, enjoyed comedies and tragedies onstage, and listened to choruses singing, all on a beautiful winter's day on the banks of the Nile surrounded by the glorious monuments of Egyptian history. It must have been spectacular.

The ancient historians who wrote about Alexander's Egyptian campaign are in disagreement about where the king went from Memphis. Some say he immediately headed north along the Nile toward the Mediterranean. But other sources claim he desired to travel south to see the ancient palaces and monuments of Upper Egypt. There are also fragmentary reports that he sent Aristotle's nephew Callisthenes deep into Ethiopia to seek the source of the Nile. None of these accounts is implausible because Alexander was intensely curious about the lands of his empire and realms beyond. A quick dash upriver to Egyptian Thebes or even to the first cataract near Aswan would not have taken more than a few weeks. Thebes would have been especially attractive as a key center of religious life in Egypt, as well as the site of many of the grandest temples in the Nile valley. To strengthen his rule in the south of the country and establish firm ties with the priestly class there, Alexander would certainly have considered a brief journey up the Nile a wise investment of his time.

Whether Alexander traveled south or remained in Memphis during these weeks, by January he was on his way north to the sea. Along this journey, only a short day's sail down the Nile, was the plateau of Giza just above the river to the west. There the three greatest pyramids of Egypt towered over the surrounding desert while the crouching Sphinx gazed unblinking toward the rising sun as it had for more than two thousand years. Oddly, none of the ancient sources mention Alexander visiting these famous monuments, but it is inconceivable that he would not have stopped to tour the site. A thousand years later most of the white limestone casing covering the pyramids would be stripped away for building materials, but during Alexander's visit the monuments would still have shone brightly in the morning sun. The king would have walked up the long causeway linking the Nile to the pyramid complex, then stared in wonder at these artificial mountains, each made of several million giant stones fitted together perfectly. Herodotus said the blocks were lifted up level by level with machines, but Alexander must have doubted this explanation given the obvious weight of the massive stones. If he entered the pyramids and made his way through the narrow, claustrophobic tunnels into the interior, he would have found the burial chambers of the ancient pharaohs long ago looted by grave robbers. Once back in the fresh air, Alexander could have toured smaller pyramids and temples in the complex as well, but he would not have missed the Great Sphinx. Over fifty feet high and carved from the living rock at the site, this looming figure with a man's head and a lion's body has always looked as if it were about to speak. Alexander surely remembered the story of young Oedipus, who was posed a riddle by a sphinx: What has four legs when young, two when grown, and three when aged? The creature killed those who were at a loss for the answer, but Oedipus knew it was a human being, who crawled as a baby, walked on two legs when grown, and used a cane when old. The Sphinx, however, asked Alexander no questions, but continued its eternal vigil as the king made his way back to the Nile.

When Alexander's ship neared Heliopolis, the river split into different channels that spread throughout the delta. But instead of taking the eastern branch back to Pelusium, the little fleet headed down the westernmost branch, known as the Canopic, toward the Greek trading post at Naucratis. The town was fifty miles inland from the sea, but for three centuries it had been the main point of contact between the Greek world and the land of the pharaohs. To Alexander, it was a small settlement too far from the Mediterranean for his dreams of a booming international metropolis. With Tyre destroyed, he needed a new port to serve as the center of trade not only for the Egyptian market but for the whole eastern Mediterranean. A harbor on the sea near the mouth of the Nile would be a natural emporium for crucial Egyptian grain exports, but also for the Arabian spice trade and goods flowing up the east African coast. With merchant traffic through the Gulf of Suez and down the Red Sea around Arabia, it could also serve as an end point for trade from Persia and India.

The sleepy little port of Naucratis would simply not do for such a vision. Alexander knew he needed an entirely new town at a site chosen for easy access to both the sea and the Nile, as well as a deep-water port easily defended against invaders and pirates, with a healthy climate, cool breezes, and plentiful fresh water. When he reached the mouth of the Canopic branch of the river and saw a broad limestone ridge to the west between the Mediterranean and Lake Mareotis, he knew he had found the site for his new city. It had a harbor on an isthmus approachable only from the east or west along a narrow shore. It was close enough to the mouth of the Nile to allow for easy access to the river and a steady supply of fresh water, but far enough away so that silting would not be a problem. Less than a mile offshore was the island of Pharos, a natural breakwater long known to the Greeks. That very night Alexander reportedly had a dream in which an old man appeared to him and quoted familiar lines from Homer:

> There is an island in the stormy sea
> in front of Egypt—They call it Pharos.

Whether he truly had such a vision or not, the king was convinced the harbor across from Pharos would be perfect for his new Alexandria.

The historian Arrian says that once again a *pothos* or desire seized Alexander, so that he decided to lay out the pattern of the city himself. The details vary according to different sources, but most agree that he was in such a hurry to begin the work that he had no time to send for chalk to mark the boundaries of the town. Instead, a soldier with him suggested using some of the barley they had brought along. Alexander thought this was a marvelous idea and eagerly began to walk the site, grain sack in hand, outlining where he wanted the fortifications, broad streets, central market, and temples. He was especially keen that there be shrines to Egyptian gods to show his respect for local beliefs. The temple of the popular native goddess Isis would be prominent, a divinity known to the Greeks as a bringer of life to the land and humanity alike.

But suddenly Alexander and his companions watched as thousands of birds from the nearby lake descended on the site and quickly ate every grain of barley he had so carefully laid out. The king was greatly worried by the implications of such an omen. Were the gods against the founding of his city? Ever quick to turn a sign from the heavens into good news, the king's favorite soothsayer Aristander proclaimed that the feasting birds were in fact wonderful portents, as they showed Alexander's new city would be splendidly prosperous and nourish all the nations of the earth.

While the king was still at Alexandria, welcome news arrived from Greece. The bearer was a Macedonian named Hegelochus, co-commander of the king's fleet in the Aegean. The admiral reported that the citizens of the strategic island of Tenedos near Troy had revolted against the Persians and forced them out. Even better, the crucial island of Chios had brought in the Macedonians to expel the Persians. There he had captured the commander of the Persian fleet, the late Memnon's nephew Pharnabazus. The operation had gone so smoothly that one of the Greek allies of the Persians, Aristonicus of Methymna on the island of Lesbos, was captured after he sailed into the harbor at Chios thinking it was still in Persian hands. The entire island of Lesbos, the key to the northern Aegean, had then been taken by Alexander's forces. In addition, the southern island of Cos near Halicarnassus had helped the Macedonians drive out the Persians. The entire Aegean and eastern Mediterranean now belonged to Alexander.

Hegelochus brought with him in chains Aristonicus and all the aristocratic leaders of Chios and Lesbos who had sided with the

Great King, but he apologized that Pharnabazus had somehow escaped while they were docked at Cos. Nevertheless, Alexander was pleased with the cowering group of prisoners before him and quickly decided their fate. The leaders from Lesbos were sent home to be judged by their own people, who subsequently tortured and executed them. Alexander then issued a decree to the people of Chios that they were now free from the oppressive rule of Persia and were to welcome home the exiles who had fled their island. He also posted a Macedonian garrison there to oversee civic affairs just in case the citizens took their freedom too seriously. But the elders of Chios wisely knew the limits of liberty and drafted a modest constitution, promptly submitting it to Alexander for approval. The king had something special in mind for the former aristocratic rulers of Chios, who had chosen loyalty to Darius over him. So that these oligarchs would feel at home in a familiar insular setting, he exiled them to the tiny island of Elephantine in the middle of the Nile River at the extreme southern border of Egypt. There near the first cataract of the river, more than a thousand miles from home, they could spend their days observing the island's famous Nilometer, measuring time as the river rose and fell every year for the rest of their lives.

With the city of Alexandria founded and political affairs in the Greek world in order, Alexander now conceived a powerful desire to visit the distant oasis oracle at Siwa. This remote shrine lay three hundred miles west of the Nile valley in the middle of the vast Sahara desert. It was an unlikely spot for a religious center, but one that had become increasingly well known to Greece. Legend says that both Hercules and the hero Perseus visited the site in ancient times, but it wasn't until a century before Alexander that the Greeks became fully aware of the oracular cult at Siwa. The divinity honored there was the deity Amun, a ruling god of the Egyptian pantheon. The Greeks, who called him Ammon, naturally saw in the god a counterpart to their own Zeus and frequently referred to the oracle as that of Zeus-Ammon. It is probable that the Aegean world became aware of the cult center of this god, who was often portrayed with ram's horns, through the Greek colony at Cyrene on the African coast west of Egypt. Caravans from the oasis would have traded at the town and brought word of the fabulous oracle of Ammon across the desert. From there, sailors spread news of the god and his power to Greece. Soon there was a temple to Ammon in Athens, while the famous poet Pindar sang his praises and set up a statue to the god in his hometown of Thebes. The oracle of Zeus-Ammon was reckoned the equal of Dodona or Delphi, though only a few made the arduous trek to the oasis itself.

Alexander's visit to the oracle at Siwa is one of the most controversial episodes of his life. Ancient writers speculated endlessly on why he made the journey and what he learned there. The details of the trip are conflicting, incomplete, and sometimes patently invented by those historians who wrote of it. But in spite of the maddening contradictions in the sources, the simple fact remains that Alexander spent several precious weeks in the middle of a war risking his life to travel across one of the most inhospitable deserts in the world to hear the words of a god.

It is difficult for modern readers to believe that religious motivation was sufficient reason to undertake such a journey at such an inconvenient time. But for us to appreciate the nature of Alexander and the world in which he lived, we must set aside our own preconceptions, skepticism, and cynical disbelief to realize that the ancient world was an age of great mystery and magic. There were doubters, to be sure, but for most people, including Alexander, the gods were everywhere and controlled every aspect of life. The flight of a solitary bird in the air, the sound of the wind blowing through the trees, a troubling dream in the night—all could be signs from the gods. These divine forces, at special places on the earth, actually spoke to people, though not always clearly. But if one was willing to make the journey to such a site, it was possible to ask a question and hear the very words of a god in response.

Alexander had many questions, but there were three that weighed most heavily on his mind. First, would he really be able to beat Darius and conquer the lands to the east? He was pitting himself against an immense and powerful empire. No matter his talent as a general and his overflowing youthful optimism, there was a very real chance that he would fail. Second, the king wanted to know if the murderers of his father Philip had all been punished. Given that many suspected Alexander himself as the force behind the assassination, this question may seem like a smokescreen to deflect suspicion from the real culprit. But assuming that Alexander was innocent, it was vital that he find and punish anyone who had a hand in his father's death. Not to do so would invite blood guilt that would stain his rule and bring on the wrath of heaven. The third and final question was the strangest and most audacious of all—Alexander wanted to know if Philip was really his father *or* if he was in fact the son of a god. His mother had told him that he was conceived by Zeus, not Philip, when the god possessed her in the form of a lightning bolt. Philip himself had dreamed that he had sealed his wife's womb with the image of a lion, a vision the prophet Aristander interpreted as a sign that she was already pregnant with a divine child.

Could Alexander really have been so vainglorious and deluded that he actually believed he was conceived by the king of the gods? This would seem the ultimate in what the Greeks called *hubris,* the quality of arrogant self-importance that was the prelude to one's own destruction at the hands of the divine. There were many Greeks who claimed descent from the gods, however distant. In the east, from Egypt to Persia to India, rulers often proclaimed their divine parentage. Was this a coldly calculated propaganda maneuver on Alexander's part to ease his acceptance by the people of Africa and Asia? Or could Alexander honestly have had doubts about who his father was? It is baffling for modern readers to think he truly believed he could be the son of a god, but again we have to put aside our own preconceptions and see Alexander in the context of his own world. To his subjects, soldiers, friends, and to himself, the idea of divine parentage was bold and daring, but not outrageous. This young man had already beaten the Great King in battle and conquered more land than any Greek had ever dreamed of. To his followers, if such accomplishments were not a sign of divine blood, what could be? We should therefore assume that Alexander's question about his parentage—however strange it might be to us and whatever uses it might serve to further his political agenda—was sincere.

From Alexandria the king and a few of his closest companions headed west with camels and local guides following the sea. The easiest route to Siwa from the Nile delta was along the Mediterranean shore for more than 150 miles to the small town of Paraetonium, one of the few safe harbors on this barren coast. Waiting for him at the town was a delegation from the city of Cyrene, many days farther to the west. These ambassadors not only represented their own town but also all the communities surrounding them. They offered Alexander the traditional crown of submission and magnificent gifts, while the king in turn warmly received their allegiance and made a treaty of friendship with them.

Cyrene was the major Greek settlement in Africa, founded as a colony from the volcanic island of Thera three hundred years earlier. Most of the later settlers were hardy Dorians related to the Spartans and other tribes of southern Greece. Cyrene was a green and fertile region on the edge of the great sandy desert, with the city itself high on a hill inland from the sea. Relations with the native Africans had been difficult at first, but the colonists had in time established hegemony over the native tribes of the region. Cyrene was famous for its horses and export of the valuable but pungent plant silphium, used in seasoning and many medicines, including contraceptives. The town even stamped a stalk of silphium on its coinage. Cyrene had been ruled for centuries by a royal family that had pledged loyalty to Persia, only to be overthrown by its own citizens. The city and its region were a remote but vital center of merchant activity connecting caravan traffic across the Sahara to the Greek world. To pledge loyalty to Alexander cost them little and diverted the Macedonian king from possibly continuing his march along the African coast. But for Alexander to have even nominal control over the region was an important factor in securing the frontier of his empire to the west. Beyond Cyrene was Carthage, an aggressive power that had already run afoul of the king at Tyre. Even now, Alexander may have been laying plans for future war against Carthage and expansion into the western Mediterranean with Cyrene as a key base.

From the seaside town of Paraetonium, Alexander and his party turned south into the desert. The guides told the king that it was almost two hundred miles to Siwa through a hellish wilderness of shifting sands and fierce south winds, but Alexander was determined to make the journey. As soon as they left behind the coastal plain, the little troop of Macedonians found themselves engulfed in a landscape unlike anything they had ever seen. Arid hills without a trace of vegetation stretched across the horizon, while the deep sand they struggled through reminded them of an endless sea. The wind stirred up the sand, driving it into their eyes and covering their clothing. Not used to desert travel, the men drank their entire water supply in just a few days with no sign of an oasis to be found. To make matters worse, their guides became lost in the blowing sand. Somewhere in the middle of the endless desert that night, the king and his friends realized they were all going to die.

But then like a gift from the gods, there was suddenly a rainstorm that broke the skies above them. Elated that they had been given a new lease on life, Alexander and his men ran around the camp with their mouths open as they collected water from holes in the ground. The rain cleared the air of dust and left a wonderful freshness across the desert, also making the sand more compact and easier to walk on. But in spite of the reprieve from heaven, they were still lost. It was then that the king saw two ravens flying overhead, common enough birds in the Libyan desert. The birds circled and turned southwest, cawing to the travelers as they went. Realizing that the ravens must be heading toward an oasis, Alexander ordered his party to follow them quickly. (His companion Ptolemy, who would later write an account of their journey, claimed that instead of ravens it was snakes that led the Macedonians to safety.) They soon came to the remote Gara Oasis, known thereafter in antiquity as Alexander's Camp. They were still far from their goal, but at least they could rest and replenish their water supply before heading onward across dry gorges and over stark gravel hills. Finally, after at least two more days, they struggled to the edge of a barren plateau and gazed down from the cliffs at the broad and unbelievably green oasis of Siwa.

Stretching fifty miles across the Sahara in a verdant valley just below sea level, Siwa was actually a series of oases and villages. The stark contrast between the barren desert and the lush pomegranate, olive, and palm trees must have been a shocking but welcome sight to Alexander and his friends. Beyond the fruit groves and springs bubbling from the ground was an arid wasteland stretching in all directions, but here at Siwa there were flocks grazing, children laughing, and a rich culture flourishing in splendid isolation. The Ammonii, as the Greeks called the inhabitants, were never a part of Egypt, although they traded with the Nile valley. All around the oases were rich deposits of salt, highly valued by the priests of Egypt for religious rituals. The natives would regularly load the salt into baskets woven from palm leaves and transport it by camel east to Memphis. (A special type of rock salt found at Siwa valued for its chemical properties was known far and wide as the salt of Ammon—thus our term *ammonia*.) Along with the salt the natives shipped dates, slaves, and other merchandise arriving at their settlement by caravan from far across the Sahara.

One attraction at Siwa that Alexander would have known from Herodotus was the Spring of the Sun. The pool in the center of a grove sacred to Ammon supposedly poured forth warm water at sunrise, cool water at midmorning, and cold water at noon. As the day passed and the sun sank over the sand hills to the west, the spring would warm until it started the cycle over again at the beginning of the next day. But Alexander was in too much of a hurry to play tourist. He had marched hundreds of miles across the desert to consult the oracle of Ammon, so without even changing clothes, he marched straight to the rocky citadel at the center of the oasis where the temple of the god stood above the trees. The hill also housed the ancient dwelling of the ruling family of Siwa, with walls separating the quarters of the chieftain from those of his wives, concubines, and children. Alexander apparently took no notice of the local nobility as he climbed the citadel and walked boldly into the sanctuary of the great god Ammon.

The high priest was waiting for him there. Normally an important pilgrim would have been welcomed by a chorus of native women singing hymns to the god, who was represented not by a statue as in a Greek temple but by a little golden boat with silver cups hanging from the side. The priest had scant warning the visiting king was coming and no time to organize the usual festivities, but he wanted to make a good impression on Alexander nonetheless. He apparently knew enough Greek to converse with the occasional visitor from across the sea, but his accent made him difficult to understand. As the king's friends stood witness outside the door of the sanctuary, the priest greeted Alexander with a paternal *O paidon,* meaning "O my child"—but with his sibilant pronunciation he changed the last letter so that it came out *O paidos.* Alexander smiled at this mistake, but saw in it a sign from the god. To the king, it sounded like *O pai dios,* which in Greek meant "O child of Zeus." Alexander had wanted to know who his real father was. This slip of the tongue was his first clue.

Ptolemy and the king's other companions waited outside as Alexander walked into the temple and shut the doors. What exactly happened next is a mystery subject to endless speculation, but what we can say with certainty is that Alexander's experience before the oracle of Zeus-Ammon changed him profoundly. All the questions and doubts that had plagued him during his short but turbulent life were put to rest. He would later write to his mother that he had heard astonishing news in the sanctuary, but would tell her the details in person when he returned to Macedonia. Since he never did return home, the ancient reports we possess are based on words the king let slip to friends in later years or on propaganda invented by early writers. Whatever the case, the sources say that Alexander first asked if the murderers of his father had been punished. The oracle, mostly through a series of nods in response to questions from the king, indicated that it was not possible to kill his true father, since his sire was not human. But the prophet continued that Alexander could put his mind to rest since the assassins of Philip had indeed all been punished. The king now had no need to ask about his paternity since the question had already been answered, so he instead posed a final query asking if he was destined to be master of all the world. To this the oracle gave a simple but profound nod of assent. It was, as the historian Arrian says, the answer his heart most desired.

Now at last Alexander knew who he was and what destiny stretched before him. He gave splendid gifts to the priest of Zeus-Ammon as thanks and departed from the citadel. Soon he would begin to call himself a son of the god whose voice he had heard at Siwa. He would even strike coins showing the characteristic ram's horns of the deity on the sides of his own head. He was still a man who could bleed and die like any other, but from that day forward Alexander knew a spark of the divine burned inside him.

Alexander spent little time in Siwa after his visit to the oracle. Spring was fast approaching and Darius would be waiting for him somewhere in Mesopotamia. After his sojourn in the western desert, it was imperative that he return to his army at Memphis as quickly as possible. He still needed to organize the government of Egypt and settle military affairs in the province before he departed the Nile valley. Most ancient sources say he returned the way he had come, back across the desert to Paraetonium, then on to Alexandria and up the Canopic branch of the Nile to Memphis. But Alexander's companion Ptolemy says the king chose the shortest route directly east across the desert. This was still more than three hundred miles through some of the most desolate terrain on earth. The eastern route was the very path long used by the inhabitants of Siwa to trade with the land of the pharaohs, so it is reasonable to assume Alexander recruited several locals to act as guides. The direct route was perilous, but given Alexander's record of taking risks, it is exactly the sort of challenge he would have relished.

With a last look back at the green valley and the temple of Zeus-Ammon, the king's camel caravan left behind the desert paradise of Siwa and struck east toward the Nile. The trail was every bit as bleak as the route Alexander had taken from the Mediterranean coast. The men passed over barren gravel flats and towering dunes, then rode beside sandstone formations that had been eroded faster at the bottom than top, making them look like giant mushrooms springing from the desert. For the first two days after leaving Siwa there was no sign of water, so that the Macedonians must have wondered if the guides were leading them astray. But soon they found a series of small oases scattered among the sand dunes. The men of Siwa would have warned them, however, to fill their water sacks to the brim at the last pool they visited as it would be more than a hundred miles before they would again see so much as a blade of grass. The little party rose the next morning and plodded on beside the camels day after day through the sun, sand, and wind. Finally, after at least a week of trudging toward the rising sun, Alexander and his companions saw the oasis of Bahariya on the horizon.

Bahariya was the main stop on the trade route between Siwa and the Nile, but it was also an important commercial center for a string of oases stretching like a great arch through the western desert. Beyond the town the ground was black from the eroded rubble of ancient mountains, but the town itself was much like Siwa, with abundant fruit trees, grapevines, and fields of wheat. There were also hot and cold springs that Alexander must have visited to wash away the layers of dirt he had collected in the wilderness. Trade was very much on the king's mind as he traveled throughout Africa and Asia, so he surely inquired about distant cities and valuable commodities from the merchants he met at Bahariya. In later ages, archaeologists would discover a small chapel to the cult of Alexander on the edge of town along the route leading to Memphis, a sanctuary that may have been founded on the king's stopover by natives eager to impress the visiting sovereign.

But there was no time to linger in Bahariya for worship or relaxation. His army was waiting for him, so Alexander set out again northeast over more inhospitable desert until finally he reached the fertile valley of the Nile and the city of Memphis. The grueling journey to Siwa and back had taken at least a month, but aside from the new confidence it gave Alexander in his divine birth and ability to conquer the world, it must have been a grand adventure that the young king and his friends would remember for the rest of their lives.

Back at Memphis, there was much to do but little time remaining until Alexander had to leave Egypt. He first held a festival to honor Zeus the King, whom he now regarded as his father, and celebrated more athletic games and musical festivals for his army before the business of war was to begin yet again. Antipater, ruling in his name in Macedonia, had sent an additional force of mercenaries and Thracian cavalry to meet him on his return from Siwa, but this was fewer than a thousand men, an indication that affairs in Greece were unsettled, especially with King Agis of Sparta still causing trouble from his base in the Peloponnese. Whatever the size of the Persian army waiting for him in Mesopotamia, Alexander would have to face it with the troops he now had on hand.

New embassies from the Aegean were also waiting for him on his return. One from Miletus reported that the sacred spring at Didyma near their city that had long been dry had miraculously sprung to life. The Persians had deported the priestly Branchidae family of Didyma to central Asia years ago, but the new priests and their oracle were working overtime predicting favorable news for Alexander. They asserted that he would defeat Darius in a major victory and that the Great King would soon meet his death. Sparta, they declared, would continue in its rebellion but would fail. As soon as they heard about the king's experience in Siwa, they suddenly remembered that their oracle had foretold the very same thing, affirming that Alexander was indeed fathered by Zeus. Not to be outdone, another delegation from the nearby Ionian town of Erythrae declared that their prophetess at the temple of Athena had also foretold that Alexander was the son of Zeus. The king realized perfectly well that these new oracular pronouncements were simply different cities trying to curry his favor, but he was willing to use them to further his own ends. If they spread the news to the Greeks that he was the child of Zeus, so much the better. Perhaps the citizens of Athens, Sparta, and Thebes would then think twice before causing him any more trouble while he was busy fighting in Asia.

The final bit of business in Egypt was the appointment of military and civilian rulers over the province. It was a tricky situation since the land along the Nile was large, heavily populated, and immensely rich. Any satrap he selected to rule would have the potential to become a mighty king in his own right if he revolted. He therefore applied the same prudent measures of dividing powers that he had used at Sardis in Lydia, but on a grander scale. To keep the native Egyptians happy, he appointed two puppet rulers, Doloaspis and Petisis, to continue the ancient forms of governance along the river valley. Petisis declined this empty honor, but Doloaspis was happy to play his part. The peasant farmers of Egypt would continue to farm the same land and pay the same taxes as they had since the time of the first pharaohs, only now the revenue would go to the Macedonian treasury. Local officials were largely kept in place. One grateful Egyptian bureaucrat named Petosiris praised Alexander in a hieroglyphic inscription as the righteous "prince of Egypt" for his actions, as opposed to the oppressive and unjust Persians who came before.

Alexander split control over the regular troops he was leaving behind between two trusted Macedonian officers, one at Memphis and the other at Pelusium. An officer from northwest Greece would command the mercenaries, but he would share power with a Macedonian who would keep a close eye on him. Watching both mercenary commanders would be two overseers reporting directly to the king. Another officer would have autonomous command of the navy, protecting the mouths of the Nile with a fleet of thirty triremes. In a further division of power, the African coast west of Egypt and the Arabian regions around the Sinai peninsula were given to separate administrators, the latter to a Greek from the colony of Naucratis named Cleomenes. There were so many different men in charge of Egypt and nearby regions that Alexander was confident it would prove impossible for any one to gain control. This would later prove a mistake, but for the present it was an effective policy.

With great fanfare, Alexander, pharaoh of Egypt, left Memphis on a spring morning sailing down the Nile to Pelusium. The event was marred only by the death of one of the king's friends, Hector, the youngest son of general Parmenion. The youth was so excited by the festivities that he jumped in one of the smaller boats and tried to race Alexander's trireme down the river. But the craft was top heavy with men and supplies, overturning in the river with the loss of almost everyone on board. Macedonians were not known for their swimming skill, but Hector struggled valiantly in his waterlogged clothes until he at last crawled half dead onto the riverbank. There, worn out by exhaustion, he collapsed and died. The king was genuinely heartbroken at the loss of his friend, though he had little affection for the rest of Parmenion's family. Alexander's last, sad memory of Egypt would be the body of young Hector burning atop a funeral pyre on the banks of the Nile.

# 6

# MESOPOTAMIA

ON THE FOURTEENTH DAY OF THE MONTH
TASHRITU . . . ALEXANDER, KING OF THE WORLD,
ENTERED BABYLON.
—BABYLONIAN ASTRONOMICAL DIARY

Two hundred desperate men, women, and children made their way through the desert canyons west of the Jordan River clutching their few belongings as they fled deep into the mountains. The refugees carried with them precious jewelry, silver coins, seal rings, fine linens, and legal documents on papyrus proving their privileged status as the honored aristocracy of their people. They were Samaritans, a group regarded by their Jewish neighbors as semi-pagans who had strayed from the true faith ever since they had mixed with foreigner settlers in the land three hundred years earlier. The Samaritans, on the other hand, considered themselves the true keepers of the ancient faith of Israel, although they accepted only the first five books of the Bible as a guide for their lives. And even the Jews had to admit that those religious laws the Samaritans kept, they kept scrupulously. Whereas the Jews might enjoy a good meal and short walk on the Sabbath, the Samaritans forbade warm food and stayed close to home. They considered nearby Mount Gerizim as the center of their faith instead of Jerusalem. They prided themselves on being pious and honest businessmen, not radicals prone to making trouble with the parade of ruling Assyrian, Babylonian, and Persian powers that passed through their land over the centuries. Thus as they stumbled through the wilderness, they must have wondered why they had burned alive the new satrap appointed by Alexander of Macedonia.

Alexander heard the disturbing news while he was on the march from Egypt back to Phoenicia. The previous year the king had appointed Andromachus, who had been in charge of his fleet during the siege of Tyre, as governor of the small province of Samaria. Now he received word that the normally equable Samaritans had seized Andromachus, tied him to a stake, and set him ablaze. It may be that with the change in regime, the local aristocracy had decided this was a propitious time to declare its independence. The aristocrats may have calculated that Alexander would be in too much of a hurry to meet Darius in Mesopotamia to bother with a detour into their highlands to punish the offenders. They were wrong. Alexander set out immediately into the hills of Samaria with his best troops to track down and punish those who would dare to kill his appointed governor. When he came to their capital city, he destroyed it and established a Macedonian colony at the site. Some of the Samaritans who had stayed behind bought their lives by revealing the whereabouts of the nobles who had murdered Andromachus and leading Alexander into the mountains after their countrymen.

The ragged group of refugees could hear the Macedonians approaching from the valley below as they ran up narrow passages in the rock barely wide enough for a donkey to pass. Crying and exhausted children were silenced as the parents realized the soldiers were closing in. Finally, they found a cave on the hillside with a tunnel leading deep into the darkness. Bats covered the roof while thick layers of guano on the cave floor burned the eyes of the fugitives and gave off such a stench that they could hardly breathe, but there was little choice but to keep moving as they groped their way hundreds of feet into the cavern. There they huddled in the suffocating darkness hoping against hope that the Macedonians would not find them. But Alexander had no trouble following their trail and soon reached the mouth of the cave, ordering torches brought up at once. Without any thought for the women and children or separating the good Samaritans from the bad, he led his troops into the cavern and slaughtered every living soul. The jumbled skeletons left behind for archaeologists to discover more than two thousand years later tell a story more vivid than any words of the swift and merciless vengeance taken against anyone who defied the will of Alexander.

From the hills of Samaria, Alexander marched back down to the sea and up the coast to Tyre. He was indeed in a hurry to meet Darius in battle, but there was business to take care of first in Phoenicia. It must have been a grimly satisfying experience to walk across the causeway to Tyre that he and his men had labored so hard to construct the year before. The city was slowly recovering as new inhabitants moved in to take the place of those killed or sold into slavery. The temples were still functioning, so once again Alexander sacrificed at the shrine of Hercules and made a rich donation to the god. There were also new appointments to make and justice to render. Samaria needed a new satrap, so the king selected a Macedonian named Menon to replace the murdered Andromachus. The Athenians had sent another embassy, this time in one of the city's sacred galleys, to beg once more for the release of their fellow citizens taken captive and enslaved at the battle of the Granicus River three years earlier. Whether because Alexander was growing tired of their pleas or because there were few of these slaves left alive after so long in the mines, he granted their request. He also received reports of King Agis and the Spartans launching a new revolt in the Peloponnese and on Crete. He sent an old family friend, Amphoterus, whom he had used for difficult missions in the past, to help the Greeks who were loyal to him deal with Agis. Alexander was not particularly worried about the Spartans, but the last thing he wanted as he marched deep into Asia was to leave an ongoing rebellion stirring to his rear. He trusted Amphoterus and his regent Antipater to deal with any further trouble in Greece.

There was also the problem of Harpalus. His childhood friend had absconded to Greece just before the battle at Issus two years earlier with as much gold as he could stuff into his traveling pack, but now he was begging Alexander to receive him back into his good graces. Harpalus, who had been given charge of the king's finances instead of a military command because of a physical handicap, swore that it was all a misunderstanding and that he had been led astray by a conniving Greek colleague. For some reason Alexander had a soft spot for Harpalus and not only allowed this scoundrel to return to his camp but once again set him in charge of his treasury, now a much more lucrative position since his victory over Darius and conquest of Egypt.

The king made other appointments and sorted through more petitions from cities in Greece and Asia Minor, but he also found time to organize another series of athletic and dramatic contests for his troops. He knew that the most difficult struggle his army would face was just ahead on the plains of Mesopotamia and he wanted his army to enter this critical period of the campaign in a good humor. The kings of Cyprus were eager to curry favor with Alexander and offered to fund the celebration. There were classic tragedies as well as comedies and choral songs in honor of the god Dionysus. The king enjoyed the productions immensely and was in a generous mood. When the Greek comic actor Lycon inserted a line in his play asking for money, Alexander laughed along with the rest of the audience and gave him the gold. An enthusiastic student of Greek theater, Alexander was especially keen on the tragic drama contest between two actors, Athenodorus and Thessalus, the former having joined him in Egypt for the earlier festivities at Memphis. Athenodorus was one of the most famous and sought-after artists in the Greek world, having won numerous contests over the past twenty years. Thessalus, on the other hand, was a longtime companion of the king who may not have been as talented as Athenodorus but was unswervingly loyal to Alexander. Philip had arrested Thessalus years before and thrown him in prison when he served as Alexander's messenger to King Pixodarus in Caria proposing a secret marriage alliance. Alexander did not wish to show preference for his friend and so allowed the judges to award the crown, which they gave to Athenodorus. The king hated to see Thessalus lose the contest so much that he later claimed he would rather have given up part of his kingdom than see Athenodorus win. But Alexander was not one to hold a grudge over artistic matters. When he found out that Athens had levied a huge fine on Athenodorus for breaking his contract and canceling a performance in their city to play before him, he cheerfully paid the penalty from his own treasury.

The shortest path from Tyre to Babylon was fewer than five hundred miles along a straight line east from the Mediterranean coast. However, only a madman would have led his army on this route, across the desert wastes of Arabia. Alexander instead followed patriarchs and kings throughout history by taking an arching route along the Fertile Crescent north beneath the mountains of Lebanon, then east across the highlands of Assyria, and finally south along the Tigris and Euphrates to Babylon. The distance was almost twice as far, but it was the only practical route, especially in summer, as it provided ample water, forage for horses, and cooler temperatures.

It was probably during this journey that the wife of Darius, whom the Macedonians had captured after the battle at Issus, suddenly died. The ancient sources present a confusing picture of the timing and cause of the queen's demise. Some say she died earlier during the siege at Tyre just a few weeks after she was taken, while others place her death during the long traverse to Mesopotamia. The cause is listed by some as exhaustion and grief, but several historians claim she died as a result of complications from childbirth. Given that it had been two years since she had seen Darius, this tradition paints a darker picture of her relationship with Alexander, one in which the king did not treat her with as much deference as he once claimed he would. In any case, all the sources agree that Alexander gave her a splendid funeral.

It was also on this journey that a battle took place, though not precisely between Macedonians and Persians. As with all ancient armies, there were large groups of camp followers that trailed behind Alexander's soldiers wherever they went on campaign. These were merchants, pimps, prostitutes, and assorted civilians who provided services to the army on an unofficial basis. Generals may not have approved of them, but they were as much a part of warfare as dusty sandals and dysentery. One evening when business was slow and the workers were bored, the camp followers divided themselves into two groups and placed commanders over themselves, calling one Alexander and the other Darius. They started by throwing all the dirt clods they could find at each other, then progressed to hitting their opponents with fists before they finally took up sticks and stones to begin killing each other for real. The king heard of the fight almost immediately and rushed to the scene. It was a delicate situation. If Alexander couldn't control the motley band of civilians following his army, the disorder and lack of discipline might spread to his troops. So, in a brilliant move once again displaying his understanding of human nature, he called the two leaders of the factions forward and made them fight in Homeric single combat before the entire army. This not only defused a tense situation, but provided welcome entertainment for the troops. As thousand of soldiers gathered around, the pseudo-Alexander and false Darius fought each other. The army—always as superstitious as village grandmothers—began to see the outcome of the fight as an omen of the great battle to come. Luckily for the king, the counterfeit Alexander won the contest after an exhausting brawl. The real Alexander then rewarded the victor with a Persian cloak and appointed him governor of twelve villages.

After several weeks of marching, the Macedonians at last reached the town of Thapsacus on the Euphrates at the beginning of August. Even along the Fertile Crescent, the temperature was scorching and the cool water of the river must have been a welcome relief to the weary soldiers. The Euphrates rises in the mountains of Armenia and flows south to the Persian Gulf roughly parallel to the Tigris, which is many miles to the east. The fertile land between the Euphrates and Tigris was called Mesopotamia ("the land between the rivers") by the Greeks. Alexander had sent his best friend, Hephaestion, ahead earlier with an engineering corps to build a pontoon bridge across the river. His companion had succeeded admirably and the bridge was ready, but Hephaestion had deliberately left the last span on the far side unfinished to prevent the enemy across the river from attacking it.

Beyond the wide Euphrates, Alexander could see several thousand Persian horsemen watching, the first soldiers of Darius he had seen for almost a year. They included a large contingent of Greek mercenaries led by Mazaeus, satrap of Babylon. Their mission was not to prevent his army from crossing; instead they were an advance force assigned to watch the river and report to Darius when Alexander crossed. Since in the mind of the Great King there was little doubt the Macedonians would follow the Euphrates south, he had already given Mazaeus orders to burn all the crops along the river on his way back to Babylon.

But by now Darius should have learned that Alexander delighted in doing the unexpected. The Macedonians did cross the river, but instead of turning south, Alexander marched his men northeast beneath the mountains of Armenia toward the Tigris and the old Assyrian capital of Nineveh. Mazaeus left at once to report the news to Darius, who was not pleased at this turn of events. He had spent the last two years planning a confrontation with Alexander on the plains north of Babylon. The Great King expected Alexander to behave like any rational general and lead his army along a well-watered and established road. Instead, the Macedonian king was making a long, slow detour in the wrong direction. It was obvious that Alexander was now intending to lead his army all the way to the Tigris before turning south. It was also clear that Darius would quickly have to change his plans.

While Alexander and his army marched across northern Mesopotamia, the Great King was moving his army. He may have been caught off guard by his enemy's unexpected shift to the east, but he was fully able to adapt—a testament both to Darius and the skill of the Persian military commanders. The Great King had learned many lessons at the battle of Issus two years earlier. The first was never allow superior numbers to be negated by fighting on a narrow plain. He believed that if he had forced Alexander to battle on a broad field as he originally had intended, he would have eliminated the Macedonian threat before the Macedonians had ever left Asia Minor. Another lesson was to increase the number and quality of his heavy cavalry forces as a response to Alexander's superb infantry. With their speed and maneuverability, well-armed horsemen could be an effective counter to the Macedonian foot soldiers and their sarissa spears. Darius had also realized that the long spears of the Macedonians gave their infantry an important advantage over his foot soldiers, so he had ordered extended lances be distributed to his men on the ground as well. The final lesson the Great King had learned at Issus was to take full advantage of the many nations of his empire to gather together a vast army. Darius was determined to outthink, outride, outfight, and absolutely overwhelm Alexander with superior numbers. With these goals in mind, he led his enormous army north along the Tigris in search of the perfect battlefield.

Alexander had at his command a little fewer than fifty thousand fighting men, mostly Macedonians, with a fair contingent of Thracian and Thessalian auxiliaries. Darius, on the other hand, had at least twice that number of soldiers, perhaps many more, drawn from the best warriors of lands stretching from Syria to India and north to the steppes of Asia. He was particularly strong in highly skilled cavalry from the east of his empire. There were also Indians from the highlands near the Khyber Pass who had brought war elephants with them—the first time any army from the Mediterranean world would face these beasts in battle. Mountain tribesmen from distant Bactria and Sogdiana were present, led by a kinsman and potential rival of Darius named Bessus, who served the Great King as satrap of Bactria. The mounted archers of the Sacae were also there, fierce and independent warriors from the plains of Scythia who prided themselves on fighting as allies, not subjects, of Persia. Arachosian tribesmen from the frontier mountains west of the Indus had made the long journey to Babylon, as had Parthians and Hyrcani from the highlands south of the Caspian Sea. The Medes, cousins of the Persians, were also on hand, along with their neighbors the Cadusians, Sacesinians, and the Albani from near the Caucasus Mountains. Arab horsemen from the shores of the Red Sea had traveled to fight with Darius. Local Babylonians also joined in the campaign, as did Armenians and Syrians, along with Cappadocians from Asia Minor, who had supposedly surrendered to Alexander two years earlier. There were many Greek mercenaries on the march as well, professional soldiers who still preferred service to the Great King over fighting for an upstart Macedonian ruler. And, of course, thousands of Persians formed the heart of the army around Darius, brave men with a long tradition of cavalry warfare.

The Macedonians arrived at the Tigris in mid-September. Though it was still summer, the river ran fast and deep through the only ford in the area. Alexander had not prepared a bridge, so he led his infantry into the water himself, struggling up to his chest through the current. After the men saw the king on the far bank, they were willing to try the river, but they foolishly placed on their heads bundles containing the spoils they had collected over the last three years, which threw them off balance in the water. Alexander told them to forget about every-thing but their weapons and that he would make up for any losses, but the Macedonians were not about to let go of their treasures. The king cursed their stubbornness, but waded back into the river and ordered them to lock arms as they crossed, forming a movable human chain supporting one another against the power of the stream. He also sta-tioned cavalry upriver from the foot soldiers to help break the current. Once the exhausted army was across, Alexander made camp and gave everyone a day to rest on the far bank of the Tigris.

Soon after, on the night of September 20, 331 B.C., an extraordi-nary event occurred that the Macedonians would long remember. As the men were finishing their evening meal under a clear desert sky, they noticed that the full moon was slowly becoming darker. It was not long before the entire lunar face was covered by the color of blood. It was a lunar eclipse, something most had seen before, but the timing of the event on the eve of battle threw even the most skeptical among the army into a panic. A contemporary but fragmentary Babylonian tablet recorded this very event, hinting at the disaster it foretold:

TOTAL ECLIPSE . . . JUPITER SETS . . . WEST WIND
BLOWING THROUGHOUT ECLIPSE, THEN EAST WIND . . .
DEATH AND PLAGUE.

Educated men like Alexander knew that the earth, moon, and sun were spheres and that an eclipse occurred when the earth was between the sun and the moon, casting its shadow on the lunar surface. But to most common people, certainly to the Macedonian soldiers, the movements of the heavenly bodies were a divine mystery. They began to fear that the bloodred moon was a sign from the gods that they would be slaughtered in the upcoming battle. Alexander heard the shouts of panic in his command tent and marched to the center of the camp with his seer Aristander to address the frightened troops. The blood on the moon, he assured them, was indeed a sign from the gods, but one that was favorable to them. Aristander had proclaimed that the darkened moon was a symbol of the Persians, who that very month would be eclipsed by the army of Alexander in battle. It was a delicate moment for the king that required a keen sense of mass psychology and crowd control, but as a cheer went up from the troops, he knew that they had believed him and been encouraged by the favorable omen. Alexander then sacrificed publicly to the sun, moon, and earth as a thanksgiving for this divine sign of victory.

The Macedonians continued their march south across the plains with the mountains of Armenia on their left and the Tigris on their right. There was no sign of Persian forces until four days after crossing the river the scouts spotted a contingent of enemy cavalry in the distance. More scouts reported that there were no more than a thousand of these Persian horsemen, who were an advance guard of the main army. Alexander ordered several squadrons of his own cavalry, including Ariston, leader of the Paeonian cavalry, and his men from the highlands north of Macedonia, to follow him in pursuit of the riders. Ariston was a prince of the royal house of Paeonia and had proven himself in battle at both the Granicus and Issus. These highlanders prided themselves on their skill fighting from horseback and waged war with a barbarian ferocity foreign to civilized Greeks. Alexander, however, cared little for niceties as long as the job got done.

As soon as Alexander and his men came over the hill, the Persians turned and galloped away as fast as their horses could carry them. The king caught up with them and began to cut them down on the run, killing most but keeping a few alive for questioning. The Paeonians were at the forefront of the fight and slew as many Persians as they could catch. Ariston had his eye on the enemy commander, a Persian named Satropates. The Paeonian captain charged his foe with spear held high and slammed the weapon straight through the man's throat, knocking him from his horse onto the ground. Ariston then leapt off his mount and cut off the Persian's head with his sword. With joy and pride, the prince then rode to Alexander and cast the head of Satropates at his feet, much to the delight of the king. The event became so celebrated in Paeonian lore that the local mint back home in the Balkans struck a coin with the god Apollo on one side and Ariston on the other, spear poised above his fallen foe.

From the captured prisoners, Alexander learned that Darius and his army were close by, beyond the hills to the east of Nineveh, not far from the town of Arbela. They were camped on a broad plain at a site called Gaugamela. It was a small, quiet village with a name meaning "camel's house" from the story of an ancient king who had once escaped from his enemies on a swift camel and fled there. He was so grateful to the animal that he built a home for it and commanded the villagers to care for it for the rest of its life. The camel was long gone, but the plain on which it grazed in contented old age still spread out for miles on the grasslands between the mountains and the Tigris. Unlike at Issus, there was plenty of open space for Darius to deploy his army. The Great King had spent the last few days meticulously leveling out dips and rises in the ground to give his cavalry and chariots a smooth surface on which to fight the upcoming battle. Darius would be taking no chances at Gaugamela.

Once he knew the location of the Persian army, Alexander ordered his troops to leave behind all their gear except weapons and prepare to move out by night. The Persians were still about seven miles away, but hills separated the two armies so that neither had yet seen the other. They were only three miles apart at dawn when the Macedonians came over the last hill and gazed down onto the plain of Gaugamela. At least a hundred thousand Persians were encamped below them. A shudder ran through the army and even Alexander seemed worried. He called his generals together to ask their counsel. Should he attack now and gain the element of surprise over the Persians or wait? Parmenion urged the king to delay the battle and survey the field before committing to a fight since it was known that the Persians had readied hidden stakes and ditches. The general advised that it would be prudent to learn the lay of the land before they engaged the enemy. For once Alexander agreed and ordered his men to make camp drawn up in battle order to save time when they marched out the next day.

Meanwhile the king took a squadron of cavalry and light-armed troops down into the plain to see the battlefield for himself. It was risky to draw so close to the Persian archers, but Alexander was determined to examine the ground his men would be fighting on the next day. When he returned to camp he again called his commanders together to give them their marching orders. There was no need for long speeches or flowery words of encouragement on the eve of battle, said Alexander. They were brave and competent leaders who had proven themselves repeatedly in action. But tomorrow they would be fighting not for Syria or Tyre or Egypt but for the sovereignty of all of Asia. Everything depended on the outcome of this battle. If the Persian army could be destroyed here and the Great King killed, the world would be theirs. They were outnumbered, but if they fought as he knew they were able then they would gain victory. But there must be no mistakes. Order and discipline were essential in the attack. The men must be silent when he ordered silence, shout when they needed to shout, and howl like wolves to inspire terror in the hearts of the Persians when the moment was right.

The king dismissed his generals and ordered the army to have a good meal and rest, then retired to his own tent for the evening. Parmenion came to him there alone with a bold suggestion that was at odds with his more public advice—why not attack the Persians that very night while it was still dark? Alexander quickly rejected this suggestion with the retort that he did not steal victories. But there were more practical matters to consider in his decision to wait until morning. Night attacks were very rare in the ancient world for the simple reason that they were too unpredictable. The attacking army might gain the element of surprise at the onset, but the battle could quickly descend into chaos with soldiers killing their own comrades by mistake. In addition, Alexander was right that he could not afford to steal a victory from Darius. If the Macedonians did win in a night battle, news would spread that he was afraid to face the Great King in a fair fight. This could fan the flames of resistance for years to come. No, he needed to beat Darius openly in the light of day to prove that he was, as the Persians called their ruler, King of Kings. In spite of his words to his commanders, Alexander had no illusions that the rest of the empire would effortlessly fall into his hands even with a victory at Gaugamela. But to crush the mighty Persian army in open battle would be a great advantage in dealing with struggles yet to come.

Nonetheless, Parmenion may have given Alexander a valuable idea. The king would not attack that night, but why not let the Persians think he would? The ancient sources say that Darius was expecting Alexander to launch an assault in the dark and kept his men ready and awake all night in preparation. It could be that Alexander allowed word to spread through the ever-present network of Persian spies that the Macedonians were planning a surprise attack. Thus while his own men rested and prepared for the fight that was coming the next day, the Persian soldiers would be forced to remain awake all night under arms, waiting for an assault that would not come until sunrise. They would be exhausted, but the Macedonians would be ready to fight.

Alexander, however, did not fall into an easy sleep that night. He knew that the Persians outnumbered him at least two to one and that they had chosen a field of battle that played to their strengths. In a broad plain, the tens of thousands of horsemen drawn from every corner of the empire would easily stretch beyond his front lines and would certainly outflank him, enveloping his infantry until every last soldier was cut down. Or they could mass into an unstoppable wedge and force their way through his infantry. He had to think of a way to break through the Persian lines with his own cavalry and attack Darius directly. If he could kill the Great King or even drive him from the field, the Persian forces would collapse. But with so many heavily armored cavalrymen on the Persian lines extending beyond his own front line on both the right and left, it seemed an impossible situation. Then, sometime in the night, Alexander had an idea—a brilliant, daring, absurd idea. From that point on, the king slept peacefully.

When Alexander's officers arrived at sunrise the next morning, they couldn't believe the king was still in bed. They didn't dare wake him, so they ordered the men to all have a good breakfast. Finally, with the sun rising in the sky above the mountains to the east, Parmenion at last entered Alexander's tent and called to him loudly two or three times before the king opened his eyes. The indignant old general asked how he could be sleeping so soundly as if he had gained a victory when the battle was still ahead. Alexander only smiled and said, "Why, don't you know we've already won?" But there was no more time to rest. Alexander quickly ate breakfast himself, then donned his splendid armor and strode forth from his tent to the cheers of his troops. With the seer Aristander standing beside him dressed in white, he offered sacrifice before the army. Then he called his officers together and revealed to them the plan that he had devised that night.

The army of Darius stretched out before the Macedonians across the plain in two broad lines, with cavalry in front and infantry behind. Alexander could see the legendary Bactrian horsemen facing his right along with other riders from central Asia commanded by Bessus. Cavalry units from many nations formed the long center of the front line, along with scythed chariot squadrons, thousands of archers, and the elephants the Indians had brought. Facing the left of the Macedonian army was again a solid wall of cavalry. Behind the horsemen were the infantry, ready to advance against his men when the cavalry broke through the lines. Darius himself was across from the Macedonian right, surrounded by his loyal Persians and tough Greek mercenaries, just as he had been at Issus two years earlier.

Parmenion commanded the Macedonian left, Alexander the right. The king stationed the Thessalian horsemen with Parmenion, but also kept a large contingent of cavalry for himself. There was also a second line of infantry, mostly his own Greek mercenaries, behind the center in case the Persians broke through, but they would not be able to hold for long if the front line collapsed. The heat was intense even at the end of September and the soil stirred up by myriads of men and horses threatened to cover the plain of Gaugamela with a choking cloud of dust. It was not long before both armies were in place, waiting for the other to make the first move.

While Alexander was inspecting the lines and encouraging his men, he had ridden any one of the fine horses he kept. But now that the battle was set, he mounted Bucephalas. The stallion he had first mastered beneath Mount Olympus so long ago was now past his prime, but he still had fire in his heart. Alexander would not dream of riding another horse into battle on that fateful day.

As in past fights, Alexander intended to strike first with the right side of his line to draw the enemy formation away from their center and open a space to drive into their heart. But with so many Persian soldiers stretching beyond his lines on both sides, he would have to try something no other general in history had ever done. He now set out with his cavalry force on the right side of his line not toward the Persians but parallel to their forces, riding farther and farther to the right of the battlefield without ever coming into contact with the enemy. This must have seemed ridiculous to Darius, as if the Macedonian king were hoping to circle around his superior forces. But Alexander had a plan. If he could draw enough of the Persian army away from their center after him, he might create a gap in their lines. At that moment, he would wheel his horsemen around and dash back to the opening before the Persian troops pursuing him could follow.

There was so much that could go wrong with this plan that Alexander probably tried not to consider the consequences of failure. It depended on Darius sending enough troops after him to thin the Persian center. Then Alexander would have to turn his cavalry back fast enough to beat the enemy that would be chasing him. If he could make it, he would still have to force his way through a mass of Persian soldiers to attack Darius directly. All this time, the superior forces of the Great King would be attacking the rest of his army with everything they had. It was absolutely essential that Parmenion hold his troops together under the most punishing conditions long enough for Alexander to break through the hole he hoped to open in the Persian lines. If Darius refused to take the bait or Alexander could not break through or the Macedonian line collapsed, they would all die.

Fortunately for Alexander, as soon as Darius saw him heading to the far right of the battlefield, he sent Bessus and his cavalry after him. The Great King was worried that if Alexander was able to reach the part of the plain he had not leveled during the previous days, his own horsemen might not be able to keep up with the Macedonians. As they were nearing the edge of the field, the Persians pulled ahead of Alexander and began to move around him on his right, threatening to strike him from behind. In response Alexander ordered his Greek mercenaries and the Paeonian cavalry under Ariston to attack Bessus and his men in a furious effort to keep them engaged on the far side of the battlefield.

Meanwhile Darius had launched the main body of his force against the Macedonian left. The Persian plan was to use the scythed chariots—deadly vehicles with blades attached to their wheels—first to tear through the enemy and throw the lines into confusion, opening their own hole in the Macedonian army. What Darius didn't realize was that Alexander had been drilling his men for weeks on how to face these terrifying machines. As the chariots drew near, the Thracians in front of the line launched a deadly volley of javelins at the drivers and killed many of them while they were still charging. Others were able to snatch hold of the reins as the chariots drove past and pull the drivers down. Those that made it past the Thracians found that the Macedonian infantry neatly stepped aside to allow them through, only to close the line again behind them. It was not a perfect plan as some of Alexander's men were eviscerated by the spinning blades, but casualties were relatively light. Nonetheless, the chariots were just the forefront of the Persian attack. Soon massive numbers of cavalry were striking the Macedonian lines, followed by infantry. Alexander's men on the left were holding for now, but the Persians were threatening to break through at any moment.

At last Alexander saw what he had been waiting for—a thinning in the Persian center. He ordered his men to turn sharply back and charge the opening in a wedge formation. The Persian forces on the right of the battlefield were kept in place by the Greek mercenaries and Paeonians, leaving the king free to race toward Darius. With a loud battle cry, Alexander and his men flew toward the Great King and charged into the Persian lines. Darius had not dreamed that Alexander would be able to break through as he had at Issus, but now he saw the young Macedonian king fighting his way through spears and swords to get to him. It was a brutal struggle on both sides, with Persian nobles laying down their lives to keep the Macedonians away from Darius. But at last Alexander and his men were drawing so close that the Great King ordered his charioteer to turn and flee the battlefield.

At this joyous moment, Alexander received word that Parmenion and his men were in grave danger. The Persians under the Babylonian satrap Mazaeus had broken through the line with Bactrians and Indians behind them. They had torn through his army all the way to the Macedonian baggage train in the rear and were freeing the Persian hostages, with many of these prisoners joining in to kill their Macedonian captors. But more important, Parmenion's men were being slaughtered and needed help. Alexander faced a tortuous decision. If he chased Darius and captured him, it would be a tremendous blow to the Persians. But if he pursued the Great King, half of his own army would perish with the battle still raging. Alexander had no choice but to turn his men around and rush to Parmenion's aid, eventually surrounding the Persian attackers and cutting them down. When he and Parmenion had destroyed the last of the Persian resistance, the Great King was long gone.

The Macedonians were victorious in one of the greatest battles in history. As the broken Babylonian tablet again records:

> ON THE 24TH OF THE MONTH ULULU . . .
> IN THE MORNING, THE KING OF THE WORLD . . .
> THEY FOUGHT EACH OTHER AND A GREAT DEFEAT OF
> THE TROOPS . . . THE SOLDIERS OF THE PERSIAN KING
> DESERTED HIM AND TO THEIR CITIES . . .
> THEY FLED TO THE LAND OF MEDIA.

The Persians had lost tens of thousands of men, with Alexander capturing a host of rich spoils—not to mention a few elephants. Macedonian losses were comparatively light, though Hephaestion and several of the commanders were badly wounded. Many of their horses were also killed in the close fighting. But even more than a military triumph, Alexander's greatest prize was glory. He had risked everything and won, defeating in open battle the largest Persian army ever assembled. True, he had not killed or captured the Great King, but the humiliation of being driven from the field yet again made Darius a gravely weakened ruler. The road to the fabled city of Babylon was open, with the wealth of Susa and Persepolis just beyond. The fight for Persia was not yet over as others would surely rise to defend the heart of the empire and the rich lands to the east, but the awesome royal glory had now passed to Alexander.

Throughout Alexander's campaign, whether he was in Egypt, Mesopotamia, or India, there was a constant stream of messengers riding back and forth between the Macedonian camp and the rest of his empire. Dispatches home to his mother at Pella were especially frequent, but there were also instructions to various satraps and military commanders, letters to allies and foreign cities, and the propaganda produced by Aristotle's nephew Callisthenes for the Greek cities. Wherever Alexander happened to be at the moment was the effective capital of his realm. His ability to control millions of subjects depended on his knowledge of local events from the latest grain harvest in Cyrene to reports of tribal movements along the Danube. Likewise, it was essential that all the provinces know where the king was, what he was doing, and that his army was successful fighting against his enemies. Victories in one part of the empire served to discourage trouble elsewhere.

Thus when news reached the Aegean that Alexander had defeated Darius at Gaugamela, the citizens of Greece were horrified. Most had hoped that the Great King would obliterate Alexander and remove the Macedonian threat forever. The League of Corinth would happily be forgotten and all the Hellenic cities could go back to squabbling with one another as they had since time immemorial. But with Alexander victorious, there seemed to be no way to loosen the Macedonian grip on Greece.

Not that some weren't willing to try. Even before Gaugamela, the appointed ruler of Thrace, an experienced and spirited leader named Memnon, had launched a rebellion that stirred up the tribesmen from the mountains east of Macedonia. Memnon gathered together a large and aggressive army so that Alexander's regent Antipater was forced to march against him with all the soldiers at his disposal. King Agis of Sparta was watching events in Thrace carefully and decided this was the moment to issue a call for the Greeks to unite and throw off the Macedonian yoke. Messengers went out to cities from Athens to Thebes, but as usual, most of the citizens were lukewarm about actually taking up arms. The Athenians in particular hesitated, depriving Agis of vital naval support. The Spartan king did sway a few cities to follow his banner, but most Greeks were content to wait on the sidelines and see whether the Spartans had any success before committing themselves.

As soon as Antipater got word of the Spartan uprising, he struck a quick peace deal with Memnon in Thrace and marched his men south into Greece. Even with the flower of Macedonian youth in the east following Alexander, Antipater still had forty thousand troops under his command, including many loyal Greeks, more than twice the total number serving Agis. At Megalopolis north of Sparta, the two forces met for a bloody clash that killed thousands on both sides. Antipater was determined to wipe out Greek resistance once and for all, but Agis was just as determined to restore freedom to the land. As the battle turned against him, the Spartan king was in the front lines fighting against the Macedonians as bravely as his forefathers who had stood against the Persians at Thermopylae. But with numerous wounds, he was at last carried off the field by his comrades. Even then the enemy was surrounding the last Spartan holdouts. Agis ordered his friends to make their escape as best they could through the enemy lines, but leave him a sword. His injuries were so grave that he could not stand as the Macedonians closed in on him, but he rose to his knees and slashed at any of Antipater's soldiers who came near. Finally, the last of the noble kings of Sparta was slain by a spear thrust and perished on the field of battle.

After the battle at Gaugamela, Darius fled first to the nearby town of Arbela, but only briefly as he knew Alexander would be close behind him. From there he struck east into the mountains toward the old Median capital of Ecbatana. This summer residence of the Great King sat atop a high citadel with a magnificent palace adorned with gold, silver, and intricate woodwork. Ecbatana also lay on the main road connecting Mesopotamia with the provinces of central Asia. As he traveled into the highlands, Darius collected survivors of the battle. The Bactrian cavalry under his kinsman Bessus were with him from the beginning, along with his closest relatives and his personal guard, known as the Spearmen of the Golden Apples for the fruit-shaped bulbs at the butt end of their weapons. Two thousand Greek mercenaries also joined him, led by their captains Patron and Glaucus. They knew they would not be welcome at the camp of Alexander because of their betrayal of the Hellenic cause.

Darius armed all the soldiers who had lost their weapons from the storehouses of Ecbatana and sent out messengers to the neighboring tribes demanding soldiers to carry on the fight. He also dispatched letters to the satraps of central Asia to confirm their loyalty to him. His plan was to move east into the deserts and mountains of Parthia, Bactria, Sogdiana, and the borderlands of India to wage a guerrilla campaign against the Macedonians. He assured his followers that they were far from defeated. Alexander had taken the Mediterranean coast and was marching through Mesopotamia, but half the Persian Empire was still untouched. Darius would personally lead his band of mobile warriors on glorious battles against the foreign invaders. They would live like their ancestors of old, riding hard and sleeping under the stars. Persians did not need palaces and riches. Let the Macedonians glut themselves on the whores of Babylon and waste away their manhood eating grapes peeled by perfumed eunuchs.

The followers of Darius were less than thrilled at the prospect of an endless insurrection waged from caves and isolated mountain villages. They could not believe that the Great King would so willingly surrender the wealth of Babylon and the Persian winter capital of Susa to Alexander. He had no plans even to fight for Persepolis and the heartland of Persia. Despite the assurances of Darius that wars were won with brave men and steel, not cities and gold, the nobles of the empire had grown quite accustomed to a life of privilege and luxury, lording over their subject people. To suddenly become a ragged band of poor but heroic warriors eating half-cooked goat meat in the wastelands of Bactria did not appeal to them. They maintained their outward loyalty for the present, but it must have been at Ecbatana that many of the officers began to talk among themselves—and especially with Bessus—about the need for a new Great King.

Darius was in such a hurry to leave Arbela and flee to Ecbatana that he left behind an abundant store of food, jewels, and a fortune in silver. Alexander found it there the next day and hauled it in wagons back to his camp near the battlefield. He quickly conducted solemn funeral rites for his fallen soldiers, but the stench of thousands of Persian corpses rotting in the sun prompted him to march toward Babylon as soon as the last sacrifice was made to the gods of the dead.

Alexander was anxious to reach southern Mesopotamia, but there were local dignitaries to receive and marvels to see along the way. The road to Babylon took the Macedonians along the Tigris through fields that had been cultivated since the Mesopotamians first discovered the art of agriculture millennia earlier. They passed ancient cities in which writing had been invented and the course of the stars charted across the heavens, when the ancestors of the Greeks were still pastoral nomads.

At one town the king was shown a pool of bitumen bubbling to the surface to form a small pool in the desert. This petroleum was a great novelty to Alexander, who had read about the liquid in Herodotus but had never seen it for himself. There were few sources of petrochemicals in the Aegean world, where heating and energy were provided almost exclusively by the burning of wood. Even in Mesopotamia, oil was used to seal boats (as in the biblical story of Noah) or as mortar in walls, not to burn for warmth or cooking.

The citizens of the bitumen-rich town were anxious to impress the king and so took buckets of the liquid and poured a trail of the sticky tar along the street leading to his quarters. When darkness fell, they lit the first patch near Alexander. He watched as a blazing trail erupted instantly in the dark night, moving faster than any fire he had ever seen. He then walked along the lighted pathway to his lodgings, following a continuous line of flames.

The king was so taken by this novel liquid that one of his bath attendants, an Athenian named Athenophanes, suggested they apply it to a homely servant named Stephanus to see what would happen when it burned on a human body. The young man was eager to please and gladly anointed himself with bitumen for the experiment. Alexander cannot have been so foolish as to think this would be harmless to the lad, but his curiosity evidently overcame both his compassion and common sense. When Stephanus, covered in pitch, touched a nearby lamp, he burst into flame. The king flew from his seat and tried to put out the fire, but it was like no other conflagration he had ever dealt with. Even the jars of water for his bath standing conveniently at hand were scarcely able to extinguish the flames. What had started as a humorous science experiment left a poor young man near death, covered with horrible burns.

Alexander continued the march south along the Tigris past Ashur and Takrit out of the highlands of Assyria into the broad and fertile land of Babylonia. The pastures between the Tigris and Euphrates were said to be so rich in nourishing grasses that the flocks of the area had to be restrained from eating themselves to death. Here in southern Mesopotamia, the two great rivers were only a few miles apart, so it was easy for Alexander to cross from the banks of the Tigris west to the Euphrates. Somewhere north of Babylon the Macedonians saw a fine procession approaching them. Mazaeus, satrap of the city, was at its head. There were priests from all the temples and leading officials bearing fabulous gifts for the new king. Mazaeus, who just a few weeks before had led his troops against Alexander at Gaugamela, prostrated himself before his new lord along with his grown sons. Parmenion in particular must have yearned to impale this turncoat on a pole after losing so many of his men to the Persian in battle, but Alexander was more circumspect. It is almost certain that the meeting of the king and the satrap had been preceded by days of negotiation. If not, it is unlikely that Mazaeus would have dared to risk his life by appearing before Alexander.

Mazaeus was above all a very practical man. He knew as soon as Darius fled the battlefield that the days of the Persian Empire were over. Alexander was now the most powerful man in the world—and Mazaeus wanted to make sure they were on the same side. Many other Persians must have felt the same way, but the Babylonian satrap led the way in switching his allegiance to the Macedonian king. What Mazaeus had to offer Alexander was the richest city in the world. The Macedonians could have taken Babylon by force, but it would have been an enormous effort. Much better to avoid another siege of Tyre and instead receive the town as a gift. The price Mazaeus exacted was the continuation of his role as governor of Babylon. That Alexander agreed to this deal is proof that his war against the Persians had now changed fundamentally.

Until this point, the Macedonian king had been a crusader in a foreign land slicing away bits of the Persian Empire to add to his own domain. Even in Egypt, the native rulers he appointed were figureheads under Greek and Macedonian domination. But Mazaeus was to be a genuine satrap with real authority over the most important city in Alexander's realm. The king was no fool and appointed Macedonians as commanders of the military units in the area, but nonetheless the rise of Mazaeus marked an extraordinary change of policy. Alexander was no longer trying to conquer Persia and kill Darius—he himself was now Great King with all the privileges and responsibilities of that office. To rule the many lands of his empire he would need experienced men like Mazaeus, who knew the language, culture, people, and politics of each province. The Persians had for two centuries skillfully governed the largest dominion ever known. Their trained and capable officers were essential to Alexander—if he could gain their loyalty. By openly rewarding Mazaeus with control of such an important city, the king was sending an unmistakable signal to those who had once served Darius that the new lord of the lands was merciful and reasonable. If they joined him willingly, they could receive rich rewards for their service.

In favoring such administrators even above his own countrymen, Alexander was in no way abandoning his Macedonian roots; rather, it was essential that he begin to think of ruling in a radically new way. His realm was no longer just Macedonia and Greece, but a true international empire encompassing three continents and dozens of distinct kingdoms. Thracians, Lydians, Carians, Phrygians, Cappadocians, Syrians, Phoenicians, Jews, Arabs, Egyptians, and Babylonians were now under his direct rule with Medes, Elamites, Parthians, Bactrians, Scythians, and Indians yet to come. Although many of his Macedonian supporters vehemently resisted these changes, Alexander wanted to make them see that the feudal system used to govern their homeland was totally inadequate for ruling a vast empire. If he were to succeed in his grand ambitions, he would have to integrate native officials into his imperial government just as the Persians had before him. As he marched toward Babylon, he knew that the days of his father's Macedonian kingdom were over—the age of Alexander's Macedonian Empire had begun.

Babylon was an enormous city more than two thousand years old when Alexander approached its walls. According to legend, it was founded in the distant past by Queen Semiramis, who built massive dikes to control the floods that regularly swept down the Euphrates from the north. Herodotus claimed the city was shaped like a square, with its sides more than thirteen miles each, giving its walls an astonishing circumference greater than fifty miles, though the true figure was surely less. A deep moat formed its outer boundary next to the wall itself, which was reportedly more than seventy feet wide and more than three hundred feet high. On top of the entire perimeter of the wall was a road wide enough for a four-horse chariot to be driven. One hundred gates of bronze were said to lead into the city, but no entry was more spectacular than the fabulous Ishtar Gate, made up of hundreds of glazed blue tiles decorated with golden bulls and dragons, all surrounded by decorated bands and rosettes.

The Euphrates divided the city in half, but there was a bridge that connected the two sides. Unlike many ancient towns that had grown haphazardly over the centuries, Babylon was laid out in a grid with straight streets running either parallel or at right angles to the river. The thousands of houses inside the walls were three to four stories high, interspersed with businesses and shops that sold everything from Chinese silk to amber from the Baltic Sea. On the eastern side of the city was a second wall, surrounding the royal palace, and another protecting the central ziggurat, a steep pyramid containing the temple to Bel-Marduk, chief god of Babylon. The ziggurat was so high that the designers included a shelter halfway up to allow pilgrims to rest on their climb. On the summit was a temple that only the priests could enter. Inside was a huge bed covered with the finest linens next to a golden table, but—unlike in most temples—no statue as the god himself occupied the sanctuary. No one ever slept on the bed except a specially chosen woman who was said to be the bride of Bel-Marduk for that night.

More than a thousand years earlier, the city had been ruled by Hammurabi, who composed his famous code of laws for his subjects to follow. These were an important influence on many Near Eastern cultures for ages to come. On a stone stele beneath the figure of the sun god Shamash were carved the many laws that governed the land. Justice was simple and harsh under Hammurabi:

If a man destroys the eye of a another man, they shall destroy his eye as well.

If a man knocks out the tooth of another man, they shall knock out his tooth as well.

But there was also a degree of mercy in the code: "If the wife of a man is caught lying with another man, they shall bind them both and throw them into the water to drown. But if the husband wishes to spare his wife, the king may consent."

Hammurabi's kingdom gave way to the Assyrian Empire, then

the Neo-Babylonian age under rulers such as Nebuchadnezzar, a great builder who restored the city to its glory before the Persians conquered Mesopotamia. The invaders from the east had been deeply resented by the natives as they showed little respect for the ancient religion of Babylon. As in Egypt, the Persians considered the rich city little more than a treasure trove to be plundered. Xerxes removed a solid gold statue of Bel-Marduk from the temple, killing the priest who tried to stop him, and melted it down into coins to pay for his wars. Xerxes offended the Babylonians on an even greater scale when he later destroyed much of the temple after a rebellion in the city, leaving it a ruin of its former glory.

Alexander, on the other hand, was determined to show respect for the religious traditions of Babylon, though he was also cautious. He gave strict orders to his men that there was to be no looting and that no Macedonian soldier would enter a Babylonian house uninvited. He hoped to take Babylon peacefully and maintain good relations with the natives, but he was ready for trouble if it occurred. Thus beneath the city walls crowded with thousands of men, women, and children throwing flowers to the soldiers below, Alexander entered the city that bright autumn day through the Ishtar Gate at the head of his troops in full battle formation. There was no hostility from the inhabitants, who, like the Egyptians, were pleased to see the Persians removed from power even though they did not yet know what sort of rule the Macedonians would impose. Instead of spears and arrows there were garlands and perfumes, followed by gifts of precious frankincense and cages filled with lions and leopards. The native priests sang hymns in ancient tongues to welcome the new king while music filled the air. The throngs of citizens joined in the procession behind the soldiers as if the entry of the army were a great holiday. Alexander had never seen anything to compare with Babylon. To his men from the poor villages of Macedonia, it was as if they had entered another world.

The king first went to the temple of Bel-Marduk and ordered the damage Xerxes had done to the sacred precinct repaired. Then, carefully following the instructions of the priests, he sacrificed to the

god, surrounded by cheering natives. Then he and his officers retired
to the palace at the northern end of the city near the Ishtar Gate and
settled into a life of splendid luxury for the next month. He marveled
at a pillar in the palace listing the dining requirements of Darius' royal
entourage, including dozens of cakes of honey, hundreds of bushels of
flour, barrels of sesame oil and vinegar, and baskets of finely chopped
cardamom. Alexander ordered the inscription destroyed to show a
break with the wasteful Persian ways of the past and told his officers
that those who indulged in such extravagant ways were quickly defeated in battle.

   With his copy of Herodotus in hand the next day, Alexander
toured the strange and wonderful city. As he passed through the
streets, he noticed that family members and friends would carry sick
people into public squares and leave them there to talk with those
walking by. The Babylonians did not trust physicians, but instead relied on the advice of strangers, who would approach the sick and offer
a remedy. Many had suffered from the same illness themselves and
had learned firsthand an effective treatment, while others had heard
of a cure elsewhere. Given the international nature of the city, with
visitors from almost every land, there was no shortage of medical
wisdom and quackery available to the sick.

   One of the first places visited by Alexander's men, if not by the
king himself, must have been the temple of the goddess Ishtar, known
to the Greeks as Aphrodite, who ruled over the sexual aspects of life.
It was an unbreakable rule in Babylon that every woman of the city
must sometime in her life offer herself to a man at the temple as
an act of worship. Rich and poor women alike would come to the
sacred precinct and sit with wreaths of cords on their heads to mark
their availability. Visiting men would walk up and down the pathways
among the women looking for an appealing devotee. When they
found the right lady, they would toss silver into her lap and call her
to come in the name of the goddess. A waiting priest would collect
the money for the temple treasury and escort the couple to a nearby
room in the temple. No woman could refuse any man, so that a poor
shepherd in from the countryside could enjoy the favors of a noble

lady of the court, at least on that single occasion. Beautiful women never had to wait long, but those lacking in appeal might sit in the temple courtyard for years before being chosen. Prudish Greek writers reported that the whole enterprise was nothing but prostitution on a grand scale, but to the citizens of Babylon it was as much an act of genuine devotion as the most solemn sacrifice to Athena or Zeus.

Alexander would least of all have missed the Hanging Gardens of Babylon, ranked along with the Great Pyramid at Giza as one of the wonders of the world. Centuries earlier, an Assyrian king ruling in Babylon had built the gardens for his foreign wife, who longed for the woods and groves of her native land. There in the middle of a desert city, the king built a series of raised platforms above the streets supported by massive columns. Tons of soil were carried to the terraces by an army of slaves and water was continuously piped in from the river and drawn up by huge screws to circulate through the gardens. Fruit trees, palms, and conifers were planted throughout, growing into a living forest rising high above the city. In the most intense heat of summer, visitors could walk through the cool groves and picnic in the shade on the lush grass.

As always, Alexander seems to have taken an interest in religious matters that went beyond the mere politics of ingratiating himself with the locals. There was in Babylon a special quarter of the city given over to the Chaldeans, the ancient priest-philosophers of Mesopotamia famed especially for their precise study of the stars. Their records of astronomical events reportedly went back thousands of years, but as they were written in a cuneiform script unknown to the Greek world, the king had to take the priests' word on the matter. Unlike most numerical systems, mathematics as taught by the Chaldeans was based on the number sixty rather than ten—a way of measuring time and space passed on to later civilizations as the sixty-minute hour, the sixty-second minute, and the 360-degree circle (six times sixty). Long before Alexander, the Babylonians had discovered how to use complex fractions, quadratic equations, and what would come to be known as the Pythagorean theorem. Many of the advances in later

Greek mathematics in fact derived from the encounter that began in Babylon that autumn with the arrival of the Macedonians. As the Chaldeans were also experts in divination, Alexander took several of them along with him for the rest of his campaign to read the signs of events to come. He must have also talked with them about their views of the gods and the origin of the world. If so, he would have learned of a remarkable similarity between Babylonian creation myths, with their stories of successive generations of gods battling one another for control of the universe, and the tales he had read in the Greek poet Hesiod of Cronos castrating his father, only to be violently displaced in time by his own son Zeus.

But Alexander could not spend all his time in Babylon seeing the sights and visiting with native scholars. There were also appointments to be made and military affairs to be arranged. Almost fifteen thousand new recruits had just arrived in the city following a long march from Macedonia. These included cavalry and infantry sent by Antipater and led by Amyntas, the veteran commander dispatched to Macedonia by Alexander many months before to bring back additional troops. The king was sorely disappointed that Amyntas had not arrived with the much-needed soldiers before the battle at Gaugamela, but he knew there would be plenty of opportunities for fighting yet to come. The commander also brought with him fifty sons of leading Macedonian nobles to serve as royal pages under the king. These lads were to wait on the royal table, attend the king in hunting and battle, and stand guard outside his chambers at night. It was an honored position for ambitious young men that served as an important training ground for future Macedonian leaders.

Before leaving the city, Alexander appointed Agathon from the coastal Macedonian town of Pydna as commander of the citadel at Babylon with a thousand troops under him. Overall command of military affairs in Babylonia was assigned to another Macedonian, Apollodorus from Amphipolis, along with two thousand soldiers and money to hire more. Asclepiodorus, probably a Greek, was put in charge of collecting taxes from the province, while the former Persian satrap Mazaeus was reconfirmed in his previous office. To keep the army happy—and perhaps to lure them away from the pleasures of the city—he gave each of his Macedonian cavalry the equivalent of a year's pay as a bonus. Foreign horsemen received almost as much and Macedonian infantry each pocketed more than they would earn in six months. Alexander wanted to give his men no cause to grumble as they continued the march into Persia. They knew there would be more to come from their generous king on the road ahead.

Once the last of his soldiers was rounded up from the brothels of Babylon, Alexander set out with his enlarged army to the winter capital of the Persian Empire at Susa. Darius was still at large in the snow-covered mountains of Media, but the most pressing matter for Alexander was to secure the treasuries at Susa and Persepolis as soon as possible. Susa was the closer of the two capitals, more than a hundred miles down the royal road that ran all the way back to Sardis in Lydia. The town was so notoriously hot in summer that lizards trying to cross its roads baked before they reached the other side, but in the cooler months it was a most pleasant city. The journey there took the Macedonians to the north of the endless marshes where the mouths of the Tigris and Euphrates met the Persian Gulf, a land known in antiquity as Sumer. From here, the biblical patriarch Abraham was said to have set out on his journey to the land of Canaan. The Sumerians, who had built cities three thousand years before Alexander, were one of the oldest civilizations on earth. The king must have heard stories from his new Chaldean traveling companions about the glories of ancient Sumer. From the city of Uruk on the Euphrates, a great king named Gilgamesh once ruled. The story may have been lost by Alexander's day, but if it had survived once again he would have been surprised by similarities with the earliest Greek literature. Gilgamesh, like Homer's Achilles, was part god and part man, a great hero seeking glory who fought monsters and gods alongside his beloved friend Enkidu. Like Achilles' companion Patroclus, Enkidu died suddenly, plunging his friend into deep despair. But unlike Achilles, who took out his frustration on the Trojan warrior Hector, Gilgamesh instead set out in search of eternal life. His quest at last took him to the island of Utnapishtim, a man who had once survived the great flood sent by the gods to destroy humanity and been rewarded with immortality. Gilgamesh failed the test that would grant him eternal life, but the lessons he learned were a comfort to readers for millennia.

The city of Susa was the old capital of the kingdom of Elam, a land of southern Mesopotamia stretching into the Zagros Mountains of Persia to the east. It was once a large territory encompassing parts of Persia before the ancestors of Cyrus the Great took over the highlands. Elam served as the main conduit of trade between the east and Mesopotamia for goods such as timber and minerals. The people of Elam, like the Sumerians, wrote on clay tablets in cuneiform script thousands of years before Alexander. Once the Persians brought the Elamites of the Mesopotamian plain into their empire in the sixth century, they made their tongue one of the official languages of state. The language of Elam was unrelated to any other in the area, though it may have shared a common origin with those spoken in ancient times in parts of India. In any case, it was an important means of communication in Alexander's new empire and required that the king employ scribes who were fluent in the language.

After a march of twenty days from Babylon, the Macedonian army arrived at Susa. The royal palace spread out there on three steep hills was the setting for the biblical tale of Esther, while just below the citadel lay the tomb of the prophet Daniel. Chief among the features of the Great King's palace was the open audience hall with dozens of pillars more than sixty feet high. Suppliants approaching the royal chamber would climb a series of stairs past stunning gold reliefs of the king's guard and a larger-than-life statue of the first Darius himself. Tribute from the whole empire was built into the palace as a reminder of the awesome power of the king—cedar wood from Lebanon, ivory from India, walls decorated by Egyptians, stone shaped by Greek workers from the Aegean coast. Inside the hall was an explosion of color, with golden images of sphinxes and lions, while the capitals of the columns were carved like the heads of gigantic bulls. Across the river next to the vast complex stood the smaller palace of the Great King Artaxerxes II, built in the time of Alexander's grand-father. This Persian king constructed a less imposing but still opulent structure as a retreat from the endless demands of the royal court. An inscription there prayed that the gods would grant him and his palace protection from all evil, that the place might be a *paradayadam* for him. In later Persian, the same word would become *pairidaeza* and pass into Greek as *paradeisos,* or paradise.

Alexander had sent one of his officers directly to Susa after the battle at Gaugamela with a demand that the local Persian satrap, Abulites, prepare the city for surrender along with a stern warning to leave the treasury untouched. The satrap had complied and now sent his own son to meet the king and escort him to the city by way of the nearby Choaspes River—an important symbolic gesture as this was the stream from which the Great King drank. Abulites met him there formally to surrender Susa and bestow on its new king regal gifts of the finest purple cloth, dromedaries, and imported Indian elephants. More important to Alexander, the satrap also brought along a staggering forty thousand talents of gold and silver bullion, enough money to fund the Macedonian army and indeed the whole empire for years to come. Alexander must have appreciated the ad-ditional gift of thousands of minted gold coins commonly known as darics that depicted the first Great King Darius as an archer. The king now had treasure at his disposal beyond his wildest dreams.

When Alexander climbed the stairs to the citadel of the city and entered the royal audience hall, he stared in disbelief at the glorious decorations and spoils collected for two centuries from throughout the empire. He noticed on one side the statues of the two Athenian youths Harmodius and Aristogiton taken by Xerxes during his inva-sion of Greece. The young men had plotted to assassinate a ruling tyrant of Athens, but were killed and later elevated to the status of heroes. Alexander ordered the statues sent back to Athens with his compliments—perhaps as an ironic comment on the Athenian view that he himself was now the greatest tyrant of all. Nonetheless, the citizens of Athens were grateful for their return and set them up be-side the path leading to their Acropolis.

At the far end of the reception hall was the royal throne of Darius himself. It was death for anyone but the Great King to sit there, but Alexander very deliberately made a public show of mounting the dais and placing himself grandly on the throne. The only problem was that the new king was shorter than average height and his feet dangled above the lowest step. This was both embarrassing and undignified, so one of the quick-thinking royal pages pushed aside the mounting block and substituted a table of greater height on which Alexander could rest his feet in royal splendor. The king then noticed that an elderly eunuch in the corner was quietly weeping. When asked why he was so sad, the servant replied that he had long served the Great King his meals on that very table and was heartbroken to see it used as a footstool. Alexander was about to order the table removed lest he be accused of callously breaching protocol and offending the gods, when Philotas, the son of general Parmenion, urged him to stop. It is an omen, he declared, that the table once used by your great enemy has now become your footstool. Alexander saw the wisdom in such symbolism and ordered that the table from that day forward remain where it was.

The king settled into the palace and saw that the family of Darius, who had been traveling with him since Issus, was made at home in their old quarters. He had no need to drag them along behind him any longer on campaign, so he ordered that they remain in Susa and be assigned tutors to learn the Greek language. Alexander was especially anxious to leave a good impression with Sisyngambris, the mother of Darius, and made a present to her of fine cloth that had just arrived from Macedonia. To show his affection, he even offered to send her Macedonian women who would teach her and her granddaughters how to weave the splendid cloth for themselves. What the king did not know is that he had just insulted the queen mother in the worst possible way. Persian women of the royal court did not work cloth—this was a task for slaves. When he heard that Sisyngambris was sulking in her quarters and discovered why, he called on her personally and offered his most sincere apologies. In his country, he explained, queens and princesses like his own mother and sisters considered it an honor to weave fine cloth. It took much explaining, but eventually Sisyngambris understood that the gesture was not intended as an insult.

Winter was settling on the Zagros Mountains to the east as the new year began at Susa. If Darius expected Alexander to wait in comfort in the warmth of the palace, he should have known better. After only a short stay at Susa, Alexander commanded his army to prepare to march. He left behind the satrap Abulites in his previous office, following the pattern he had established with Mazaeus at Babylon, but once again appointed loyal Macedonians to command the military. Alexander had conquered the Mediterranean provinces and Mesopotamia for his empire, but the heart of Persia and the provinces to the east still lay ahead. Up until this point of the campaign, the natives through whose lands he passed saw him as a potential liberator or at least as a means to drive out the Persians. But once he crossed the mountains and moved toward Persepolis, he would be nothing but an invader in hostile territory. He knew the Persians would fight all the more bravely for their homeland. Beyond them lay the Bactrians, Scythians, and Indians—all among the best warriors in the world, who would also be fighting for their own lands. The battle for the west may have been won, but the hardest part of the war was just beginning.

# 7

# PERSEPOLIS

IS IT NOT PASSING BRAVE TO BE A KING
AND RIDE IN TRIUMPH THROUGH PERSEPOLIS?
—CHRISTOPHER MARLOWE

A few days east of Susa, Alexander and his army left the warm plains of Mesopotamia and entered the snow-covered mountains of Persia. These highlands were occupied by a people known as the Uxians, whose king, Madates, was a cousin of Darius. Although related to the royal family, they were a people apart who granted passage through their lands only to those who paid their price. Every Great King since Cyrus had given gold to the Uxian brigands to allow his men to travel the narrow gorges that were the only practical road between Susa and Persepolis. It was a bitter humiliation for the king of Persia to pay tribute to bandits, but given the inaccessible nature of the mountains no army had ever been able to subdue them or drive them out.

Messengers from the Uxians came to Alexander at his camp in the foothills and greeted the king with respect. They welcomed him to their land and—lacking loyalty to any but their own—had no objection to his passing through the mountains to attack Persepolis. But there was the small matter of the tribute payment. They would let his army cross in peace as long as he paid the same toll as the Great King.

Alexander must have been a study in self-control at this moment, for he smiled and bid them to wait for him in the mountain pass, where they would receive his payment.

Darius and his predecessors may have given in to these highland bandits, but Alexander was not about to start his march into Persia by submitting to blackmail. He intended to teach the Uxians a lesson they would never forget. The king took several thousand of his best troops and led them through a narrow backcountry trail into the mountains accompanied by guides from Susa. There he found a number of Uxian villages nestled in the high valleys. One by one, he fell on them in the night and killed everyone he could find, many of them still in their beds. He took what little goods they had, mostly fine horses and sheep, but his real object was terror.

As he moved toward the pass where the Uxian warriors were guarding the main road, he sent his trusted lieutenant Craterus with a brigade of crack mountain troops into the peaks above them, knowing this is where the natives would retreat when he struck. The Uxians trusted the inaccessible terrain of their mountain home to protect them from enemies, but they had never dealt with men from the highlands of Macedonia and Thrace. These soldiers had grown up in mountains as rough as those they found themselves in now and felt perfectly at home scrabbling over rocks and ledges where wild goats were at home.

Alexander suddenly swept up from below toward the Uxians guarding the pass, so surprising them with his speed that they fled into the surrounding hills—only to find Craterus and his men waiting for them there. Many were killed outright by sword and spear, while others were thrown off the rocks to their deaths. A few escaped to spread the news of the unstoppable new king and his ferocious army. Alexander was right behind them with his men, destroying village after village as they made their way through the highlands. Their king Madates was so distraught that he sent messengers by a secret path to Susa to plead with the mother of Darius, his own mother-in-law's sister, to intervene with Alexander and save his people. Sisyngambris was reluctant to get involved in military affairs, but for the sake of family she consented and sent a letter to Alexander begging him to spare the Uxians from destruction. The king was probably still feeling guilty about the misunderstanding with Sisyngambris over weaving cloth, so he gave in to her plea and pardoned Madates and all those Uxians who would surrender. He left their remaining villages intact with the provision that they would now pay to him as tribute one hundred horses each year along with five times that many transport animals and thirty thousand sheep. In mere days, Alexander and his men had done what the Persian Empire was unable to accomplish in two hundred years.

The Macedonians continued their march eastward ever deeper into the frozen mountains separating them from Persepolis. The direct route into Persia lay through a high pass called the Persian Gates, a narrow gap surrounded by impassable cliffs on all sides. The only other option was a long detour to the south, but this would take many extra days of travel. Alexander knew from scouts that the local Persian satrap, Ariobarzanes, was waiting for him with a considerable force guarding the Gates, but he didn't believe their numbers would be significant. Still, they had the advantage of terrain and would be difficult to dislodge. Ariobarzanes was an experienced war leader who had fought against Alexander at Gaugamela and was still loyal to Darius—but more to the point, he was still loyal to Persia. He was determined to prevent the invaders from moving into his homeland.

Alexander considered the situation and once again made an unexpected move. He decided to split his forces, sending most of the army the long way around with Parmenion to approach Persepolis from the south. It may be true that the king was looking for an excuse to once again operate independently from the old general, but his main concern was reaching Persepolis before the Persians were able to remove the treasury. The only way he could do this was to push rapidly with a minimal force through the heavily protected Persian Gates. Ariobarzanes clearly expected him to turn his whole army south when he heard the pass was guarded, thereby buying time for the defense or at least the evacuation of the capital. Knowing this, Alexander did just the opposite and gave up the advantage of his superior numbers for a risky attack. It was not a plan any reasonable general would have attempted, but, once again, Alexander was not a reasonable general.

With only a few thousand Macedonian and Thracian mountain troops, Alexander set off at a breakneck pace up the valley leading to the Persian Gates. The approach was through a steep defile with cliffs rising on both sides. The king could see in the distance that Ariobarzanes had built a wall across the gap leading over the pass. There were a great many Persian soldiers manning the wall, but Alexander believed his men could overcome them and moved into formation into the narrowest part of the valley just before the wall.

Suddenly, there was a thunderous crash from the ridges above as boulders came crashing down onto his tightly packed men. Missiles launched from catapults in the hills above, javelins thrown by Persian soldiers, and arrows from thousands of archers fell like rain on the Macedonians as they tried to clamber up the snow-covered cliffs to get at the defenders. But the cliffs were so precipitous they kept sliding back on top of their own companions, all while hundreds of their fellow soldiers were dying around them. Alexander had led his men into a perfect trap. Ariobarzanes allegedly had forty thousand men guarding the pass, but even if there were a quarter of this number, no enemy—not even Alexander—could hope to take the Persian Gates in a direct assault. The king ordered his soldiers to raise their shields above their heads in a protective tortoise formation, but men still kept falling under the massive stones from above. Alexander at last had no choice but to order a retreat, leaving the bodies of many of his best soldiers lying broken in the narrow gorge before the wall.

Alexander was not accustomed to defeat and the shame bore heavily on him. The reckless overconfidence that had served him so well in the past had cost the lives of hundreds of his bravest men. He considered calling on Aristander the prophet to ask the gods if he had somehow offended them, but decided that it was more important at the moment to inspire confidence in his discouraged men. To lose a battle was hard enough for them, but to be forced to abandon the broken corpses of their friends was unthinkable. The dearest duty for any soldier was to bury a fallen comrade so that he might journey on to the underworld. Alexander knew that Ariobarzanes would probably permit him to retrieve the dead under a flag of truce, but the humiliation would be too much to bear. He decided to leave the bodies behind and follow Parmenion around the long southern route to Persepolis—or somehow find a way to outflank the Persians holding the Gates.

The Macedonians had managed to capture a few prisoners during the assault and Alexander ordered them brought before him. Under threat of the most horrific tortures imaginable, he asked them if there was any way around the Persian Gates. All shook their heads, but there was one man among them who spoke Greek. He was a native of Lycia in southern Asia Minor who years before had been captured and exiled to this distant corner of Persia. He labored in the local mountains as a shepherd and had been drafted by Ariobarzanes to help defend the pass. He told Alexander that there was a rocky trail that led behind the Gates, but it was a narrow backcountry track suitable only for summer travel by a few sheep, not by an army of thousands. Alexander looked him in the eye with what must have been a terrifying intensity and asked him again if there was any way his soldiers could make it through this secret path. The Lycian repeated that it was simply impossible.

It was now that Alexander remembered a prophesy he had heard when he was still a boy. At some point when he was dreaming of war against the Great King, he had sent to Delphi to ask if he would ever conquer Persia. The messengers returned from the oracle with word that he would be led into Persia by a wolf. He had forgotten this curious response for years, but with this man from Lycia before him it began to make sense. The Greek word for "wolf" was *lykos*, practically the same as Lykios, a Lycian. In Alexander's mind this could not be a coincidence. He told the prisoner that his entire army would be following him over the sheep trail that very night. The man begged Alexander to be reasonable. Men in full battle armor would never make it through the path and would certainly blame him for their failure. The king replied that whatever a shepherd could do for his flock, the army of Alexander could accomplish for the sake of eternal glory.

The king left Craterus behind with most of the infantry and all of the cavalry. He was under orders to light as many fires as if the whole army were still camped before the pass, then wait for a trumpet signal to charge the wall. Alexander then ordered the rest of his men to load provisions for three days into their packs and prepare for the toughest climb of their lives. With a whispered prayer to the gods, the king and thousands of his soldiers set off in the night single file up the trail.

The path was covered in snow so deep that the men sunk repeatedly up to their chests as if they had fallen in holes. Their friends who tried to pull them out of the drifts fell in themselves. Hidden ravines and deep gorges were everywhere, while thick pines blotted out the stars on all sides. The wind was bitterly cold and whipped the frozen branches against the faces of the miserable soldiers. But Alexander had ordered his men to move over the mountain in absolute silence, so there were none of the usual complaints of cold and weary soldiers on the march. Hour after hour they struggled through impossible conditions over unknown trails in complete darkness, trusting their lives to a single Lycian shepherd and their king, who believed in a childhood prophesy.

At last, as the new day was beginning, they reached the summit of the trail well above the Persian Gates. Here Alexander ordered his exhausted men to rest and eat while he conferred with his officers. His plan was to split his forces yet again, sending a sizable detachment under Ptolemy directly down the mountainside to strike at the side of the wall at the right moment. With the rest of the men, Alexander continued down the trail to the back of the pass, a passage that was scarcely less difficult than the climb to the summit. When he reached the main road behind the Gates, he surprised a Persian guard unit stationed there, killing them all except for a few who fled down the mountain.

Night had fallen again as Alexander put his men into formation and advanced against the Persians. He ordered a trumpet blast that carried to Craterus at the far side of the Gates as a signal to begin the

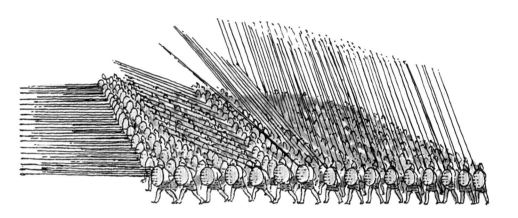

The sarissa spear formation used by Philip and Alexander. The exceptionally long spears prevented attackers from reaching the Macedonian troops.

Mount Olympus, home of the Greek gods, as viewed from Dion in northern Greece. In the fields of Dion, Alexander tamed his horse Bucephalas.

The Acropolis of Athens, which Alexander visited when he was eighteen years old. Athena's great temple, the Parthenon, stands at the center.

The tomb of Philip at Vergina in northern Greece. Archaeological excavations have revealed magnificent jewelry and weapons deposited here.

The ruins of Troy, Alexander's first stop in Asia, in modern Turkey.

The dedicatory inscription to Athena from the temple at Priene near the Turkish coast of the Aegean dating to around 330 B.C. It is one of the few surviving documents from Alexander's lifetime that mention him by name. (The top line reads: "King Alexander.")

The harbor and town of Halicarnassus, modern Bodrum in southwest Turkey. Alexander's defeat of this key city opened Asia Minor to his army.

The Phoenician town of Tyre on the coast of modern Lebanon, which Alexander took after a brutal siege in 332 B.C. The causeway built by Alexander's army became the isthmus still connecting the city to the mainland.

The Alexander mosaic from Pompeii. Bareheaded Alexander on the left raises his spear to strike down King Darius on his chariot with outstretched hand at the battle of Gaugamela in northern Iraq.

The pyramids of Giza. When Alexander visited Egypt in 332 B.C., these massive monuments were almost as old to him as he is to us.

The palace of Darius at Persepolis in modern Iran, capital of the Persian Empire, taken and burned by Alexander in 330 B.C.

The tomb of Cyrus the Great at Pasargadae near Persepolis. Alexander admired this founder of the Persian Empire and ordered the monument restored.

The towering Hindu Kush mountains of Afghanistan and Pakistan. Alexander crossed this range with his entire army in winter.

Coin celebrating the victory of Alexander over the Indian king Porus on the Hydaspes River in 326 B.C. Alexander is riding Bucephalas to attack Porus as he retreats on his elephant.

Coin *c.* 300 B.C. minted by Lysimachus, one of the generals who divided the empire, showing Alexander with horns of the god Zeus-Ammon. Only twenty years after his death, Alexander was already becoming a god.

attack from his end. At the same time, Ptolemy and his men hit the
Persians from the side after their own hike down the steep mountain. It was now Ariobarzanes who was caught in a trap. Some of his
men tried to make a stand while others tried to flee, but Alexander's
surprise was so complete that almost all were slaughtered. Only the
satrap himself and a handful of his men managed to escape by horse
into the hills. It was one of the most horrendous battles imaginable,
fought in darkness in a narrow, snow-covered pass. Thousands of Persians died in defense of their native land, hacked down by bone-tired
but determined Macedonian and Thracian warriors who had made
an impossible trek over the mountains in the depths of winter. The
frozen corpses of the men who had died in the earlier battle before
the wall were at last given funeral rites. The Lycian shepherd who had
led them was rewarded lavishly by Alexander and warmly praised by
the men whose lives he had held in his hands. The Persian Gates had
fallen and the road to Persepolis now lay open before them.

It was now a race to reach the capital before the Persians could set up
an effective defense or evacuate the treasury to the north. Alexander
had already sent Philotas ahead to bridge the Araxes River on the
way to the city. He had also just received a letter from Tiridates, the
royal treasurer at Persepolis, who was probably a eunuch, informing
the king that he would hand over the town and treasury to Alexander
if he could arrive quickly. But it was essential that the Macedonians
beat Ariobarzanes and his men to the city or they would surely fight
for control of the capital. Tiridates was obviously hoping for the same
sort of preferred treatment that important officials who had willingly
given over their cities had received from the king in the past.

The Macedonians rushed at full speed down from the Zagros
Mountains toward Persepolis, but when they were almost at the city
they saw something that caused Alexander to pause in spite of his
haste. Before him on the road was a procession of eight hundred elderly men and women bearing branches of supplication. They were a
hideous and pitiable sight as each one of them had been mutilated.
Some lacked hands, others feet, some were without ears or noses. To

add to the shock, they all cried out to the king in Greek. Their spokesman explained that they had been carried away to this place many years before by an earlier Persian king as punishment for deeds in their homeland. They formed a colony of Greek exiles on the doorstep of the Persian capital to serve as a visible reminder for those passing by of the price of disloyalty to the Great King. Many of the refugees were craftsmen, so that their Persian masters had spared those limbs necessary for their particular work, but all were disfigured.

Alexander was so moved by the story of these aged and broken souls that tears ran down his face. He promised that he would do everything he could to help them return home to Greece. The exiles thanked him and asked if instead they might stay where they were. In Greece, they explained, they would be scattered into small groups and treated as objects of scorn. But here in Persia, they were a community with a common bond of misfortune who all looked out for one another. All they asked from Alexander was help in taking care of themselves. The king gladly agreed and ordered all be given enough money to see them comfortably through the rest of their lives, along with clothing, oxen, sheep, and bushels of wheat. He exempted them from taxes and gave strict orders to the officials ruling the region to treat them with the greatest respect.

Persepolis lay in a broad plain ringed by distant mountains at the heart of the Persian homeland. There were other capitals—Susa, Babylon, Ecbatana—but these were conquered cities that had been taken over during wars of expansion. Persepolis, on the other hand, was the soul of the empire. Here was the place the Great King and his nobles came to remember what they had accomplished over two centuries. In the days of the young Cyrus the Great, the Persians were a minor subject people, a band of highland warriors who had swept in from the lands to the north to live on the edge of civilization. They were fierce fighters and men of honor, but they were little more than country cousins to the Medes, who ruled them, and nothing but barbarians to the ancient cultures of the Fertile Crescent. They had no written language and no skill in building great monuments. But then in the course of a single lifetime they had conquered the Medes and spread into Asia Minor, Mesopotamia, Egypt, and central Asia. No empire in history had accomplished such a wondrous achievement. At Persepolis, where once the Persian clans had gathered in tents, they built a magnificent city using the talents of the civilized peoples they ruled. Here they stored the tribute and treasure collected from distant provinces to fund their armies and administer their empire. The first Great King Darius was the earliest architect of Persepolis, declaring on a wall inscription at the site:

> I AM DARIUS, THE GREAT KING, KING OF KINGS,
> KING OF NATIONS, KING ON THIS WIDE EARTH,
> SON OF HYSTASPES, THE ACHAEMENID.
> KING DARIUS PROCLAIMS: ON THIS PLATFORM WHERE
> THIS FORTRESS HAS BEEN BUILT, NO FORTRESS HAS
> BEEN BUILT BEFORE. BY THE FAVOR OF AHURAMAZDA,
> I BUILT THIS FORTRESS AS AHURAMAZDA AND ALL THE
> GODS WITH HIM WILLED IT. I BUILT IT, COMPLETED IT,
> MADE IT BEAUTIFUL AND SECURE,
> EXACTLY AS I DETERMINED.

Alexander and the army of Macedonia approached this great city at the end of January, almost four years after they had left Europe and crossed into Asia. By rapid marches over impossible terrain, tenacity in battle, and sheer determination, they had beaten Ariobarzanes at the Persian Gates and reached the walls of Persepolis unopposed. The turncoat treasurer Tiridates kept his word and opened the gates to the king. But unlike at Babylon, there were no welcoming crowds lining the streets. The citizens of the city hid in their homes praying to their gods, fearing for good reason the worst at the hands of this young king from the edge of the world.

The city that Alexander entered was not like Babylon in its ancient, vibrant grandeur or even like Susa with its magnificent palace complex and rich heritage of Elamite culture. Persepolis was a new city, monumental in the truest sense, a stately sermon in stone proclaiming the awesome power of the Persian Empire. The large palace complex was located on a rock terrace rising above the plain and was approached by a broad double stairway guarded by statues of giant bulls to ward off evil, a borrowing from earlier Mesopotamian iconography. Climbing onto the terrace, the visitor would see the audience hall on a platform with magnificent relief carvings of Persian soldiers and subject nations approaching the royal throne. Petitioners to the Great King passed beautifully detailed carvings of nobles in their chariots and imperial guards on one side. On the other side were Arabs leading camels and Indians bearing gifts, along with suppliant Parthians, Bactrians, Egyptians, Scythians, Greeks, Syrians, Babylonians, Lydians, Elamites, Medes, and others. Everyone who was granted the honor of an audience with the Great King would have to climb past these testimonials of Persian might.

Near the audience hall was another immense gathering space with one hundred columns, as well as the large and well-guarded treasury constructed of deceptively plain mud bricks. The palaces built by the first Darius and his son Xerxes were on the southern side of the terrace. That of Darius was Egyptian-inspired, small and compact, lined with walls polished to such a finish that it was known as the Hall of Mirrors. The palace of Xerxes occupied the highest part of the complex and was much grander than the structure of his father. Dozens of small chambers filled the back of the building, probably containing the harem of the king. Here the many wives and concubines of the Great King lived in splendid isolation. These ladies of the court were Persian nobility or the daughters of subject princes pledged as symbols of fealty to the empire. As a king had to be absolutely sure of the paternity of his sons, the women were guarded night and day by eunuchs.

The palace complex of Persepolis was an administrative and diplomatic center, a residence of the Great King and his entourage, a treasure house, and a ceremonial site of great importance. It was probably here that the Persian New Year ceremony was celebrated annually on the spring equinox, when gifts were given and the king confirmed as the earthly representative of the great god Ahuramazda. The majority of the population lived outside the grounds of the palace in the surrounding city. These were government officials, businessmen, and merchants who owned luxurious homes furnished with beautiful works of art. The people of Persepolis were the elite of the Persian world and had profited greatly from the tribute pouring into the capital for two hundred years.

Alexander had been generous with his army during the campaign, ensuring they were well paid when possible and given an ample share of booty along the way. But now as the men entered Persepolis, they were restless. They saw all around them riches beyond measure and knew that the private homes they passed held incredible wealth. They were, however, a disciplined lot and restrained themselves so as not to anger Alexander. Nevertheless, the king knew that even the self-control of his soldiers had its limits. Armies in the ancient world firmly believed it was their natural right to pillage any city they conquered. After all, they put their lives on the line fighting for king and country. Glory was all well and good for princes and nobles, but they longed for tangible treasure to spend while they were still young enough to enjoy it and gold to buy that farm they had always had their eye on back home. As for captive women, in the minds of the soldiers they were nothing more than the spoils of war and were to be treated as such.

Alexander had made the situation at Persepolis even more volatile by his depiction of the capital city as the ultimate goal of their campaign. The king roused his men to continue the march through deserts and mountains to Persepolis to seek revenge, calling it the most hated city in Asia. By the time the army actually reached the Persian capital, they were so embittered toward the town as the symbol of all that was evil in the world that they had no eye for the beauty of palaces or any interest in building good relations with the natives for the sake of Alexander's new empire. They wanted to seize everything of value for themselves and watch the rest burn.

After Alexander had taken possession of the royal terrace overlooking the town, he felt he could no longer constrain his men. Rather than have a riot on his hands, he gave his army free rein to sack the great city of Persepolis, sparing only the palace complex for himself.

His army had plundered cities before from Thebes to Gaza, but this was the first time he allowed a town that had peacefully surrendered to be ravaged. It was a radical change in his policy toward conquered peoples and not at all conducive to building trust among his subjects. It was also a dangerous precedent to allow such license to an army, but the king believed the alternative was more perilous.

All that day and throughout the night the soldiers ran wild through the streets of Persepolis in an orgy of ferocious greed rarely equaled in history. The Macedonians burst into every private house and killed the men inside, then took turns raping the women and girls. When they wearied of this, they bound their captives to sell into slavery. At the same time, they stripped the homes of anything remotely valuable, even fighting among themselves for the best objects. Some hacked the limbs from golden statues when they found they could not carry away the heavy objects whole. Not a few of the men were killed by their comrades quarrelling over fine purple cloth or silver jewelry. Some even had their hands cut off by men they had long fought beside as they tried to grab a bit more treasure for themselves. A few of the Persian households tried to fight back, but it was no use. The bravest among the citizens saw what was coming and set their own houses on fire with themselves and their families inside before the Macedonians could break down the doors. Others put on their finest clothing and threw their wives and children from the roofs to their deaths in the streets below, then followed themselves. Finally, after a full day and night of horror for the people of the capital, Alexander ordered his men to cease from looting the city and stop the killing. But by then, there was little left to steal and few lives left to spare. Persepolis was a smoking ruin filled with the dead, an indescribable scene of horror as naked widows and orphans were led away in the winter cold to the slave markets. Alexander at last had his revenge against the Great King's empire, but the Persians would never forget what he had done.

While his men were still ravaging the city, Alexander walked through the palace taking an inventory of his new possessions. The first thing he noticed was a statue of Xerxes that had been carelessly overturned by some of his men. This was the Persian king who had invaded Greece early in the previous century, slaughtered the Spartans at Thermopylae, and burned Athens to the ground. And yet, Alexander knew that Xerxes had many admirable qualities, not least of which was a gift for building the magnificent palace around him. He stopped in front of the toppled statue and spoke to it as if it were alive, asking if he should set it up on its pedestal again even though he had done such harm to Greece. He pondered the problem for a long time in silence as his friends stood near, then walked away.

The king next entered the throne room and approached the seat of the Great King, a grandiose piece of furniture on a raised platform covered by a golden canopy. The pages had apparently already placed a footstool of appropriate height before the throne in anticipation of Alexander's entrance, for the ancient sources don't mention his feet dangling above the floor as they did in Susa. It was a moving moment for Alexander and all those present. Here at last the king fulfilled his dream of sitting on the throne of the Great King at Persepolis. For four years he had fought his way across the Persian Empire defeating armies and sacking cities to earn this right. Demaratus of Corinth, his old family friend, burst into tears at the sight. He declared that he pitied those Greeks who had died before they could see Alexander seated on the throne of Darius.

From the palace Alexander moved to the treasury, where he gazed in awe at the tribute collected by the Great Kings of Persia for two centuries. The royal treasury at Susa had held an unbelievable store of gold and silver, but the abundance of wealth contained in this simple mud-brick building at Persepolis made the coffers at Susa look small by comparison. There was row after row of boxes filled with gold coins collected from all the nations of the empire. Alexander thought it best to remove the money from Persepolis and so ordered it transported to the treasury at Susa. But the load was so immense that the Macedonian quartermasters had to send for thousands of mules and camels from Mesopotamia to bear the treasure.

Alexander also visited the royal center at Pasargadae just a few

miles to the east of Persepolis. This was the place where Cyrus won
his final victory over the Medes, prompting the first Great King of
Persia to build a palace there. This was also the holy site where each
new Persian king was crowned. Each man who would lead the empire
entered the sanctuary there and laid aside his own cloak, taking up
instead the garment that Cyrus had once worn. The coronation rituals
seemed strange to outsiders, but the new king first ate a fig cake, then
chewed on turpentine wood, and finally drank a cup of sour milk. It is
likely that each king began his reign in this way to remember that in
spite of golden palaces and the comforts of civilization, most important, he was the leader of a highland tribe of warriors nourished on
simple and sometimes bitter fare.

Alexander appropriated the treasury at Pasargadae to add to the
caravan heading for Susa, but he was even more interested in visiting
the tomb of Cyrus. It was a small, rectangular stone structure at the
top of a platform of stairs. A garden surrounded the tomb tended by
a permanent staff of priests. The door to the tomb was narrow and
small, so that even a short man like Alexander had difficulty squeez-
ing through the single opening. Inside was a golden sarcophagus
containing the body of Cyrus. Beside it was a couch covered with a
Babylonian tapestry and surrounded by purple carpets over the cold
stone floor. Next to the couch were laid out Median trousers and royal
robes, along with a table holding swords and jewelry. The hereditary
family of priests who tended the tomb received daily a sheep and
grain for their own needs, along with a horse each month to offer
as a sacrifice to the spirit of Cyrus. On the outside of the door was
an inscription in Persian cuneiform that the priest interpreted for
Alexander:

MORTAL MAN, I AM CYRUS, SON OF CAMBYSES,
FOUNDER OF THE PERSIAN EMPIRE AND KING OF ASIA.
DO NOT BEGRUDGE ME THIS SMALL MONUMENT.

Alexander was deeply moved by his visit to the tomb of Cyrus
and commanded that the wishes of the first Great King be forever

honored. The priests were to continue in perpetuity the royal ceremonies due to Cyrus and the tomb was to remain inviolate.

It may have been the stench of the burned city or shame at having allowed his soldiers to rampage through Persepolis that soon moved Alexander to leave the city for a trip to the Persian countryside. He knew Darius and the remnants of the Persian army were in Media waiting to see what he would do next, but he was in no hurry to chase them across Asia just yet. After four years of campaigning, he felt his men needed a rest. The winter snows still covered the mountains to the north and the king knew there would be many difficult marches ahead, even if many of the soldiers thought the campaign was over and they were soon returning home. It seemed best to let his army regain their strength in Persepolis and perhaps their appetite for battle before beginning the campaign once again in the spring.

But the restless nature of Alexander did not abide remaining long in any one place. There were reports of primitive tribes in the hills that refused to acknowledge his sovereignty, but this was little more than an excuse to explore more of Persia on his own. Leaving his army behind, he took with him his closest companions and a small force of only a thousand cavalry and light-armed infantry into the rugged mountains. The weather was horrible and the paths were covered with snow and ice. As they climbed into the highlands, the men began to feel as if they had reached the end of the world. There were no farms or houses, no people or animals, only endless sky and fading light. There was something strange and disturbing about these mountains even for men who had been raised in the highlands of Macedonia. At last a group of soldiers dared to approach Alexander and begged him to turn back.

Instead of berating his frightened men, the king jumped down from his horse and pressed ahead up the trail by himself over snow and slippery patches of ice. He took a pick and broke up the ice covering the path as he made his way forward. All his men watched and were filled with shame. First his friends joined him in blazing the trail, then his officers, and finally the rest of the soldiers. They slowly made their way through the forest and over the mountains until at last they saw traces of human civilization once again. The bands of herdsmen who lived in these inaccessible hills did not expect to see outsiders in the middle of winter and certainly were unprepared for a small army to descend upon their valley. Many of the tribesmen killed their own people to spare them from the invaders, and fled themselves higher into the mountains.

The Macedonians then moved even deeper into the highlands to the isolated land of a people known as the Mardi, a tribe left over from another age. They lived in caves in the mountains and fed their families on sheep and wild animals. Their women were as tough as the men, wearing tunics that barely covered their thighs and binding their bushy hair with slings. When the need arose, the women would pull off the slings and fight alongside the men with devastating effect. To Alexander, it was as if the trek from Persepolis had become a grand hunting expedition with humans as prey instead of beasts. There were few spoils aside from a handful of scrawny sheep, but nonetheless the hapless Mardi were tracked down and killed for the amusement of the king and his men. On their return to the city after thirty days in the wild, Alexander celebrated the excursion by giving each of those who had accompanied him gifts to remember their month traversing the mountains of Persia.

It was a fine Greek tradition to blame women for the foolish deeds of men. Helen was the face that launched a thousand ships full of warriors to fight and die before the walls of Troy. Pandora allowed evil into the world when she opened her forbidden jar (box is a mistranslation). Likewise at Persepolis that spring, it was an Athenian prostitute who would enter history as the woman who led Alexander to destroy the palace of the Great King.

As the story is told by Plutarch and other ancient authors, there was a drunken party one night not long after Alexander returned from his expedition into the mountains. Wine flowed freely as always at Macedonian banquets, so that soon all the king's friends and guests were roaring drunk. Alexander's old friend Ptolemy was there along with his mistress, Thaïs, whom he would later marry and father three children with. She was not a common harlot and camp follower but a woman known to the Athenians as a *hetaira*—a beautiful, educated, and charming female who shared the bed of her sponsor but also served as his confidante and advisor. Such women did well in Greek society and often ended up as lifetime partners of their lovers. Thaïs, as an Athenian, knew the history of the Persian conflict better than most of the Macedonian soldiers around her and took this moment of revelry to make an impassioned speech to Alexander and his friends. It was a fine reward, she proclaimed, after wandering over Asia, to dine in luxury in the splendid palace of Xerxes. But it would be a so much sweeter pleasure to set fire to the house of the man who had burned down her own city. Thaïs was a moving speaker, so that applause and cheers erupted from the whole crowd and echoed through the hall. Everyone began to urge the king to lead the way in starting a blaze. Alexander eagerly agreed and grabbed the nearest torch. He himself first set afire the cedar columns and rafters of the building, then all the others ran through the halls with firebrands. Soon the whole complex was a raging inferno that lit up the plain of Persepolis. But even as the king watched the great palace of Xerxes burn, he began to regret his hasty action. He tried to put the fire out, but it was much too late. By morning, there was nothing left but scorched pillars and ashes.

This is one tradition handed down through ancient documents, but there is a darker and more sinister tale found in the historian Arrian, often our best source for the life of Alexander. What makes Arrian so believable in this instance is that he normally has a quite positive view of the Macedonian king, but he passes over the events of this night as rapidly as possible with outright condemnation of Alexander's actions. He states that the king planned all along to burn the palace and that even Parmenion tried to discourage him from such a drastic deed. The old general argued that it was foolish to destroy his own property and that the people of Asia would see him as just a rampaging conqueror with no real interest in building an empire. But in Arrian's version, Alexander counters that he wants revenge for all the evils the Persians had done to the Greek world.

Discovering the truth about what happened that night is next to impossible when the ancient sources disagree. What can be said with certainty is that the palace burned to the ground before Alexander left the city. Archaeologists found a thick layer of ash throughout the remains, but no precious gold or treasures, indicating the valuables had been deliberately removed beforehand—again suggesting premeditation. If Arrian is right and Alexander burned down the palace on purpose, was revenge a sufficient reason? Perhaps, if it were an act of propaganda designed to bolster his support in Greece, especially Athens. But the king had shown surprisingly little interest in what the Greeks thought of his war since he left the Aegean coast. It may be instead that the primary audience was the Persians in an effort to show them that the old days were finished and that Alexander was now Great King. In this scenario, the burning was meant to discourage further resistance before he resumed his campaign against Darius. And yet, after slaughtering the population of Persepolis, did the Persians really harbor any doubts that opposing Alexander was dangerous and ultimately futile? In the end, we simply cannot know whether or not the king deliberately burned down the palace of Xerxes. But we can be sure that most of the ancient historians who wrote of the episode were deeply uncomfortable with Alexander's actions and preferred to blame the events of that night on too much wine and the silken tongue of a woman.

The game now was to capture the king. Darius had spent the winter at the Median capital of Ecbatana, almost four hundred miles north of Persepolis, waiting to see what Alexander would do next. The Persian ruler had gathered an impressive army of perhaps ten thousand soldiers, including his loyal Greek mercenaries. He knew he did not have enough men to face the Macedonians in open battle, but he planned to withdraw east across the mountains into Bactria, burning the fields as he went. Since the area had few reliable crops to begin with, this devastation would make it difficult for Alexander to feed his army while pursuing him. Once in Bactria, he would lead a rearguard effort to retake the empire. Given the sheer size and rugged terrain of the lands from the Caspian Sea to the Indus River, it was a reasonable plan. Darius could hold off the Macedonians for years in the mountains and valleys of the Hindu Kush, all the while wearing down Alexander and diverting his attention and resources from potential problems elsewhere in his new realm.

Alexander understood the strategy of Darius quite well and appreciated the threat it posed to his rule. He also knew that in a very real sense he could not be Great King in the eyes of Asia until Darius had abdicated or was dead. It was therefore essential that he overtake Darius before he could escape into Bactria. As he explained to his officers and men, the war against Persia could not be finished until the *shah*, as the Persians called their king, was *mat*, or finished. The endgame had to be *shah mat*, a Persian phrase that would evolve in time into *checkmate*.

As soon as most of the snow had melted between Persepolis and Ecbatana, Alexander readied his army for a lightning march up the eastern side of the Zagros Mountains. He once again appointed a Persian as local satrap, this time a noble named Phrasaortes, but also left behind a strong Macedonian garrison at Persepolis under the command of a trusted officer. Alexander then set out with his men across the edge of the great desert of the central Persian highlands toward Ecbatana. He pushed his men over twenty miles a day past parched hills and scattered oases in an attempt to reach the doorstep of Darius before the Persian king could flee. After almost two weeks at this blistering pace, Alexander heard that Darius had decided to make a stand at Ecbatana as the Persian had been joined by reinforcements from Scythia and tribesmen from near the Caspian Sea. This was just what Alexander was hoping for. He separated the supply train to follow at a slower pace while he and the army moved even faster toward the north. But just a few days later he received an updated report that the Persian reinforcements had not in fact arrived, prompting Darius to change his plan from fight to flight. The Persian leader had sent ahead his harem and supply wagons to a pass called the Caspian Gates in the mountains east of Rhagae (Tehran) leading to Bactria. Three days out of Ecbatana, a Persian noble named Bisthanes arrived at the camp of Alexander. This man was the only son of the previous Great King, Artaxerxes III, who had escaped the bloody purge engineered by the scheming eunuch Bagoas that had led to the ascension of Darius. He had no love for the Persian king and had decided, along with many others, to take his chances with Alexander. Bisthanes reported that Darius had now fled the Median capital and was on his way to the Caspian Gates. He also had in his wagons enough gold to pay his men and hire local warriors for years to come.

Alexander was now becoming seriously worried. If Darius made it over the mountains with his soldiers and treasure he could carry on the war indefinitely. It was therefore essential that Alexander move even faster with a rapid force. But in spite of the hurry and indeed using it as an excuse, he seized the moment to make a radical change in his command staff. First he announced that he was sending the cavalry units from Thessaly back home to Greece. These men had served bravely as the contribution of their nation to the war effort against Persia. They would all depart in honor with a large bonus and would be escorted back to the Mediterranean to be carried by ship to the Aegean. Once home they could rejoin their families and live out their lives in peace and prosperity. On the other hand, if any of them wished to sign on to his army as paid volunteers rather than subject soldiers, he would welcome them with an even larger bonus. Most of the Thessalians jumped at the chance to remain and were transferred to a new commanding officer.

It is no mere coincidence that the reassigned Thessalian cavalry were the backbone of Parmenion's support in the army. They had fought with him for years and were stubbornly loyal to the old general. In removing them from Parmenion's command, Alexander was cutting off his father's oldest friend from his power base among the soldiers. The king then called Parmenion to his tent and informed him that he was sending him to Ecbatana to guard the treasury and keep an eye on Harpalus, who would now be running Alexander's finances from the Median capital. It was an important position, Alexander assured Parmenion, and besides, at over seventy years of age, the heroic general deserved a rest from chasing fugitive Persians across the mountains. In time, he would certainly call on the general to join him in the east.

Parmenion realized exactly what Alexander was doing. The king had slowly whittled away his supporters and family members from positions of power during the campaign, leaving one here as satrap and another there as garrison chief. Now the only significant players left from his faction were himself and his two sons. Finally, in one quick stroke with no time to debate the issue, the king had severed Parmenion from his soldiers and cashiered the old man to guard duty away from the army. Parmenion had served his purpose and was to be set aside like an aged horse put out to pasture. There was no point in arguing as Alexander was leaving immediately to pursue Darius. The son of Philip had yearned for years to be his own man and silence forever the voice of his father whispering in his ear through the lips of Parmenion. In the last few years the king had gained confidence in his own innate leadership skills and grown in experience leading an army. Now, he hoped, the great battles were over and much of the empire conquered; Alexander didn't need Parmenion anymore.

Alexander set out from Ecbatana after Darius with a strong but fast-moving force of cavalry and infantry. He was so eager to overtake the Persians that many of his men fell behind as he rushed across the arid highlands on the way to the Caspian Gates. The horses were pushed so hard that they began to die. They reached Rhagae in only eleven days and at last saw the towering Elburz Mountains rising before them. But there was no time to stop as they raced eastward, only to find that Darius had passed through the Caspian Gates several days ahead of them. Alexander camped at the pass that night, sending a battalion forward to prepare supply caches as he had heard the lands beyond were even more desolate.

While he was still in camp, a Babylonian named Bagisthanes came to him along with Antibelus, one of the sons of Mazaeus, his own satrap at Babylon. They had just left Darius and brought valuable information to Alexander. Bessus, the satrap of Bactria and kinsmen of Darius, had arrested the Persian king with the support of another eastern satrap named Barsaentes and were fleeing with him, un-harmed at present, as a captive in a wagon. Alexander had been fear-ing something like this might happen. A coup in the Persian ranks only complicated his goal of capturing the king and ending the war. If Bessus killed Darius and took the throne, that would drag out the fight, especially as the satrap was a skilled warrior and general who had the loyalty of the Bactrians and other eastern provinces.

Alexander's response was to strip down his troops even more and pursue Bessus with a smaller, faster force of horsemen and picked infantry. He didn't even wait for the supply caches to be readied, but set off from the Caspian Gates with orders that the remainder of his soldiers were to follow as fast as they could. He traveled all night and stopped only at noon when his men and horses were exhausted. He had reached the camp where Darius had been arrested. Then he discovered from Persians remaining behind that Bessus had assumed the title of Great King with the support of the Bactrian cavalry. Some Persian troops remained loyal to Darius and refused to follow Bessus, including the Greek mercenaries who had set off into the mountains to try to make their way home. The plan of Bessus was that if the Macedonians ceased their pursuit, to strike a deal with Alexander and surrender Darius to him in exchange for favorable terms. But if the Macedonians continued to pursue them, they would retreat into the mountains and stage a guerrilla campaign against Alexander, forming a Persian government in exile in the highlands of Bactria.

The Macedonians were some of the toughest soldiers in the world, but by this point in the chase they were spent. Still, Alexander pushed them on through the night and into the next day. He reached the camp where the Persians had stayed just the previous day, but they were still well ahead of him. He asked the local inhabitants if there was any shortcut through the desert by which he could overtake Bessus. There was, but it was a waterless route traveled only rarely by camel caravans. Alexander then dismounted five hundred weary cav-alry and put his most fit infantry on their horses, setting off into the night at full speed. With this small force he covered almost fifty miles in the darkness and at last saw the Persians in the distance at dawn.

Most of the Persians fled in panic when they saw the Macedonians closing in, though they must have far outnumbered Alexander's men. A few attempted to delay the approaching enemy by turning back and fighting, but they were swept aside. For a short time, Bessus continued to haul Darius in the wagon behind him, but he soon realized that he would never be able to stay ahead of his pursuers. With Alexander practically on top of him, the satrap rushed to the wagon and stabbed Darius with a spear, leaving him for dead. He also killed two loyal slaves accompanying the king and wounded the horses pulling him. Then with his Bactrian cavalry, Bessus fled east into the mountains.

The scene was a confusion of men, horses, and carts racing in all directions with the Macedonians close behind. The cart bearing Darius no longer had a driver, so the injured horses wandered off the road in pain and confusion, finding their way to a small oasis in a nearby valley. Alexander immediately sent search parties into the hills to find Darius. And so it was that a weary young Macedonian soldier named Polystratus came upon the cart as he stopped to collect water in his helmet. He saw the wounded horses and wondered why anyone would be so cruel to helpless animals. Then he heard groans from inside and pushed aside the curtains to find the two dead slaves and the bloody form of Darius, barely alive.

Later traditions make much of the final scene in the life of the king. In some versions, Alexander himself is there to bid Darius farewell and to weep at the death of his adversary. In these stories, Darius commits his family and kingdom into the care of Alexander and then breathes his last. In other stories, Darius adresses Polystratus in broken Greek, asking him to give his blessing to his king and thank him for being such a noble opponent. But the truth, as far as it can be known, is simpler and sadder. Darius saw Polystratus enter the wagon and kneel beside him. He motioned for water, which the young man gave to him from his own helmet. Then—with only a single enemy soldier in attendance in a barren desert valley—the Great King of Persia closed his eyes and died.

# 8

# BACTRIA

ALEXANDER ADVANCED NONETHELESS, WITH
GREAT STRUGGLES, THROUGH DEEP SNOW AND
WITH FEW SUPPLIES, BUT STILL HE PRESSED ON.
—ARRIAN

Alexander had never wanted it to end this way. In his mind, he saw Darius captured and coming before him still dressed in the robes of the Great King. Alexander would rise and greet the Persian leader with respect, embracing him like a brother. Darius would formally abdicate and hand over his empire to the Macedonian king. He would give Alexander his own daughter in marriage to cement the bonds between the two houses. Then he would retire in honor with his servants to some out-of-the-way corner of the world where he would live out the rest of his days under close guard.

But now, the King of Kings was dead in the back of a common wagon, betrayed by his friends and deserted by his allies. Alexander wept as he wrapped his own cloak around Darius and ordered the body transported back to Persepolis to be buried there in the family tomb carved in the rocky hillside. As Alexander watched the caravan bearing the Persian leader leave camp and move south, he could only curse fate that things had turned out in the worst possible way. To have captured Darius would have been ideal. There would have been a smooth if forced transition of power from one king to another. To have killed Darius in battle, even in a skirmish, facing down and overcoming his foe like Achilles on the plains of Troy, would have been acceptable. The Persians respected martial strength and would have acknowledged that Alexander was the rightful ruler by victory in combat. But to have Darius rejected and murdered by his own people meant that the war would go on. Alexander had always planned to continue the march east and consolidate his territory, but now he would have to fight for it against Bessus and whoever else in Bactria, Sogdiana, or India rose up to challenge his legitimacy as Great King. What he had hoped to accomplish in a season or two of quick campaigning could now drag on for years.

But to the Macedonian army, the death of Darius was wonderful news. They had followed Alexander thousands of miles across deserts and over mountains to destroy the Persian Empire. The largest cities of the kingdom were captured and the Great King was now dead. It was time to go home. All of them had made more money than they had ever dreamed of when they were shepherds and farmers in the hills of Macedonia. Now, after four long years in Asia, they could go back to their parents, wives, and children as heroes and wealthy men.

The army was so excited at the prospect that rumors quickly spread through the camp that they were indeed going home. Men began to pack up their tents and load their gear onto wagons. It was as if someone had sounded a signal to begin the march. Alexander heard the noise and realized immediately what was happening. The men longed for home, but he somehow had to convince them to continue the campaign to the east. He therefore strode to the assembly grounds and called his soldiers to him. He looked out at them with pride in his heart and spoke to them as both their king and fellow soldier.

Do you remember, he asked, all that we have gone through together the last few years? Do you remember how we beat the Triballi on the way to the Danube and how we crushed the Persians at the Granicus, then at Issus and Gaugamela? Have you stopped to think of all the lands we have conquered together? Asia Minor, Syria, Phoenicia, Egypt, Mesopotamia, Persia, and all the rest. We, the army of Macedonia, a land that in my father's day was little more than a backward kingdom on the northern rump of Greece, have done the impossible. We have conquered the world, my friends.

But listen to me carefully—although we have accomplished miracles, everything we have done, all the blood you and our dear fallen comrades have shed, could come to nothing. Don't you think I want to go home as well? I would love to rush back to my mother and sisters at Pella and leave this desolate land behind. But the truth is that the enemy is just waiting for us to relax our guard. Bessus now claims to be Great King and many people are willing to follow him. He is an accomplished general who commands thousands of soldiers from the lands to the east. Yes, we could go home now, but no sooner than we were settled beside our hearths back in Macedonia, we would see the armies of Bessus rising up behind us. Would you rather fight Bessus here and end this or do you want to face him when he crosses the Hellespont and ravages Macedonia? You can deal with Bessus now or later, but unless you want to see your families slaughtered in their beds by hordes of Bactrian cavalry, you had better finish it now. Come now, we're only a few days away from Bactria. That's nothing to men who have crossed countless rivers and snow-covered peaks. We can destroy Bessus and be home for next year's harvest. Then, at last, we will truly be free of the Persian threat.

It was a beautiful performance, so much more so because it was all a lie. Bactria was hundreds of miles away and Alexander knew very well that it could take years to subdue the eastern provinces. And while raids by Bessus and his men might prove a nuisance to the borders of Persia, they were no more a threat to Macedonia than were the warriors of Britain. And even now, the king was dreaming of lands beyond the borders of the Persian Empire with no plans to return home anytime soon, even if he crushed Bessus that summer. Fortunately for the king, his men were easily persuaded to continue the march for a few more weeks, especially after Alexander offered them a generous bonus to carry on. But it was a risky proposition to mislead an army. Sooner or later they would realize that their king was taking them farther and farther into the wilds of Asia with no thought of returning home. Alexander had won them over for now, but the challenge for the king would be to keep them going.

The road to Bactria lay due east, but Alexander decided first to take a brief detour north over the mountains to the land of Hyrcania on the southern shore of the Caspian Sea. The Macedonian army climbed out of the deserts and over the high Elburz Mountains towards a semi-tropical paradise full of fig trees, grapevines, and fields of grain. Hyrcania was a breadbasket of the Persian Empire, heavily populated by a number of tribes. Alexander had to establish his control here before he moved on to the eastern provinces.

Alexander divided his forces into three groups as he marched into Hyrcania. He sent Craterus forward with one group and put another officer in charge of the main body of the army and its supply train. He himself took the light-armed soldiers and headed up the steepest road to reach Hyrcania first. While he was making camp at the crest of the mountains, a Persian noble named Nabarzanes came to him along with several other important officials and surrendered. Nabarzanes had been with Bessus at the arrest of Darius and conspired with him in the murder of the Persian king. It seems unlikely that Alexander would have allowed him to live were it not for the intervention of a remarkable young man named Bagoas. No relation to the man who had plotted the overthrow of Darius' predecessor, this Bagoas was a handsome eunuch of great influence at court who had been a sexual favorite of the Great King. Alexander was evidently charmed by the courtier as well, for he not only spared Nabarzanes for the moment but began an affair with Bagoas that would last the rest of his life.

When the Macedonians finally descended from the mountains and stood on the shores of the Caspian Sea, they must have stared in wonder at the vast waters stretching before them. A few merchants and soldiers from the Aegean may have traveled this way before, but the Caspian was virtually unknown to the Greek world. There were stories of sea monsters in its depths and fish of strange colors, though few locals reportedly sailed on the sea. Herodotus had described it as a large inland lake, but most ancient writers believed it was an inlet of the great ocean that encircled the world. In theory, a voyager could board a boat in Hyrcania and sail west to the Atlantic or east around Asia to India. Some thought it was connected to the Black Sea, while other Greeks mistakenly believed that the Oxus and Jaxartes rivers flowed into the Caspian from central Asia. Alexander would learn in time that these rivers instead ended at the even more distant Aral Sea.

This remote corner of Asia was a curious gathering place of many displaced nobles, refugees, and wayward souls. Artabazus appeared one day, the old friend of Philip who had sought sanctuary in Macedonia when Alexander was a boy. Alexander knew him well and welcomed him to his camp. He was just the sort of Persian the king was hoping to bring into his new empire—a respected figure who had been tenaciously loyal to Darius but now saw Alexander as the rightful heir to the throne. It also didn't hurt that the old man's daughter, Barsine, was still Alexander's mistress. Envoys from the Greek mercenaries who had served Darius also met him there to inquire about terms. The king said that only unconditional surrender was acceptable, but when the fearful soldiers laid down their arms he held no grudge and enrolled them into his army at full pay. Even some Spartan ambassadors to Darius were rounded up who apparently did not know that their cause was now hopeless. They were arrested along with a delegation of roving Athenians who were still trying to convince the Persians to give them money to rebel against Alexander.

Also in Hyrcania, one of the strangest meetings between Alexander and a visiting envoy took place—or didn't, depending on which ancient sources one believes. The guest was a woman named Thalestris and she was the queen of the Amazons. According to Greek tradition stretching back to the days of Homer, the Amazons were a tribe of warrior women living on the northern edge of the civilized world. From time to time they had invaded the Aegean lands, fighting at Troy or even rampaging through Athens. The name *a-mazon* means "no breast" and supposedly derives from a legend of their removal of a single breast in order to throw a javelin unimpeded. Myth says they lived without men, allowing only occasional conjugal visits for procreation. Resulting male children were killed or sent away, while females were raised as warriors. According to Plutarch, Diodorus, and others—most of whom had serious doubts about the story—Thalestris ruled a country to the north of Hyrcania between the Black Sea and the Caspian. She had heard of the extraordinary abilities of Alexander and came to him with an escort of three hundred women warriors and a proposition. Being the bravest and most beautiful of women, she proclaimed that she wished to have a child by the king, the greatest man in the world. In contrast to his previous inclinations toward women, Alexander was supposedly enthusiastic about the idea and spent thirteen exhausting nights trying to satisfy Thalestris. Then the queen rode away to her home, convinced that she would bear a child by the king. Although there is occasional evidence of women warriors in ancient societies, the story probably reveals more about timeless male fantasies than it does about any historical event. Years later, a young companion of Alexander's named Lysimachus, who was present with the king in Hyrcania and would rise to great power, was listening to the Amazon story as told by a writer named Onesicritus. As the historian finished the tale, Lysimachus smiled and asked, "And where was I when all this happened?"

Whether the story has an element of truth or not, the king soon left all his guests behind and took a contingent of forces west along the coast of the Caspian to confront a tribe known as the Mardi, unrelated to the primitive tribe of the same name near Persepolis. These proud horsemen were unimpressed by the Macedonians and refused to offer tribute to Alexander. With eight thousand soldiers they held the passes leading into their lands, until the king broke through and killed many of them, driving the rest into the mountains. In retaliation, the stubborn Mardi struck back at Alexander in an unexpected way. One day while the royal pages were leading the king's horses outside camp to graze, a group of Mardi rushed the troop and stole the finest horse they saw, which just happened to be Bucephalas. To the Mardi this was a matter of honor, counting coup on the foreign king to earn his respect and perhaps a few concessions. But they had picked the wrong man and the wrong horse. Alexander would rather have lost half his kingdom than the horse he had trained and loved since he was a boy. He sent out his soldiers into the mountains with orders to destroy the country, cutting down every precious tree in the Mardi's territory. He also sent word to the tribesmen that unless they returned Bucephalas unharmed he would continue until their home was a wasteland, then he would hunt down and slaughter every man, woman, and child in their nation. The Mardi realized he was deadly serious and quickly sent a delegation leading Bucephalas back to the king. They included many rich gifts brought by fifty of their leading citizens to beg forgiveness of Alexander. The king ceased from devastating their country, but he kept several of the men as hostages to guarantee the good behavior of the tribe in the future.

Alexander spent another two weeks in Hyrcania settling administrative matters, sacrificing to the gods, and holding athletic contests for his soldiers. He then led his army back across the mountains to begin the long trek to Bactria. He held to the highlands along the northern edge of this arid wilderness through the land of the Parthians, relatives of the Persians who would one day become a mighty empire in their own right. Two hundred miles and many days later he was at the city of Susia in the province of Aria. There he met the Persian satrap Satibarzanes, a veteran commander at Gaugamela, who promptly surrendered to him. This Persian nobleman informed Alexander that Bessus had reached Bactria and was gathering allies from as far away as Scythia. Bessus had taken to wearing his cap upright in the manner of the Great King and went about arrayed in royal clothing. He was also styling himself as Artaxerxes V, King of Kings, heir to Darius. It was just the sort of news Alexander did not need. Perhaps because of his haste in pursuing Bessus, Alexander quickly confirmed Satibarzanes in his old post as satrap of Aria. He also appointed his Macedonian companion Anaxippus as leader of an honor guard of forty mounted spearmen to accompany the governor back to the regional capital of Chortacana (modern Herat). The king and the army then continued their march toward Bactria.

It may have been the news of Bessus dressing in the garb of the Great King that prompted Alexander to accelerate a policy that he had been developing for some time. Up until the conquest of Persepolis, the king had been an invader warring against a foreign empire. But now that Persia was beaten and Darius was dead, Alexander began to feel the responsibilities of the Great King resting on his own shoulders. He realized that if he were to rule the Persian Empire as its rightful lord, he could no longer simply be a Macedonian king. To have sovereignty over many nations, he would have to become the Great King not only in substance but in style as well. The Persians, Medes, and all the other peoples of the East expected their ruler to be surrounded by pomp and ceremony worthy of a mighty lord. A Macedonian chieftain could join his men around the campfire and sing bawdy songs of women and war, but the ruler of the largest empire in the world must be a man apart. On the other hand, Alexander's power resided in his role as military leader of the Macedonian army. These officers and soldiers from the hills and plains around Mount Olympus by long tradition revered their king as war leader and would lay down their lives for him, but he was the first among equals in a body of free men. If they had a problem or complaint, they claimed the right to come to him and be heard without pretentious rituals. The men loved Alexander as they had his father before him, but he was the conquering king of Macedonia to them, not the lofty lord of Asia.

It was therefore troubling to many in the army when they saw Alexander gradually taking on the ways of a foreign king. On the march, he was still just Alexander, as likely as a common soldier to help pull a stranded mule out of a mud hole. But when camp was made and he was surrounded by the increasing number of Persian courtiers accompanying the campaign, he became someone else. He began to wear a purple diadem on his head just like the Great King, not a simple Macedonian fillet as he had in years past. He wore a white robe and sash in the manner of Darius, though he did draw the line at Persian trousers. For his correspondence with Greece and Macedonia, he sealed his letters with the ring he had inherited from his father, but messages to Asia were impressed with the seal he had taken from Darius. He also began to keep a royal harem of 365 concubines, one for each night of the year, from the most beautiful women of Asia. Though he had little interest in these women, he felt it was important to keep up appearances for the sake of his Persian subjects. He even began to encourage his officers to take on Persian dress, though most found this distasteful. Alexander tried to walk a thin line between living up to the expectations of his Asian subjects and preserving the old Macedonian ways for the sake of his army. It was an impossible position to maintain and one that would cause him endless problems in the years to come.

Somewhere during the march to Bactria, Parmenion's son Nicanor died, presumably of natural causes. He had been a loyal soldier of Alexander's since before the battle at the Granicus, but the king was not necessarily grieved to see him pass away. With Nicanor gone, his brother Philotas was the only leading figure in the Parmenion faction still present with the army. As there was no time to stop for a proper funeral, Alexander left Philotas and a large contingent of soldiers behind in Aria to conduct the proper rites and catch up with the army as soon as possible.

Just as he was approaching the borders of Bactria, Alexander received news that made him regret his hasty decision to reappoint Satibarzanes as satrap of Aria. As soon as the Persian had put a few days travel between himself and the Macedonians, the governor massacred Anaxippus with his forty cavalry and defected to Bessus. His plan was to join the would-be Great King in his guerrilla war against Alexander from the eastern provinces. Taking a strong contingent of cavalry and archers, Alexander left Craterus in charge of the main force with orders to follow him and turned south across the high desert to Chortacana. Again the king was relying on his remarkable gift for speed to reach an enemy before he had time to organize an effective defense. Alexander raced almost seventy miles in two days and threw the city into panic when he arrived suddenly at the gates. Satibarzanes fled with a few of his local horsemen, while most of the troops deserted their posts in town and hid at a nearby wooded mountain. The king chased after the satrap but was unable to catch him, so he turned back to the mountain, where the majority of the soldiers had taken refuge. Craterus and the army had arrived by this point and were set to besieging Chortacana while Alexander surveyed the nearby mountain site to see how best to force the enemy out of hiding. It was a steep crag with cliffs and numerous precipices, making it exceedingly difficult to take by direct assault. The top was a grassy plateau, but the sides were covered by trees. At first Alexander tried cutting down a few of these to build a road to the top, but then a simpler plan occurred to him. He ordered his men to continue felling trees and place them in a giant circle around the whole forested mountain. Then, with a fire kindled, he set the mass ablaze. Flames shot up the sides of the peak on every side, setting the encircling forest on fire and choking the defenders in thick smoke. Some of the men tried to escape through the flames, but the Macedonians cut them down. A few threw themselves over the cliffs, though most died on the mountain, roasted alive.

Alexander returned to the city of Chortacana and began to construct siege towers. When the inhabitants saw these and heard of the fate of the men on the mountain, they sent messengers to the king begging him to reserve his anger for Satibarzanes. They quickly surrendered and were pardoned by the king, who was in too much of a hurry to waste time. He left behind a garrison and renamed the city Alexandria-of-the-Arians, the first of many namesake towns he would establish in central Asia. Alexander was also gladdened by the timely arrival of reinforcements fresh from Antipater in Macedonia. There were almost seven thousand new troops, including over two thousand of the famed cavalry of Lydia. With these added forces, he decided on a change in plans. As he had already come so far off his original path, he decided to move against Bessus from the south, through the lands of Drangiana and Arachosia. It was a longer journey, but time spent securing these lands would deprive Bessus of soldiers and support. However, before he could deal with an enemy in the distant mountains, he had to first face a threat in the heart of his own camp.

Philotas had caught up with Alexander after burying his brother and took up his place again as the leader of the old guard faction among the Macedonian troops. He was respected if not loved by most of the army, who regarded him as a brave and generous commander, but one who thought more of himself than modesty recommended. He enjoyed fine clothes and rich surroundings, prompting even his father, Parmenion, to warn him more than once that he should take care not to provoke the envy and disdain of those around him. Alexander had known Philotas for as long as he could remember but never liked him, though even he had to admit that he was as good a soldier as his father in a tight spot. The family of Parmenion and Philotas came from old Macedonian stock with connections to almost all the leading figures at court. If anything had happened to Alexander on the Persian campaign, it was almost certain that Parmenion would have taken his place. With the army behind him, he would have become the new king of Macedonia and all the lands they had conquered.

Alexander was aware of the standing and power of Parmenion's family, which was one reason he had worked so hard ever since the invasion began to reduce the influence of the old general. With Parmenion far away in Ecbatana guarding the treasury he was less of a direct threat, but he still had thousands of troops under his command and all the money necessary to hire new soldiers. If Parmenion decided to stage a coup, there was a decent chance it could succeed, especially with Philotas already in place to take command of the army. Alexander knew the bloody history of his country better than most and could never forget that few of his ancestors had died in peaceful old age. Conspiracy and assassination were second nature to the Macedonian nobility—and the king who ignored the signs of a plot usually ended up dead. But now the rewards for a successful insurrection were not just the kingdom of Macedonia, but an empire that stretched across much of the known world.

Alexander had heard rumors of plots by Parmenion and Philotas ever since Egypt, but he had dismissed these as the usual camp gossip spread by those who resented the influence of the general's family. Nevertheless, the king had arranged to keep an eye on Philotas through an unexpected source. When Parmenion had captured the treasury at Damascus three years earlier, one of the prizes he gave his son was a beautiful slave girl from Greece named Antigone. Philotas was prone to self-flattering pillow talk and frequently told Antigone that Alexander was little more than a boy who owed all his success in war to himself and Parmenion. The slave girl repeated these claims to her confidants until word finally reached Alexander through his companion Craterus. The king brought the girl before him for a private briefing, then ordered her to report directly to him in the future anything of interest Philotas said as they lay together in bed. Over the months and years that followed, the general's son continued to complain about Alexander, but revealed nothing that was truly damning about himself or his father. Still, Alexander watched patiently and waited for signs of trouble.

While the army was outside Chortacana on the way to Bactria, a Macedonian named Dimnus instigated a plan to assassinate Alexander. His motives are a mystery, but he told his lover Nichomachus of the plot in an intimate moment and mentioned the names of those involved. Nicomachus wanted nothing to do with a conspiracy against the king and so told his own brother Cebalinus about the matter and begged him to get word to Alexander. Cebalinus apparently did not have access to the king and so told Philotas of the plot, expecting him to inform Alexander immediately. Whether because Philotas put little stock in the chain of rumors or because of darker motives, he dismissed Cebalinus with the retort that Alexander was too busy to be bothered by baseless accusations. He then withheld the information from the king during their meetings over the next few days. Cebalinus, however, was not to be put off so easily. Through another associate he did get word to the king, who ordered the arrest of Dimnus. When the soldiers came for him, Dimnus fought back and was killed, confirming his guilt in the eyes of Alexander.

The companions of the king who had so long disliked Philotas now saw a perfect opportunity to be rid of the man. They came to Alexander and suggested that the role of Philotas in the conspiracy had been much deeper than initially reported. The king needed little encouragement to pursue a course of action close to his own heart. He may have suspected a plot was afoot, since he had recently begun to open mail from his soldiers back to Macedonia. He called Philotas before him and demanded to know why he had not reported the rumors of a conspiracy against him. There was little Philotas could say except that he did not give the reports enough credit to bring them before the king, as they seemed to him to spring from just another tiresome lovers' quarrel. He apologized and said that it would never happen again. Alexander made sure that it wouldn't when he had Philotas immediately arrested and taken off for interrogation under torture. The king also posted guards on all the roads out of camp to stop any word of his son's arrest from reaching Parmenion.

Alexander listened behind a screen as Philotas was mercilessly flogged and beaten under the direction of Craterus. Torture broke Philotas as it would any man so that soon he was ready to confess to anything to stop the pain. He did, however, retain a bit of the old wit when he asked Craterus what exactly it was he wanted him to confess, so he could be sure to get it right.

With a forced confession but no hard evidence against him, Philotas was summarily brought before the Macedonian army for trial by the assembled soldiers according to ancient tradition. It was a risky move for Alexander as many of the men respected Philotas as a commander even though they thought him a pompous ass in his private life. But Philotas made a grave mistake when he responded to the charges in proper Greek rather than the Macedonian dialect of the rank and file soldiers. They thought this pretentious and turned on him, condemning him to death in spite of flimsy proof. Alexander was pleased and watched as Philotas was stoned to death along with several others who had been implicated in the plot.

Philotas was dead, and it was certain that Parmenion would soon hear of his son's execution and quite probably rise up against Alexander in response. It was unthinkable that the father could remain alive once the son was dead. Therefore the king sent his trusted friend Polydamus with a few Arab guides on racing camels back to Ecbatana at breakneck speed. They reached the Median capital after many days of travel and brought a letter in great secrecy to Parmenion's four lieutenants, including Alexander's companion Cleander. They read their orders in disbelief, but told the messenger they would carry out the king's commands. Parmenion knew Polydamus and liked him, so he was surprised but pleased to see the man accompanying his commanders as they approached him while he strolled in a beautiful grove near his residence. It had been weeks since he had received any word from Alexander and he was anxious for news of both the campaign and his only surviving son. Polydamus first gave him a letter from the king reporting on his ambitious war plans in the east, to which Parmenion commented that Alexander ought to slow down after already achieving so many conquests. Then Polydamus handed him a letter supposedly from Philotas that Parmenion began to read with pleasure. It was then that Cleander pulled out his sword and stabbed the old general in the side, then plunged the blade into his throat to silence his cries. The other commanders joined in, leaving Parmenion, one of the greatest soldiers in Macedonian history, a bloody corpse in the gardens of Ecbatana.

When the general's soldiers heard what had happened, they rushed to the scene with swords drawn ready to kill Parmenion's murderers. Cleander had their leaders brought in and read to them a letter direct from Alexander issuing the orders for Parmenion's death and explaining the reasons. The troops were fond of Parmenion, but when they heard the claims of Alexander that the general and his son had been plotting against him they grudgingly accepted the news. They did demand that they be given the body of Parmenion for a proper burial, allowing Polydamus to take the head back to Alexander for verification of death as was the custom.

Had Parmenion and Philotas really plotted against the life of Alexander? Ancient historians differ on the matter considerably, with most seeing the charges as little more than a trumped-up excuse to eliminate longtime rivals. As is often the case, final judgment regarding the alleged conspiracy is impossible to reach. Nevertheless, if there were to have been a successful coup against the king, Parmenion and his son would have been the most likely instigators. It may well be that Alexander took advantage of an unrelated plot to stir up feelings against the pair and eliminate once and for all a potential menace. Leaving Parmenion in a position of power as the army headed into the wilds of central Asia for what could be years of fighting would have been dangerous in any case. Whether or not there was any truth to the conspiracy of Philotas, Alexander had removed a very real threat to his throne.

Alexander and his army had marched almost fifteen hundred miles since they left Persepolis the previous spring. They had traveled from the Persian homeland north to Media, chased Darius east across Parthia and taken a detour into Hyrcania on the Caspian Sea. Assuming they were making a short trip straight to Bactria, Alexander had then instead led his men south into the highlands of Aria and onward to the borders of Drangiana. Any sensible commander would have made a winter camp at this point and given his men several months to rest. But whether because of his determination to catch the rebel king Bessus or because he thought that a prolonged period of inactivity so soon after the Philotas affair might serve to fan the fires of discontent, Alexander decided to press on through the winter snows toward the peaks of the Hindu Kush.

The Drangians were subdued easily enough, but Alexander received word that there was trouble back in Aria, once again stirred up by Satibarzanes and his band of Persian renegades. The king had suffered enough from the rebel satrap, but he did not want to turn his entire army around yet again to deal with him. Instead, he sent back his old friend and trusted cavalry commander Erigyius of Lesbos along with a force of more than six thousand men, including his Persian companion Artabazus, to confront Satibarzanes. The details are sketchy, but there was a fierce battle in which the satrap and his men fought bravely with the Macedonian soldiers until Erigyius and Satibarzanes finally faced each other in single combat. The Greek commander struck the satrap in the face with a spear and killed him, prompting the rebel soldiers to flee into the mountains.

The path that Alexander took to Bactria followed the Helmand

River through an arid plateau, a reasonable choice as fresh water for a large army was always a serious concern. Just as the river began to curve north into the mountains, the king founded another Alexandria, accompanied by the usual sacrifices to the gods. This city commanding the southern approaches of the Hindu Kush would thrive through the centuries, preserving a trace of its original name in the much modified form of Kandahar. To recruit citizens for his colony, Alexander relied mostly on volunteers, including a large group of camp followers who must have taken one look at the icy peaks ahead and decided the location of this Alexandria seemed promising. The pioneers who settled these cities in distant Asia profited from generous grants of land and the chance to begin a new life. A weary soldier who was a nobody back in Macedonia might build a fine house and sit on the city council in a such a place. A poor wine seller who had trailed after the army for thousands of miles could become a wealthy merchant on this promising frontier, while a struggling prostitute might marry an officer with plenty of gold in his pockets and settle down to become a leading matron of the town. For Alexander, these foundations served as crucial garrisons throughout his empire. They were indeed islands of Greek civilization in the East that would have great influence on local cultures for hundreds of years, but most important to the king, they were military settlements to keep the natives in line.

The Macedonians had never imagined mountains like the Hindu Kush rising before them north of Kandahar. Stories about these peaks had filtered west to Greece for years, so that educated men like Alexander knew there was a lofty range of mountains on the eastern borders of the Persian Empire higher than anything in the Aegean world. Greek scholars sometimes called them the Caucasus, thinking they were an extension of the mountains between the Black Sea and the Caspian, perhaps even a branch of the same peaks that rose in central Asia Minor. But even soldiers from the rugged Balkans were unprepared for the Hindu Kush, a towering range extending southwest from the Karakorum and Himalayas. These mountains averaged almost fifteen thousand feet in height, with the highest peaks soaring well above twenty thousand feet. They cut off Persia, Aria, and Drangiana from Bactria to the north and the valley of the Indus River to the east. The only way through these peaks was a small number of high passes such as those used by caravans crossing from the south to Bactria or the Khyber Pass linking the region to India. The valleys of the Hindu Kush were inhabited by fiercely independent tribes who barely acknowledged Persian rule. They made their living through pastoralism, brigandage, and export of the few resources they had to offer, including pistachios and lapis lazuli—the Hindu Kush being the only known source for this precious blue stone in the ancient world.

The journey north from Kandahar to the valley of Kabul took weeks of struggle over snow-clogged passes and icy peaks. The Macedonians were tough as nails, but even they were susceptible to altitude sickness and snow blindness. Their eyesight became so bad that often they would not realize they had stumbled into a mountain village with its distinctively cone-shaped houses until they were practically on top of it. Then they would force the surrender of the frightened inhabitants and take whatever supplies were available, leaving the villagers to starve until the next harvest. On the march between villages, many of the men would become so fatigued by the altitude that they lay down on the ice and refused to go on. It was only with the greatest effort that their companions were able to rouse them to continue the march. But in spite of the enormous difficulties, town by town, valley by valley, Alexander subdued the tribes of the Hindu Kush through the harsh winter months.

When the army finally reached the Kabul valley in early spring, Alexander gave his men a brief but much needed rest. Between them and Bactria were still some of the highest peaks in the Hindu Kush. It would have been prudent to wait in Kabul until early summer when the snow in the passes north had begun to melt, but the king wanted to catch Bessus off guard. He did take the time to establish another garrison town nearby, Alexandria-in-the-Caucasus, populating it again with conscript locals, army volunteers, and those too weary or injured to continue. The choice before the king then was which of the several passes to the north to take. The logical choice—if any choice could be called logical under such conditions—was one of the western corridors rising to an altitude of no more than ten thousand feet. But this was precisely what Bessus was expecting him to do, though not so early in the season. The Persian leader had already applied a scorched-earth policy to the lands north of these passes and had his men waiting to strike the Macedonians as they struggled across the mountains. The most unlikely option was the easternmost route, the Khawak Pass, at twelve thousand feet above sea level the highest and most difficult trail north through the Hindu Kush into Bactria. It was a precipitous crossing with little shelter over deep snow that not even the locals would have attempted that time of year. But, of course, this was exactly the path Alexander chose. With tens of thousands of men behind him, the king led his army out of Kabul and up into the highest mountains any of them had ever seen.

It was still deep winter in the Khawak Pass as the Macedonians entered the steep valley leading into Bactria. The journey over the pass was almost fifty miles long, but the path was so narrow up the mountainside that most of the time the men were forced to walk single file. For an army the size of Alexander's, this meant the line of men and horses stretched back for many miles. There was little food to be stolen from the natives in these heights, so the men and animals were forced to carry all their supplies and fodder up and over the mountains. The packhorses and mules that could not keep up were quickly devoured, often raw, as there was little wood available for cooking.

Somewhere in this area the native guides showed Alexander a peak rising almost three thousand feet above the trail on which they said a god had been chained when he stole fire from the heavens. They even pointed out the scratches on the stone made by the eagle sent by the angry lord of the gods to peck at the thief as punishment. Alexander immediately recognized this tale as the Greek myth of Prometheus, the Titan who had stolen fire from Zeus to give to men and was punished by being chained to a pillar in the distant eastern mountains. His liver was eaten every day by an eagle, only to grow back again each night. At last he was rescued by Hercules, a reputed ancestor of Alexander. The king must have taken comfort that he was passing through the same lands that Hercules once traveled, daring the impossible just like his legendary forefather.

Alexander at last reached the frozen summit of the pass and found it unguarded by Bessus, who had never dreamed the Macedonians would dare such a difficult route. The view to the north stretched for miles over more mountains and valleys, but the king knew that at the end of the trail were the plains of Bactria leading to the Oxus River and the steppes of central Asia. It would take days for his entire army to move over the pass and down to the warmer lands below, but Alexander had the satisfaction of knowing he had not only outflanked Bessus, but had crossed the mighty Hindu Kush.

As the army came down from the Khawak Pass, the Macedonians moved from winter ice to blistering summer heat in a matter of days. To make the situation worse, little food or fodder was available in a land that had suffered the scorched-earth policy of Bessus. The few cities of Bactria quickly fell to Alexander, but even here supplies were limited. And worst of all for the king, Bessus was nowhere to be found. He had chosen a strategic retreat across the Oxus River into Sogdiana accompanied by Spitamenes, a Sogdian lord who had served the Persians for years. They brought with them thousands of Sogdian cavalry perfectly suited for hit-and-run strikes against Alexander on the endless plains of central Asia. Most of the Bactrian warriors, however, when they learned that Bessus was abandoning their homeland to the Macedonians, deserted the satrap and returned to their villages in the hills.

Alexander appointed his old family friend Artabazus as the new satrap of Bactria and headed north to the Oxus after Bessus. The farther north they marched under the summer sun the worse conditions became. The land was covered with barren sand dunes stretching to the horizon, so that experienced travelers moved only at night using the stars to guide them—a trick Alexander quickly learned. But so little water was available that the journey soon became a hellish trek for the men. Just a few weeks earlier they had been freezing to death in the Hindu Kush, but now they were dying of thirst and heat under the desert sun. Most of the soldiers trudged along mindlessly putting one foot in front of the other, while others simply stopped moving and stood fixed to whatever spot they found themselves. A few of the men broke into the wine stores and drained the skins, but this only made their thirst worse in the end. Day after day the army marched on toward the Oxus, with the weaker soldiers falling by the wayside to die in an empty land far from home. One of the scouts the king had sent ahead to the river came back with a skin full of water for his sons in the ranks, but when he saw Alexander he poured a cup and offered it to him. The king refused and bade him save the water for his children.

When at last the army reached the Oxus, they were strung out for miles behind Alexander. He lit a fire on a nearby hill to guide the stragglers to camp and stood by the road himself to encourage the troops. Many of the men who struggled to the banks of the river plunged into the stream and began to drink greedily, even though they knew better. Some vomited and others choked to death, as their parched bodies were unable to handle so much water so quickly after a long period of thirst. When the remainder of the soldiers arrived at last, some had had enough. The historian Arrian says only that Alexander decided to decommission some of the older Macedonian veterans and Thessalian cavalry and send them home with large bonuses, but this cannot be the whole story. These were the very soldiers who had been closest to Parmenion. The march across the Bactrian desert must have been the last straw for men already on the verge of mutiny at the murder of their old commander. Rather than face an open rebellion, the king bought them off and sent them away, even though it left him with a shortage of men just as he was entering a crucial phase of the war.

The Oxus was swift, cold, and deep because it was fed by melting snows at its headwaters in the high Pamir Mountains to the east. Alexander's trusty corps of engineers at first tried to drive piles into the stream for the foundation of a bridge, but the current soon tore these apart. Even if they had been able to build a bridge, there was not enough wood available in the surrounding desert to span a river half a mile wide. To make matters worse, Alexander had no boats and Bessus had made sure there were none to be found in any of the villages along the river. The king therefore resorted to the same trick he had used on the distant Danube six years earlier. He ordered his men to stuff their tents with whatever dry straw and grass they could find and use these as floats to swim downstream across the river. The first soldiers across the river stood guard as the rest of the men paddled with all their might, but the army was so large that it took five days to complete the crossing.

Once in Sogdiana, the Macedonians must have felt that they had reached the very edge of the world. To the north was the Jaxartes River and the great steppes of central Asia, a boundless grassland stretching seemingly forever. In the east were more mountains and deserts. Sogdiana was a strange and beautiful land, but unnerving to men unaccustomed to endless horizons.

It may have been this deeply unsettled feeling that led Alexander to commit one of the most barbaric acts of the entire campaign. As they were moving north, they came to a village on the steppe and were surprised to be greeted in Greek by the inhabitants. These were the descendants of the Branchidae, priests of Apollo at Didyma near Miletus on the Aegean coast of Asia Minor. Alexander had visited the ruins of the oracle five years earlier and must have marveled to find the great-great-grandchildren of the priests so far from home. Their ancestors had been deported by Xerxes in the previous century to protect them from the hostile Greeks after they had collaborated with the Great King and burned down their own temple. But this was ancient history to their descendants, who had become citizens of Persia and embraced their new land, though they still maintained their old language, religion, and many of their customs. They were thrilled to see a king from the Aegean world, though they had never even visited their ancestral home, and welcomed Alexander warmly, surrendering their city to him with celebration.

However, when Alexander had retired to his tent for the night, he called together the soldiers of Miletus serving in his army and asked them what he should do about the Branchidae. These men of Miletus had been raised since childhood with an abiding hatred for the traitorous priests and wanted revenge, though some felt the events happened so long ago that they were best forgotten. The king thanked them and said he would consider what to do during the night. The next morning, Alexander entered their town and was again welcomed by all the people. But their joy turned to horror when they saw the soldiers entering behind him with swords drawn. Every man, woman, and child was killed in spite of their cries for mercy in Greek and the olive branches they held before them. The town was sacked and the houses as well as the city walls were flattened. Even the nearby sacred grove was cut down and the stumps pulled up so that no trace remained of the Branchidae.

When the Sogdians heard that Alexander was in their country, they began to have second thoughts about Bessus. His credibility was already at a low point, as he had abandoned Bactria without a fight, so there was little objection when Spitamenes and his men entered his tent one night and arrested the satrap. They then sent a message to Alexander saying they would gladly hand over Bessus to him if he would send a party to lead him back to the Macedonian camp. The king suspected a trap, but the opportunity to seize the murderer of Darius without a fight was too tempting to resist. He sent his friend Ptolemy with a strong force into Sogdiana on a fast ten-day march to retrieve the prisoner. While he was approaching the village where Bessus was being held, Ptolemy received a message that Spitamenes was now uncertain about whether he should hand over his captive, so Ptolemy surrounded the village with his soldiers. By this point the Sogdian leader and his officers had fled, so the Macedonian captain left most of his troops encircling the area and entered the town with only a handful of men. It was a tense situation with the potential for ambush, but Ptolemy dealt with the matter boldly, marching into the hut where Bessus was detained and dragging him away before anyone had time to object. He then sent a messenger back to Alexander asking what he should do with the captive satrap. The king told him to put a wooden collar on Bessus and tie him naked to a pole along the road that the army would soon pass.

When Alexander arrived at the village, he got down from his horse and approached the prisoner. He asked by what right he had seized the Great King in the first place, betraying a sacred trust that bound him to a man who was both his relative and benefactor. How had he dared put him in chains, then murder him like a slave? Bessus could only weakly respond that he had not acted alone and that he thought Alexander would be pleased. If the satrap still entertained any hopes that his story would have a happy ending, they soon vanished. The king first had him flogged, then cut off his ears and nose, the traditional Persian punishment for traitors. He then ordered the mutilated prisoner to be delivered into the hands of Darius' family. When Bessus arrived, the former Great King's brother and other relatives inflicted every possible torture and humiliation on him, then cut him to pieces.

The crossing of the Hindu Kush and the parching deserts of Bactria had been hard on the men, but it had also taken an enormous toll on the horses. Alexander now took advantage of moving through some of the finest horse country in the world and acquired new mounts for his cavalry. These animals would prove especially effective in the upcoming battles on the steppes of Sogdiana. The king then led his army almost two hundred miles north across the plains and highlands to the ancient walled city of Marcanda, or Samarkand, a royal city of the Persians in central Sogdiana. In centuries to come this town would become one of the major trading centers of Asia, but for now Alexander made it one of his key garrisons in what he assumed would be a quick campaign in the northern reaches of his new empire.

From Samarkand the king struck north to the Jaxartes, like the Oxus a major river running from the great Himalayan massif to the Aral Sea. The Jaxartes was the farthest boundary of the Persian Empire in central Asia. Beyond it lay the untamed land of the Scythians, as the Greeks and Persians called all the tribes of the steppes stretching back to the lands north of the Danube in Europe. It was here that things first began to go wrong for the king in this wild region. Alexander had assumed that the surrender of Bessus by Spitamenes meant that the Sogdian lord had acknowledged him as the new Great King. All he would need to do now was show the flag in a few forays around the country, perhaps found a city or two, then head back to Bactria so he could be on his way to India before the snows began to fall. Even the sudden massacre of some of his Macedonian foraging parties by local tribesmen was dismissed as a random act by impetuous barbarians. Still, it was not the sort of thing Alexander could allow to go unpunished. The king took a large contingent of his fastest troops and attacked the Sogdian warriors as they hid on a mountainside. These men of the steppes were not easily intimidated, however, and drove back the first Macedonian assault with a shower of arrows. Many of the king's soldiers were injured, including Alexander himself, who suffered a shot in the right leg that broke his fibula. His physicians patched the wound as best they could, then the king struggled back to the mountain and directed the fight until his men finally took the high ground and killed most of the Sogdians. For the next few days, the Macedonian cavalry and infantry argued over the right to carry the wounded king in his litter until Alexander finally settled the matter by having them bear him in turn on alternate days.

As he recovered back on the Jaxartes, Alexander laid out both his immediate and long-term plans for Sogdiana. The Persians had established seven garrison towns on the river to fortify their northern border against Scythian raids. Alexander planned to strengthen these and establish new posts of his own, most important a city called Alexandria Eschate ("Alexandria the Farthest") near the site of the largest of the Persian forts. The city was well positioned, guarding the western edge of a large basin leading to the steppes, with high mountains to the east. But Alexander's plan was not merely to defend the borders of his kingdom. His stated ambition was to use the town as a base to invade Scythia in the future. This is the first hint we have in the ancient sources of the young king's scheme for expansion after he had secured all the provinces of the Persian Empire. Cyrus and his successors had fought in this region for two hundred years, but they never intended anything more than to hold the frontier against the tribes beyond the Jaxartes. Alexander dreamed of conquests greater than those of any of the previous Great Kings, reaching even into the endless steppes of Asia. And as he had only just celebrated his twenty-seventh birthday, he could reasonably hope that there were still many years ahead of him to lead his army to the ends of the earth.

But diplomacy had its uses as much as war. While he was on the Jaxartes, delegations came to him from various Scythian tribes, including the Abii on the steppes far to the west of Sogdiana. The Abii were known to the Greek world, probably through their colonies on the Black Sea, as a poor but honorable people who waged war only in self-defense. Alexander greeted all the envoys warmly and affirmed his desire for friendship with their people. As proof of his good intentions, he sent back with them several of his Macedonian companions, including a man named Derdas who was a relative of his treasurer Harpalus. These men were in for the adventure of their lives as they traversed the steppes of Asia with their new Scythian friends. But before sending them off, Alexander called them aside and ordered them to gather all the information they could on the tribes, their military capabilities, distances, major rivers, water and food resources, and anything else that might be useful to an invading army in the future.

At this point Alexander invited Spitamenes and the other Sogdian lords to a conference across the Oxus in Bactria. He was anxious to clear up any misunderstandings aroused by his slaughter of the Sogdian rebels on the mountainside earlier and to settle affairs in the province before he set out for India. But the local nobles were understandably hesitant about walking into a fortified Macedonian town. Often in the ancient world such settings were a prelude to arrest or murder of the guests. They had no way of knowing this was not Alexander's style. He might ride fifty miles in a night to kill them all in their beds, but he would never violate the sacred duty of a host. Nevertheless, Spitamenes and his fellow lords refused, sending the whole province of Sogdiana into rebellion. The seven cities of the Persians along the Jaxartes were quickly retaken and their Macedonian garrisons massacred.

Alexander's response was characteristically swift and decisive. He struck north and personally led his army back to the Jaxartes to recapture the frontier outposts. The Sogdians were great horse warriors, but they had little experience at defending a besieged town. The first city the king attacked, ironically named Gaza, had only low earth walls. Unlike the town of the same name in Palestine that had put up a fierce resistance to the Macedonians, the Sogdian fort fell almost immediately as Alexander's men climbed over the walls with hastily constructed ladders. The men of the town were killed while the women and children were added to the army's spoils. The next day he moved to the second city and took it in similar fashion, then went on to seize the third the following day. He sent a large cavalry force on to the fourth and fifth cities to take them before they had time to organize an effective resistance, so that within a week the king had recaptured five of the seven frontier forts and enslaved thousands of Sogdian women and children.

The sixth town was named Cyropolis after the first Great King, who had died in battle not far away fighting the Scythians across the Jaxartes. This city was the greatest of all with high walls and defenses designed by the Persians. Alexander had his engineers bring up siege engines to batter down the walls, but the fortifications turned out to be more substantial than the king had anticipated. It was then he noticed that the river flowing into the city exited the walls through a narrow channel. There might be just enough space in this opening for a man to squeeze through and enter the town undetected. He therefore led a small group of soldiers down into the channel and under the walls while the main force of his army distracted the defenders with a full-blown assault on the front gates. Once he was inside, Alexander and his men overpowered the guards and opened the gates to his troops. But the thousands of Sogdian warriors in the city did not give up so easily. They knew the fate of their comrades in the other cities and so put up a fierce street-by-street defense against the

Macedonians. One Sogdian defender enjoyed a moment of delight before his death when he threw down a heavy stone, smashing Alexander square on the face and neck, knocking the king to the ground unconscious. His men feared he was dead, but he arose and showed them he was still alive, although he must have suffered a terrific headache for days. Adding this injury to his still-unhealed leg wound did not put the king in a good mood. At first he had planned to spare the city, as it had been founded by Cyrus, but now he ordered his troops to slaughter everyone in the town—the texts do not mention sparing the women and children—as well as all the inhabitants in the seventh city, which he took soon after.

The frontier posts were once again in his hands, but Alexander's troubles were far from over. Spitamenes and his fellow chieftains were now besieging Samarkand, so Alexander sent a force of mercenary infantry along with a few hundred cavalry to rescue the town, led by a Lycian diplomat named Pharnuches, who had served the Persians and spoke the local languages. Meanwhile the king stayed on the Jaxartes and supervised the construction of his new city, a project he now viewed as more important than ever as a military center for the region. He even held athletic games for his men to distract them from the fact that they were cut off from retreat to the south by thousands of Sogdian warriors.

The Scythian tribes north of the river had heard about the rebellion and rushed to the border, hoping for a chance to cross over and do some raiding while the Macedonians were distracted. The king's forces, however, were stationed in strength along the Jaxartes to discourage the Scythians from attempting the river. But they did remain on the far side and delighted in taunting the Macedonians, daring Alexander to cross the river so they could teach him a lesson about Scythian prowess in war. After almost three weeks of this endless harangue, the king was ready to strangle the Scythians with his bare hands. He sacrificed to the gods in preparation for his own raid across the river, but his prophet Aristander said the omens were bad. The king ordered him to try again in hope of better signs, but the entrails continued to speak of danger to him if he attacked the Scythians. It must have entered Alexander's mind that Cyrus had died in a similar raid to the one he was now being warned against by the gods, but he was determined to risk death rather than be a laughingstock to barbarians.

The king ordered hide boats prepared and stationed his artillery on the bank opposite the enemy. While the Scythians, who had never seen such devices, continued to hurl insults at the Macedonians, the catapults launched their missiles across the river and struck the warriors from a great distance. Several were wounded and one of the leaders killed, so the surprised Scythians pulled back from the bank while the battery continued. Alexander then launched his boats, placing his slingers and archers in the first to cross so that they could set up screening fire to protect the rest of the men as they landed. The Scythians were accomplished horsemen and put up a strong defense, striking the Macedonians then pulling away, but soon the Macedonian cavalry was across and the king struck out against the enemy, killing at least a thousand as they fled. It was so hot as Alexander chased them across the steppe that the army, which had apparently forgotten to pack water skins, drank from whatever stagnant puddles they could find. The king himself did likewise and almost immediately was struck with crippling dysentery, forcing him to break off the chase and be carried back to the city in a litter. Aristander had been proven right in his prediction of danger to the king, though in a less glorious form than Alexander might have wished.

Meanwhile the Macedonians trapped in Samarkand were fighting off constant assaults by Spitamenes. But when the Sogdian leader heard that a relief force was approaching, he wisely broke off the assault and retreated. One of the defenders, the Lycian diplomat Pharnuches, chased him for many miles, but failed to appreciate that he was now on the steppes where the Sogdians were trained from childhood to fight. To make matters worse, the Sogdians had been joined by six hundred Scythian cavalry so that they now outnumbered the Macedonian forces. They led Pharnuches on until his men and horses were exhausted, then wheeled around and attacked, shooting arrows from horseback in deadly nomad fashion. The Macedonians fell apart, with Pharnuches explaining to the officers that he was a diplomat, not a soldier. The soldiers did their best, hiding in groves along a river to avoid arrows, but the Sogdians and Scythians were relentless. In a few hours almost all the Macedonians lay dead on the steppes, with only a few hundred escaping back to Alexander's camp.

This debacle was a propaganda disaster for the king, who knew that word would swiftly spread across the plains that the Macedonians were vulnerable. To counter this bad news, Alexander struggled from his sick bed and led a large but swift force of horsemen back to Samarkand, where Spitamenes had returned to continue the siege. The king covered almost two hundred miles in an incredible three days, approaching the city at dawn on the fourth day. The Sogdians fled in panic at his unexpected arrival, with Alexander close behind them. He rode past the site where the Macedonians had recently been massacred and took the time to bury them, but then carried on the chase across the steppes. Spitamenes and his men, however, knew the country too well and had faster horses, so the king was unable to catch them. In frustration and anger Alexander turned back and began to burn every Sogdian village he could find, killing all the natives because he suspected them of sympathizing with Spitamenes. After the last town was nothing but ashes, he posted garrisons throughout the land and brought his main force back across the Oxus to Bactria for the winter. His quick campaign in Sogdiana had now turned into a grueling guerrilla conflict with Spitamenes, the most dangerous opponent he would face in all his years at war.

It had been months since Alexander had crossed the Hindu Kush into Bactria and Sogdiana. In that time he had lost hundreds of men to guerrilla strikes and ambushes by the elusive Spitamenes, struggled to maintain his hold on the Jaxartes frontier, and fought dozens of skirmishes against enemy cavalry who melted back into the steppes just when he began to gain the advantage. Add to this that he had been shot through the leg with an arrow, knocked senseless by a rock, and developed an ongoing intestinal disorder from contaminated water. Above all, he was no closer to securing Sogdiana for his empire than he had been a year earlier. As he sat in his tent across the river in Bactria with the snow starting to fall outside, he must have felt that the gods had deserted him.

But there was some good news that long winter. Alexander's boyhood friend Nearchus, who had been serving as satrap in Lycia, arrived along with other fresh officers and more than twenty thousand seasoned mercenaries. These much-needed troops were drawn from Greece and Syria, having marched for months from the Mediterranean to rendezvous with the army. With these recruits the king was confident that he could make a new start in his war against Spitamenes in the spring. He also received a second embassy from the Scythians who dwelt by the Caspian Sea, informing him their old king had died but that their new ruler wished to confirm their ties of friendship. These distant Scythians had nothing to do with his recent troubles on the Jaxartes, so Alexander was glad to renew his treaty with them. They brought an offer of marriage to their king's daughter if the Macedonian leader was willing, but Alexander tactfully declined, claiming he was too busy fighting a war. Another embassy arrived from the Chorasmians living south of the Aral Sea, a people both Bessus and Spitamenes had courted to join in the rebellion against the Macedonians. Instead, their king, Pharsamenes, had decided that Alexander was more useful as an ally than an enemy and therefore sought his friendship. Pharsamenes had personally ridden to Alexander's camp with fifteen hundred of his cavalry. He suggested that if Alexander wished to conquer the lands between the Aral and Caspian seas, he and his people would be glad to help. Of course, any such conquest would benefit Pharsamenes as it would eliminate his enemies and make him the most powerful ruler in the region. Again Alexander politely deferred, saying that first he must take India, but that he would certainly keep the offer in mind for a future campaign. He told Pharsamenes—and we have every reason to believe him—that his plan was to return to Macedonia after the Indian campaign and launch an attack on Scythia from the west. Combined with an assault from the east from his forts along the Jaxartes, he would squeeze the Scythians in a vise and become ruler of all the steppes of central Asia.

When the long winter was finally over, Alexander renewed his campaign against Spitamenes with a promising strategy adapted to fighting nomad warriors. Instead of chasing the Sogdians across the plains with his entire army, he divided his troops into five fast-moving divisions so that he could strike the enemy in multiple places at the same time. The king put Hephaestion in charge of one division, Ptolemy another, his companions Perdiccas and Coenus the third and fourth, while he himself led the fifth group. There are few details recorded in the ancient sources describing the campaign that long summer, but we know the different forces split up and headed into Sogdiana to destroy any centers of resistance they could find and chase down the slippery enemy cavalry. The first goal they accomplished admirably, burning and ransacking villages across the land, but they were unable to catch Spitamenes. The wily Sogdian lord had retreated across the Jaxartes into Scythia along with his troops.

As the months went by, the king may have thought he had pushed the Sogdian leader permanently into hiding, but Spitamenes soon showed he knew the value of patience. While Alexander and his divisions were distracted in Sogdiana, Spitamenes led his men across the Jaxartes all the way to the Oxus and into Bactria. With his Sogdian cavalry and hundreds of Scythian allies, he attacked one of the Bactrian forts and caught the Macedonian defenders completely off guard. He captured the outpost, killed the defenders, and took the commander hostage. Then Spitamenes moved to the key Bactrian town of Zariaspa, where Alexander had established his winter headquarters a few months earlier. He was unable to take the protected city, but he ravaged the surrounding area and carried off plenty of booty. The king had left only a skeleton defense in Zariaspa, mostly men recovering from their wounds along with some mercenaries, royal pages, and a few noncombatants, including Aristonicus, a harpist who had served in the Macedonian court since Philip's day. These men were so incensed by the raid that they gathered together as many horses as they could find and set off to attack the Sogdians. They managed to surprise an isolated group of the raiders and killed quite a few, collecting the loot they had stolen before heading back toward the city. They were brave men, but lacking effective leadership they were easy prey for Spitamenes once he heard the news. The Sogdian lord ambushed them outside the city and slew almost everyone, including Aristonicus. Alexander later ordered a statue erected in honor of the bard at Delphi portraying him with a harp in one hand and a spear in the other.

The king was still far away, but Craterus set out after Spitamenes when he heard about the ambush and chased the Sogdians and their Scythian allies out into the steppes. It was a risky move to enter the plains where the enemy felt so at home, but Craterus and his men overtook the raiders and killed more than a thousand of the Scythians, though Spitamenes once again disappeared into the steppes.

At the end of the summer, Alexander left his lieutenant Coenus in northern Sogdiana with a large cavalry force to protect the province and—hoping against hope—to capture Spitamenes if he continued his raids into the winter months. Then the frustrated king returned to Samarkand to rest and catch up on administrative matters throughout his empire. Once again he was no closer to a solution of the Sogdian situation than he had been the previous autumn. He had spent two full campaigning seasons in the lands between the Oxus and Jaxartes without bringing stability to the region. He was desperate to move on to India, but he could not leave his northeastern frontier unsettled with a clever enemy like Spitamenes ranging through the province at will. He had to find a way to defeat the man, but in spite of his best efforts and gifted generalship, he had at last met a foe he could not beat.

The Trojan War began when the goddess Strife rolled an apple into a banquet held by the gods. The message on the apple said it was for the most beautiful, leading to a quarrel among three goddesses, the judgment by young Paris, and the kidnapping of Helen from Greece. Now in distant Samarkand, an apple was again the cause of anger, death, and bitter regret. Alexander had set up an extensive postal service throughout his empire to deliver letters and orders, but on occasion the service also brought luxuries from home. On this autumn day, a shipment of fruit arrived all the way from Greece. Among the goods were beautiful apples that so impressed the king he sent for Cleitus to come and share them with him. He had known Cleitus, nicknamed the Black, since he was a boy, when Cleitus' sister, Lanice, was Alexander's wet-nurse. Though not as old as Parmenion, Cleitus had been an officer in Philip's army and had also served Alexander in various senior posts since the expedition began. Alexander had always liked and trusted Cleitus, in spite of his being part of the old guard faction of conservative Macedonians, all the more so since he had saved the king's life on the battlefield at the Granicus River.

Cleitus was in the middle of a sacrifice when he received Alexander's message, but one did not ignore a summons from the king and so he left the altar. The sheep he was about to offer to the gods had already been prepared with libations poured over them, but sheep being sheep, they blithely followed Cleitus as he made his way toward Alexander's tent. It must have been an amusing sight, but when the king heard of it he was horrified. Such occurrences were omens from heaven, so he called his soothsayers to ask what it meant. They declared that sacrificial sheep following so close behind Cleitus could only bode ill for the Macedonian officer. Alexander was greatly troubled now, as he had had a dream just two nights earlier that Cleitus had been seated in black robes beside Parmenion and his sons, all dead. He therefore ordered sacrifices to be made to the gods for the protection of his old friend.

After Cleitus washed up and joined Alexander in his quarters, a banquet began with the usual fine food and excessive drinking. The war in Sogdiana had not gone well the previous two yeas and the Macedonian officers, including the king, had been seeking solace in wine even more than usual. That night one of the court bards had composed a song satirizing the Macedonian generals who had failed to capture Spitamenes—carefully omitting the fact that Alexander had been equally unsuccessful in his attempts. The younger offices and the king delighted in the verses, laughing and encouraging the poet to continue. But the older officers were insulted as the song went on and grumbled among themselves that they were being blamed for an impossible situation. Some of Alexander's sycophantic companions even began to insult his father, Philip, saying his son was an incomparably better soldier.

Cleitus at last rose to his feet, as drunk as everyone else, and declared that it was shameful, even in jest, to insult loyal Macedonian soldiers in front of barbarians. Persians and the other foreign rabble at the king's table were laughing at his friends, far better men than any of them. Alexander was amused, still seeing the whole affair as a harmless diversion, and teased Cleitus that he was just offering excuses for himself and his failure to capture Spitamenes, blaming his own lack of success on ill fortune instead of cowardice. Cleitus exploded at this and asked if it was his cowardice that had saved the king's life at the Granicus or perhaps the king had forgotten all the Macedonian blood spilled so that he cold turn his back on Philip and claim an Egyptian god as his father?

Now Alexander was truly angry as the mood in the tent turned to ice. He accused Cleitus of trying to stir up factions in the court, Macedonians against foreigners. Cleitus shot back that it was too late for that, since loyal Macedonians were already second-class soldiers who had to beg some Persian chamberlain for an audience with their own king! Alexander then lunged at Cleitus, but both men were restrained by their friends before they could come to blows. The king apologized to some Greeks standing near him for the crude behavior of his Macedonian officers, but Cleitus roared back that he should speak freely to all his guests, not just those toadies who bowed and scraped before him and his fine Persian clothes.

Alexander lost control at this point and looked around for a weapon. Not seeing his sword—a prudent bodyguard had hidden it when the trouble began—he grabbed one of the imported apples and threw it at Cleitus. Still looking for his sword, the king raged and called out in the Macedonian dialect to sound the alert and summon his guards. The trumpeter was still sober and bravely refused, earning himself a beating from Alexander. But Cleitus would not back down and continued to hurl insults at the king. As he was dragged from the tent by his friends, he shouted at the king a line from the playwright Euripides:

Oh, how rotten things are in Greece . . .

Alexander, who knew Euripides well, would have had no trouble filling in the rest of the speech:

> . . . when the army sets up trophies of victory over the enemy,
> but the people don't give credit to those who did the work.
> Instead the general receives the honor.
> He carries his spear as one among many,
> yet he did no more than a single soldier!

Cleitus was halfway out of the tent when he broke away from his companions and stumbled back in to continue his tirade against the king. But before he could say anything more, Alexander shook off his own bodyguards and grabbed one of their spears. He then launched himself at Cleitus and ran him through.

Almost immediately the king was filled with regret. He cried in agony that he had murdered his friend and pulled the spear from the dead body of Cleitus, bracing it against the floor so that he could throw himself on it. It was only the struggles of his friends and bodyguards that prevented the king from killing himself. They then dragged him to his quarters, where he collapsed in despair.

For three days Alexander lay on his bed weeping and lamenting Cleitus, refusing all food and drink. By now the army was becoming disturbed at the king's behavior. They were far from home in a dangerous land and needed firm leadership. If word got out that Alexander had lost his mind, they would be vulnerable to attacks on all sides, especially from Spitamenes. The prophet Aristander at last entered the king's quarters and assured him that the death of Cleitus had been foreordained long ago and that Alexander was merely acting as an agent of the gods' will. The king had always been susceptible to whatever nonsense this soothsayer conveniently revealed to him and so brightened a bit at the news. After this, Aristotle's nephew Callisthenes, the expedition historian, arrived and gently began to argue that the Cleitus affair was not as bad as it seemed. But then the philosopher Anaxarchus barged into the tent and demanded that Alexander stop behaving like a sniveling slave. He reminded he king that he was ruler of most of the known world and better start acting like it. Being a prince among men, he could do whatever he wanted to his subjects even if it meant skewering them with a spear when angry. That's the way things work, chided the philosopher, and if he wanted the respect of his army he had better pull himself together.

This Machiavellian advice was just what Alexander needed to bring him out of his depression. The king still felt horribly guilty and ordered that Cleitus be given a fine funeral, but he finally left his quarters and took up leadership of the army once again. The officers and men were greatly relieved, but they were deeply troubled as well. In spite of the extenuating circumstances of anger and drunkenness, the fact remained that Cleitus—one of Alexander's most loyal and faithful friends—had been murdered by the king because he dared to stand up to him and say what was on the mind of many of the Macedonian soldiers. Each of them must have wondered who would be next.

In spite of the gloom at Alexander's camp, events in the field were looking up for the Macedonians. Spitamenes was starting to feel hemmed in by Alexander's garrisons scattered throughout the land, so he once again retreated to the borders of Scythia. There he recruited three thousand Scythian horsemen for a raid into Sogdiana. He expected it would be a quick and easy strike into his homeland since all the Macedonians were settled for the winter at their camps, but he did not reckon on the daring of Alexander's lieutenant Coenus. Instead of fruitlessly chasing Spitamenes once he had already launched his raid, Coenus used his local intelligence network to get word of the strike before it happened and rode out to intercept the raiders. He surprised them on their own ground and killed more than eight hundred of them in battle. This defeat was enough to shift public opinion in the enemy camp. The Sogdians deserted Spitamenes, as did most of his Bactrian followers, who surrendered themselves to Coenus. The Scythians in his army remained loyal, but they plundered the baggage train and rode with the Sogdian lord into the steppes.

When the end came for Spitamenes, it arrived from a most un-expected source. He was cunning and resourceful, but his weakness was, as the Roman historian Curtius puts it, an *immodicus amor* for his wife. This immoderate love took the form of dragging her through the steppes and over mountains with him on his raids, whereas most Sogdian commanders would have left their wives at home. The poor woman was at the end of her wits after two years of such affection and begged Spitamenes to surrender himself to Alexander and trust in the mercy of the Macedonian king. She had borne him three children, she implored him, now grown into men. End this conflict and let them go home rather than wearing away their lives in a pointless war of at-trition against an unbeatable foe. But instead of giving in to her pleas, Spitamenes felt betrayed by his wife and pulled out his scimitar to kill her, only to be stopped by her brothers. He told his wife to get out of his sight, threatening her with death if he ever saw her again.

For a few days Spitamenes slept only with his concubines, but at last his love for his wife overcame him and he admitted her back into his good graces. She in turn declared that her earlier outburst had been due to her feminine weakness and that from now on she would be a submissive and dutiful wife. The Sogdian lord celebrated their rapprochement with a banquet, from which he was carried back to his tent roaring drunk. As soon as he was asleep, his loving and attentive wife took his sword and cut off his head. Then, with the collusion of a trusted servant, she wrapped it in a cloth and rode off to the Mace-donian camp. When they at last arrived, she went to Alexander's tent and told the guard she must speak to the king personally. Alexander saw her enter with a blood-spattered robe and presumed it was yet another local noblewoman complaining of abuse at the hands of his troops. When the woman called in her servant with the bundle and unrolled the wrappings, the surprised king saw the head and asked whose it was, the object being an unrecognizable mess at this point. When the identity was confirmed, Alexander was torn between relief at the death of his greatest enemy and shock that his wife would do this to him. He was grateful, but he sent the woman away lest she be a poor example for the women in his entourage.

At least that is the story according to Curtius. The version recorded by Arrian is a more plausible account of politics and betrayal. In this version the Scythians who had remained loyal to Spitamenes began to worry when they heard Alexander was coming for them. Their faithfulness was limited only by their devotion to saving their own skin, so they cut off their leader's head and sent it as a present to the Macedonian camp. Whichever account is true, resistance along the northern borders of Sogdiana fell apart with the death of Spitamenes. The Scythians sued for peace, as did the Sogdians, turning over to Alexander any of the officers of Spitamenes remaining in their territory.

The king wasted no time celebrating his victory as he wanted to settle affairs in the province quickly before he set out for India. He took his army into the mountains of eastern Sogdiana where some of the highland tribes still refused to accept his sovereignty. It was a strange winter among these peaks, with daytime thunderstorms turning to ice and snow at night. The hail was so heavy that the Macedonians used their shields to protect themselves. During one horrendous day, many of the soldiers became disoriented in the thick forest and almost two thousand died of exposure. The rest wandered aimlessly, hiding as best they could among trees to shelter themselves. Alexander went out like a shepherd, gathering those he could find and sending them to nearby mountain huts to thaw out. He found some frozen to trees, huddled together in death.

When he had collected all the soldiers he could find, he went back to his camp and collapsed on his throne in exhaustion. It was then that a young Macedonian infantryman more dead than alive stumbled through the door of his tent, not knowing where he was or whose quarters he had entered. The king leapt from his seat and led the poor man over to his throne to warm up by the fire. For a long time the man was in a stupor, but Alexander plied him with hot drinks and covered him with blankets. At last the soldier recognized the king and saw where he was sitting. He was horrified that he had taken the royal throne and jumped up in terror. Alexander calmed him and ordered him to sit down again. He then told the young man that he was lucky he had not seated himself on the throne of the Great King of Persia, for it would be a crime worthy of death. But here, it was just the chair of a Macedonian king.

Alexander gathered his men together to rest and warm their bones before he began the last push into eastern Sogdiana. There was a series of mountain fortresses in the region controlled by local lords who still held out against the king, hoping he would pass them by on his way to India. But Alexander hated to leave an enemy in a position of strength behind him, so he decided to take these citadels that winter no matter the cost. The first and most heavily fortified was a stronghold known as the Sogdian Rock on top of a mountain hundreds of feet high surrounded on all sides by precipitous cliffs. The tribesmen there had a secure source of water and enough food to survive a long siege. They were so confident of the impregnability of their fortress that they called down to Alexander saying he would never take the place unless his soldiers had wings.

This was just the sort of taunt that made the king more determined than ever to achieve his goal. He addressed the army and asked for volunteers to scale the mountain. Each man who made it to the top would receive a generous reward from the king. By now many of the soldiers were experienced in climbing difficult cliffs; three hundred stepped forward. They took with them only lengths of linen rope and their tent pegs to drive into the cliffs for handholds. They climbed through snow and ice at night on the unguarded, sheer face of the mountain. Thirty of them fell to their deaths during the ascent, their bodies lost in the crevices below, but by sunrise the rest were on top of a peak rising up just behind the fortress. Alexander then sent a message to the defenders saying they should turn around and look up, because he had found soldiers who could fly. The Macedonians above them grinned and waved linen flags. The tribesmen could not believe that anyone could have scaled their mountain and were so terrified that they surrendered without a fight. The other mountain fortresses of Sogdiana quickly gave up in turn when they heard the news. By spring, the whole province was in Alexander's hands at last.

Among the captives from the Sogdian Rock was the family of Oxyartes, a Bactrian nobleman who had fought against Alexander. One of his daughters was a maiden named Roxane, who seemed to the Macedonians to be the most beautiful woman they had ever seen. In spite of his tepid response to women in the past, the king was apparently smitten with the teenager and fell in love with her. He could have taken her as his prisoner to his bed whenever he wished, but he saw in Roxane something special and decided to make her his wife. Alexander had been turning down proposals of marriage for years, so one might wonder why he suddenly decided to marry a Bactrian woman at this point in his life. The answer is probably a mixture of politics and passion—two forces that are not necessarily mutually exclusive. Alexander was now twenty-eight years old, a king of many lands without an heir. As everyone around him had been saying for years, it was high time for him to get married and bring sons into the world. And as his father, Philip, had shown, there was no reason why a Macedonian king had to wed a bride from his own country. Alexander's own mother was a foreigner from Epirus. And again as with his father, there was also no reason Roxane could not be the first of many royal brides, including perhaps a proper Macedonian woman in time. There was also the matter of cementing alliances with an important Bactrian lord. Family ties were a sure way to bind Oxyartes and his family to Alexander, securing his hold on a restless land. It would also be a grand gesture to the natives of his empire that their new king did not think himself above marriage to one of his foreign subjects. It was important propaganda that could serve him well for years to come, even though the old guard among the Macedonians would grumble that the king was going native on them yet again. And there was love. Like many Greeks and Macedonians, Alexander preferred the company of men for his sexual affairs, but this did not mean he could not feel passion for women as well. The king, like most people in the ancient world, would have found modern distinctions of sexual orientation baffling.

And so Alexander, king of Macedonia and ruler of all the lands from Egypt to the Hindu Kush, married Roxane, daughter of the Bactrian lord Oxyartes, beneath a soaring mountain in the distant land of Sogdiana. According to ancient Macedonian custom, attendants carried a fresh loaf of bread before the couple, which the king cut in two with his sword and shared with his new bride. Oxyartes was present and surely thrilled at the prospect of calling Alexander his son-in-law. Persians, Lydians, Syrians, and Babylonians, along with soldiers and courtiers from the whole empire, rejoiced at the sight of their young king marrying a wife from the heartland of Asia. Only the Macedonian officers disapproved of the union, but they feigned pleasure and offered the king their warmest congratulations. Since the murder of Cleitus, they had learned to hold their tongues.

# 9

# INDIA

OF ALL THE PEOPLE OF THE KNOWN WORLD,
THE INDIANS OF ASIA LIVE FARTHEST TO THE EAST
AND THE CLOSEST TO THE RISING SUN. BEYOND
INDIA IS NOTHING BUT AN UNINHABITABLE
DESERT OF SAND.

—HERODOTUS

Alexander's wedding to Roxane in the seventh year of the campaign was only the first of several controversial steps the king took to unite the disparate factions of his empire as he prepared to move toward the borders of India. One of the most farsighted was his decision to train thirty thousand native youths from throughout the empire as Macedonian soldiers. This plan was motivated by necessity, since Alexander knew—even if most of his officers refused to accept the fact—that the small nation of Macedonia simply could not produce enough troops to control all the lands he had conquered and hoped to conquer yet. Like the Persians before him, the king realized that he needed to draw on the manpower of the many nations under his control to secure and expand his dominion. These selected youths would be taught the Greek language, equipped as Macedonian soldiers, and trained to fight as members of his army. They would not be foreign auxiliaries, as was common enough in the ancient world, but an integral part of the new Macedonian army, including leaders at the top levels. It was a boldly innovative plan beyond anything that had been attempted in military history. Alexander took pains to assure his current troops that this action would not lessen their importance, but they did not believe him for a minute. Anyone could see that the king was planning to turn the Macedonian army from a provincial into an international force. As the soldiers grew older and the new crop of native recruits came of age, the men who had fought with him for so long would be sent home to Macedonia with a bag of gold and a pat on the back. Their sons and grandsons would also serve under Alexander, of course, but as members of an imperial army of which Macedonians were just one part. Their future commanders would as likely be from Persia, Babylon, or India as Pella. It was a bitter blow to his loyal troops, officers and common soldiers alike, who did not share Alexander's vision of a new world empire.

But even more disturbing to many Macedonians was the immediate problem of homage before the king, a ritual known to the Greeks as *proskynesis*. Herodotus says that when two Persians met on the street, it was always possible to know their respective social status by watching how they greeted each other. Equals would kiss each other on the mouth, but a man of slightly lower rank would receive a kiss on the cheek from his superior. Persons of greatly inferior standing, however, would prostrate themselves on the ground before their betters. The same ritual applied to the Great King at court, though as he was superior to all others, it was expected that everyone would fall on the ground before him except a select few. Scenes from Persian art show high-ranking officials approaching the king on his throne and blowing him a kiss with their right hands, but most supplicants—and certainly all Greeks—were expected to fall on their faces before the awesome royal glory.

To Greeks and Macedonians, such degrading behavior before any king was inconceivable. Free Greeks did not bow down before kings, but only before gods. To fall prostrate on the floor before a man was the posture of a slave before his master or a worshiper before a divinity. Even in prayer, the people of the Aegean normally stood in reverence before the image of a god with no more than a slightly bowed head. The Persians did not view proskynesis to the Great King as an act of worship, but as a profound mark of reverence and submission to royal authority. The Greeks knew this, but they could never in good conscience bring themselves to perform such obeisance when they appeared before the Persian throne. One clever Theban envoy to Persepolis had once approached the Persian king and let his ring drop to the floor, then stooped to pick it up, excusing himself in his own mind that he had simply fallen to the ground to retrieve his personal property. Some Spartan visitors to the court at Susa, however, had been more obstinate. When the royal bodyguards told them to prostrate themselves, they refused. When the guards tried to push them onto the floor, they fought back, saying it was not their custom to fall down before any mortal man. Greek resistance to this Persian ceremony was deeply ingrained in the national psyche, so that many preferred to risk death rather than submit to such degradation.

But to Persians and others at the royal court, proskynesis was a normal part of protocol. From the first time they had come before Alexander, the Persians had fallen to the ground as an act of respect, in spite of the fact that the Macedonians looked upon their performance with amusement and contempt. This created an untenable situation for Alexander. His Asian subjects regularly performed proskynesis before him and refused to change their ways, while the Greeks and Macedonians treated the ritual as an impious and degrading barbarian observance. By the time Alexander was preparing for the invasion of India, he knew he had to resolve the situation. His hope was to introduce proskynesis gradually to the Macedonians, perhaps in a modified form, so that they would come to accept it as a purely ceremonial rite with no religious connotations. Alexander had no desire to be worshiped as a god by his countrymen or even enjoy the same elaborate court rituals that traditionally surrounded the Great Kings of Persia, but it was ridiculous and divisive to have half his court performing ritual obeisance before him and the other half treating it as a bad joke.

The king's attempt to introduce proskynesis among the Greeks

and Macedonians turned out to be a miserable failure, thanks largely
to the court historian Callisthenes. Callisthenes hated to lose an argument and took pride in portraying himself as the defender of liberty
in the face of Oriental despotism. Many among the old guard Macedonians admired his outspoken stance in favor of tradition because
he spoke what was on their own minds, but the historian mistakenly
believed he was untouchable. Even Aristotle had commented that his
nephew was a marvelous orator, but had no common sense.

Callisthenes sealed his fate one night at a banquet when Alexander tried to introduce a form of proskynesis acceptable to his
Macedonian officers and friends. The king passed a cup of wine to
his nearest dining companion, who then would bow down to a small
shrine of a god conveniently located just behind the king. Each guest
would then receive a kiss from Alexander and return to his place on
the dining couch. When it was Callisthenes' turn, he took the wine
but did not perform proskynesis to the shrine. Alexander was busy
talking with Hephaestion at the moment and did not notice, but one
of his friends pointed out the omission to the king. When Alexander
confronted him, Callisthenes impertinently responded that he would
do without a kiss.

Alexander had arranged the death of his greatest general and his
son, then killed one of his most loyal friends in a fit of anger. Callisthenes was a fool if he thought the king would hesitate to punish
a mere historian for such willful insubordination. But Alexander was
also shrewd and knew he could play on Callisthenes' vanity to hasten
his doom. He therefore challenged him to offer an impromptu ora-
tion in praise of Macedonian valor. Callisthenes was only too happy
to comply, lauding the glories of the sons of Macedonia while they
applauded and threw garlands at his feet. But then, to test his skills
in a time-honored fashion taught at all Greek schools of rhetoric, the
king asked him to take the opposite stand and denounce Macedonian
virtue. Callisthenes took the bait and responded with gusto, decrying
the faults of his hosts with biting recriminations. As Alexander's generals did not appreciate the nuances of Greek rhetorical performance,
they took the criticisms at face value and grew furious at Callisthenes.

Thus with one stroke, Alexander succeeded in alienating him from his most ardent supporters. Now all he had to do was wait for the right time to silence Callisthenes forever.

The opportunity soon presented itself when one of the royal pages, a dull-witted young man named Hermolaus, concocted a plan to gain eternal fame by killing Alexander. The page had earlier offended Alexander when he killed a boar during a hunt ahead of the king, earning the boy a flogging. Hermolaus was humiliated and wanted revenge. Just as Pausanius had hoped to win fame by killing Philip years earlier, Hermolaus now wanted to make his mark on history as the assassin of a famous king. When he told some of his friends of his plan, the foolish youth was quickly betrayed and arrested. Alexander knew this was just a harebrained plot by a boy who should never have been a royal page in the first place, but he saw a perfect chance to rid himself of Callisthenes. Even though Hermolaus did not implicate the historian under torture, it was no trouble to entangle Callisthenes in the plot, given that he was friendly with all the pages. Before he knew it, Callisthenes was arrested and placed in chains with no objections from the old guard Macedonians he had so recently insulted. Some sources say he was immediately hanged, others that he died months later of disease, but all agree that his career as court historian met a fatal end on the borders of India. Nevertheless he had managed to prevent Alexander from permanently introducing the ritual of proskynesis among his Macedonian followers. In the end, the king decided it was not worth the trouble.

In the late spring of the seventh year after crossing into Asia, Alexander and his army left Bactria to begin the invasion of India. He crossed the mountains to the south in ten days, much faster than his trek north two years earlier by way of the Khawak Pass. He spent several days in the Alexandria he had founded north of the Kabul valley and replaced a governor there who had ruled poorly in his absence. It is easy to see Alexander as nothing but a general and conqueror as this is how he is usually portrayed in the ancient sources, but he spent a great deal of time fretting over the administrative details of his empire. Whether he always made wise choices is debatable. He was in the habit of choosing a governor for a city or province quickly, then replacing the appointee after he built up a glaring record of mismanagement. At Alexandria-in-the-Caucasus, he chose a solid Macedonian as the new ruler of the city, but almost as an afterthought selected a Persian named Tyriespis as satrap of the region. True to form, Alexander would replace Tyriespis two years later and execute him for corruption.

While he was still in Sogdiana, Alexander had sent messengers to the closest cities in India to summon the local kings to attend him and submit to his authority. These rulers met him as he moved east through the Kabul valley and pledged their allegiance. The ruler of the important Indian city of Taxila, just beyond the Indus River, was among them. He had no more love for Macedonians than he had for the Persians, but he saw an opportunity to use Alexander to help him defeat his enemies. To prove his sincerity to the Macedonian ruler, he presented him with twenty-five battle elephants to use in the upcoming campaign.

At this point, Alexander divided his army in two and sent Hephaestion with a considerable force along the relatively easy road east across the Khyber Pass with orders to subdue rebellious tribes along the way, and most important, to reach the Indus River as quickly as possible and build a bridge, as he had at the Euphrates, for the rest of the army to cross. The Indian kings and a large squadron of engineers accompanied his best friend on this route. Alexander himself took the remainder of the army northeast into the mountains on a circuitous trek to pacify the highland tribes of the eastern Hindu Kush. As usual, the young king delighted in taking on the most difficult tasks.

The expedition through the mountains took months of trudging over narrow trails and across raging streams. If there was an inaccessible fortress that refused to surrender to the Macedonians, Alexander took it, no matter how difficult. The records of this highland campaign tell the same story repeatedly—Alexander demanded the surrender of a town, the citizens refused, the Macedonians stormed the city after a great struggle, and the inhabitants were slaughtered. But there were variations in the routine from time to time. One day early in the march Alexander was shot in the shoulder with an arrow, adding to his many wounds. At another point he and his army were ambushed by tribesmen who charged out of nowhere just as the Macedonians were making camp for the evening, forcing them to withdraw to a nearby hill. But then Alexander struck back and pushed the warriors behind their city walls, having killed many of them. These were the toughest opponents the king faced on this campaign, but after four days of assaulting their city, he forced them to surrender and spared their lives on the condition they join his army as auxiliaries. They agreed, but when they tried to sneak away that night, the suspicious Alexander waylaid and killed them, then captured their city.

As he moved east through the towering peaks and beautiful forests of the Swat valley, the king continued to seize fortresses and force the submission of local tribes. But when he arrived at the town of Bazira, he found that the soldiers and townspeople had fled to a nearby mountain called Aornus. As with the defenders at the Sogdian Rock, the natives of the region believed this refuge was a perfect defense against invaders. It was surrounded by sheer slopes several thousand feet high with only one precipitous and well-defended path to the top. On the summit was a wide plateau suitable for growing abundant grain along with plentiful wood and a perennial water supply. The local guides with Alexander said that even Hercules had been unable to take the mountain on his travels. This was just the encouragement the king needed.

Unlike the Sogdian Rock, Aornus could not be taken by climbers but only by direct assault up the impossible path along a narrow ridge. The guides were able to lead Ptolemy and some troops to a part of the mountain that they could hold against the enemy, but the position was not secure enough for a direct attack against the main fortress. Ptolemy held the post against a fierce assault while Alexander and his engineers set to work building a road to the top. They were able to fight their way near the summit, but there was a steep ravine before the final approach that blocked their progress. The king ordered his men to cut thousands of stakes to hold the soil and began to extend a large mound of packed dirt hundreds of feet across the gap under constant fire from the defenders above. It took days of torturous effort, but at last they had constructed a narrow causeway. The astonished tribesmen sued for peace and offered to surrender the next day. But once again, the enemy tried to sneak away by night, only to find Alexander waiting for them. He killed many as they fled, while others fell over the cliffs, then the king stormed the walls and took possession of the mountain at last. Alexander was tremendously proud that he had managed to conquer a place that had defeated even Hercules.

The king turned south from Aornus and continued the march toward the Indus, finding time for a wild elephant hunt along the way. But his greatest surprise during the march came when he neared the town of Nysa. The local people and even the flora seemed strangely out of place in these mountains. The Nysians placed their dead in cedar coffins in the trees—some of which Alexander accidentally set on fire—and made wine from grapes, unlike other tribes in the area. The natives met Alexander and begged him not to harm their town as they were descendants of settlers that the god Dionysus had placed there generations before. Their prolific ivy, a plant sacred to Dionysus that grew nowhere else in the mountains, was proof they were a people blessed by the god. This was just the sort of story that appealed to Alexander. They showed the king the grove of Dionysus, covered with ivy, where Alexander and his soldiers decked themselves with wreaths and sung hymns to the god of wine. Although the divinity worshiped by the people of Nysa was more likely Shiva or another Eastern deity than a misplaced Greek god, Alexander accepted the tale and treated the natives kindly, taking their presence in those remote mountains as a sign that he had now arrived at the very limits of the ancient wanderings of Dionysus. This was proof in his mind that he was nearing the edge of the earth.

When he at last came down from the high mountains and arrived at the Indus, Alexander found that Hephaestion had finished a large pontoon bridge of boats across the wide river. On the other side was India, a mythical land barely known to the Greek world. The earliest stories of India in the West were brought back by a sailor named Scylax from Caria in Asia Minor. The first Great King Darius commissioned him almost two hundred years before Alexander to explore the Indus River in preparation for a Persian takeover. Scylax sailed down the Indus to the sea and then around the Arabian peninsula to Egypt. His work survives only in scattered fragments, but the intelligence he gathered allowed Darius to add the Indus valley to the Persian Empire as the twentieth satrapy. By the time of Alexander, Persian control of the Indus was only nominal, but Alexander considered it subject to the Great King and therefore part of the domain he had to secure.

A Greek physician also from Caria named Ctesias wrote briefly about India in a history of Persia just a few years after Scylax, drawing on the mariner's voyage and his own examination of Indian animals brought to the Persian court. His work likewise survives only in fragments, but Alexander would have read the complete accounts of both men. The king also would have been familiar with the references to India in Herodotus. The Greek historian did not visit India as he did Egypt and Babylon, so his account is limited and even more imaginative than usual. He described India as rich in gold, contributing more to the Persian treasury than any other province, but claimed the gold was dug from the ground by ants. He related that there were many nations living along the Indus who spoke different languages and had diverse customs. Some reportedly ate only raw meat, while others would never kill any animals. Herodotus also claimed that some Indians ate the bodies of their dead fathers as a sign of respect and were disgusted when they heard that Greeks cremated their dead. But the one constant thread regarding India in Herodotus and the other sources that Alexander would have read was that the country lay at the easternmost edge of the world, separated from the great encircling ocean by only a thin strip of desert. None of the ancient writers until the time of the Macedonian invasion had any idea that India extended far beyond the Indus.

Thus Alexander approached India believing that if he could conquer the valley of the Indus, his realm would reach the limits of the inhabited world. Just a short march across the desert and he would stand on the shore of the great eastern ocean. Some Greeks even believed that this sea could be glimpsed from the summit of the Hindu Kush. It must have been when the king of the Indian city of Taxila arrived at his camp in Bactria and began to speak of his country that Alexander learned just how wrong he had been. The Indian prince would have described to him the geography of the Punjab, the land of five rivers stretching like the fingers of a hand across the northern Indus valley. But then he would have told Alexander of the lengthy Ganges River flowing through a vast land beneath the Himalayan mountains down to a large gulf. Along the banks of the Ganges were ancient, powerful, and wealthy kingdoms. To the south of the Ganges was the enormous mass of the Indian peninsula stretching out into the ocean, with the fabled island of Taprobane (Ceylon or Sri Lanka) just off the southeastern coast. The king of Taxila would also have known of another immense peninsula beyond the mouth of the Ganges extending far into the southern sea toward fabulous islands where rare spices grew. It was probably also at this meeting that Alexander became the first man from the Aegean to hear about the Seres, or silk people, who lived between two great rivers in a distant land beyond the Himalayas. It must have been disorienting in the truest sense to Alexander to discover that his vision of the lands of the East was woefully inadequate. And yet, even if the edge of the world did not lie just days beyond the Indus, the idea of a whole new world of rich lands and prosperous kingdoms must have stirred his imagination and endless ambition.

Alexander and his army crossed the Indus on the bridge Hephaestion and his engineers had constructed by lashing together dozens of boats large and small and building a roadway on top. In this region of the world, where torrential monsoon rains flooded the lands each summer, permanent bridges were impracticable. After pausing to offer sacrifices and celebrate athletic contests as thanks for a safe transit of the river, they continued south to Taxila through the low hills. They were still several days away from the city when its king sent gifts of silver, cattle, sheep, and elephants to show his goodwill. The ruler of Taxila was not the same man Alexander had met earlier in Bactria but rather his son, Omphis, as the old king had recently died. The new king had shown as much as his father every sign of cooperating with the Macedonians, having supplied Hephaestion and his work crews with grain, though he surprisingly had not left his city to greet Alexander's friend personally.

As the Macedonians drew near to Taxila, Alexander was alarmed to see an army coming out to meet him. There were thousands of Indian troops in battle formation with decorated elephants so large they looked like moving fortresses. He immediately ordered his trumpeters to sound the call to arms and sent his cavalry to the wings to prepare for the coming attack. The surprised King Omphis saw what was happening and guessed that his grand display had been misinterpreted. He ordered his army to halt and he rode forward to meet Alexander with just a few men at his side. It was a tense moment, especially as neither king could speak the other's language, but eventually an interpreter was found and Omphis explained that he was merely greeting his new lord in the traditional Indian manner. The Indian king pledged his loyalty to Alexander and surrendered his kingdom to him. Alexander in turn gave back Taxila and the surrounding territory to Omphis.

Alexander rode into Taxila at the head of his army and inspected a major Indian city for the first time. It was a haphazard town of rough limestone and mud-brick houses lining irregular, wandering streets—more of an overgrown village than the capital of a wealthy kingdom. Still, what was lacking in architectural grandeur was made up for by the vibrancy of the people and hospitality of his host. Omphis entertained Alexander and his officers at a banquet for three days and presented the king and his companions with more gifts, including a fortune in coined silver. Alexander graciously thanked the king, but in a gesture of royal generosity returned everything to Omphis and added silver and gold vessels, Persian robes, and an astonishing amount of gold from the treasury. This prompted one of Alexander's Macedonian companions, Meleager, to congratulate the king for having traveled all the way to India to find a man deserving of so much money. Alexander took this sarcasm poorly, but after the death of Cleitus he had learned how to restrain himself, coldly telling Meleager that jealous men only tormented themselves. What his companion failed to appreciate was that Alexander was buying loyalty, a precious commodity in a land so far from the center of his empire. He needed to secure both Taxila and its king before he could move down the Indus. If it cost him a fraction of the vast treasure he had accumulated from the Persians, so be it.

Omphis was eager to be accommodating as he was in a permanent state of war with the neighboring kingdoms, including a powerful state to his south beyond the Hydaspes River ruled by Porus, king of an Indian people known as the Paurava. The young ruler of Taxila wanted to expand the borders of his own kingdom at the expense of Porus and was happy to use the gold and army of Alexander to accomplish his goal. His prospects seemed even more promising when an envoy Alexander had sent to Porus returned to Taxila. The Macedonian king had demanded that the Indian lord pay tribute to him and meet him at the borders of his realm when he moved south. Other local rulers had submitted, but Porus replied that he would not be giving Alexander any tribute, though he would be happy to meet him at the Hydaspes with his army ready for battle.

This was a serious blow to Alexander's plans for a quick and peaceful march through India. His intelligence network had already informed him that Porus had a large army, including more than a hundred war elephants. Alexander was confident he could beat such an adversary, but it would not be easy, especially as the monsoon had just begun. The Macedonians didn't mind rain, but they had never experienced anything like the deluge that poured on them from the Indian sky. Adding to their misery was the unbearable heat, creating the rare and thoroughly miserable sensation of being hot and wet at the same time. Day after day the rain continued with no respite. Streets turned to rivers, fields became lakes, and thick mud covered everything. The Indians were perfectly cheerful in the rain as the monsoon was essential for their crops, but the Macedonians began to despair that they would ever be dry again. The local people assured them that the rain would stop in a few months, but Alexander could not afford to wait that long. He appointed a Macedonian as commander of a permanent military garrison at Taxila—just in case Omphis wavered, in spite of the gold—and led his very wet army to the Hydaspes River.

Alexander and his soldiers marched south over a low range of mountains for several days until they suddenly came to a pass leading down to the plain of the Hydaspes. From this gap they first saw the vast Punjab plain, an utterly flat landscape stretching south and east all the way to the Ganges River. Below they could see the Hydaspes River, almost a mile wide, fast-moving and swollen by both the monsoon and the melting snows of the Himalayas. Porus was on the far side of this flood with an army smaller than that of Alexander, but the Indian ruler knew the territory well and possessed many trained elephants that would terrify any horses that approached.

Alexander took one look at the Hydaspes and sent Coenus back to the Indus to dismantle the pontoon bridge that Hephaestion had built and bring the boats to him in pieces. Meanwhile the king made camp on the north bank of the river and considered how he might cross such a stream undetected by Porus. He had to find a spot along the river that was out of view of the southern shore. After days of searching, his scouts located a likely place several miles to the east near where a ridge of mountains approached the Hydaspes. Across from this headland was a large island in the river surrounded by several smaller islands, all covered with thick trees that hid the north shore from the troops of Porus, constantly patrolling the opposite side. Alexander realized this was the perfect location to launch his amphibious assault, but he had to make sure the Indian king didn't know the attack would come so far to the east. To keep Porus guessing, Alexander ordered units of his army to move back and forth along the northern shore for many miles. He would shift troops to the west, then the east, then back again to his main camp. The Macedonians also built campfires along the river and made a point of being noisy as they went about their duties. The Indian troops across the Hydaspes were driven to distraction by this constant motion and eventually gave up trying to keep track of every movement of the Macedonian soldiers—just as Alexander intended. The king also ordered tons of grain from the surrounding countryside transported to his camp as if he planned to stay there until the autumn when the rain would stop and the river subside. He also announced to his troops—and to the Indian spies among them—that they would wait at least two months to move across the river. When Porus heard the report, he was unconvinced, but Alexander was not seeking to deceive the king as much as he was to keep him off balance.

When the ships were at last ready, Alexander left Craterus in charge of the main camp opposite Porus with a strong force and orders not to move unless the Indian king shifted east to the site of the upcoming crossing. Then in darkness Alexander led his toughest troops silently upriver to the embarkation point. He must have felt the heavens favored him as the normally steady showers had turned into a violent storm. The crashing of thunder and the pounding rain covered the noise made by the Macedonians as they prepared to launch the boats, though several were reportedly killed by lightning.

Thousands of troops slipped into the boats and began to paddle across the raging river and around the large island as best they could. When at last they reached land, they poured out of the landing craft ready to face Porus, only to find that in the darkness they had not reached the southern bank but one of the many smaller islands in the river. It was an absolute disaster as the storm was now breaking and the sun rising, leaving the Macedonians visible to the Indian scouts. With no time to lose, Alexander ordered his men into the deep channel separating them from the southern bank. The heavily armored soldiers were up to their necks in swift water and the cavalry horses could barely swim through the current, but at last they struggled out of the river onto land.

At this point word reached Porus that a large force of Macedonians was crossing several miles to the east, leaving the Indian king with a difficult decision. He could see that many of the enemy were still directly across from him in Alexander's camp. Was the eastern attack a ploy to draw him away so that the western force could cross and attack him from behind, or was it in fact the main thrust of the assault, outflanking him to the east? There was no time to send out more scouts, so Porus ordered his son upriver with a chariot brigade to prevent the landing if possible or delay it if not. Then he followed with the main force of his army, leaving only a small detachment with a few elephants behind to hinder the remaining Macedonians from crossing.

Porus was a brave and capable leader, but he was in an impossible situation. Outnumbered, he now found himself facing Alexander's superbly trained troops, who were so tired of being wet and miserable that they were ready to massacre every Indian they found. The one advantage Porus had was his elephants, who just as Alexander feared caused havoc among his cavalry and trampled his men. But by now the Macedonians had developed a defense against these creatures. Although it cost the lives of many of their countrymen, Alexander's troops would encircle an elephant and stab it with their long sarissa spears while the archers shot out its eyes. Then the maddened and blinded beast would charge wildly, as likely at friends as foes.

Alexander surveyed the Indian battle order and decided to deploy a classic envelopment tactic to surround the enemy troops. He sent his cavalry to the left and right with orders to come up behind the Indians while the main army attacked from the front. It was a brutal battle waged savagely in mud and blood with heavy casualties on both sides. At one point, Alexander was riding Bucephalas when the old horse was struck by a spear and mortally wounded. The king was too busy to mourn, so he switched to another mount and continued the fight. When the Indian lines began to break, Craterus quickly crossed the river and came up behind to cut off the Indians' retreat.

Only Porus continued the fight from the back of his giant elephant. Alexander so admired the man's courage that he sent a messenger to the king begging him to surrender and be spared. Unfortunately the envoy was Omphis of Taxila, whom Porus bitterly hated and tried to kill with a spear. Then Alexander sent another messenger who at last persuaded the Indian king to lay down his arms. As the two rulers met, the elephant Porus was riding knelt down in spite of its wounds

to allow the king to dismount. Alexander approached Porus and marveled at the stature of the man, more than six feet in height, as well as
his regal bearing even in defeat. Alexander asked how he would like
to be treated, to which Porus replied, "Like a king." The victor allowed
him to retire from the field to seek medical treatment, then gave him
back his kingdom, even adding nearby lands, much to the chagrin of
Omphis. The Macedonians held funeral rites for their dead, offered
sacrifices, and celebrated athletic games on the banks of the Hydaspes in honor of their costly victory. Then, in memory of Bucephalas,
Alexander founded a city near the site of the battle and named it for
his beloved horse.

Alexander meanwhile sent a work party into the mountains to cut
wood for ships. His plan was to build a great navy and sail down the
Hydaspes to the Indus, then follow the river to the sea, subduing
kingdoms along the way. As this grand construction project would
take weeks if not months, the king announced to his men that in the
meantime they would invade eastern India. His army still must have
believed that the great sea lay just over the horizon, even though by
now Alexander had learned the true extent of the Indian subcontinent. The problem was once again how to keep the troops moving.
This was especially challenging as the monsoon was still raging as
they moved into a region where the ground was so thick with snakes
that the men took to sleeping in hammocks like the locals. Yet the
king marched on with his loyal but increasingly disgruntled troops
behind him.

The westernmost tributary of the Ganges was two hundred miles
away, while the mouth of that great river system lay more than a
thousand miles to the east. Still Alexander was determined to lead his
army all the way to the Ganges delta, taking the rich kingdoms along
its banks. His first stops were the cities near the borders of Porus,
thirty-seven towns in the shadow of the Himalayan mountains. He
conquered these easily enough and gave them to Porus as part of his
expanded kingdom. Then he advanced to the Acesines, one of the
largest and swiftest rivers of the Punjab. He loaded his troops onto

their transportable boats and launched out into the stream, only to find that the current ripped many of the craft to shreds, drowning a number of his men. Afterward he moved forward to the Hydraotes River, just as broad as the Acesines but not as swift. The natives on the far bank put up only token resistance, then submitted to the Macedonians. But beyond the Hydraotes was the land of the Cathaeans, a warlike tribe with the city of Sangala as their capital. The Macedonians heard tales that the Cathaean widows were encouraged rather forcefully to burn themselves alive on the funeral pyres of their husbands, a suttee ritual reportedly initiated after one local woman poisoned her husband. These Indians placed wagons in front of their city to block the Macedonian charge and manned their walls to shower arrows and spears on the attackers. But Alexander's men were finally able to break through the brick walls and take the city by storm, aided by Porus, who had recently arrived with a brigade of elephants.

The king of the next country along the sodden march was Sopeithes, who wisely surrendered before the Macedonians drew near to his capital. Alexander gave him back his kingdom to govern in his name, then enjoyed the hospitality of the Indian ruler for the next few days. The unusual customs of the country surely reminded Alexander of Spartan society or the ideal city laid out in Plato's *Republic*. At birth, the children in the kingdom of Sopeithes were separated into two groups, the most fit and beautiful of which were carefully reared, while the rest were killed. As the survivors grew, they were placed in arranged marriages with those mates that would likely produce the finest offspring for the state. Sopeithes was also proud of the hounds raised in his land and gave Alexander more than a hundred of these animals, so fierce they were said to have tiger's blood in their veins. To prove this to his guest, the Indian king staged a fight pitting four of the dogs against a full-grown lion. The canines were winning when Sopeithes sent a servant in to cut off the right leg of one of the dogs that had a death grip on the lion. Alexander rose up to object, but the hound did not even flinch as its leg was severed, keeping its jaws clamped on its prey even while it slowly bled to death.

By now, after weeks of fighting their way across the Punjab, the ever-victorious Macedonians were starting to feel like Sopeithes' dog. Alexander pushed them on to the kingdom of Phegeus on the Hyphasis, the last of the great rivers of the Punjab. This Indian ruler also submitted and received back his throne, much to the relief of Alexander's soldiers, who had no desire for another battle in the rain. Alexander questioned Phegeus about the country ahead and learned there was a wide desert to the east, followed by a deep river leading to the Ganges. Beyond this was the great kingdom of the Gandaridae ruled by Xandrames, who reportedly possessed two hundred thousand infantry, twenty thousand cavalry, and four thousand war elephants. Alexander couldn't believe these numbers, so he sent for Porus and questioned him separately. Porus assured his new lord that the report was accurate, adding, however, that Xandrames was a lowly born son of a barber who had seized his throne through treachery and murder. This news only fired the desire of Alexander to march on and conquer lands no other Western ruler, not even the Great Kings of Persia, had dared to dream of. He reminded himself that the oracle at Delphi had said he was unbeatable and that Zeus-Ammon at Siwa had confirmed his rule over the whole world.

Alexander was so excited that he led his troops down to the banks of the Hyphasis to begin the crossing to the other side. He launched into a magnificent speech extolling the bravery of his fine Macedonians and their allies, enticing them with promises of spoils from the rich cities that lay ahead. There were armies and elephants to the east, of course, but they were nothing compared with what they had already overcome. Eight years ago, the king declared, we crossed the Hellespont together, then conquered Asia Minor, Syria, Egypt, Babylonia, Persia, Bactria, Sogdiana, and more. We have marched ten thousand miles and accomplished the impossible. There is no limit to what men of noble spirit can accomplish. All of Asia lies within our grasp if we press on a little farther. The eastern sea is there, just beyond the horizon, waiting for us to bathe our feet in its waters. Then we can return home, knowing that our new empire is secure and rejoicing that our names will live forever. Of course, if you want to stop here, you certainly can. You may run home and tell your children that you deserted your king in a distant land. But as for myself, I will go on even if I march alone. But those who come with me to the fabulously wealthy lands ahead will be the envy of all when they return home to live like kings.

This sort of speech had always worked for Alexander before, so he waited in anticipation for the rousing cheers he knew would follow. But to his surprise, there was a complete silence as his men hung their heads, not daring even to raise their eyes to look at their king. At last Coenus, Alexander's most senior surviving general, who had served him so faithfully as he had his father, Philip, before him, rose to speak. The old soldier spoke for the entire army when he told Alexander that they had been honored to follow him for so long amid all the toils and dangers they had faced together. But now they were exhausted and their spirits broken. So many of their friends had died, so many of those who survived bore the scars of battle. Their own clothing had worn away long ago so that now they were forced to wear Persian and Indian garments beneath their armor. They wanted to see their parents, if they were still alive, and to embrace their wives and children once more. He urged the king to return to Macedonia with them and lead back a new generation of soldiers, young men to follow him to the glorious victories that surely lay ahead. But as for themselves, they could go no farther.

Now a great cheer rose up from the army in support of Coenus as the men openly wept at the thought of going home. Alexander, however, was so furious that he dismissed the assembly and stormed off to his tent, not seeing even his closest friends for three days. He waited for his men to change their minds and come to him as they had in the past, begging him to forgive them, swearing that they would follow him to the ends of the earth—but no one came. At last the king had to accept that his dream of marching down the Ganges was dead. To save face, he held a public sacrifice to seek the counsel of heaven. After examining the entrails before them, the soothsayers wisely declared that the omens were poor for crossing the river. Alexander then stood before the army once again and declared that he would not fight the will of the gods as well as his men. They were all going home.

Before he left the Hyphasis, Alexander ordered his army to erect twelve towering altars, one for each of the Olympian gods. These were in thanksgiving to the gods for having carried him so far, but also as lasting memorials to his own accomplishments. Some stories say he also constructed an enormous fort with beds more than seven feet long and feeding troughs twice the normal size so that future generations of Indians would think the Macedonians and their horses were giants.

With a last wistful look to the east, Alexander began the long march back to Macedonia. They were still on the northern edge of India, more than a hundred miles from the fleet being readied on the Hydaspes. After that it was a voyage of almost six hundred miles to the sea. Alexander's plan was to conquer the remaining tribes of the Indus valley on his journey rather than return by way of Bactria. He must have used considerable charm and persuasion to convince his officers and troops that the fastest road home lay to the south. From a military point of view, it also made perfect sense to complete the conquest of western India. From the Indus delta he would send his fleet along the coast to rendezvous in Persia with the army he would be leading overland. This would close the great circle the king had begun when he left Persepolis four years earlier to chase Darius, but also give him the opportunity to establish a trade route between his provinces in India and the rest of the empire. What the troops did not know—and Alexander himself did not realize—was that some of the toughest fighting of the long campaign still lay ahead, as well as one of the most grueling desert marches in military history.

The journey back to the Hydaspes was uneventful, aside from the surrender of a few remaining Indian kings who decided that fighting was unnecessary now that the Macedonians were withdrawing. Alexander was also pleased with the arrival of a sizeable group of reinforcements who had journeyed all the way from Greece to join his army. These included thirty thousand infantry and six thousand cavalry, along with wagonloads of medical supplies and twenty-five thousand sets of armor inlaid with gold and silver from his treasurer

Harpalus. These were much appreciated by the men, whose original armor was falling apart. A sad note was struck by the sudden death of old Coenus. In spite of the timing, it is likely that he died of natural causes. In fact it may have been a sense of his approaching demise that had given Coenus the courage to face down Alexander at the Hyphasis.

When the army arrived back at the Hydaspes, the king was thrilled to see that the fleet was ready. There were more than a thousand ships prepared for the voyage, including large warships, horse transports, and cargo vessels. Alexander recruited the seafaring Phoenicians, Cypriots, Carians, and Egyptians in the army to serve as sailors and appointed his boyhood friend Nearchus as admiral. A few days later at dawn when everything was finally in order, Alexander sacrificed to Zeus and Hercules as well as to many other gods, including the divine powers ruling the rivers of India. He poured libations into the Hydaspes from a golden bowl, much as he had done in the middle of the Hellespont before crossing to Troy. There was not enough room on the ships for most of the army, so Alexander sent Hephaestion and Craterus to lead the rest of the men on opposite banks following the fleet. These two companions of the king had developed an intense mutual hatred and had even drawn swords on each other once, so Alexander considered it prudent to keep a river between them.

The departure was a great ceremony, with the ships moving in perfect formation down the wide stream with the sound of drums and oars striking the water. The local Indians had never seen such a spectacle and were especially impressed by the sight of horses riding in boats. The locals all came down to the banks to cheer the Macedonians and sing songs in celebration. Alexander was deeply touched by the beautiful farewell the Indians were giving him, taking it as a sign of their affection, but they were undoubtedly thrilled to see him and his army sailing away.

The first few days of the voyage south along the Hydaspes provided Alexander with a welcome opportunity to relax. With thousands of miles of marching behind him and constant life-or-death decisions to make, it was a rare luxury to sit on a ship gently drifting down a river in India. He passed some of the time listening to his old friend Aristobulus reading from a history of the expedition he was composing. The Greek writer was reciting aloud from a recent section he had composed on the battle against Porus. In his version, Alexander fought in glorious single combat with the Indian king and personally killed his elephant with a spear. The king grabbed the book and threw it into the river, saying he should toss overboard the man who wrote such nonsense as well.

After five days the Macedonian fleet came to the confluence of the Hydaspes and Acesines. Here the two wide, gently flowing rivers entered a single, narrow channel that produced swift currents and turbulent whirlpools. The sailors were accustomed to storms on the Mediterranean, but no one, least of all Alexander, had any experience running rapids. The small round ships used for transport managed well enough as they twisted and turned in the stream, but the larger warships were tossed like corks. They quickly turned sideways and ran into one another as their oars snapped off. Men that had faced barbarian warriors and trumpeting elephants with determined silence screamed in terror as they were thrown into the river, with many drowning in the roiling water. Alexander himself panicked when his flagship hit the rapids. He threw off his clothes and jumped naked into the swirling eddies even though he had never learned to swim. His friends leapt in after him and pulled him to shore, thankful they had been able to save his life. The king was so grateful to the gods for having spared him that he sacrificed to them as if he had just won a deadly battle. After a little rest he was even able to joke about the experience, boasting that he had now won a contest of strength against a river, just like his hero Achilles in the Trojan War.

After they had repaired the damaged ships, Alexander sent Nearchus ahead to the next river juncture while the king and most of the army marched overland to the realm of the Malli, one of the most feared tribes of the Punjab. These Indians had prepared for the arrival of the Macedonians by river, but in typical fashion Alexander snuck up on them from behind by crossing a waterless desert at night. He struck their first city by surprise while the few soldiers were relaxing outside the town, then stormed the walls and seized the citadel, killing all two thousand natives who had taken refuge there. Those few that had escaped to the nearby marshes were hunted down and slaughtered. A second and third city followed, with Alexander bravely—or recklessly—climbing the first ladder to reach the walls and personally leading the fight against the defenders.

The remaining Malli had all fled to the strongest of their cities to make a final stand against the invaders. Alexander arrived at the town near sunset and told his troops to rest in preparation for an assault at dawn. He divided his troops into two forces, leading the first himself and entrusting the second to his companion Perdiccas. The Indians were so terrified at the approaching army that they deserted their posts and retreated to the inner citadel of the city, leaving the outer walls unguarded. Most of the Macedonians thought they had taken the whole town as they poured through the gates only to see the natives holding a much stronger position at the central fortress. The soldiers tried to find a way into the citadel, but failed to breach the walls. Alexander soon became frustrated and grabbed a ladder himself, held his shield in front of him, and began to mount the wall. His attendant Peucestas went up behind him, carrying the sacred shield the king had taken from the temple of Athena at Troy. He was followed by two more men, Leonnatus his bodyguard—whom he had sent to console the women of Darius after the battle of Issus—and Abreas, a common soldier.

Alexander reached the top of the wall and stood there fighting off Malli defenders while his three companions scaled the ladder behind him. The rest of the soldiers below were so ashamed that they had allowed themselves to be left behind that they all clambered up the ladder at once, breaking it under their weight. This left the king and the three others who had made it to the top in a desperate struggle. Rather than remain a perfect target poised on top of the wall, Alexander decided to cast caution to the wind and jumped into the city. When the soldiers outside saw him disappear, they were horrified. Out of their sight, Alexander positioned himself with his back to a large tree and stabbed anyone who approached him. After he killed several defenders, the Malli backed away and formed a semicircle around him just out of sword range. The king then picked up stones lying on the ground and hurled them at anyone who dared to draw near. The natives countered by grabbing their own rocks and throwing them back.

At this point, the three companions who had made it to the top of the wall with Alexander saw what was happening and leapt down themselves into the fray to defend the king. Abreas was killed almost immediately by an arrow in the face. Then Alexander was struck by an arrow shot at close range that penetrated his armor and went into his chest, puncturing a lung. He continued to defend himself, but he was bleeding so profusely and struggling so hard to breathe that he collapsed onto the ground. Leonnatus took up position on one side of the king while Peucestas held the Trojan shield above him to ward off the stones and arrows that rained down on them.

The Macedonians outside the walls were meanwhile frantically trying to find a way into the citadel. Some stuck pegs into the mud bricks and climbed the wall like a mountain cliff. Others stood on the shoulders of their comrades to reach the top, while more pushed on the gate until the bar holding it finally snapped. When they at last reached Alexander, they found him in a pool of blood beneath the tree with Peucestas still standing over him. The soldiers were not an educated lot, but they knew battlefield injuries and could see that the king was critically, perhaps mortally, wounded. In their fury they turned against the Malli inside the citadel and cut down every man, woman, and child.

Alexander was carried to his nearby ship, where some sources report that Critodemus, a physician from the Greek island of Cos and a descendant of the legendary healer Asclepius, removed the arrow. Others say that no doctor was available, so that Perdiccas cut out the projectile with his knife. In either case, the king began to hemorrhage profusely when the arrow was finally removed and slipped into unconsciousness. Rumors ran through the army that Alexander was dead, so that wailing and lamentation echoed through the camp.

Once again the men began to wonder who could lead them home if the king died. Deep in enemy territory as far from Macedonia as anyone could imagine, the situation seemed hopeless to the distraught soldiers. As the days passed with no word, the army fell into despair. Finally the command staff announced that the king was alive and would soon make an appearance, though most of the men thought this was a lie to cover up the fact that Alexander had already died. Then at last the curtains on the ship opened and the army watched as the motionless body of the king was carried on a litter down the ramp. He seemed dead to all who were standing on the shore, but the moment the litter reached the bank Alexander held up his hand and waved to the crowd. Shouts and cries were raised to heaven while some of the toughest fighters in the world broke down and wept like little children at the sight of their king still alive. Alexander's officers had brought another litter to transfer him to the dock, but instead the king ordered a horse led forward. In what must have been one of the most courageous acts of his life, the still gravely injured king pushed his friends away and climbed slowly up onto his horse to reassure his men that he was fine. The army was beside itself with joy, clapping in unison and showering Alexander with the fresh flowers that were blooming all around them. Men strained to touch even the hem of his garment as he rode through the ranks. Then with the greatest of efforts, he dismounted and walked under his own power into his tent to collapse onto his bed.

Once he had regained some of his strength, his officers began to chide him that his performance on the wall was a brave but foolish act for a king. It was not the job of a commander, they said, to risk his life in such a way when there were plenty of men in the army who could do the same thing. Alexander did not know how to tell his friends that for him such actions were an essential part of being a king. Faced with such criticism, he walked out of his tent into the camp. A grizzled veteran from Boeotia in central Greece who had heard about the rebukes of Alexander's companions approached him. The man looked the king straight in the eye and said just a few words in his rural dialect—"Alexander, brave deeds are what true men do."

The king embraced the old soldier and considered him a friend for the rest of his life.

Alexander's often brutal campaign in India did not hinder his ongoing fascination with native religions. As early as his visit to Taxila he had gathered together Indian wise men to question them about their beliefs. The king was fortunate to visit a land with such a rich collection of religious traditions. Some aspects of Indian religion, such as belief in a multitude of gods, would have been familiar to anyone from the Mediterranean world, but many of the ideas he encountered would have been quite puzzling to Alexander.

Followers of the native Jain tradition sought to release the soul from the cycle of pain and reincarnation through the practice of asceticism. The most devout became monks who wandered naked through the land owning nothing but a small pot for washing. All Jains sought to follow the teachings of masters from the past who had achieved enlightenment. The latest had been Mahavira, a former warrior who lived along the Ganges two centuries before Alexander. Other Indians were devotees of a teacher named Siddhartha Gautama, who had lived near the Himalayas at about the same time as Mahavira. Siddhartha had been born a prince, but had abandoned his previous life when he first encountered old age, disease, and death. Underneath a bodhi tree he gained enlightenment and release from the cycle of rebirth, becoming the Buddha—literally "the one who is awake"—and devoting himself thereafter to guiding his followers along the path of escape from suffering and rebirth. There were also many religious traditions known under the collective term of Hinduism that traced their origins to the arrival of the Aryan tribes in India many centuries before. These invaders brought with them the hymns of the Vedas and many gods similar to the Persian pantheon, but their beliefs were also shaped by contact with the rich traditions of the natives they met in their new land. Hindus worshiped Vishnu, Brahma, Shiva, and many other deities, but shared with Jains and Buddhists the desire to attain release from the endless cycle of reincarnation.

To Alexander, the teachings of these spiritual masters—lumped together by the Greeks as *gymnosophistai*, or "naked wise men"— seemed most like those of Diogenes, the Cynic philosopher, whom Alexander had met living in his jar in Corinth ten years earlier. One story tells how Alexander met a group of these religious teachers living under the open sky in a meadow. When he approached them, they stood and beat their feet on the ground. Alexander asked them through an interpreter what this action meant and was told that each man alive holds no more earth than he stands on. They urged him to remember that even though he was busy conquering the world, one day he too would die and possess no more land than that which held his bones.

Two of the most venerated Indian religious teachers in the region were Dandamis and Calanus, who each lived quietly by themselves in the forest. Alexander sent Onesicritus—a follower of Diogenes and one of his resident philosophers on the campaign—to find and question them. Dandamis received his visitor warmly and asked about famous Greek philosophers. Onesicritus explained the teachings of Socrates, Diogenes, and Pythagoras (who also believed in reincarnation) to Dandamis, but the wise man said that although each had his good points, they seemed too concerned about following rules. When Onesicritus reached Calanus, the Indian teacher yelled at him to take off his clothes and sit naked before him or he would say nothing, even if Zeus himself sent him. Onesicritus did so and listened to his teachings, then persuaded Calanus to return with him to visit Alexander. When he arrived, the king asked him how best to govern an empire. The holy man threw an ox hide on the ground and pressed down on one edge, only to have another rise up. Then he stood in the center so that the whole hide lay flat—the lesson being that Alexander should stay close to the center of his realm and not wander about the borders. The king was so impressed by Calanus that he invited him to accompany him on the remainder of the expedition. Although the other Indian wise men disapproved of such involvement in secular affairs, Calanus accepted his invitation.

Alexander ordered even more boats constructed during his conva-
lescence to carry his troops the remainder of the journey down to
the sea. When these were ready, he once again loaded thousands of
his men on board while the rest marched along the banks. The wide
Acesines was joined a few days later by the Hyphasis flowing in from
the east, then at last the fleet entered the Indus. At this final juncture
of the rivers, the king founded another Alexandria with expectations
that it would one day grow into a city known throughout the world.
He constructed dockyards and laid out streets, then left behind troops
to garrison the new metropolis, including many veterans from the
mountains of Thrace who would live out their lives far from home on
the banks of the Indus.

The army then drifted along the broad plains for several weeks in
relative peace until it came at last to the kingdom of Musicanus just
above the Indus delta. This local king surrendered and once again Alexander gave him back his realm to rule in his name. Things did not
go so well, however, at a nearby land ruled by a king named Sambus.
One of his towns was a holy center of the Brahmins, the priestly caste
of India. These religious leaders urged resistance against the Macedonians and sent warriors into battle with weapons smeared with a
poison derived from dried snake venom. The drug caused sharp pains,
convulsions, and a horrible, lingering death. The king's friend Ptolemy
was one of the many dying from the poison when Alexander reportedly had a vision of a local plant that could counteract the drug. He
plastered it on Ptolemy's body, then ground up the rest in a drink for
his friend, which cured him. Alexander continued the war against the
city of the Brahmins, who had now been joined by Musicanus, sens-
ing that the Macedonians were at a disadvantage. Alexander quickly
dispelled this notion by storming the city and hanging Musicanus
and the leading Brahmins as rebels.

At last the army arrived at the city of Patala, where the Indus split
into two branches, both flowing through an enormous delta into the
great southern sea. The king found the city deserted, but was eventually able to persuade the local inhabitants of his goodwill so that
they returned from hiding in the nearby countryside. Here Alexander

split his army into three parts. The first, under Craterus, would march northwest overland back to Kandahar and join Alexander in Persia. He would take with him all the elephants and the Macedonian veterans soon to be decommissioned. The second group, under Nearchus, would sail the fleet along the coast all the way to the Persian Gulf once the winds were favorable. The king himself would lead the main force of the army back to Persepolis by a southern route through the Gedrosian desert.

Though he was nearing the end of his Indian campaign, Alexander could not resist one final bit of exploration. He sailed down one branch of the Indus and anchored not far from the ocean. There the king and his men received a shock when over a period of just a few hours the sea surged many feet and damaged their ships. Alexander had never heard of tides. In the Mediterranean, the sea rose and fell each day only a few inches at best, so even educated men had no idea that along a sea coast the water could ebb and flow so rapidly. But after repairing his ships and bracing himself for the twice-daily repetition of this strange phenomenon, he continued his journey down to an island called Cilluta at the mouth of the river. From there he proceeded to another island in view of the open sea. Alexander and his men gazed in wonder at the vast ocean before them—a sight few from the Aegean world had ever beheld. But this was not enough for the king. Taking a single ship, he sailed many miles out into the ocean to see if there were any more lands to conquer. When he was finally convinced that nothing lay beyond, he sacrificed to Poseidon and cast a golden bowl into the waters in thanksgiving to the gods for having brought him to the very edge of the world.

# 10

# BABYLON

As he crossed the Tigris River with his army
on the way to Babylon, Alexander was met
by the Chaldean soothsayers who drew him
aside from his friends and begged him, for
his own sake, not to continue the march
to the city.
—ARRIAN

The monsoon rains had returned to India in the months it took
Alexander and his army to descend the Indus and conquer the
land. Craterus had already left with many of the Macedonian veterans
and elephants to return to Persepolis along a northern route. Now after
ten years in Asia, the king himself was anxious to begin the journey
back to Persia, but the fleet under Nearchus was not able to leave the
Indus River port of Patala for the long voyage to Mesopotamia until
the winds were once again favorable. The impatient king therefore
bade good-bye to his old friend with careful instructions to explore the
northern shore of the great ocean and look for rendezvous points along
the coast where Alexander's army would have dug freshwater wells for
the sailors and where his own men would receive much needed food
supplies from the ships. It was to be a carefully coordinated land-sea
journey with both components dependent on the other for survival.

Alexander knew the march ahead through the Gedrosian desert would be extremely difficult for his army, but he was determined
nonetheless to lead his men through one of the most desolate land-
scapes on earth. Some scholars, ancient and modern, have suggested
that the king wanted to punish his soldiers for forcing him to turn
back from the conquest of the Ganges valley. By this line of reasoning, Alexander was deliberately trying to kill off his army in the wilderness that lay ahead. This was certainly not his intention. Alexander
could be petty and vindictive, but it is unreasonable to suggest that
he wanted to eliminate the very force that made it possible for him
to create and control his empire. The answer to the mystery of the
Gedrosian desert journey is plainly stated by the historian Arrian and
is perfectly consistent with what we know of Alexander from other
episodes in his life. First, as a practical matter, he wanted to keep
in close contact with the fleet as it moved west through the Indian
Ocean. The exploration of the coast and the opening of a trade route
between India and Persia was an essential part of his future plans. But
second, and perhaps even more important, Alexander wanted to lead
his army across the Gedrosian desert because no one had ever done it
before. There were stories that the Babylonian queen Semiramis had
once brought an army back this way from India, but only twenty of
her men survived the journey. The first Great King Cyrus had reportedly tried the same route, with only seven of his soldiers living to
tell the tale. The historical accuracy of these tales is doubtful, but the
challenge they would have stirred in the imagination of Alexander
was real enough. If he could bring his army back from India through
the wastelands of Gedrosia, it would be a story of glory that would
live forever. To Alexander, that was reason enough.

More than fifty thousand Macedonian and allied soldiers left
the Indus River in late summer accompanied by a vast train of camp
followers, including most of the women and children who trailed
after the army wherever it went. The land and climate were pleasant enough at first as they moved west along the shore and over low
mountains into the territory of the Arabitae. Alexander sent parties
to dig wells for the fleet on the shore and took time to launch a series

of surprise attacks on natives in the area who had not yet submitted to his authority. After two weeks he arrived in a well-watered valley near the coast that was the home of the Oreitae, who fled at his approach. Their chief village of Rhambacia was a promising site for a trading post and colony, so Alexander left Hephaestion behind to establish it as another Alexandria—the last such city he would found in the East.

The king discovered the natives hiding in the hills to the west of their home waiting to attack the Macedonians. But when Alexander brought forward just a small force to meet them, they immediately deserted their posts and sent their leaders forward to surrender on their behalf. He accepted their submission and assured the natives that they would be allowed to live in peace in their own land under the rule of a Macedonian satrap and garrison. The king also left behind his companion Leonnatus to await the arrival of the fleet and clean up any remaining resistance in the area. By this point, Hephaestion had caught up with the army as the men left the mild valley of the Oreitae and began the trek west into the desert.

Gedrosia, straddling the border of modern Iran and Pakistan, was the poorest and least hospitable of all the provinces of the Persian Empire. It consisted of little more than an arid wilderness of salt flats surrounded by mountains too dry to support agriculture. Only the Phoenician traders traveling in the army's wake seemed impressed by what the desert had to offer. There were unusually tall myrrh trees in scattered locations that yielded priceless gum, which the merchants loaded onto their pack animals. They also gathered ginger grass, though most of it was crushed by the feet of the passing army, leaving a delightful fragrance wafting over the countryside. The soldiers were able to dine well at first on rabbits that snared themselves in the plentiful thornbushes as they fled from the army, but soon even these were left behind. The few natives who lived in Gedrosia clustered along the seashore and lived a life as primitive as anything the Macedonians had ever seen. They were called the Ichthyophagi, or Fish Eaters, because their only nourishment came from whatever small fish they were able to collect offshore and dry in the sun. These natives let their hair grow into long mats and never trimmed their nails. Their clothing was made of fish scales and their primitive houses of shells and skins stretched over whale ribs. The Fish Eaters were so destitute that Alexander didn't even bother to plunder their villages for supplies.

But as there was still no sign of Nearchus and the fleet along the coast, Alexander began to despair. There was not enough food for the army without the supplies brought by sea. After the grain supply was gone, men began to eat their pack animals. The king sent messengers on racing camels to the nearby satrapies with orders to dispatch provisions to him as quickly as possible, but the distances were too great for these calls to be easily answered. When the water ran out, the soldiers were totally dependent on whatever oases they could find in the desert, though these were few and far between. Once a waterhole was discovered, the first men there would rush in and drink all they could scoop into their hands, becoming sick from overdrinking and fouling the water for the rest of the army. Thereafter Alexander made a rule that every camp would be at least two miles from a water source and access strictly limited.

As days turned into weeks, men began to fall by the wayside by the hundreds, then thousands, from sickness, heatstroke, and thirst. Many simply gave up and refused to rise from their bedrolls. Those who pulled themselves together after the army departed would try to follow in the tracks of their companions, but most of these were lost in the desert just like men fallen overboard into the sea.

One night the army made camp in a dry riverbed with a welcome trickle of water running through the sand. But as darkness fell, a wall of water suddenly coursed down the stream from a thunderstorm in the distant hills. The flash flood caught the soldiers by surprise, but most were able to escape, though many with only their weapons at hand and the clothes on their backs. The civilians were not so fortunate. Most of the women and children who had dragged themselves on this hellish trek through the wilderness had no time to flee and were drowned in the very water they so desperately craved.

Toward the end of the march, when officers and men alike had all but given up hope of escaping the desert alive, some scouts found a small spring with only enough water to fill a single helmet. The patrol was so thankful that they had found even this that they brought it before Alexander, who was as thirsty as anyone. As wretched as his own state was, however, he knew his men were suffering even more. Therefore, just as he had done in the desert crossing in Bactria four years earlier, Alexander refused to drink when his army could not. He took the helmet of precious water and poured it on the ground in full view of his army. To the parched men, for their king to share in their suffering in this way meant more than the water soaking into the sand. They were so heartened, says Arrian, it was as if they had each drunk every drop that he poured on the ground.

Alexander then turned back to the sea in one final attempt to find water and rendezvous with the fleet. The ships were nowhere to be seen, but the army was able to dig wells along the shore for their own needs and travel for a week with adequate water supplies. At last the king realized in shame that his fleet must have been lost somewhere along the trackless shore of the southern sea. He had failed Nearchus and condemned his whole navy to death. The army that had followed him through the desert for two months was little better off. Perhaps half his soldiers had perished in the sands of Gedrosia and almost all the civilians had been lost. He then led the men in a final push north away from the sea more than a hundred miles to the provincial capital at the shabby frontier town of Paura on the road to Persepolis. The emaciated and exhausted Macedonians who stumbled through the gates of the city must have been a frightening sight to the natives, who nevertheless welcomed them in peace and provided them with food, water, and much needed rest.

The final leg of the journey from Paura to Persepolis was almost five hundred miles long, but the countryside, while still arid, promised a steady supply of food and water for Alexander's remaining troops. Several ancient authors report that the king was so relieved after his march through the Gedrosian desert that he led his army along the road as in a Dionysian parade with pipes playing and soldiers bedecked with garlands. Alexander also held festivals and contests to celebrate their crossing, including a singing and dancing competition won by the Persian eunuch Bagoas, who had been one of the king's lovers since they had departed from Persepolis several years earlier. After the contest, Bagoas in full costume marched through the theater and sat down at Alexander's side, to the delight of the army. The men shouted and called loudly on the king to kiss the winner, which he gladly did.

Alexander was now back on the edges of civilization and could turn his mind to matters other than mere survival. It had been five years since the Macedonians had left the heartland of Persia for the campaign in the eastern provinces. Many of the governors and officials Alexander had left behind doubted he would ever return—most, in fact, hoped he would not. Reports began to reach the king that his appointees had taken advantage of his long absence to set themselves up as virtually independent rulers in their satrapies, indulging in extravagant lifestyles and enforcing their will with private militias. Alexander spent the next few months purging his empire of corrupt officials—natives, Greeks, and Macedonians alike—including his old friend Harpalus. This unregenerate shyster had been given charge of the treasury and squandered countless talents of gold on exquisite luxuries and expensive women. He imported rare delicacies from distant lands for his table and bought celebrated Athenian courtesans for his bed. When news reached him that a very angry Alexander was on his way back to Persia, he panicked and fled to Athens with six thousand mercenaries and all the money he could load onto a fast ship. Demosthenes and his anti-Macedonian allies in the Athenian assembly were at first reluctant to risk the wrath of Alexander by granting refuge to Harpalus, but a generous bribe convinced them it was worth the consequences. But when one of Alexander's admirals showed up beneath the Acropolis to demand his extradition, the Athenians had Harpalus arrested, though they did keep his money. He soon escaped and made his way to Crete, where he was murdered by Macedonian agents.

While Harpalus was still in flight to the Aegean, Alexander and his army made their way through the land of Carmania near the

Straits of Hormuz at the entrance to the Persian Gulf. Here Craterus arrived at last with his veterans and elephants safely in tow after the march along the northern route from India through Kandahar and eastern Persia. It was also near the straits that a small party of filthy, sunburned men arrived at the edge of Alexander's camp with long hair and clothes covered in brine. No one recognized them at first, though they carried themselves like Macedonian officers. The leader then spoke in a raspy voice and declared that he was Admiral Nearchus, just arrived from India, and asked to be led to Alexander himself to tell his tale.

The story of the voyage of Nearchus is one of the best-preserved travel accounts from ancient times, largely because the log of the expedition was copied almost word for word by the historian Arrian. Nearchus and his fleet left the Indus River port of Patala in September, several weeks after Alexander had departed by land. The monsoon rains were still falling, but the admiral was eager to catch up with the army and decided to risk travel in spite of the unfavorable conditions. After the usual sacrifices to the gods, the fleet sailed down the delta for several days until they at last reached the open sea at the mouth of the Indus. From here they turned west and followed the coast along the land of the Arabitae until they arrived at an island called Crocala. It was the habit of Nearchus to sail as close to the shore as possible, anchoring at protected bays or nearby islands at night to avoid the risks of making camp on the mainland. The next day they found a well-protected harbor near an island called Bibacta. Nearchus was so struck by the tranquil setting that he named the spot Alexander's Haven. A strong monsoon wind was still blowing in from the ocean, forcing the fleet to delay their departure. As the unfavorable winds continued unabated, Nearchus realized he would have to wait out the weather at Bibacta and so built a fort on the island surrounded by stone walls to guard against raids by the natives. The trade winds that would carry them across the Indian Ocean were late that year, forcing the fleet to tarry almost a month at the island. Nearchus must have been frantic at this point, realizing that such a delay would put him well behind the march of the army. Still, there was nothing he could do until the weather changed. The sailors themselves were more sanguine and enjoyed the weeks on their tropical island hunting for mussels, oysters, and other shellfish, though they did complain that the fresh water tasted brackish.

As soon as the winds shifted from west to east, Nearchus weighed anchor and sailed along the coast to a desert island called Domai, where his men searched in vain for water. This was the primary concern of the admiral throughout the voyage and the main reason he was so dependent on the well-digging parties of Alexander that had preceded him. However, it seems that only in rare instances was Nearchus able to find the wells that the army had dug, leaving him on his own to supply water for his thirsty sailors. This problem was solved at Domai and elsewhere by sending armed patrols inland, sometimes many miles, to collect fresh water in large jars and skins for transport back to the ships.

At one point during the next few days, Nearchus sailed so close to the coast that his ships were barely able to squeeze between the beach and the rocks just offshore, forcing the men to strike the oars against solid ground on both sides. But the fleet passed this dangerous spot and found a safe haven in a small bay named in the local language Woman's Harbor for a queen who had once ruled there. Dodging large waves and shifting tides, the fleet advanced briefly along a more hospitable shore lined with a thick forest to the mouth of the Arabis River. This marked the end of the lands ruled by the Arabitae and the beginning of the territory of the Oreitae, who had earlier fled in panic from Alexander's army.

The seas were rough as they continued up the coast, forcing Nearchus to anchor well offshore to protect his vessels from being dashed against the rocks. Three ships nonetheless were lost in the waves as the sailors struggled to keep the fleet away from the breakers. The men became so seasick in the constant swell that after a few days the admiral took the risk of building a fortified camp on a mainland beach to allow his men a night's rest on steady ground. At this point Nearchus was delighted to find Alexander's companion Leonnatus, whom the king had left behind to await the fleet and secure the area. Things had not gone well in the land of the Oreitae since Alexander's departure, forcing Leonnatus to kill several thousand local warriors in a battle that also took the life of the satrap Apollophanes. But the general had been faithful to his charge of preparing for the fleet and had stockpiled enough food to supply the sailors for at least ten days. Nearchus also took the opportunity to repair some of the damaged vessels and rid himself of the more troublesome sailors, leaving them with Leonnatus and replacing them with men from Leonnatus's command.

The shore became more mountainous as the fleet moved west up the coast of Gedrosia while the land grew ever more arid. Water was a pressing concern, forcing even longer journeys into the interior to dig wells. At a welcome stream called the Tomerus, the fleet for the first time met the primitive Fish Eaters, whom the army had encountered along the same coast. Nearchus described them as more warlike than did Alexander, perhaps because of their recent experience with the Macedonian land force. A people who had rarely had contact with the outside world for generations were suddenly forced to deal with a second invasion by a large foreign force in as many months. Six hundred angry natives were waiting to attack the sailors when they came ashore, but Nearchus could see that their wooden spears would be a threat only at close range. He therefore sent his best swimmers among the light-armed troops over the side into the shallow surf and ordered them to advance together with weapons drawn into battle. With a loud cry to Ares, the men swept forward against the natives protected by a volley of arrows from the ships. The half-naked Fish Eaters were terrified and fled inland to the wilderness to escape. The few that were captured were a source of fascination to the Macedonians. Nearchus noted, as had Alexander, that they let their nails grow long, but observed that this was not out of a lack of hygiene but rather that they might use their nails as other people would iron tools, since they lacked the skill to forge metal blades.

The coast of Gedrosia was the southernmost point reached by any of Alexander's men, so Nearchus, observant sailor that he was, commented on the unusual stars visible in the sky over the ocean. The fleet was so far south that the familiar northern constellations they had all grown up with dipped below the horizon and new stars appeared.

But astronomical observations did little to distract Nearchus from his increasingly perilous situation. The coast was ever more rocky and inhospitable with water increasingly difficult to find. Day after day the thirsty sailors traveled west along a barren coast relieved only by the occasional appearance of a Fish Eater village. These natives had little to steal, but the fleet did manage to haul off a few scraggly sheep. As there was no grass in this land for grazing, the animals were fed on dried fish, giving the mutton a distinctly maritime taste, according to the Macedonians. Most of the villages were deserted before the fleet could pull ashore, but at one small harbor Nearchus found an experienced native sailor to guide them along the remainder of the Gedrosian coast. Near the harbor was also a welcome source of fresh water to restock their supplies.

The coast from this point onward was marginally better, with more reliable water sources and natives who, according to Nearchus, did not quite live like animals. There were date palms cultivated by the local inhabitants and gardens that yielded flowers woven into wreaths by villagers. The local fishermen paddled their boats like canoes rather than using oars mounted on pins like Greeks. The natives wanted to avoid conflict with the Macedonians and brought them all the food they could spare, including cooked fish and cakes made from dates. Nearchus nonetheless took the town by force and stripped the poor villagers of whatever food he could find hidden in their homes. Unfortunately for the sailors, the villagers had only fish-meal flour along with a small amount of wheat and barley used for special occasions.

Setting out to sea once again, the fleet was surprised one morning by a spout of water blown up from a pod of whales off their bow. Similar animals in the Mediterranean were small, but these cetaceans were enormous by comparison. Ever superstitious, the Egyptian, Greek, and Phoenician sailors who made up the majority of the crews were terrified at the sight of these creatures so close to the ships. They dropped their oars and huddled together, wondering what the gods had in store for them. Nearchus, however, went along the deck encouraging the men to remain firm and—in a move that must have struck the frightened sailors as sheer madness—ordered the helmsmen to turn their bows toward the whales in attack formation. He set a fast rowing pace for the oarsmen directly toward the sea creatures with trumpets blaring and battle cries raised above the waves. The puzzled whales merely slipped beneath the water and swam away from the noisy intruders, but the Macedonians counted their battle with the monsters of the deep as a great victory.

Farther along the coast the fleet came to an island called Nosala several miles offshore that their local guide said was sacred to the sun god. No one dared to land there, he reported, and those few who had were swept onto its shores and never returned. The island was supposedly the home of a sea goddess who welcomed castaway sailors into her bed for a night of passion, then turned them into fish the next morning. This sounded to Nearchus like a tale out of Homer's *Odyssey*, but the next day when one of his ships manned by an Egyptian crew went missing near the island, the admiral decided to investigate for himself. He rowed near the shore and called out the names of the sailors, but no one answered. He then forced his crew to land on the island and went ashore himself, searching in vain for his missing men. Whether lost in the waves or turned into fish by a goddess, they were never seen again. Nearchus returned to the fleet safely and set sail ever westward up the coast.

After traveling almost five hundred miles along the shore of the Indian Ocean, the fleet finally passed the barren land of Gedrosia and was now entering the Straits of Hormuz opposite the Arabian peninsula. One morning they sighted a distant headland off their port bow only a day's sail away, marking the entrance to the Persian Gulf. Nearchus knew he had now fulfilled his commission to explore the unknown coast for Alexander. He also knew the king must be beside himself with worry after months with no word from the fleet. He therefore brought his ships ashore at the straits and ordered his sailors to build a stockade while he took a handful of men inland in search of the army. Almost immediately they came across a man wandering by himself wearing a Greek cloak and speaking the same language Nearchus had grown up with on Crete. The surprised vagabond said he was a soldier of Alexander who had become separated from the army a few days earlier. The main camp of the Macedonians, he reported, was only a few days away, with the king in residence there. Nearchus was thrilled at this piece of good fortune and set out with his men through the desert.

When he finally arrived at the camp and convinced the guards that he was indeed the admiral the king had been searching for, Nearchus was brought before Alexander. The king was so delighted to see his old friend that he broke into tears and could not speak for several minutes. Nearchus and his companions were so gaunt and tattered that Alexander assumed the whole fleet had been lost except for these few survivors. His guilt at failing to meet the ships and supply them properly threatened to overwhelm him until Nearchus understood the cause of his grief and explained that the fleet was safely harbored just a few days away. Alexander then wept again, this time from joy, and declared that the deliverance of the fleet made up for the horrible losses he had suffered on his own trek through the Gedrosian desert. After sacrifices of thanksgiving, Alexander ordered Nearchus to remain behind while one of his lieutenants led the ships on the remainder of the voyage up the Persian Gulf. But Nearchus begged the king to let him finish what he had begun and sail all the way to Susa with the fleet. Alexander granted his request and sent him on his way with plenty of supplies, grateful that he had such a man to serve under him.

Almost six years after leaving Persia and a full decade since he left Europe, Alexander at last returned to the heartland of his empire just as winter was descending on the hills around Persepolis. His trek through Hyrcania, Parthia, Bactria, Sogdiana, India, Gedrosia, and Carmania had covered thousands of miles over blistering deserts, towering mountains, and steaming jungles. No other army in history had made such an extended campaign nor had any previous expedition discovered and recorded so much new information about distant lands and peoples. When Alexander had left Persepolis, he was twenty-six years old. Now he was in his early thirties, a proven general and ruler of the largest empire the world had ever known— greater even than that of his Persian predecessors. There were still many lands left to conquer, but his first task was to establish firm control over the realms he governed. The lax administration of the provinces during his long absence had to come to an end as the king returned to his throne.

Alexander's first stop was Pasargadae to visit again the tomb of the first Great King, Cyrus, a man for whom he had gained a new respect, having fought against many of the same barbarians as this previous ruler in the distant east. As he stooped down and entered the small chamber, he was appalled to see that it had been looted. Everything except the royal couch and sarcophagus itself had been stolen. The lid of the great stone coffin had been pried off and the preserved body of Cyrus thrown carelessly on the floor. The robbers had even tried to break the sarcophagus into sections to take it out the entrance, but had failed and left the pieces scattered about inside. Alexander was livid. He seized the whole family of Magi priests he had charged to care for the tomb and put them to torture to reveal the culprits, but to no avail. He immediately set his old friend Aristobulus the task of restoring the monument to its original condition. This gross insult to the memory of Cyrus was an affront to his own honor as Great King.

From Pasargadae, Alexander rode the few miles to the city of Persepolis in a very bad mood. There had been much rebuilding during his absence, but the charred ruins of the palace still loomed over the town. Again the king deeply regretted that he had burned down the royal halls of Darius and Xerxes. Parmenion had been right that it was foolish to destroy his own property and stir up ill will among the Persians. In his renewed frustration, he struck out at the local satrap Orxines and accused him of treason. This governor had welcomed the king on his return just a few days before at Pasargadae with splendid gifts for his whole entourage. After bestowing fabulous presents on all of Alexander's friends, he conspicuously omitted any gift to the eunuch Bagoas, a man highly regarded by the king for both his practical advice and skill in the arts of love. When quietly admonished by one of Alexander's companions concerning this lapse in protocol, Orxines replied that he gave gifts only to the king's friends, not to his whores. After word of this comment reached Bagoas, the eunuch and experienced palace courtier quickly carried out his revenge. He whispered in Alexander's ear that it was in fact Orxines who was behind the looting of Cyrus' tomb as well as many other crimes. The king was in the mood to blame someone for the poor administration of the province, so it seemed logical to fault the satrap—who was undoubtedly guilty of many genuine indiscretions during his term. The Persian was led out into the courtyard at Persepolis and hanged, much to the delight of Bagoas. In his place Alexander appointed his bodyguard Peucestas, who had saved his life when he held his shield above Alexander inside the walls at the Indian city of the Malli. Peucestas was as solid a Macedonian as they came, with absolute loyalty to the king. He had also made a great impression on Alexander as one of the few officers who had openly embraced his policy of accommodating himself to the new political order. He had learned the Persian language fluently and dressed in local clothing when appropriate, exactly as the king had hoped his administrators would do. He was well liked by the Persians for these efforts and held great promise as a mediator between the Macedonian elite and the still-powerful natives of the region.

As Alexander made his way from Persepolis to Susa in Mesopotamia, he was brimming with plans for future conquests. Most men would have been content to consolidate their rule and enjoy the fruits of such a vast empire, but Alexander could not cease from dreaming of new horizons. As Arrian says, he always searched for something more, in competition with himself in lieu of another rival. The reports of Nearchus concerning the nearby coast of Arabia served to strengthen the desire he had long nursed to extend his control of the seas from the Indus River around the peninsula of Arabia to Egypt. The Greek mariner Scylax of Caria had made the long ocean journey from India to Egypt two centuries before for the first Great King Darius, so Alexander knew his plan was possible. He also wanted to conquer the coastal kingdoms of Arabia at the same time. The interior of the enormous peninsula offered little more than sand, but the tribes bordering the more hospitable lands along the Persian Gulf, the Indian Ocean, and the Red Sea had long been known as lucrative sources of pearls, cinnamon, frankincense, and myrrh, which were transported by caravan through the deserts to Palestine and Syria. Why not eliminate the middlemen and bring these riches under his direct control?

As if this wasn't enough, Alexander conceived a longing to retrace the Phoenician voyage he had read of in Herodotus and circumnavigate Africa itself, sailing from the Tigris around Arabia and down the eastern coast, following the shore of the continent until he at last arrived at the Pillars of Hercules at the western entrance to the Mediterranean Sea. He had no idea of the immense distances involved in such a trip, though the fact that it took the Phoenicians three years to complete the journey should have been warning enough. He became so excited by the possibility of the maritime conquest of Arabia and a voyage around Africa that he ordered sailors and pilots assembled and a fleet of galleys constructed on the Euphrates in preparation for the expedition.

But the king's plans did not end there. He had nursed a grudge against Carthage for aiding Tyre ever since his siege of that doomed city. He also knew that the next logical step of expansion west into the Mediterranean beyond Cyrene would bring him into conflict with this powerful mercantile kingdom of North Africa. He decided that it was both expedient and necessary to crush Carthage and seize control of the whole African coast, as well as the islands and cities it governed. He also knew of the rising power of a small town on the Tiber River in central Italy. These natives, known as Romans, had beaten back Gaulish invaders earlier in the century and were now beginning to spread their power, by war and diplomacy, throughout the Italic peninsula. They might become useful subjects—they had a reputation as fine fighters—but they could not be allowed to expand their influence independently in such a key region of the Mediterranean. The Greek colonies of southern Italy and Sicily would have to be brought into the fold as well, along with the Samnites and other Italic peoples. Spain with its rich mines of silver and gold lay just beyond and would form a natural boundary for the western edge of his empire—unless he sailed beyond the Pillars of Hercules into the Atlantic, adding even Britain and Ireland to his kingdom.

Once he was finished in the west, he longed to return east and complete the conquest of Scythia as he had planned during his wars in Sogdiana. North through the Black Sea the Macedonian fleet would sail, then the army would march east across the steppes to the banks of the Oxus and Jaxartes with the help of their allies among the Scythian kings. At the same time he commissioned a fleet of open-decked Greek galleys in Hyrcania to explore the Caspian Sea with orders to discover whether it connected to the great ocean encircling the world. When these northern adventures were complete, the kingdoms of the Ganges valley in India were still waiting, in spite of however many battle elephants they might dare to muster. Alexander scoffed at the idea that the Medes and Persians had called themselves kings of Asia, having left so much of the continent unconquered. He, however, would create the first true universal empire encompassing Europe, Africa, and Asia and stretching from Spain and the unknown shores of Africa to Scythia and the great eastern sea, perhaps even to China. It was a stunning vision of world domination. If the gods granted him enough time, he just might be able to make it come true.

When Alexander arrived at Susa, he summoned the satrap Abulites and demanded to know why he had not sent him supplies in the Gedrosian desert as requested. The Persian governor had no ready response for this lapse nor for the poor administration of his province during the king's long absence. He tried to mollify Alexander by offering him an enormous bribe in gold coins, but the king simply set the money before his horses. When the animals ignored the treasure,

Alexander asked him what good such money was in place of the provisions they had needed in the desert. He then threw Abulites into prison and executed him. Then he personally ran through one of the satrap's grown sons, Oxathres, with a spear.

At this point, the Indian wise man Calanus who had accompanied Alexander from the Punjab suddenly fell ill with an acute intestinal disorder and decided to put an end to his own life. He was more than seventy years old and had lived all that time in ascetic simplicity and had avoided sickness. Rather than suffer the torments of a wasting disease in a foreign land, he told the king he was planning to burn himself alive while he still had his wits about him. Alexander, who had grown quite fond of the old philosopher, argued with him and tried to dissuade him from such a drastic step, but Calanus would not be moved. So the king at last agreed and ordered his friend Ptolemy to construct a massive funeral pyre for Calanus.

On the morning of the grand immolation, Calanus was carried to the pyre in a litter as he could no longer walk long distances. The teacher cheerfully dismounted and stood at the foot of the wooden structure, saying his good-byes and giving away to his Macedonian friends all the rich gifts that Alexander had presented him. He cut a lock of his hair and threw it on the logs, then slowly climbed the pyre and lay down on top. While the whole army watched, Calanus began chanting hymns to the Indian gods in his native tongue just as the fire was lit. The king led the men in a rousing shout as if they were charging the enemy, while horns blared and elephants trumpeted battle cries. All this while, as the inferno engulfed him, Calanus did not move a muscle, but remained motionless until he was consumed by the flames. Afterward some of the soldiers commented that the aged guru must have been mad to undergo such torment, while others thought he was overly prideful about his ability to bear pain. But most—Alexander surely among them—marveled at his courage and disregard for death.

The king followed the funeral of Calanus with a mass wedding that winter at Susa. This was yet another attempt by Alexander to integrate the Macedonian and native factions under his command, though on a grander scale than anything he had previously attempted. The king himself took two Persian brides, Stateira, the daughter of Darius, and Parysatis, the daughter of the former Great King Artaxerxes. He bestowed another daughter of Darius, Drypetis, on his best friend, Hephaestion, so that their future children might be cousins of his children. Craterus received a sister of Alexander's first wife, Roxane, while Perdiccas, Ptolemy, Nearchus, Seleucus, and dozens of other companions were given brides from the native aristocracy of Persia, Media, and Bactria. The ceremony itself was deliberately Persian rather than Macedonian in style, with chairs for the bridegrooms placed near one another. After toasts were drunk to everyone's good health, the brides entered and sat down beside their intended husbands. Each couple held hands as the groom kissed his new wife—or in Alexander's case, wives—then led them home to bed. The king had granted all the women fine dowries to make the unions even more appealing to his Macedonian officers.

It was a great show and a noble effort on Alexander's part, but as with most of his programs to bring together the quarrelsome members of his court, it was a miserable failure. None of the Macedonians was enthusiastic about taking native brides. Foreign women were fine for amusement, but Alexander's officers wanted respectable wives from their homeland. Few of the marriages consummated at Susa would endure. The king had better luck with the rank-and-file soldiers. Many had willingly taken on native women as they marched across Asia and fathered children in the camps. Alexander now formally recognized these unions and gave each of the couples splendid wedding presents. He also paid off the debts his soldiers had accumulated over the last few years from moneylenders, wine merchants, and prostitutes—no questions asked—even though it was a huge drain on the treasury. The men were suspicious at first when they were asked to write down how much they owed, fearing it was some sort of trap. But when they realized the king was sincere and not even recording their names as he handed over the money, they were immensely grateful.

The mood turned sour, however, when the thirty thousand Persian boys he had been training as Macedonian soldiers for the last few years arrived at Susa ready to take their promised place in the new imperial army. These youths had been tutored in the Greek language and schooled in Macedonian fighting techniques and military management until they were the equals of any lads from the hills around Mount Olympus. They performed their drills before the king and his officers in expert fashion, dressed and equipped as traditional Macedonian soldiers, delighting Alexander but sending a shiver through the rest of the army. These Successors, as the king ominously called the boy troop, were to become in time officers of Alexander's international force to rule the empire and expand the king's power to new lands. The Macedonians were filled with resentment and fear at the thought of being replaced by these native youths, whom they contemptuously called the "war dancers." What was the point of conquering the world if they were to lose their rightful place to foreign children?

The crisis came to a head when Alexander decided that now was the moment to decommission many of his veterans and send them home. He had traveled north from Susa up the Tigris to the town of Opis to supervise the removal of dams the Persians had constructed on the river to hinder any naval force invading Mesopotamia from the south. These dams made shipping on the Tigris difficult and were, as Alexander said, marks of an empire lacking military supremacy. He summoned his Macedonian troops to him at Opis and announced that he was sending away all who were unfit for further service due to age or injuries. They would be amply rewarded for their past service, while those that remained would become so rich that they would be the envy of all in Macedonia. The king had assumed his news would be greeted with joy by those leaving and staying alike, but his words met with stony silence. The soldiers who had fought so long with him were brokenhearted at being dismissed, even though they had long wanted to go home. Those who were selected to remain could only wonder when he would decide to be rid of them as well. Alexander's integration of foreign forces into the army, his adopting Persian ways, his forced marriages—all of this was at last too much for the common soldiers. Instead of applause for the king, shouts arose from the troops calling on him to send them all home since he didn't need them anymore. Let him fight alongside his new father, Ammon, some cried.

Alexander grew furious at this insubordination and leapt off the platform where he had been standing. He ordered his guards to arrest the dozen or so most prominent agitators and haul them off for immediate execution. Then he climbed back on the stage and began one of the most impassioned speeches of his life to the stunned soldiers before him. He chastised them for their gross ingratitude after all he had done for them. He reminded them that they were nothing before his father, Philip, accepted them into his army, only goatherds clothed in animal skins fighting off wolves and Illyrian bandits. Under his father they had spread Macedonian power throughout Greece and the Balkans. Then under his own banner they had invaded Asia and taken the Mediterranean from Troy to Cyrene, adding the Aegean coast, Syria, Phoenicia, and Egypt to their empire. From there it was on to Persia itself, followed by Bactria, Sogdiana, and India. They had become rich men while he kept no luxuries for himself. He had eaten the same food and shared the same labors as the lowliest infantryman. Did they have wounds to show him? He would strip and show them his injuries as well. There were scars on every part of his body just as on theirs. He had toiled with them through everything. He had paid their debts and legitimized the children they had fathered with camp followers. If any man among them had died along the way, he was honored with a splendid funeral and his family back home in Macedonia spared from future taxes. Therefore, he shouted, all of you get out of my sight. Every one of you go home to Macedonia whether you are old and infirm or not. *I don't need you anymore.* Just be sure to tell your families back home that you deserted your king, handing over him and the empire you won to the care of the very barbarians you defeated.

Alexander then stomped off the platform and retired to his tent for three days, refusing to see anyone. This was the same trick he had used at the Hyphasis River in India to prompt his army to march down the Ganges. It had failed miserably then, but Alexander now knew the measure of his men. To drive home his point, he called in his Persian followers and began to divide up command of the army among them. By this time, all the Macedonians were beside themselves and had gathered outside his headquarters, having thrown down their weapons, begging him to see them. They declared they would stay there day and night until the king admitted them. At last Alexander emerged and saw his repentant soldiers before him. One of their number, an old Macedonian cavalryman named Callines, came forward to speak for the men. He urged the king to reconsider sending them all home and take pity on them for their rash words earlier. They could not bear to see him embracing Persians while they stood by shunned. Alexander then took Callines in his arms and kissed him to the wild applause of the crowd as tears rolled down their faces. The king wept as well and welcomed all of them to come and receive his blessing with a kiss. All was forgiven. Only those who were truly unable to fight any longer were sent home to Macedonia and these went willingly, with plenty of gold and silver in their saddlebags. His faithful comrade Craterus would accompany them home as a sign of the honor he held them in. Alexander asked only that they leave their camp wives and children with him rather than take them home. In Macedonia, these foreign wives and offspring would stir resentment among their kin. He would see to their care and raise their sons as true Macedonian soldiers, proud heirs of the fathers who had sired them. There must have been many tears as the native wives and children said their good-byes, but the soldiers knew that the king was probably right. Better to start again with the old wife or a new young bride in Macedonia rather than bring a wild Bactrian or Indian woman and her children home to meet the family.

Back in Macedonia, Craterus was also to handle a delicate situation that had arisen between Alexander's mother, Olympias, and his aging regent, Antipater. These two headstrong personalities had never liked each other but were forced to endure one another's company while the king was away on his eastern conquests. Both had sent a constant stream of letters to Alexander all the way from the Hellespont to the Indus and back accusing the other of every imaginable impropriety. Antipater claimed that Olympias was a willful, sharp-tempered shrew, forever interfering in the affairs of government. Olympias shot back that Antipater had forgotten who appointed him and that he was behaving more like a king than a governor. Alexander had listened to this verbal war for the last decade from a blissful distance, but now it was time to settle the troublesome affair once and for all. Antipater had been a loyal and useful servant during the expedition to Asia, but he was still a threat. With Parmenion's faction eliminated, only Antipater and his well-entrenched family back in Macedonia could endanger Alexander's control of the homeland. The king could not easily repudiate his own mother, as much as he might like to at times, so he chose to remove Antipater from power. He sent orders to his regent to turn the governance of Greece and Macedonia over to Craterus once he arrived and make his way to Babylon along with a new draft of Macedonian troops. There he would be greatly honored for his service and enjoy a blissful retirement amid the gardens of the city. When Antipater received the letter, he knew it was his death warrant.

Rather than surrender to fate, Antipater sent his son, Alexander's boyhood friend Cassander, to Babylon to negotiate with the king and buy time. This meeting went exceedingly poorly when Cassander was led before the king and laughed at a group of Persians bowing their faces to the ground. Alexander jumped up from his throne, grabbed Cassander by the hair, and smashed his head against a wall. Antipater's son recovered soon enough, but years later back in Greece the sight of a painting or statue of Alexander would still send him into a fainting spell. Even with Cassander fearful, it remains that Antipater's other son, Iolaus, was cupbearer to the king—a trusted position in which the holder of that office could easily slip a lethal potion into the royal wine bowl. Antipater may well have decided that if negotiations failed, he would have Alexander poisoned before the king could kill him.

To escape the heat of the approaching summer, Alexander did what all the Persian kings before him had done and retreated to the royal capital of Ecbatana in the cool mountains of Media far above the

Mesopotamian plain. There he held splendid athletic and musical competitions during the day for his men and epic drinking parties at night for his companions. Three thousand actors and artists arrived from Greece for the festivities, which went on for days at a time. Alexander's closest friend, Hephaestion, was more interested in the evening revelries than the contests, but the king attended most of the contests himself with genuine enjoyment. After one party, Hephaestion fell ill with a fever and was sternly warned by his personal physician, Glaucias, not to indulge himself further at the risk of his health. Hephaestion grudgingly agreed while the doctor stayed by his bed for seven days, but as soon as Glaucias was confident that Hephaestion would recover and had departed for the theater himself, Alexander's friend jumped out of bed and ran to the dining room. There he ate a whole boiled chicken and drank an entire container of chilled wine at one sitting. He collapsed almost at once and was rushed back to bed. Alexander quickly received word that Hephaestion was gravely ill and ran from the stadium to his companion's side, but by the time he arrived his dearest love was dead.

The ancient sources relate different versions of what happened next, but all agree that Alexander was beside himself with grief. He immediately had Hephaestion's doctor crucified, blaming him for not caring for his patient properly. He then ordered all the manes and tails of the horses and mules shorn as a token of mourning after a custom practiced by Thracians and Persians alike. He commanded that all music in the city cease and the temple to Asclepius, the god of healing, in Ecbatana be burned to the ground. For the next day he lay prostrate, weeping, on the body of his friend, neither eating nor drinking until his companions finally had to carry him away. At last, like his hero Achilles lamenting for his own Patroclus, slain by Hector before the walls of Troy, Alexander cut his hair and drove the body of Hephaestion himself in the funeral procession.

Alexander sent to the oracle at Siwa in Egypt to ask if Hephaestion might be honored as a god, but this was too much even for the compliant priests of Zeus-Ammon to endorse. They did, however, consent that his friend might be honored as a divine hero with his own cult. The king settled for this, at least at first, and ordered that shrines be constructed in Egypt and elsewhere for Hephaestion. His friend's post as military commander was left vacant in his honor and extravagant funeral games were planned. The king's surviving companions tried to outdo each other in showing respect to Hephaestion, dedicating themselves and their arms to his memory while commissioning ivory and gold statues of the deceased. A few bold friends tried to comfort Alexander with the suggestion that he had others, such as Craterus, who cared for him as much as Hephaestion had. He responded that Craterus loved him as king, but Hephaestion had loved him for himself. His boyhood friend had even stood up to Alexander's mother—who was always jealous of the close relationship between the pair—and warned her in a letter to cease from trying to stir up enmity between them, for Alexander meant more to him than anything in the world.

The king commanded a tomb be built for Hephaestion that rivaled any previous memorial in cost and lavishness. It was to be in the shape of a Babylonian ziggurat with a base more than six hundred feet square and ascending levels almost two hundred feet in height. The best artists were imported for its decoration, which included carvings of warring archers, wild animal hunts, and eagles with outspread wings. On the monument were the golden prows of ships, lions and bulls in Persian fashion, and hollow sculptures of Sirens, in each of which a living person could stand and sing songs of lamentation for his dead friend. Even for those of Alexander's supporters who had liked Hephaestion, this was all too much—though they did not dare to share their thoughts with the king. Aristotle had taught both Alexander and Hephaestion as young men that friendship was one of the greatest goods in the world, but that moderation in all things was the goal of a worthy man. To all who watched the funeral preparations for Hephaestion, it was clear that Alexander had gone too far. Such ostentatious grief for a friend, even with the best of intentions, was an affront to the gods. And as they all knew, the gods would have their revenge.

Alexander's mourning for Hephaestion continued for weeks into the winter until everyone in the court realized they had to find a way to bring him out of his depression. Fortunately an opportunity for military action—the one thing guaranteed to appeal to the king—presented itself at this moment in the form of a rebellious tribe known as the Cossaeans who lived in the mountains southwest of Ecbatana. Like their neighbors the Uxians, whom Alexander had faced years before, these highland warriors had never submitted to the Persians but had demanded payment from the royal treasury for passage across their land. When approached by Macedonian envoys demanding their surrender, the Cossaeans refused. For Alexander, this was like waving a red flag in front of a bull. Much to the relief of his companions, the king rose from his despair with a renewed spirit and determination to teach these mountain tribesmen a lesson. In the past the Cossaeans had retreated deep into the hills of their homeland when confronted by an army, only to reappear and renew their raids when the threat was past. But now Alexander, aided by Ptolemy, surrounded their lands and isolated their villages, then launched a series of devastating attacks against the Cossaeans throughout the snow-covered mountains for forty days. Alexander declared that those slain were offerings to the spirit of Hephaestion, just as Achilles had sacrificed Trojan youths to the dead Patroclus. The few who survived the Macedonian assaults were captured and enslaved, so that soon their leaders sued for peace. They agreed to become subjects of Alexander and submit to his authority thereafter.

As spring was beginning and the Zagros Mountains were blooming with wildflowers, Alexander at last began the march from Ecbatana to Babylon. Along the way envoys arrived from distant lands to offer their congratulations on his many conquests and to express their sincere hopes that he would form ties of friendship with them. At the very least, they wanted to gauge his intentions and prepare themselves for any conflict to come. There were ambassadors from Africa west of Cyrene bearing a crown of submission and Ethiopians from the lands south of Egypt. The Carthaginians also came, with more reason to worry than most. The tribes of Italy were there as well—Bruttians, Lucanians, and Etruscans—including envoys from Rome, according to some Greek sources, though later Roman records omitted any reference to homage they might have offered Alexander. The Celts sent ambassadors, just as they had done during the king's first campaign along the Danube twelve long years before. Iberians arrived from distant Spain, as did Scythians from the lands to the north of the Black Sea. Some of these peoples Alexander had met before, but others were new to the Macedonians. The king welcomed them all with good cheer and warm assurances of friendship, along with promises of peace that could be broken later if he deemed it expedient.

As Alexander at last drew near to the walls of Babylon, he was met by a group of Chaldean priests, who begged him not to enter the gates of their city. They had received an oracle, they claimed, from the great god Bel-Marduk warning the king that he should avoid Babylon at all costs. Alexander respected the Chaldeans, indeed he had taken a party of them with him on his march to the East, but he was also suspicious of their motives. He knew from reports that his command to restore the temple of Bel-Marduk had been ignored during his trek to India and that the priests were quiet happy with this situation. The enormous amount of money set aside for the restoration still remained in the temple treasury, available for use and abuse by the Chaldeans. If the king entered Babylon and forced them to start construction, their riches would rapidly dwindle. At first Alexander tried to laugh off the prophesy, quoting a line from the Greek playwright Euripides that the best prophet is one who guesses well, but he was still a man of his times and superstitious enough to be cautious when it came even to questionable warnings from the gods. When the Chaldeans saw that their plan wasn't working, they quickly changed tactics and urged the king at least not to enter the city facing the west and the setting sun, the universal symbol of death in the ancient world. This was a clever ploy to keep Alexander out of Babylon altogether as the priests knew their city was surrounded by a huge marsh, making entry from another direction difficult. The king therefore sent some of his men into the city while he led the rest around through the swamps to approach the town from the opposite side. If the Chaldeans thought they would keep Alexander out so easily, they were sadly mistaken. A few days later he walked through the gates of Babylon and took up residence at the royal palace.

But once inside the city, the ill omens from the gods only increased. When one of his friends was sacrificing on behalf of the king, the animal was discovered to have a malformed liver, always an ominous sign. One day ravens fought with one another above Alexander's head and some fell dead at his feet. Then the largest and most handsome lion in his private zoo was attacked by a tame donkey and kicked to death. A few days later Alexander briefly left the city to sail along the river, guiding the lead boat himself after the pilot became lost. He was sailing past the flooded tombs of some ancient Assyrian kings when suddenly the wind snatched the cap from his head along with the crown he had jauntily placed on top of it. The diadem caught on a sturdy reed that grew out of an old tomb so that one of the sailors jumped in to rescue it. The man snatched the treasure from the plant, but found he couldn't swim while holding it above the water. He therefore put the crown on his head, swam back to the boat, and handed it to the king. Alexander was grateful and gave him a rich reward, but he also ordered him punished for daring to place the diadem on his own head. Some sources say the man was flogged, while others say he was decapitated. Whatever the punishment, the king evidently saw the incident as a warning that he was in danger of losing his crown permanently.

But the most disturbing episode came one day when Alexander had returned to the city and was playing ball with his friends. Spring had arrived with a vengeance and the weather was unbearably hot, so the king had taken off his robes and laid them on the back of his nearby throne. When he returned from exercise, he saw a man sitting on his royal chair wearing his cloak and crown. The intruder seemed strangely dumbfounded and responded to questions only after a round of intense torture. His name was Dionysius and he hailed from the Greek city of Messenia, near Sparta. He said he was an escaped prisoner and had long been bound in chains, but a god had come and freed him, bidding him to put on the king's attire and sit silently on the throne. As Alexander may have known, the episode bore an uncanny resemblance to a local Babylonian custom in which a condemned criminal acted as a substitute king to draw down the wrath of heaven on himself and spare the real king misfortune. Alexander was uncertain whether the incident was a stroke of good fortune or not, but he played his part and had the scapegoat prisoner executed, hoping that the sacrifice of this one man would satisfy the gods.

As May turned to June, Alexander busied himself with plans for his upcoming expedition to Arabia. Hundreds of ships were given their final fittings and the crews drilled with races along the Euphrates River. Scouts reported that there was fresh water along the Arabian coast, as well as offshore islands along the Persian Gulf convenient for anchorage. It would be a grand expedition down the gulf and through the straits, then around the southern shore of the peninsula, seizing the lands of frankincense and myrrh, then up the Red Sea to Egypt. The king could not wait to begin.

Alexander spent his days organizing the details of the voyage, but the nights were replete with banquets and drinking parties in true Macedonian style. One evening the king gave a feast for his admiral Nearchus, then was heading home to bed when he ran into his friend Medius from Thessaly, who invited him to a late soiree with a few companions. Alexander joined them till the wee hours, but was up early the next morning to perform the customary sacrifices. The next evening he was back at the house of Medius for a celebration in honor of Hercules. There he topped off the night by drinking a whole beaker of unmixed wine in a single gulp, after which he shrieked as if hit by a blow and was led back to his bed by his friends. The next morning he was suffering from a fever, though he still was scrupulous about the required sacrifices to the gods even though he had to be carried to the altar on a litter. He issued orders to the fleet concerning the departure for the Arabian expedition a few days hence and commanded the infantry to be ready a day before the sailing. He was then borne to the river and rowed across to a favorite garden to bathe and rest. The next day he was still incapacitated, but carried out the sacrifices and ate only sparingly. He told his officers to meet him the next day for a conference, but spent the whole night with a high fever. He rose the next morning to perform the sacrifices, then bathed and talked with Nearchus about the departure of the fleet. The following day he carried out his duties to the gods, though he was growing ever weaker. He still believed he would rise again soon to sail with his ships to Arabia, though his companions were now becoming deeply concerned. He was so stricken with fever that he took to resting in the cool bath house instead of his room at the palace. For the next few days he carried on his routine of sacrifices, military meetings, bathing, and resting, all while his generals began to gather around him.

Word had spread to the army that the king was gravely ill. Some even suggested, as they had in India, that he had already died and his demise was being covered up by his senior officers. To put an end to these rumors, Alexander ordered the soldiers admitted to his presence to see for themselves that he was still alive, though by that point he was struggling even to speak. The men filed past his bed in silence and tears, each receiving a nod or at least a smile from their commander and king. No one could believe that the great Alexander, who had outwitted death on the battlefield at every turn, would die in his bed in Babylon. Some of his companions wanted to carry him to a nearby temple in hope that the gods would spare his life, but others thought it best not to move him. His fever raged on, the pain increased, and soon even Alexander—just short of his thirty-third birthday—knew that the end was near. He took off his royal signet ring and gave it to his friend Perdiccas so that he might act temporarily as regent, but the ultimate succession was unclear. His Bactrian bride Roxane was pregnant, he hoped with a boy, though the child would not be of age for many years to come even if the Macedonians would accept a half-barbarian ruler on the throne. The situation promised chaos for the empire unless the king made clear his wishes. At last, his companions approached his bedside and implored him to name his successor: *To whom do you leave your kingdom?*

They leaned close to hear his words. With great effort Alexander answered in a whisper: *To the strongest.*

With that, the king of the world closed his eyes and breathed his last.

# 11

# TO THE ENDS
# OF THE EARTH

IT SEEMS THAT THERE WAS NO NATION, NO CITY
IN THOSE DAYS, NO PERSON IN ANY LAND THAT
THE NAME OF ALEXANDER HAD NOT REACHED.
—ARRIAN

Even before the body of Alexander had grown cold, rumors began to circulate that the king had been murdered. Stories grew that Antipater had ordered the poisoning through the agency of his son Cassander, who was still in Babylon recovering from the beating he had received from Alexander. As Antipater was highly motivated to save his own life and as he had access to the king's wine through his younger son, the royal cupbearer Iolaus, it was a plausible accusation to many. Some sources say the poison, perhaps strychnine, was smuggled into the palace in the hollowed hoof of a pack mule. The fact that the lover of Iolus was none other than Medius—who had invited Alexander to the fateful party in which he cried out in pain after drinking—made the charges more credible. Whether or not Aristotle, a friend of Antipater, was involved at a distance in the assassination of his former pupil continued to be debated in ancient times.

As attractive as conspiracy theories are in any age, it is just as likely that Alexander died of natural causes. He may have suffered from malaria for years, at least since his collapse in the Cydnus River at Tarsus just before the battle of Issus. He had cheated death a dozen times since with wounds and illnesses that would have killed most men. The endless bouts with dysentery and especially the punctured lung he suffered in India at the city of the Malli would have weakened his resistance to disease. Add to this the sheer exhaustion of twelve long years of marching through swamps and over mountains along with the heavy drinking expected of any Macedonian king and it's a wonder Alexander lived as long as he did. If malaria, a lung infection, or liver failure didn't kill him, typhoid fever is another possibility, given the symptoms of abdominal pain and high fever during his final days.

There is a sad and charming story that when Alexander realized he was dying, he secretly dragged himself from his sickbed out of the palace to throw himself into the Euphrates so that he might vanish from the world without a trace. He hoped it would strengthen his claim to be the son of a god if he disappeared mysteriously rather than died like any other man. But the story has it that his wife Roxane saw him at the last moment struggling toward the water and stopped him, prompting Alexander to complain that she was denying him the eternal fame he so desired. In any case, whether by poison or the infirmities of disease that claim most mortals, the king was dead and the living remained to mourn him.

Macedonians and natives alike wept at the news of Alexander's death, running through the streets in panic. Persian subjects shaved their heads, as was the custom on the Great King's passing, while the mother of Darius reportedly starved herself to death as if she had lost her own son. The Macedonian soldiers quickly fell to fighting among themselves about whose faction they would support—Perdiccas, the ambitious ring bearer; Meleager, the infantry commander and conservative stalwart; or perhaps general Ptolemy, the childhood friend of the king. After much blood was spilled, the different leaders agreed to meet in peace to decide how to rule the empire. The soldiers then marked the death of the king with an ancient Macedonian custom of marching between the two halves of a disemboweled dog on the plain outside Babylon. At the subsequent meeting, it was agreed that Alexander's mentally handicapped half brother Arrhidaeus, who was resident in Babylon, would ascend to the throne as King Philip III until such time as Roxane's expected child, should it be a boy, would come of age and take his father's place. No one took Arrhidaeus seriously as a ruler, viewing him only as a temporary and expendable symbol of the Macedonian royal dynasty. What the major players needed was time to consolidate their own positions in the part of the empire each desired for himself. Neither did the generals expect Roxane's child to be anything more than a political pawn. Alexander's illegitimate young son Hercules by his Persian mistress Barsine was not even worth considering as a possible heir.

One outcome of the meeting was a division of the empire. Ptolemy received Egypt, while Seleucus, a friend of Perdiccas, would hold the bulk of Asia for the time being. Antipater and his son Cassander would retain Macedonia and Greece, and the king's former bodyguard Lysimachus would take over Thrace. Alexander's body would be embalmed and returned to Macedonia for a royal burial, though this plan was thwarted when Ptolemy hijacked the funeral procession and took the king's remains to Egypt. There his tomb in Alexandria remained a favorite destination for Greek and Roman tourists, among them the emperor Augustus, until the early Christian era.

Civil wars soon began in earnest when Perdiccas had Meleager murdered in the sanctuary of a temple where he had sought refuge. Many of Meleager's followers were cast before the army's elephants to be trampled. It was an inauspicious beginning to years of fighting in which each side sought only to strengthen itself, with little care for the fate of the millions under their rule. Of those who had known and served Alexander, few died peacefully in their beds. Roxane quickly poisoned Stateira, the daughter of Darius whom Alexander had married in Susa, along with her sister and threw the bodies of both women down a well, all with the approval of Perdiccas. The Bactrian queen's own child turned out to be a boy and was named Alexander IV. Perdiccas championed both mother and child to further his own ends until he himself was killed in Egypt fighting Ptolemy. Roxane and the young prince fled to Macedonia and were welcomed by Olympias. But soon Cassander, who had taken over Macedonia after the death of his father, Antipater, had them murdered, thus ending the line of Alexander. Olympias continued to plot throughout the struggles of succession, killing many of the nobility of Macedonia and earning their undying hatred. When finally she was captured by Cassander, who had promised to spare her life, the soldiers he sent to slay her admired her dignity in her last moments and watched while she arranged her hair and clothes even as she bled to death from the wounds they had given her.

The fate of most of the remaining friends and family of Alexander was equally violent. The king's half bother Arrhidaeus was slain by a Thracian guard after he returned to Macedonia, reportedly under orders from Olympias. Barsine and Alexander's surviving son Hercules were apparently poisoned at Pergamum in Asia Minor, where they had retired in a futile attempt to live a quiet and deliberately apolitical life. Aristotle was forced to flee from Athens in the wake of anti-Macedonian uprisings following the death of Alexander. Referring to Socrates, he claimed he didn't want to give the Athenians a second chance to sin against philosophy. Instead he died in exile of a digestive disease. The orator Demosthenes, Alexander's most vociferous foe in Greece, also escaped Athens after he was accused of bribery in the Harpalus affair and committed suicide on a small Aegean island, assassins sent by Antipater hot on his trail. Craterus, Alexander's loyal lieutenant who had fought with such vigor during the eastern campaign, died in battle early in the wars when he was thrown from his horse. King Porus of India held on to his satrapy after the death of Alexander, only to be treacherously killed several years later by one of Alexander's generals. One-eyed Antigonus, left behind in Asia Minor early in the campaign to deal with rebellious natives, turned his province into a private kingdom until he grew so fat he could no longer lead troops in battle. Seleucus, having rid himself of his friend Perdiccas, extended his personal rule over much of Alexander's former empire, from the Aegean to the steppes of central Asia. The dynasty he established would continue for many years to come, until engulfed by the Parthians in the east and Rome in the west. Ptolemy likewise consolidated his control of Egypt and lived to write his memoirs of the great campaign with Alexander from the Danube to the Indus. His family passed on the throne of the pharaohs for generations until the death of his descendant Cleopatra, who killed herself with the bite of an asp and surrendered Egypt to Rome.

The legacy of Alexander and the powerful influence of Greek culture that he initiated with his short-lived empire spread quickly over Asia, Africa, and Europe in the following centuries. It seems safe to say that without the Macedonian king and his conquests, the philosophy, art, and literature of ancient Greece that have so influenced our lives for more than two thousand years would instead have been only one of many voices in a chorus of ancient civilizations. Alexander's plan to spread Greek culture across three continents was never anything more than a practical and limited means of military control over a diverse population. Like the Persians before him and the Romans after, he didn't particularly care which language the natives spoke or which gods they worshiped as long as they followed his rules. The Hellenic customs he introduced into cities across his realm were largely for the benefit of his Macedonian and Greek colonists, who became the ruling citizens of their regions. He wanted his followers to feel at home whether they served him in Bactria or Babylon. Even the thousands of native youths he trained in the Greek language as part of his new officer corps were never meant to be cultural ambassadors to their people. But the successors of Alexander, especially the heirs of Seleucus, turned the spread of Greek civilization into a tool of sometimes ruthless political dominance, aided greatly by the members of the local nobility who saw that adopting Greek ways was the key to power, wealth, and prestige in the new Hellenistic age.

In India, the influence of Greek culture spread even as direct political control by the Macedonians waned. The kingdoms of the Ganges valley fell under the sway of a powerful ruler named Chandragupta, who founded the Mauryan empire and extended his rule to the Indus River. Twenty years after Alexander had fought so hard to gain control over the area, Seleucus met Chandragupta and ceded sovereignty of his Indian possessions up to the Hindu Kush in exchange for five hundred war elephants to use against his enemies in the west. Seleucus sent an ambassador named Megasthenes to the Indian court who, like Herodotus before him, mixed firsthand observations with dubious local stories to produce the most extensive and influential account of India available to the ancient Mediterranean world.

But even with the withdrawal of Seleucid power from the Indus valley, Greek culture and influence survived in the distant East for centuries. The great Buddhist king and grandson of Chandragupta, Ashoka, expanded the Mauryan empire over much of the subcontinent and set up inscriptions in Greek proclaiming his power. Under the influence of Hellenic artists, images of the Buddha appeared for the first time, dressed like the god Apollo in Greek clothing. The descendants of Macedonian and Greek soldiers continued to dwell in the many Alexandrias the king had established in the East. The largely male population of settlers married local women and created a vibrant hybrid culture. Archaeological excavations at Ai Khanum on the Oxus River have revealed a magnificent city with a Greek theater, a gymnasium, and a mint producing Greek-inscribed coins. In time the Mauryan empire lost control of the upper Indus valley to a series of Greco-Bactrian states ruled by Greek-speaking descendants of Alexander's colonists. Rulers such as Demetrius I maintained contact with the Aegean world, but were much more at home among their mixed Greek and native courts in Bactria and Sogdiana. Even after the rise of the Parthians in Persia severed relations between the Greco-Bactrians and the Mediterranean, the heirs of the original veterans and merchants flourished. The greatest of the Greek rulers of the East was Menander, born near Kabul, who conquered the Punjab and invaded the Ganges valley. He became a Buddhist in spite of his success at war and sponsored a fusion of Greek and Indian art and culture that would long survive the collapse of the Greco-Bactrian kingdoms two hundred years after the death of Alexander.

In Persia, Alexander has long been remembered as both a hero and villain. In the medieval *Shahnameh,* Alexander—or Iskandar, as he came to be known in the Middle East—is a noble Iranian prince of the royal line, but is also vilified as the destroyer of Persian power. The slightly later *Iskandarnameh* portrays the king as an ideal ruler of Greek origin, a philosopher and scientist as well as a warrior, who marries Roxane, daughter of the Great King Darius, and takes the throne, then travels to China and journeys to Mecca. But to the Zoroastrians who still practice the old religion of the Persian kings, he is Alexander the accursed, who destroyed their holy books and soaked the earth in blood. The burning of Persepolis is not forgotten as they tend the sacred fire of Ahuramazda yet today. Even among Muslims in modern-day Iran, Alexander appears as a character in village parades along with the wicked scoundrels of history including Uncle Sam, while mothers threaten naughty children that Iskandar will get them if they misbehave.

Throughout the Middle East, the legacy of Alexander endures. He appears in the Koran as Dhul-Qarnayn, literally "the two-horned one," in reference to his image on ancient coins wearing the horns of his divine father Zeus-Ammon. In the words recorded by Mohammed, he was a philosopher-king "whom God made mighty in the land and gave the means to achieve all things." The Greek learning Alexander introduced into the region survived well into Muslim times and exercised a particular influence on the intellectual history of Shiite Islam.

Jewish culture was also ambivalent about Alexander and the value of Greek civilization. The Jews had prospered under Persian rule and many did not look kindly on the invader from the north. In the biblical book of Daniel, the Macedonian king appears as the last in a line of foreign rulers:

There shall be a fourth kingdom on earth,
that shall be different from all other kingdoms;
it shall devour the whole earth,
and trample it down, and break it to pieces.

As in the Koran, the biblical Alexander has horns, though they are ten in number, representing the evil rulers of the Seleucid line who contended for control of Palestine after his death. Most notable among these was Antiochus IV Epiphanes, who sought to spread Greek culture actively among the Jews. This vision was endorsed by many influential Jewish leaders, who gladly accepted a Greek gymnasium and educational institutions even in Jerusalem. Young Jewish men competed naked in athletic contests alongside Greeks in the shadow of the Temple. Some, ashamed at the circumcision that set them apart from their Greek friends, even underwent a painful operation to restore their foreskins. For the small but dedicated group of Jewish pietists, all this was blasphemy. They launched a war against the Seleucid king, but were beaten down by his troops and a garrison of his soldiers was established on a citadel north of the Temple. Antiochus outlawed Jewish worship and defiled the Holy of Holies, prompting even the most accommodating Jews to rise up against him. They were led by the Hasmonean family, who with their band of guerrilla warriors known as the Maccabees, drove the hated Seleucids and their Greek ways from Jerusalem and reinstated Temple worship—an event still celebrated by the feast of Hanukkah.

But not all Jews were opposed to the influences introduced by Alexander. In Egypt, Jews flocked to the newly established city of Alexandria on the Mediterranean coast and helped transform it into the greatest metropolis of the age. Only a century after the death of the king in Babylon, the Jews of Alexandria were translating their sacred scriptures from Hebrew into Greek as they became more comfortable with the language of Socrates than their native tongue. The result was the Septuagint, a rendering of the Hebrew Bible that became the standard edition for Greek-speaking Jews (and Christians) after them. But the Septuagint was just one of many notable products of the magnificent Hellenistic culture that grew up in Alexandria with the support of the Ptolemaic kings. The city became the center for Greek scholarship in the ancient world, outshining even Athens. Citizens were recruited from all over the Greek world who, along with the Jewish residents and the decidedly second-class native

Egyptians, formed a cosmopolitan center unparalleled in history. The city's famous museum and library became the home of the greatest scientists and scholars of the Hellenistic age. Aristarchus of Samos, who first theorized that the sun was the center of the solar system and the earth revolved on its own axis, was resident in the city, as was the geographer and polymath Eratosthenes of Cyrene, who calculated the circumference of the earth with great accuracy.

But of all the lands that benefited from Alexander's legacy, the one that most embraced Greek culture was a country Alexander never conquered—Rome. The legions seized Macedonia and Greece for their empire two centuries after Alexander, but the captured land in turn exerted a powerful influence on its captors. Any Roman who dared to call himself educated became fluent in Greek and immersed himself in Hellenic philosophy and literature. Not that Romans weren't suspicious of foreign ways and mistrustful of any Greeks bearing cultural gifts inside their walls, but the allure of Greek civilization was too pervasive and powerful to resist. Hellenistic culture spread throughout the Roman world from Syria to Britain. Julius Caesar studied Homer and Herodotus as carefully as any Greek scholar and wept when he saw a statue of Alexander on display at a temple in Spain on the shores of the Atlantic. The Roman general explained his tears by saying he had accomplished so little by the age at which Alexander had died. Augustus also admired Alexander, but more for his unmatched military skill than his ability to govern an empire effectively. Many succeeding emperors modeled themselves on Alexander and tried to match his conquests in the East, though none was able to extend Roman rule beyond Mesopotamia.

The spread of Alexander's Hellenistic culture throughout the Roman world and beyond became a prime factor in the eventual success of Christianity. The New Testament and most other popular early Christian literature were written in the Greek language, not the native Aramaic of Jesus of Nazareth. The almost universal knowledge of Greek allowed the Gospels to be read with equal ease in Jerusalem, Egypt, and Rome. When the Apostle Paul wrote his New Testament letters to the native people of Asia Minor, Greece, or to the Romans themselves, they were composed in the tongue of Alexander. Indeed, one could make a persuasive case that without the conquests of the Macedonian king, the Christian religion would have remained a local phenomenon.

The Greek language was also the initial means for the dispersion of the most famous version of the story of Alexander himself, *The Alexander Romance*. Only a century after the king's death, a collection of entertaining and highly imaginative tales of his life had been published, probably in Egypt. These stories became incredibly popular and were translated over the following centuries into Latin, Aramaic, Hebrew, Arabic, Armenian, Sanskrit, Persian, and many other languages, including Icelandic and the Middle English of Chaucer's age. The stories go far beyond anything recorded in Arrian and the other ancient historians. The Alexander of the *Romance* ascends into the air in a basket carried by eagles, explores the ocean depths in a diving bell, and searches for the fabled Water of Life. Through this collection of stories the classical and medieval world came to know Alexander as the greatest of ancient kings. The legend of Alexander spread even to medieval West Africa, where the famous prince Sundiata listened eagerly to tales of the Macedonian ruler.

There was scarcely a country in the world that did not have its own stories of the great king Alexander. But, as in Persia, not everyone in history has viewed him in a positive light. The Italian poet Dante placed him in the seventh circle of Hell, boiling forever in the very blood of others he so freely shed. Many others since have readily agreed that Alexander was nothing more than a murderous tyrant with a gift for generalship. Views of Alexander have swung back and forth like a pendulum over the centuries, depending on the flow of history and the predisposition of those who have written his story. For the British Victorians, he was a mirror of themselves as enlightened purveyors of civilization through a superior culture backed by a powerful military. This rosy view of Alexander collapsed with the devastating wars of the twentieth century, when the horrific reality of absolute power swept away any romantic notions of benevolent tyranny. Today many modern scholars prefer to see Alexander as little more than a "drunken juvenile thug," as one prominent historian has recently characterized him.

This view of Alexander is much too simplistic. He was a man of his own violent times, no better or worse in his actions than Caesar or Hannibal. He killed tens of thousands of civilians in his campaigns and spread terror in his wake, but so did every other general in the ancient world. If he were alive today, he would undoubtedly be condemned as a war criminal—but he did not live in our age. Like the heroes of Thomas Love Peacock's marvelous satirical poem "The War Song of Dinas Vawr," Alexander conquered much of the ancient world simply because he could:

> The mountain sheep are sweeter,
> But the valley sheep are fatter;
> We therefore deemed it meeter
> To carry off the latter.
> We made an expedition;
> We met a host, and quelled it;
> We forced a strong position,
> And killed the men who held it.

Alexander himself would not have disputed such reasoning nor would those who fell beneath his sword. If the Great King Darius could have crossed the Hellespont and slaughtered every Macedonian in his path to add their land to his empire, he would have done so without remorse.

Whether we approve of Alexander's often brutal tactics, every reasonable student of history must agree that he was one of the greatest military minds of all time. No one but a true genius in battle could have taken on the entire Persian Empire at long odds and fought his way across Asia all the way to India. As for his motives, we err greatly when we try to make Alexander anything more than a man of supreme military ability who wanted passionately to rule the world. Views of the Macedonian king as Prometheus bringing the light of

Greek civilization to the poor masses of Asia are both unsound and insulting to the advanced cultures of the ancient east. To truly understand Alexander we must realize that—perhaps more than any man in history—he hated to lose. Alexander was and is the absolute embodiment of pure human ambition with all its good and evil consequences. We can condemn the death and destruction he left in his wake as he strode across the world like a colossus, but in the end we can't help but admire a man who dared such great deeds.

# GLOSSARY

*Achaemenid:* The Persian royal house from the region near Persepolis. All Persian kings claimed descent from the supposed founder of the line, Achaemenes. The term is used interchangeably for the royal line of kings and the empire itself.

*Achilles:* Greatest Greek hero of the Trojan War. Alexander claimed ancestry from him through his mother and emulated him in his quest for undying fame.

*Ada:* Satrap of Caria until removed by her brother Pixodarus. She was restored to power by Alexander and adopted him as her son.

*Agis:* King of Sparta and devoted foe of Alexander. Tried to reassert Spartan power in Greece in a coalition against Macedonian rule, but was killed in battle against Antipater at Megalopolis in 331.

*Ai Khanum:* Possibly a colony founded by Alexander, this Bactrian Greek city on the banks of the Oxus (Amu Darya) in northern Afghanistan was excavated by the French, who unearthed evidence of a thriving settlement that survived until the mid-second century B.C.

*Alexander IV:* Son of Alexander by Roxane. He was used as a pawn in the wars of succession and killed along with his mother in 310.

*Alexander of Epirus:* Brother of Olympias and king of Epirus. His ties to Macedonia were strengthened when he married Philip's daughter, Cleopatra. He died fighting in Italy in 331.

*Alexandria* (Egypt): Founded by Alexander in 331 on the Mediterranean coast near the westernmost edge of the Nile delta. Ptolemy built a tomb for Alexander here after hijacking his body on its journey back to Macedonia. The city grew to be a major center of Hellenistic civilization with more than a million inhabitants, including a large Jewish community. It was famed for the Pharos lighthouse, museum, and library.

*Alexandria:* The name given to a number of cities founded by Alexander from the Mediterranean to India.

*Ammon:* The major Egyptian god Amun identified by Greeks with Zeus. His oracle at the oasis of Siwa on the modern border between Egypt and Libya was visited by Alexander in 331.

*Antigonus:* A Macedonian nobleman known as Monophthalmus ("one-eyed"), who was a contemporary of Philip's. Alexander appointed him satrap of Phrygia in Asia Minor. He was a major player in the wars of succession after Alexander's death.

*Antipater:* Trusted Macedonian nobleman and lieutenant under Philip. Alexander appointed him regent of Macedonia and Greece while he campaigned in Asia. He defeated Agis of Sparta when he revolted, but later fell from favor and faced replacement by Craterus. An important figure in the struggle for power after the death of Alexander.

*Arabia:* The modern Arabian peninsula that in ancient times was a major source of incense and spices. Alexander was preparing to conquer it when he died in Babylon in 323.

*Aristander:* An influential seer from Telmessus in Lycia skilled at interpreting omens to favor Alexander.

*Aristobulus:* An engineer and architect who accompanied Alexander on his expedition. In his old age, he wrote a flattering account of Alexander that was a major source for Arrian.

*Aristotle:* Student of Plato, tutor of Alexander, and one of the most influential and learned thinkers of ancient times. Born in Stagira in northern Greece in 384, he was the son of the court physician to Alexander's grandfather, King Amyntas III. He spent part of his childhood at the Macedonian court at Pella. He taught Alexander and his young companions at Mieza in Macedonia and maintained contact with his royal pupil throughout his campaigns, receiving scientific specimens from many parts of Asia.

*Arrhidaeus:* Half brother of Alexander and son of Philip II by one of his seven wives, Philinna of Thessaly. Reportedly mentally impaired, he was unexpectedly proclaimed king at Babylon in 323 along with Alexander's infant son. He was a pawn in the hands of the successors and was later murdered by Olympias.

*Arrian:* Most influential ancient biographer of Alexander, Arrian was born in Bithynia and served the Roman government in important political and military offices in Asia. A student of the Stoic philosopher Epictetus, his *Anabasis of Alexander* and *Indica* remain key sources for modern biographers of Alexander.

*Artabazus:* Persian nobleman who revolted against the empire and fled to the Macedonian court in 352. He later returned to Persia and was loyal to Darius until the king's murder. He then joined Alexander and was appointed satrap of Bactria. His daughter Barsine married Memnon and had a long affair with Alexander that produced a son.

*Artaxerxes III:* Also known as Ochos, he ruled Persia from 359 to 338. He put down a revolt of satraps in Asia Minor and reconquered Egypt before he was assassinated. Alexander married his daughter in 324 at the mass wedding in Susa.

*Artaxerxes IV:* Son of Artaxerxes III, he ruled Persia from 338 to 336. He was assassinated and followed on the throne by Darius.

*Athens:* Longtime antagonist of Macedonia, it was one of the major cities of Greece and famed for its naval power.

*Attalus:* Macedonian nobleman and son-in-law of Parmenion. He questioned Alexander's legitimacy as a worthy heir to the throne and was killed soon after Philip's assassination.

*Babylon:* An ancient and celebrated city of Mesopotamia on the Euphrates south of modern Baghdad. It was the capital of the Neo-Babylonian Empire and an important city of the Persian Empire. Alexander visited it in 331 and died there in 323.

*Bactria:* Region in central Asia between the Oxus River on the north and the Hindu Kush mountains to the south, it included much of modern Afghanistan. An important Persia satrapy. Alexander faced some of his fiercest resistance here.

*Bagoas:* Not to be confused with the grand vizier of the same name who murdered two Persian kings, this eunuch, noted for his beauty, was the lover of Darius, then Alexander.

*Barsine:* Daughter of Artabazus and widow of Memnon, she had an affair with Alexander that produced a son named Hercules (Heracles).

*Batis:* Eunuch and governor of Gaza who resisted Alexander's takeover. This so infuriated Alexander that he was dragged behind a chariot around the city walls of Gaza until dead.

*Bessus:* Satrap of Bactria under Darius, he murdered the Great King and assumed the Persian throne to lead resistance to Alexander in the east. He was captured, mutilated, and executed by Alexander.

*Brahmins:* Priestly caste of India, some of whom resisted Alexander and paid with their lives.

*Bucephalas:* Thessalian stallion with an ox-shaped mark tamed by Alexander as a boy and ridden by him in his conquests across the Persian Empire. He died in India and was honored by Alexander, who named a city after him.

*Calanus:* Indian holy man who accompanied Alexander back to Persepolis. He died there in a spectacular public suicide.

*Callisthenes:* Born in Olynthus, a town destroyed by Philip, he was a nephew of Aristotle and official historian of Alexander's expedition. He fell from favor after he opposed Alexander's *proskynesis* policy and was executed for his alleged involvement in the Pages' Conspiracy.

*Caria:* Coastal region of southwest Asia Minor in modern Turkey conquered by Alexander in 334. The chief city was the port of Halicarnassus.

*Carthage:* Phoenician colony and naval power in modern Tunisia founded from Tyre in the early first millennium B.C. It supported Tyre in resisting Alexander and was reportedly on his list for conquest at the time of his death.

*Celts:* A collection of related tribes dominating central Europe at the time of Alexander. Celtic envoys met Alexander on the Danube in 335 and established a treaty of friendship with him.

*Chaeronea:* Town in central Greece where in 338 Philip defeated the Greek forces, including the Sacred Band of Thebes. It was also Alexander's first major battle.

*Chares:* Chamberlain of Alexander from the Greek island of Lesbos who wrote a long and colorful history of court life under the king.

*Cilicia:* Coastal region in southeast Asia Minor near the modern border between Turkey and Syria. Alexander took Tarsus, the chief city of the area, in 333.

*Cleitarchus:* late-fourth-century B.C. historian of Alexander whose lengthy work was a major source for later historians.

*Cleitus the Black:* Macedonian nobleman and brother of Alexander's nurse. He saved Alexander's life at the Granicus but later criticized him at a drinking party in Samarkand and was killed by the drunken king.

*Cleopatra:* A common female name among the Macedonian nobility. One so named was the full sister of Alexander married to Alexander of Epirus, while another was the niece of Attalus and seventh wife of Philip.

*Coenus:* Noted Macedonian soldier who was the son-in-law of Parmenion. He sided against his brother-in-law Philotas in 330, but spoke up for the troops at the mutiny on the Hyphasis River in 326. He died soon thereafter.

*Corinth:* Strategic Greek city west of Athens that was the setting for Philip's League of Corinth, established after the battle of Chaeronea in 338. It provided nominal independence and a unified voice to member Greek city-states, but was in fact dominated by Macedonia.

*Craterus:* Important commander of Alexander's at Issus, Gaugamela, and in the eastern campaigns. He participated in the removal of Philotas and Parmenion. Alexander sent him back to Greece just before his death to escort decommissioned troops and replace Antipater in Greece.

*Curtius Rufus:* Roman historian of the second century A.D. known in his history of Alexander for his rhetorical flourishes and frequent criticisms of the king.

*Cyrene:* Greek colony on the north coast of Africa west of Egypt in modern Libya. It submitted to Alexander in 331.

*Cyrus the Great:* King who founded the Persian Empire and rose during the mid–sixth century from ruler of a small territory subject to the

Median king to master of an empire stretching from central Asia to the Mediterranean.

*Danube:* European river rising in the Alps and emptying into the Black Sea. Alexander crossed it in 335 and subdued the tribes on his northern border before his invasion of Asia.

*Darius I:* Persian nobleman who seized control of the empire in 522 and invaded Greece in 490, only to be defeated by the Athenians at Marathon.

*Darius III:* Became Persian king in 336 after the murder of Artaxerxes IV and fought Alexander at Issus and Gaugamela. He was murdered by Bessus in 330.

*Delphi:* Famous oracle of Apollo in the mountains of central Greece. Alexander visited the holy site soon after becoming king and extracted a favorable prophesy from the priestess of the god.

*Demaratus:* Native of Corinth and veteran of wars in Sicily, he was a friend of Alexander's father who some say bought the famous horse Bucephalas for Alexander. He later accompanied Alexander to Asia and died shortly before the Indian campaign began.

*Demosthenes:* Famed Athenian orator and vociferous opponent of both Philip and Alexander.

*Dion:* Sacred site in southern Macedonia at the foot of Mount Olympus. It was here that Alexander acquired his horse Bucephalas.

*Ecbatana:* Modern Hamadan in western Iran, it was the Median capital and major palace center under the Persian Empire.

*Elam:* An ancient kingdom in the southwest of modern Iran conquered by the Persians. Susa was its largest and most prosperous city.

*Epirus:* Roughly modern Albania, this mountainous region west of Macedonia was the homeland of Alexander's mother, Olympias.

*Gaugamela:* Near modern Mosul in northern Iraq, it was here in October of 331 that Alexander won his decisive victory over Darius.

*Gedrosia:* Inhospitable desert region in southeastern Iran through which Alexander marched his army on the return from India to Babylon.

*Gordian Knot:* Gordium was the capital of ancient Phrygia in central Asia Minor. A famously difficult knot around the yoke of an ancient wagon was undone here in 333 by Alexander, some say by unloosing and others by slashing through it with his sword.

*Granicus:* Modern Kocabas River in northwest Turkey, where Alexander won his first great battle against the Persians in 334.

*Halicarnassus:* Now Bodrum on the southwestern coast of Turkey, it was an important Greek city of Caria holding the celebrated tomb known as the Mausoleum. Alexander took the city after a difficult siege in 334.

*Harpalus:* Boyhood friend of Alexander's from upper Macedonia who served the king as treasurer. He deserted Alexander before the battle of Issus, but was forgiven and reinstated, only to desert him again in 324 before Alexander returned to Babylon.

*Hephaestion:* Boyhood friend and intimate companion of Alexander who rose to important military commands later in the Asian expedition. When he died suddenly at Ecbatana in 324, Alexander was inconsolable and buried his friend with extravagant honors.

*Hercules:* In Greek, Heracles. This is the name of both the famed divine hero of Greek myth—considered an ancestor by Alexander—and the son of the king by his mistress Barsine.

*Herodotus:* Greek historian of the fifth century B.C. from Halicarnassus who wrote a colorful history of much of the known world.

*Hindu Kush:* A mountain range stretching from northern Pakistan to northeast Afghanistan with peaks soaring up to 25,000 feet. Alexander crossed the high passes of this range several times during his campaign.

*Homer:* Famed Greek poet of the eighth century B.C. who composed the *Iliad* and *Odyssey.* Alexander modeled himself on the hero Achilles from the *Iliad* and reportedly slept with a copy of the poem under his pillow.

*Hydaspes:* The modern Jhelum River in Pakistan, where Alexander defeated the Indian king Porus in 326.

*Hyphasis:* The modern Beas River in northern India, where a mutiny of his men forced Alexander to turn back from his planned invasion of the Ganges valley.

*Hyrcania:* Region on the southern shore of the Caspian Sea in modern Iran. Alexander conquered the area in 330.

*Illyria:* Roughly the former Yugoslavia, it was an ancient region of the Balkan peninsula north of Epirus and west of Macedonia. Philip gained control over these lands for Macedon, while Alexander confirmed his power there in an early campaign in 335.

*India:* The ancient name for the lands stretching from the Indus river valley to the East, especially the region of Punjab. For Greeks such as Alexander, the term encompassed the entire subcontinent, including both modern Pakistan and India.

*Isocrates:* Athenian orator and early advocate of a united Greek invasion of Persia.

*Issus:* Along the coastal border between modern Turkey and Syria, in 333 it was the site of a decisive victory of Alexander over Darius.

*Jaxartes:* Flowing into the Aral Sea, the modern Syr Darya was the northeastern boundary of the Persian Empire and the scene of fierce fighting by Alexander. He founded the city of Alexandria Eschate ("the farthest") on its banks.

*Justin:* A Roman who may have lived in the third century A.D. who wrote an epitome of the now lost history of the rule of Alexander's father Philip by Pompeius Trogus.

*Leonidas:* Severe boyhood tutor of Alexander with a reputation for frugality who once rebuked Alexander for using too much incense at a sacrifice. With this in mind, Alexander sent him plentiful frankincense and myrrh seized during his Asian campaign.

*Lydia:* Region of western Asia Minor near the Aegean coast in modern Turkey famous for its cavalry. Its capital Sardis was a key city of the Persian Empire in the west.

*Lysimachus:* One of Alexander's boyhood tutors. He had a special affection for Homer that he instilled in Alexander from his early years. He was rescued by his former pupil when threatened with death from exposure in the mountains above Tyre. This is also the name of one of Alexander's commanders who ruled Thrace after the king's death.

*Macedonia:* The region of modern Greece north of Mount Olympus bordered in ancient times on the east by Thrace, on the south by Thessaly, and on the west by Epirus and Illyria.

*Magi:* Though their exact function is poorly understood, these religious professionals performed sacred rituals and preserved oral history among the Medes and Persians. In Greek tradition, as in the

New Testament nativity story, they were frequently associated with astrology.

*Malli:* A powerful tribe of the Indus River valley. Alexander was almost killed at one of their cities during an assault on its walls.

*Marathon:* Coastal site to the east of Athens where in 490 the Greeks defeated the invading army of the first Great King Darius.

*Mazaeus:* Persian nobleman who served Darius at the battle of Gaugamela, but then quickly switched sides and helped Alexander take over Babylon. Alexander made him satrap of Babylonia, the first Persian he appointed to such a high post.

*Medes:* In Greek thought, Medes were often confused with their cousins the Persians, but they were in fact a separate people from the northern area of modern Iran. Ecbatana was their capital. Cyrus the Great conquered their kingdom and freed the Persian tribes from their control.

*Memnon:* Greek general from the island of Rhodes who served Darius well until his untimely death in 333. He was married to Barsine, daughter of the Persian satrap Artabazus. He fought at the Granicus and held Alexander back at Halicarnassus before eventually withdrawing to continue the war in the Aegean.

*Nearchus:* Boyhood friend of Alexander from Crete. He first served as a satrap in Asia Minor, then as a naval commander on the rivers of India. He led Alexander's fleet back from India to the Tigris, later recording his exploits in a lost text that was a major source for the historian Arrian.

*Olympia:* Town in western Greece where the Olympic games were held every four years.

*Olympias:* Wife of Philip and mother of Alexander. Born in Epirus, she was brilliant, resourceful, ambitious, and sometimes cruel as she strove to assure Alexander's place on the throne of Macedonia. After Philip's death, she remained in Macedonia, though in close communication with Alexander while he conquered Persia.

*Olympus:* By tradition the seat of the gods, this towering mountain almost ten thousand feet high marked the southern boundary of Macedonia.

*Olynthus:* Greek city on the Chalcidic peninsula to the east of Macedonia destroyed by Philip in 348 after it intrigued with Athens against him. It was the home of Alexander's official historian, Callisthenes.

*Onesicritus:* Greek student of the philosopher Diogenes who served as helmsman for Alexander's fleet. His lost work described India and portrayed Alexander as a philosopher as much as a warrior.

*Oxus:* The modern Amu Darya, which rises on the northern border of Afghanistan and flows into the Aral Sea. It was the northern border of ancient Bactria.

*Pages' Conspiracy:* An alleged murder plot in 327 by the sons of Macedonian nobles who served Alexander as attendants. Callisthenes was falsely accused of conspiring with the pages and executed.

*Parmenion:* Macedonian nobleman and chief general of Philip who also served Alexander. He is frequently portrayed in the ancient sources as overly cautious in contrast to the daring young Alexander. He was killed on Alexander's orders in 330 soon after the execution of his son Philotas.

*Pasargadae:* Royal Persian burial site near Persepolis where the tomb of Cyrus the Great still stands.

*Pausanius:* A young bodyguard of Philip who murdered him in 336 after reportedly suffering vile abuse at the hands of Philip's companions.

*Pella:* A notable city of Macedonia as revealed by archaeological excavations. It replaced Vergina (ancient Aegae) as administrative capital in the late fifth century B.C.

*Perdiccas:* A common name among Macedonian nobility, Perdiccas, son of Orontes, was a military leader and bodyguard of Alexander's who succeeded Hephaestion as cavalry commander in 324. He was chosen as guardian of Alexander's son by Roxane, but perished in the wars of the successors.

*Persepolis:* A chief residence of the Persian kings in the heartland of ancient Persia near modern Shiraz, Iran. Alexander burned the palace there in 330, but accounts of his motives vary. Excavations have revealed an impressive city with stunning royal reliefs.

*Persians:* A people of Indo-Iranian speech related to the Medes and more distantly to the tribes of northern India. They were originally warlike tribesmen from the region around Persepolis, but through Cyrus and his successors gained control of the largest empire the world had yet known.

*Peucestas:* A Macedonian who saved Alexander's life during an assault on an Indian city of the Malli. He was promoted to bodyguard and eventually satrap. He was one of the few important Macedonians genuinely to embrace Alexander's policy of orientalism.

*Philip of Acarnania:* Greek physician who saved Alexander's life in 333 before the battle at Issus.

*Philip II:* Alexander's father, husband of Olympias, and man chiefly responsible for turning Macedonia from a struggling secondary power into a mighty empire. He was murdered in 336.

*Philotas:* Oldest son of Parmenion, he was condemned to death by Alexander's order in 330, closely followed by the murder of his father.

*Phoenicia:* Roughly equivalent to modern Lebanon, this coastal land of the cities Tyre and Sidon was the home of the wide-ranging Phoenicians.

*Plutarch:* Born in the mid–first century A.D., a biographer of famous Greeks and Romans who was a favorite source for Shakespeare. Native to Chaeronea in central Greece, he wrote a moralistic account of Alexander that is our only significant source on the king's early life.

*Porus:* King of the Pauravas in the Punjab region of India, Porus was reportedly a brave and honorable king who fought Alexander well at the battle at the Hydaspes River in 326, but was pardoned and reinstated to his throne afterward. He was later murdered by the Macedonian commander at Taxila.

pothos: A Greek word indicating a deep desire or yearning. It was used by the historian Arrian to describe the motive of many of Alexander's more audacious and questionable actions.

proskynesis: A Greek word used for religious worship, but applied to varying acts of obeisance performed before the Persian king. Alexander's efforts to incorporate proskynesis into his court ceremonies met heated resistance by the Macedonians.

*Ptolemy:* Childhood friend and trusted military commander of Alexander's on his campaign against the Persians. He later seized Alexander's body and became king of Egypt, founding a dynasty that ended with the celebrated Cleopatra. His lost memoirs on Alexander's expedition were a key source for later historians, especially Arrian.

*Punjab:* Literally "the land of the five rivers" stretching across northern regions of modern Pakistan into India. Alexander campaigned here in 326.

*Roxane:* Daughter of the Bactrian nobleman Oxyartes. She married Alexander in 327 just before his invasion of India. Her son, Alexander IV, was his father's only legitimate heir. Both she and her son were murdered in 311.

*Samarkand:* Ancient Markanda, the capital of ancient Sogdiana, lies on the old Silk Road in Uzbekistan. It was a center of Alexander's campaigns starting in 329.

*Sardis:* Ancient capital of Lydia in western Asia Minor, it surrendered to Alexander in 334.

*sarissa:* An iron-tipped wooden spear up to eighteen feet long used with devastating effect by the well-drilled Macedonian infantry.

*satrap:* A Persian term borrowed by Alexander for the governor of a province.

*Scylax:* Sailor from Caria in Asia Minor who served the first Great King Darius and explored the sea route from India to Egypt.

*Seleucus:* Known later as Nicator ("conqueror"), he served in Alexander's later campaigns and gained control of Babylonia after Alexander's death. He founded a dynasty that for a time ruled much of Alexander's Asian empire.

*Semiramis:* Legendary queen of Babylon who reportedly led an army through the Gedrosian desert, losing almost all her soldiers on the way.

*Sisyngambris:* Mother of Darius captured at Issus, she was reportedly treated with great respect by Alexander and committed suicide in grief after his death.

*Siwa:* A large oasis on the modern border between Libya and Egypt. It was home of the oracle of Ammon, visited by Alexander in 331.

*Sogdiana:* Ancient region to the north of Bactria that encompasses much of modern Tajikistan and Uzbekistan. Alexander campaigned here beginning in 329.

*Sparta:* Greek city renowned for its military prowess. It had faded in power by Alexander's day, but under its king Agis it rose to challenge Macedonian control of southern Greece, only to be soundly defeated by Alexander's regent Antipater.

*Spitamenes:* Nobleman of Sogdiana who led the resistance to Alexander after the death of Bessus. He staged an effective guerrilla war against the Macedonians for more than a year before being captured and executed.

*Susa:* The ancient capital of Elam in what is now southwestern Iran, it was an administrative capital of the Persians. Alexander took the city without bloodshed in 331 and staged a mass wedding here in 324.

*Taxila:* An ancient city in the northern Indus valley near modern Islamabad, Pakistan. Its king was an early ally of Alexander in India.

*Thebes:* Famous city of central Greece defeated and destroyed by Alexander in 335 as a warning to all who would resist him.

*Thermopylae:* Narrow pass in central Greece where the Spartans and their allies held back the entire invading Persian army in 380 before they were killed to a man.

*Thessaly:* Region just to the south of Macedonia famous for its cavalry.

*Thrace:* Land to the east and north of Macedonia inhabited by warlike tribes.

*Triballi:* Tribe on the Danube defeated by Alexander in 335 during his early campaign in the northern Balkans. They afterward contributed soldiers to his Asian campaign.

*trireme:* A type of swift and formidable Greek warship propelled by three ranks of rowers with a bronze battering ram in the prow.

*Troy:* City on the Hellespont in northwest Asia Minor that was the scene of the Trojan War of Greek legend. Excavations at its ruins near modern Canakkale in Turkey have revealed a complex site dating back thousands of years before Alexander's visit in 334.

*Tyre:* Ancient Phoenician city, once an offshore island, on the coast of modern Lebanon that was long besieged and finally taken by Alexander in 332.

*Vergina:* Ancient Aegae, this hillside town overlooks the coastal plains of Macedonia. Excavations here have revealed spectacular royal tombs of the Macedonian kings, including the burial place of Philip. It was also at the theater here that Philip was murdered.

*Zoroaster:* Greek form of the Persian prophet Zarathushtra, who established a religious tradition based on the opposition of the forces of darkness and light, with Ahuramazda as supreme god.

# Source Notes

## Author's Note and Acknowledgments

xxi   *Epigraph:* Arrian *Anabasis* Book 1, preface.


## 1. Macedonia

1   *Epigraph:* Plutarch *Alexander* 3.

1   *The solitary messenger:* Plutarch *Alexander* 3. I am indebted to Green *Alexander of Macedon* 1–3 for the image of the courier riding from Olympia to Philip's camp.

3   *he commanded a special silver coin be struck:* See Arnold-Biucchi, *Alexander's Coins and Alexander's Image*, 47.

3   *the land of Macedonia:* For two excellent and sometimes contradictory introductions to Macedonia and the early history of its royal family, see Hammond, *The Macedonian State*, and Borza, *In the Shadow of Olympus*.

4   *the savage land of Thrace:* Herodotus 5.3–8.

5   *to yell at his guards in Macedonian:* Plutarch *Alexander* 51. See also Plutarch *Eumenes* 14. The question of Macedonian language and ethnic identity is one of the most contentious topics in classical scholarship, the debate often driven more by modern Balkan nationalism than the small amount of ancient evidence we actually possess. I incline to the argument that Macedonian was a distant dialect of Greek rather than a separate language. In any case, the practical result in the age of Alexander was that the Macedonians considered themselves and were considered by others as non-Greeks.

6   *According to the Greek historian Herodotus:* Herodotus 8.137–139.

7    *when the Persians invaded nearby Thrace:* Herodotus 5.18–22.

7    *He was even chosen as Persian ambassador to Athens:* Herodotus 8.140–144.

7    *the final battle at Plataea in 479:* Herodotus 9.44.

8    *After Alexander was assassinated:* Curtius 6.11.

8    *Perdiccos was murdered by his illegitimate son Archelaus:* Plato *Gorgias* 471.

9    *an unsuccessful plot by his wife, Eurydice:* Justin 7.4.

10   *a hostage to the Greek city of Thebes:* Justin 7.5.

11   *four thousand Macedonian soldiers lay dead on the battlefield:* Diodorus Siculus 16.2.

11   *Philip quickly arrested and executed one brother:* Diodorus Siculus 16.3.

12   *Discipline came first:* Diodorus Siculus 16.3; Aelian *Varia Historia* 14.48.

13   *an attack on the Illyrians led by Bardylis:* Diodorus Siculus 16.4.

15   *"It is said that while still a young man":* Plutarch *Alexander* 2 (the text mistakenly calls Arybbas her brother, but I have accepted the emendation "brother of her father"). The exact year of this meeting and the ages of Philip and Olympias are uncertain.

15   *twin gods known as the Cabiri:* Herodotus 2.51.

16   *Later stories say that on the night:* Plutarch *Alexander* 2.

17   *an enormous snake:* Plutarch *Alexander* 2–3.

17   *the great temple of the goddess Artemis:* Plutarch *Alexander* 3; Cicero *On Divination* 1.47.

18   *Alexander's boyhood at Pella:* Plutarch *Alexander* 4–5.

18   *As Alexander said in later years:* Plutarch *Alexander* 22.

18   *He was so parsimonious:* Plutarch *Alexander* 25.

19   *Lysimachus:* Plutarch *Alexander* 5.

19   *One of the earliest stories about Alexander:* Plutarch *Alexander* 5; Curtius 6.5; Diodorus Siculus 16.52.

19   *"Boys, my father is beating me to everything":* Plutarch *Alexander* 5.

20   *Saint Paul:* Acts 16.

20   *Philip laid siege to Methone:* Diodorus Siculus 16.31, 34. An ivory miniature from Vergina identified as Philip bears a scar above

the right brow. A broken skull from the same site, claimed by some to belong to Philip, is from a man with a damaged right eye.

20   *the city of Olynthus:* Diodorus Siculus 16.8.

21   *Have any of you been paying attention:* Demosthenes *Olynthiac* 1.12–13.

21   *The embassy the Athenians sent to Pella:* Aeschines *Against Timarchus* 166–169.

22   *a horse named Bucephalas:* Plutarch *Alexander* 6; Diodorus Siculus 17.76; Gellius *Attic Nights* 5.2; Arrian 5.19; Pliny *Natural History* 8.44.

23   *"Are you fool enough to criticize your elders?":* Plutarch *Alexander* 6.

24   *"My son, you must seek out a kingdom":* Plutarch *Alexander* 6.

24   *Aristotle:* Plutarch *Alexander* 7–8; Diogenes Laertes 5.1.

27   *Plutarch describes Alexander:* Plutarch *Alexander* 4.

27   *a beautiful Thracian prostitute named Callixeina:* Athenaeus 10.435.

27   *sex and sleep:* Plutarch *Alexander* 22.

27   *only if he could compete against kings:* Plutarch *Alexander* 4.

28   *the king left his son at Pella as regent:* Plutarch *Alexander* 9.

29   *Chaeronea:* Diodorus Siculus 16.84–86.

31   *he called for a general assembly:* Diodorus Siculus 16.89; Tod *Greek Historical Inscriptions* #177.

32   *Philippeum:* Pausanias 5.20.9–10.

33   *Philip had no sooner returned to Pella:* Plutarch *Alexander* 9–10.

34   *"Look, everyone!":* Plutarch *Alexander* 9.

34   *"The bull is ready for slaughter":* Diodorus Siculus 16.91.

35   *Demaratus of Corinth:* Plutarch *Alexander* 9.

35   *Pixodarus:* Plutarch *Alexander* 10; Diodorus Siculus 16.74.

37   *Your dreams soar higher than the sky:* Diodorus Siculus 16.92.

## 2. GREECE

39   *Epigraph:* Plutarch *Alexander* 11.

39   *Pausanias:* Diodorus Siculus 16.93–94; Justin *Epitome* 9.6–7;

Plutarch *Alexander* 10.

41 *The reported actions of Olympias:* Justin 9.7. Justin (11.2) mentions a son of Philip and Cleopatra named Caranus, but most scholars believe he was a later invention.

42 *Plutarch records:* Plutarch *Alexander* 10.

42 *"The giver of the bride":* Plutarch *Alexander* 10; Euripides *Medea* 289.

42 *a grand tomb at Vergina:* Discovered and excavated by Manolis Andronikos in 1977.

43 *Alexander, from Lyncestis:* Arrian *Anabasis* 1.25; Justin 11.2.

43 *an assembly of the troops:* Justin 11.1.

44 *Attalus:* Diodorus Siculus 16.93, 17.2, 5; Justin 9.5; Curtius 7.1, 8.1.

45 *the Greek cities:* Diodorus Siculus 17.3–4; Plutarch *Demosthenes* 23.

47 *Alexander summoned the League of Corinth:* Diodorus Siculus 17.4; Arrian *Anabasis* 1.1; Plutarch *Alexander* 14.

49 *"If I were not Alexander":* Plutarch *Alexander* 14.

49 *the sacred site of Delphi:* Plutarch *Alexander* 14.

49 *There was no time for Alexander:* The best source for the northern campaign is Arrian *Anabasis* 1.1–6.

50 *Poneropolis: Fragmenta der griechischen Historiker:* 115 F 110.

52 *Ptolemy reports:* Arrian *Anabasis* 1.2.

52 *Danube:* Hesiod *Theogony* 339. See also Herodotus 4.47–51.

53 *Getae:* Herodotus 4.93–94.

53 *Darius, the Great King of Persia:* Herodotus 4.89–143.

53 *a pothos, in Greek:* Arrian *Anabasis* 1.3.

54 *The soldiers took their tent covers:* Xenophon *Anabasis* 1.5.

55 *Triballi:* Arrian *Anabasis* 1.4; Diodorus Siculus 17.3–4.

55 *The Celts:* Arrian *Anabasis* 1.4.

56 *From the Danube, Alexander struck southwest:* For Alexander's Illyrian campaign, see Arrian *Anabasis* 1.5–6.

59 *the Greek states had once again risen against him:* Arrian *Anabasis* 1.7–10; Diodorus 17.8–15; Plutarch *Alexander* 11–13; Justin 11.3–4.

60    *as Arrian wisely observes:* Arrian *Anabasis* 1.7.

63    *As Diodorus says:* Diodorus Siculus 17.9.

65    *According to Plutarch:* Plutarch *Alexander* 12.

66    *the news of the destruction of Thebes:* Arrian *Anabasis* 1.10; Diodorus Siculus 17.15.

66    *Phocion:* Plutarch *Phocion* 17.

67    *Alexander and his men marched home to Macedonia:* Arrian *Anabasis* 1.11; Diodorus Siculus 17.16.

# 3. ASIA

69    *Epigraph:* Isaiah 45.1.

69    *There was once a king named Astyages:* Herodotus 1.107–123.

72    *"Neither snow nor rain":* Herodotus 8.98. This, of course, was borrowed from the Greek historian as the unofficial motto of the U.S. Postal Service.

72    *"to ride horses, to shoot the bow, to speak the truth":* Herodotus 1.136.

72    *Alexander at last began his war against Persia:* Arrian *Anabasis* 1.11; Justin 11.5; Plutarch *Alexander* 15; Diodorus Siculus 17.17.

73    *Protesilaus:* Herodotus 9.116.

74    *When the Great King Xerxes had crossed the Hellespont:* 7.34–36.

74    *and cross from Elaeus:* Arrian *Anabasis* 1.11; Diodorus Siculus 17.17.

74    *Alexander's first act in Asia:* Arrian *Anabasis* 1.11–12; Diodorus Siculus 17.17; Plutarch *Alexander* 15.

75    *"I care little for that harp":* Plutarch *Alexander* 15.

76    *Alexander's greatest regret, he lamented:* Arrian *Anabasis* 1.12.

76    *From Troy, Alexander moved north:* Arrian *Anabasis* 1.12; Justin 11.6.

77    *the Granicus River:* Arrian *Anabasis* 1.13–16; Diodorus Siculus 17.19–21; Plutarch *Alexander* 16.

79    *Arrian describes a similar dialogue: Anabasis* 1.18, 2.25, 3.10, 18.

82    *Alexander son of Philip and all the Greeks:* Arrian *Anabasis* 1.16.

82    *He appointed his cavalry commander Calas:* Arrian *Anabasis* 17.

83    *Life on the campaign:* Plutarch *Alexander* 23.
84    *From the Granicus, Alexander marched south:* Arrian *Anabasis* 17;
      Diodorus Siculus 17.21; Plutarch *Alexander* 17.
85    *"If Croesus sends a great army against Persia":* Herodotus 1.53–86.
87    *the coastal city of Ephesus:* Arrian *Anabasis* 1.17.
87    *"Great is Artemis of the Ephesians":* Acts 19.28.
88    *The famous painter Apelles:* Pliny *Natural History* 35.92.
89    *Miletus:* Arrian *Anabasis* 1.18; Diodorus Siculus 17.22–23.
89    *The dedicatory inscription:* Tod #184. It is now at the British
      Museum in London.
91    *the reasons given by the historian Arrian:* Arrian *Anabasis* 1.20.
92    *Halicarnassus:* Arrian *Anabasis* 1.20–23; Diodorus Siculus 17.23–27.
94    *At the seaside town of Iasus:* Pliny *Natural History* 9.8; Tod #190.
98    *into the wild highlands of Lycia:* Arrian *Anabasis* 1.24.
98    *According to one story:* Polyaenus 5.35.
98    *the Xanthus River:* Plutarch *Alexander* 17; Arrian *Anabasis* 1.24.
99    *a disturbing report from Parmenion:* Arrian *Anabasis* 1.25; Dio-
      dorus Siculus 17.32; Justin 11.7; Curtius 3.7, 7.1.
99    *a very high rent for nine months in her womb:* Arrian *Anabasis*
      7.12.
100   *Mount Climax:* Arrian *Anabasis* 1.26; Diodorus Siculus 14.3.9.
101   *a local tribe known as the Marmares:* Diodorus Siculus 17.28.
101   *Pamphylia:* Arrian *Anabasis* 1.26–28.
102   *Gordium:* Arrian *Anabasis* 1.29–2.3; Curtius 3.1.9.
104   *Memnon:* Arrian *Anabasis* 2.1–2; Diodorus Siculus 17.29–31;
      Curtius 3.1.19–21.

## 4. Issus

107   *Epigraph:* Arrian *Anabasis* 2.7.
107   *The story of the Gordian knot:* Arrian *Anabasis* 2.3; Curtius
      3.1.14–18; Plutarch *Alexander* 18; Justin 11.7.
108   *There was an alternate tradition:* Herodotus 7.73, 8.138.
108   *The second year of Alexander's campaign:* Arrian *Anabasis* 2.4; Cur-
      tius 3.1.22–4.15; Plutarch *Alexander* 18.

109　*Xenophon's army:* Xenophon *Anabasis* 1.2.21.

110　*plunge naked into the Cydnus River:* Curtius 3.5; Arrian *Anabasis* 2.4; Plutarch *Alexander* 19; Justin 11.8.

110　*the Cydnus was famed for its healing properties:* Strabo 14.5.12; Pliny *Natural History* 31.11.

112　*a new silver coin:* Arnold-Biucchi #7 (page 51).

113　*Sardanapalus:* Arrian *Anabasis* 2.5.

114　*Amphilochus:* Strabo 14.5.16.

114　*Harpalus:* Arrian *Anabasis* 3.6.

114　*from reading Xenophon:* Xenophon *Anabasis* 1.4.

114　*Darius:* Curtius 3.2; Diodorus Siculus 17.31; Arrian *Anabasis* 2.8.

115　*Issus:* Arrian *Anabasis* 2.7–11; Curtius 3.8–11; Polybius 12.17; Diodorus Siculus 17.32–35; Plutarch *Alexander* 20–21; Justin 11.9.

120　*the camp of Darius:* Arrian *Anabasis* 2.11–12; Curtius 3.11–13; Plutarch *Alexander* 20; Diodorus Siculus 17.35–38.

120　*"So this is what it means to be a king":* Plutarch *Alexander* 20.

122　*Alexander called a formation:* Arrian *Anabasis* 2.12; Curtius 3.12.

122　*the Syrian city of Damascus:* Curtius 3.13; Arrian *Anabasis* 2.11, 15; Plutarch *Alexander* 21; Justin 11.10; Polyaenus 4.5; Pliny *Natural History* 7.29; Strabo 13.1.27.

124　*Pharnabazus:* Arrian *Anabasis* 2.13.

125　*Alexander broke camp at Issus:* Arrian *Anabasis* 2.13–15; Plutarch *Alexander* 24; Curtius 4.1; Diodorus Siculus 39.1–2.

128　*Sidon:* Arrian *Anabasis* 2.15; Curtius 4.1.15; Diodorus Siculus 16.45.

128　*Tyre:* Arrian *Anabasis* 2.15–24; Curtius 4.1–4; Diodorus Siculus 17.40–46; Plutarch *Alexander* 24–25; Justin 11.10.

129　*"Do you really think you are safe":* Curtius 4.2.5.

130　*Herodotus relates:* Herodotus 4.42.

131　*The Greek alphabet:* Herodotus 5.58.

131　*the high priest in Jerusalem:* Josephus *Jewish Antiquities* 11.8.

136　*a giant sea monster:* Diodorus Siculus 17.41.

139　*Josephus:* Josephus *Jewish Antiquities* 11.8.

139   *envoys from the Great King:* Arrian *Anabasis* 2.25; Curtius 4.5; Diodorus Siculus 17.48.

140   *Gaza:* Arrian *Anabasis* 2.25–27; Curtius 4.6; Herodotus 3.5.

142   *Cambyses:* Herodotus 3.9–12.

## 5. EGYPT

143   *Epigraph:* Herodotus 2.35.

143   *the writings of Herodotus:* Herodotus 2, 3.17–26, 4.181.

144   *Apis:* Herodotus 3.27–29.

145   *Alexander's fleet:* Arrian *Anabasis* 3.1; Curtius 4.7.

146   *Heliopolis:* Herodotus 2.3; Strabo 17.27.

146   *Memphis:* Herodotus 2.153, 3.27–28.

147   *where the king went from Memphis:* Arrian *Anabasis* 3.1; Curtius 4.7–8.

147   *Callisthenes deep into Ethiopia:* Rose Aristotle fragment 246.

149   *he needed a new port:* Arrian *Anabasis* 3.1–2; Plutarch *Alexander* 26; Curtius 4.8; Diodorus 17.52; Justin 11.11; Strabo 17.1.6–8.

149   *There is an island:* Plutarch *Alexander* 26 quoting Homer *Odyssey* 4.354–355.

149   *a* pothos *or desire seized Alexander:* Arrian *Anabasis* 3.1.

150   *Hegelochus:* Arrian *Anabasis* 3.2; Curtius 4.5.

151   *a decree to the people of Chios:* Todd #192.

151   *Siwa:* Arrian *Anabasis* 3.3–4; Plutarch *Alexander* 26–27; Curtius 4.7; Diodorus Siculus 17.49–51; Strabo 17.1.42–43.

152   *Pindar sang his praises:* Pindar *Pythian* 4.16; Scholion on *Pythian* 9.53, fragment 36.

156   *the Spring of the Sun:* Herodotus 4.181.

157   *O paidon:* Plutarch *Alexander* 27.

158   *as the historian Arrian says:* Arrian *Anabasis* 3.4.

158   *Ptolemy:* Arrian *Anabasis* 3.4. See also Wood 78–82 and the superb details of the *Barrington Atlas of the Greek and Roman World,* maps 73–75.

160   *Back at Memphis:* Arrian *Anabasis* 3.5; Curtius 4.8; Strabo 17.1.43.

161    *One grateful Egyptian bureaucrat named Petosiris:* Kuhrt 2007,
       1.460–461.

## 6. MESOPOTAMIA

163    *Epigraph:* Babylonian Astronomical Diary for 331 B.C. (Kuhrt
       1.447).
163    *Samaritans:* Curtius 4. 8; Eusebius *Chronicles* 2.223, 229; Cross
       "Papyri of the Fourth Century B.C. from Daliyeh."
164    *Tyre:* Arrian *Anabasis* 3.6; Plutarch *Alexander* 29; Curtius 4.8.
167    *the wife of Darius:* Plutarch *Alexander* 30; Diodorus 17.54; Cur-
       tius 4.10; Justin 11.12.
167    *camp followers:* Plutarch *Alexander* 31.
168    *the Macedonians at last reached the town of Thapsacus:* Arrian
       *Anabasis* 3.7.
169    *the Great King was moving his army:* Arrian *Anabasis* 3.7; Dio-
       dorus Siculus 17.53.
171    *The Macedonians arrived at the Tigris:* Arrian *Anabasis* 3.7; Cur-
       tius 4.9; Diodorus Siculus 17.55.
171    *an extraordinary event occurred:* Arrian *Anabasis* 3.7; Curtius
       4.10; Plutarch *Alexander* 31.
171    *fragmentary Babylonian tablet:* Kuhrt 1.447.
172    *Ariston:* Arrian *Anabasis* 3.7–8; Curtius 4.9.
173    *camel:* Plutarch *Alexander* 31.
173    *Alexander ordered his troops:* Arrian *Anabasis* 2.9–11.
176    *"Why, don't you know we've already won?":* Plutarch *Alexander* 32.
176    *The army of Darius:* Arrian *Anabasis* 3.11.
177    *He now set out with his cavalry force:* Arrian *Anabasis* 3.13–15;
       Curtius 4.12–16; Diodorus Siculus 17.57–61; Plutarch *Alexan-
       der* 33; Justin 11.14.
179    *the broken Babylonian tablet again records:* Kuhrt 1.447.
180    *the citizens of Greece were horrified:* Diodorus Siculus 17.61; Cur-
       tius 6.1; Justin 12.1.
182    *Ecbatana:* Arrian *Anabasis* 3.16; Diodorus Siculus 17.64; Curtius
       5.1; Polybius 10.27.

183     *a pool of bitumen:* Plutarch *Alexander* 25; Curtius 5.1; Herodotus 1.179; Strabo 16.1.15.

183     *the biblical story of Noah:* Genesis 6.14.

184     *Alexander continued the march south:* Curtius 5.1; Arrian *Anabasis* 3.16.

186     *Babylon:* Herodotus 1.179–200; Curtius 5.1; Arrian *Anabasis* 3.16; Strabo 16.1.5; Diodorus Siculus 17.64

187     *Hammurabi:* Pritchard 163–180.

188     *He gave strict orders to his men:* Kuhrt 1.447.

189     *dining requirements:* Polyaenus 4.3.32.

190     *Chaldeans:* Strabo 16.1.6; Plutarch *Alexander* 57; Hesiod *Theogony.* The Babylonian creation epic *Enuma Elish* is found in many translations, including Pritchard 60–72.

192     *the biblical patriarch Abraham:* Genesis 11–12.

192     *Gilgamesh:* The cuneiform tablets containing *The Epic of Gilgamesh* have been recovered by archaeologists in the last century. One of best modern editions is that of Kovacs.

193     *Susa:* Curtius 5.2; Diodorus Siculus 17.65–66; Arrian *Anabasis* 3.16; Plutarch *Alexander* 36; Allen 65–72.

## 7. Persepolis

197     *Epigraph:* Christopher Marlowe *Tamburlaine the Great Part I.*

197     *the Uxians:* Arrian *Anabasis* 3.16; Curtius 5.3; Diodorus Siculus 17.67; Strabo 15.3.4.

199     *the Persian Gates:* Arrian *Anabasis* 3.18; Curtius 5.3–4; Diodorus Siculus 17.68: Plutarch *Alexander* 37.

203     *a race to reach the capital:* Arrian *Anabasis* 3.18; Diodorus Siculus 17.69; Curtius 5.5; Justin 11.14.

203     *Persepolis:* Diodorus Siculus 17.70–72; Curtius 5.6–7; Plutarch *Alexander* 37–38; Arrian *Anabasis* 3.18; Justin 11.14; Allen 72–81.

205     *I am Darius:* Kuhrt 2.488.

209     *Pasargadae:* Strabo 15.3.7–8; Arrian *Anabasis* 6.29; Plutarch *Alexander* 69.

210    *Mortal man:* Arrian *Anabasis* 6.29; Plutarch *Alexander* 69.

213    *Thaïs:* Diodorus Siculus 17.72; Curtius 5.7; Plutarch *Alexander* 38; Arrian *Anabasis* 3.18; Strabo 15.3.6.

214    *to capture the king:* Arrian *Anabasis* 3.19–21; Curtius 5.8.

## 8. BACTRIA

220    *Epigraph:* Arrian *Anabasis* 3.28.

221    *But to the Macedonian army:* Curtius 6.2–3; Diodorus Siculus 17.74. The paraphrase of Alexander's speech to his men is based on the Curtius passage.

223    *Hyrcania:* Arrian *Anabasis* 3.23–25; Diodorus Siculus 17.75–77; Strabo 11.7.2; Curtius 6.4–5; Plutarch *Alexander* 44–46; Herodotus 1.203.

225    *Lysimachus:* Plutarch *Alexander* 46.

226    *Satibarzanes:* Arrian *Anabasis* 3.25.

227    *taking on the ways of a foreign king:* Diodorus 17.77; Plutarch *Alexander* 45; Curtius 6.6.

228    *Philotas:* Plutarch *Alexander* 48–49; Arrian 3.26–27; Curtius 6.7–7.2; Diodorus 17.79–80; Justin 12.5; Strabo 15.2.

229    *Drangiana:* Arrian *Anabasis* 3.28; Diodorus 17.81–83; Curtius 7.3.

237    *Khawak Pass:* Arrian *Anabasis* 3.28; Diodorus Siculus 17.83; Curtius 7.3. For the description of the pass, I am indebted to Lane Fox 294–297 and Wood 138–147.

238    *down from the Khawak Pass:* Arrian *Anabasis* 3.28–29; Curtius 7.4–5; Diodorus Siculus 17.83.

239    *Arrian:* Arrian *Anabasis* 3.29.

240    *Branchidae:* Curtius 7.5.

241    *Sogdiana:* Arrian *Anabasis* 3.30–4.7; Curtius 7.5–11.

249    *some good news:* Arrian *Anabasis* 4.7, 15; Curtius 7.10.

250    *Alexander renewed his campaign:* Arrian *Anabasis* 4.15–17; Curtius 7.10, 8.1.

252    *Cleitus:* Plutarch *Alexander* 50–52; Arrian *Anabasis* 4.8–9; Curtius 8.1–2; Justin 12.6; Lucian *Rhetorum Praeceptor* 5–6.

253    *Euripides:* Euripides *Andromache* 693–700.

256    *When the end came for Spitamenes:* Curtius 8.2–4; Arrian *Anabasis* 4.17–18.

256    immodicus amor: Curtius 8.3.2.

258    *the Sogdian Rock:* Arrian *Anabasis* 4.18–21; Curtius 7.11, 8.4.

## 9. India

261    *Epigraph:* Herodotus 3.98.

261    *thirty thousand native youths:* Arrian *Anabasis* 7.6; Curtius 8.5; Diodorus Siculus 17.108; Plutarch *Alexander* 71.

262    proskynesis: Plutarch *Alexander* 53–55; Arrian *Anabasis* 4.10–14; Curtius 8.5–8; Justin 12.7; Athenaeus *Deipnosophistae* 13.556b.

262    *Herodotus says:* Herodotus 1.134.

263    *One clever Theban envoy:* Aelian *Varia Historia* 1.21.

263    *Spartan visitors:* Herodotus 7.136.

265    *Alexander and his army left Bactria:* Arrian *Anabasis* 4.22–5.4; Curtius 8.9–12; Plutarch *Alexander* 57–58; Diodorus Siculus 17.85–86.

269    *Scylax:* Herodotus 4.44.

269    *Herodotus:* Herodotus 3.38, 98–106, 4.40.

270    *Alexander and his army crossed the Indus:* Arrian *Anabasis* 5.3–8; Curtius 8.12–13; Diodorus Siculus 17.86. See also Wheeler 1968, 102–122.

273    *the plain of the Hydaspes:* Arrian *Anabasis* 5.8–19; Plutarch *Alexander* 60–61; Curtius 8.13–14; Diodorus Siculus 17.87–89; Justin 12.8.

276    *"Like a king":* Plutarch *Alexander* 60; Arrian *Anabasis* 5.19.

276    *invade eastern India:* Arrian *Anabasis* 5.20–29; Diodorus Siculus 17.89–95; Plutarch *Alexander* 62; Curtius 9.1–3.

278    *Eight years ago, the king declared:* The speech is paraphrased from Arrian *Anabasis* 26, and Curtius 9.2.

280    *twelve towering altars:* Arrian *Anabasis* 5.29; Diodorus Siculus 17.95; Curtius 9.3; Plutarch *Alexander* 62; Justin 12.8.

280    *The journey back to the Hydaspes:* Arrian *Anabasis* 5.29–6.3; Diodorus Siculus 17.95–96; Curtius 9.3.

281 *the voyage:* Arrian *Anabasis* 6.4–20; Diodorus Siculus 17.96–104; Curtius 9.3–9; Plutarch *Alexander* 63–66.

282 *his old friend Aristobulus:* Lucian *Quomodo historia conscribenda sit* 12.

282 *he had never learned to swim:* Plutarch *Alexander* 58.

282 *just like his hero Achilles:* Homer *Iliad* 21.

285 *"Alexander, brave deeds are what true men do":* Arrian *Anabasis* 6.13.

286 *native religions:* Arrian *Anabasis* 6.7, 16, 7.1–2; Plutarch *Alexander* 64–65; Diodorus Siculus 17.102–103.

287 *One story tells:* Arrian *Anabasis* 7.1.


## 10. BABYLON

290 *Epigraph:* Arrian *Anabasis* 7.16.

291 *the march ahead through the Gedrosian desert:* Arrian *Anabasis* 6.21–26; Diodorus Siculus 17.104–105; Curtius 9.10; Plutarch *Alexander* 66–67.

291 *plainly stated by the historian Arrian:* Arrian *Anabasis* 7.24.

294 *They were so heartened, says Arrian:* Arrian *Anabasis* 7.26.

294 *The final leg of the journey from Paura to Persepolis:* Arrian *Anabasis* 6.27–28, *Indica* 34; Plutarch *Alexander* 67; Diodorus Siculus 17.106–108.

296 *The story of the voyage of Nearchus:* Arrian *Indica* 19–43; Diodorus Siculus 17.106; Strabo 15.5–14.

303 *future conquests:* Arrian *Anabasis* 7.1, 16; Plutarch *Alexander* 68; Curtius 10.1.

304 *the Phoenician voyage he had read of in Herodotus:* Herodotus 4.42.

305 *the satrap Abulites:* Plutarch *Alexander* 68; Arrian *Anabasis* 7.4.

306 *the Indian wise man Calanus:* Arrian *Anabasis* 7.3; Plutarch *Alexander* 69; Diodorus Siculus 17.107.

306 *a mass wedding that winter at Susa:* Arrian *Anabasis* 7.4; Plutarch *Alexander* 70; Diodorus Siculus 17.108.

308 *The crisis came to a head:* Arrian *Anabasis* 7.7–12; Plutarch *Alexander* 71; Diodorus Siculus 17.109.

309    *one of the most impassioned speeches of his life:* Paraphrased from
       Arrian *Anabasis* 7.9–10.
310    *Olympias, and his aging regent, Antipater:* Arrian *Anabasis* 7.12–
       13, 28; Plutarch *Alexander* 74–75.
311    *Ecbatana:* Arrian *Anabasis* 7.14, 23; Plutarch *Alexander* 72; Dio-
       dorus Siculus 17.110–115; Justin 12.12.
314    *Cossaeans:* Arrian *Anabasis* 7.15, *Indica* 40; Plutarch *Alexander*
       72; Diodorus Siculus 17.111.
315    *As Alexander at last drew near to the walls of Babylon:* Arrian
       *Anabasis* 7.16–30; Diodorus Siculus 17.112–118; Plutarch *Alex-
       ander* 73–77; Justin 12.13–16.
315    *the Greek playwright Euripides:* Arrian *Anabasis* 7.16.

## 11. TO THE ENDS OF THE EARTH

319    *Epigraph:* Arrian *Anabasis* 7.30.
319    *rumors began to circulate that the king had been murdered:* Arrian
       *Anabasis* 7.27; Diodorus Siculus 17.118; Plutarch *Alexander* 77.
320    *There is a sad and charming story:* Arrian *Anabasis* 7.27.
320    *Alexander's death:* The events immediately following the death of
       Alexander are best preserved, with the usual rhetorical flourish,
       in Curtius 10.5–10.
325    *he appears in the Koran:* "The Cave" 18.82–89.
325    *In the biblical book of Daniel:* Daniel 7.23.
328    *The Italian poet Dante:* Inferno Canto 12.107.
329    *"drunken juvenile thug":* Mary Beard "A Don's Life" (timesonline.
       typepad.com/dons_life/) July 3, 2009.

# BIBLIOGRAPHY

## ANCIENT SOURCES

The ancient sources for the life of Alexander are plentiful but problematic. Unlike Julius Caesar, whose firsthand accounts of the war in Gaul and struggle for Rome survive, Alexander wrote nothing himself that has come down to us aside from a few decrees recorded in inscriptions and fragments from a handful of possibly genuine letters quoted by later authors. Thus the search for accurate accounts of Alexander becomes very much like the quest for the historical Jesus or Socrates. As with these two famous figures from antiquity, our knowledge of Alexander is ultimately dependent on records left by those who knew him, whether friends or enemies. However, even the biographies of Alexander written during his lifetime or soon after his death disappeared from Greek and Roman libraries by late antiquity. This leaves us with only secondhand accounts penned by historians in Roman times who had access to these earlier sources.

None of this means that the search for the historical Alexander is hopeless—far from it. But we do have to be keenly aware of the problems associated with our sources. Even accounts written by those who knew and traveled with Alexander have their own agenda. Some contemporaries despised the Macedonian king and missed no opportunity to denigrate him as a murderous drunkard craving eternal glory at any cost. Others portrayed him as a noble and kindly soul, the paradigm of a just ruler. Like every modern historian, each ancient biographer was deeply influenced by the circumstances in which he wrote and by his own prejudices.

The ancient sources on Alexander begin with Callisthenes, the nephew of Aristotle and native of the Greek city of Olynthus, a town destroyed by Alexander's father, Philip. Alexander chose Callisthenes to accompany him on his expedition and send back flattering reports of his heroic exploits to the Greeks. Callisthenes undoubtedly harbored much ill will toward the royal house of Macedonia for obliterating his hometown, but he obliged Alexander with obsequious propaganda until the king had him executed. His reports were widely available, at least in part, to most of the ancient biographers of Alexander.

One of the most important early biographers of Alexander was his boyhood friend Ptolemy, son of Lagus, later the pharaoh of Egypt. Ptolemy was by Alexander's side from the first campaigns on the Danube to the final days in Babylon. As a lifelong companion with intimate knowledge of Alexander's life, he could hardly be a better source—except that Ptolemy had a vested interest in portraying his friend in a positive light. Writing from Alexandria in his later years, he needed a heroic and admirable Alexander to strengthen his own legitimacy as a successor and ruler of Egypt. Even so, Ptolemy was not a sycophant and was a crucial source on the details of Alexander's military conquests for later writers, especially Arrian.

Another eyewitness to Alexander's journey was the Greek engineer Aristobulus. He accompanied Alexander on his expedition and was responsible for numerous projects, such as the restoration of the tomb of Cyrus. His account of Alexander is uniformly positive, often to a suspicious degree. He may be forgiven his selective memory somewhat as he was in his eighties when he composed his history. Many stories of Alexander's chivalry, such as his treatment of the women in the Persian royal household, come originally from the pen of Aristobulus. He was not a soldier, but had a keen eye for geography and natural science, which is evident in Arrian's and Strabo's borrowings from his text.

Nearchus of Crete was another childhood friend of Alexander's who accompanied him on his campaign. He is an essential source for later writers on Alexander's campaigns in India, and the best source for his own voyage as admiral of the fleet returning from the Indus to Persia.

Other firsthand accounts of Alexander's campaigns survived in ancient times, but their subject matter ranges from dubious anecdotes to scandalous rumors. The Greek Onesicritus was a pupil of the cynic philosopher Diogenes and helmsman on the fleet returning from India. He wrote a highly flattering account of Alexander as a philosopher-king, while his descriptions of India and the Brahmans were much used by later historians. Chares, from the Greek island of Lesbos, served as court chamberlain to Alexander in his final years. His gossipy memoir of life behind the throne took up ten books and was used by several later biographers, especially his descriptions of the *proskynesis* controversy and the mass marriage at Susa. A pamphlet by Ephippus, also of Olynthus, preserved several lurid tales of luxury quoted by Athenaeus. The otherwise unknown Nicobule wrote in the same vein. Medius of Thessaly is best remembered as the host of the Babylonian dinner at which Alexander's fatal decline began. He later wrote a flattering account of Alexander, perhaps to deflect charges that he had poisoned the king. Polyclitus, another Thessalian, may also have accompanied Alexander's expedition because he offers detailed geographical data quoted by Strabo. The remaining eyewitnesses who wrote of Alexander's campaign are known only by name or in brief fragments.

Other contemporary records such as the logbooks of the expedition, the personal notebooks of Alexander, and the letters of the Macedonian leader quoted frequently by Plutarch are of questionable value at best. Some of the letters may be genuine, but others are later creations, as are the alleged logbooks and probably the notebooks as well.

One early record of Alexander comes not from an eyewitness but from someone too young to accompany the expedition to Asia. Cleitarchus was the son of the Greek historian Dinon, who wrote a history of Persia known for its sensationalism. His son continued the family tradition with an action-packed thriller on Alexander's conquests. Written just a few years after the king's death, this multivolume work was widely read in the Greek and Roman world. Cleitarchus was able to study official accounts of the expedition during his research in Athens and Alexandria, but could also draw on the oral tradition from interviews with returning veterans to gain multiple perspectives of battles and other key events.

All these earliest sources on the life of Alexander are now lost. What we do possess are the works of later historians who used them and passed their information down to us in part. One group of historians, known in modern times as the vulgate tradition, used Cleitarchus as its primary source but supplemented his work with other authors. Diodorus of Sicily wrote a forty-volume history of the world up until his lifetime in the first century B.C., which presents Alexander as a model king. Drawing on the same tradition, Diodorus' contemporary Trogus of Gaul, whose work survives only in an epitome by the third-century Latin writer Justin, more often condemns Alexander as a bloody tyrant. The Roman historian Curtius, who probably wrote during the reign of the Roman emperor Claudius, similarly criticizes Alexander in a highly rhetorical history full of invented speeches.

The biographer Plutarch also drew on the vulgate tradition, but read widely from other sources as well. He was born in the middle of the first century A.D. in the Greek town of Chaeronea, the very place Alexander's father Philip won his decisive battle against the Greeks. As he himself admits, his aim was not to write a historical biography but rather a morally instructive life story for readers. He is generally positive in his view of Alexander, but can be critical as well. Plutarch preserves our only detailed account of Alexander's early years.

Pride of place among Alexander's biographers, however, belongs to Arrian of Bithynia. He was born in the late first century A.D. and was educated by the famous Stoic teacher Epictetus and preserved the high moral teachings of his master in a handbook known as the *Enchiridion.* But Arrian was no academic recluse. He held high political office and served in the Roman army as a field commander in battles across Asia Minor. His history of Alexander is not perfect by any means, but it offers a detailed and balanced picture of a remarkable man marred by very human flaws. Arrian's primary sources were Ptolemy and Aristobulus.

Many other Greek and Latin writers from the ancient world also mention Alexander. Strabo refers to him frequently in his *Geogra-*

*phy,* while Athenaeus quotes many passages from lost authors in the course of his grand dinner party of philosophers. Non-Greek sources are rare, but there are a few native references to Alexander, such as Babylonian astronomical records.

The remaining ancient evidence for Alexander is more tangible. We possess a number of valuable inscriptions from Greece and elsewhere recording decrees issued by the king or accounts of his activities. Coins issued by Alexander as payment and propaganda survive from the Mediterranean to India. Archaeology as well has revealed fascinating details about Alexander and his world. Excavations in Turkey, Iraq, Iran, Afghanistan, and of course the dazzling discoveries from the royal Macedonian tombs at Vergina in northern Greece have brought to life the world of Alexander like nothing else.

## MODERN SOURCES

Readers wishing to explore the modern literature on Alexander have a vast array of book and articles available to them—but be aware that there are as many Alexanders as there are those who write about him.

Political circumstances have influenced modern scholars as much as ancient authors. The work of W. W. Tarn, written during the waning days of the British Empire, remains important, though his overly positive assessment of Alexander finds little favor among scholars today. Most recent writers on Alexander provide a more mixed picture of his character, though I have read few modern scholars who seriously question his military genius.

For a general introduction, I highly recommend Paul Cartledge's *Alexander the Great,* a learned and wonderfully readable collection of studies on different stages of Alexander's life. For a gripping and insightful biography there is none better than *Alexander the Great* by Robin Lane Fox. Along with Fox, Peter Green's darker portrait in *Alexander of Macedon* should be on everyone's reading list. If you want to follow Alexander's arduous path from Greece to India and back to Babylon, you should read Michael Wood's *In the Footsteps of Alexander the Great,* preferably while you watch the companion PBS video.

Just a few of the more specialized studies on Alexander that I would recommend are Waldemar Heckel's *Who's Who in the Age of Alexander the Great,* a useful book for keeping straight the many Persians and Macedonians who inconveniently bear the same name. Frank Holt's works on Alexander in Bactria and India are marvelous guides to the eastern campaigns, especially his *Into the Land of Bones: Alexander the Great in Afghanistan.* Important recent scholarship on ancient Persia includes Amélie Kuhrt's collection of primary sources in *The Persian Empire,* Pierre Briant's monumental study *From Cyrus to Alexander,* and Lindsay Allen's *The Persian Empire.* For the afterlife of Alexander and his legend, the books of Richard Stoneman are essential.

Allen, Lindsay. *The Persian Empire.* Chicago: University of Chicago Press, 2005.

Andronicos, Manolis. *Vergina: The Royal Tombs.* Athens: Ekdotike Athenon, 1993.

Arnold-Biuchhi, Carmen. *Alexander's Coins and Alexander's Image.* Cambridge, Massachusetts: Harvard University Art Museums, 2006.

Ashley, James R. *The Macedonian Empire.* Jefferson, North Carolina: McFarland & Company, 1998.

Borza, Eugene N. *In the Shadow of Olympus: The Emergence of Macedon.* Princeton: Princeton University Press, 1990.

Bosworth, A. B. *Alexander and the East: The Tragedy of Triumph.* Oxford: Clarendon Press, 1996.

———. *Conquest and Empire: The Reign of Alexander the Great.* Cambridge: Cambridge University Press, 1988.

———. *A Historical Commentary on Arrian's History of Alexander,* 2 vols. Oxford: Clarendon Press, 1980, 1995.

Bosworth, A. B., and Baynham, E. J., eds. *Alexander the Great in Fact and Fiction.* Oxford: Oxford University Press, 2000.

Briant, Pierre. *From Cyrus to Alexander: A History of the Persian Empire.* Winona Lake, Indiana: Eisenbrauns, 2002.

Brosius, Maria. *The Persians.* New York: Routledge, 2006.

Carney, Elizabeth. *Olympias: Mother of Alexander the Great.* New York: Routledge, 2006.

Cartledge, Paul. *Alexander the Great.* New York: Vintage Books, 2004.

———. *The Spartans.* New York: Vintage Books, 2004.

———. *Thermopylae.* New York: Vintage Books, 2007.

Cohen, Ada. *The Alexander Mosaic: Stories of Victory and Defeat.* Cambridge: Cambridge University Press, 2000.

Cross, Frank Moore. "Papyri of the Fourth Century B.C. from Daliyeh" in Freedman, David Noel, and Greenfield, Jonas C., eds., *New Directions in Biblical Archaeology,* 41–62. New York: Doubleday, 1969.

Cunliffe, Barry. *Europe Between the Oceans: 9000 BC–AD 1000.* New Haven: Yale University Press, 2008.

Curtis, Vesta Sarkhosh. *Persian Myths.* Austin: University of Texas Press, 1993.

Dahmen, Karsten. *The Legend of Alexander the Great on Greek and Roman Coins.* New York: Routledge, 2007.

Engels, Donald W. *Alexander the Great and the Logistics of the Macedonian Army.* Berkeley: University of California Press, 1980.

Fildes, Alan, and Fletcher, Joann. *Alexander the Great: Son of the Gods.* Los Angeles: The J. Paul Getty Museum, 2002.

Fox, Robin Lane. *Alexander the Great.* New York: Penguin, 2004.

———. *The Search for Alexander the Great.* Boston: Little, Brown and Company, 1980.

Green, Peter. *Alexander of Macedon, 356–323 B.C.: A Historical Biography.* Berkeley: University of California Press, 1991.

———. *Alexander to Actium.* Berkeley: University of California Press, 1990.

Hamilton, J. R. *Plutarch: Alexander.* Oxford: Oxford University Press, 1969.

Hammond, N.G.L. *Alexander the Great: King, Commander and Statesman.* Bristol: The Bristol Classical Press, 1989.

———. *The Macedonian State: The Origins, Institutions and History.* Oxford: Clarendon Press, 1989.

———. *Sources for Alexander the Great.* Cambridge: Cambridge University Press, 1993.

———. *Three Historians of Alexander the Great.* Cambridge: Cambridge University Press, 1983.

Hanson, Victor Davis. *A War Like No Other.* New York: Random House, 2005.

Heckel, Waldemar. *The Conquests of Alexander the Great.* Cambridge: Cambridge University Press, 2008.

———. *Who's Who in the Age of Alexander the Great.* Malden, Massachusetts: Blackwell Publishing, 2006.

Heckel, Waldemar, Tritle, Lawrence, and Wheatley, Pat, eds. *Alexander's Empire: Formulation to Decay.* Claremont, California: Regina Books, 2007.

Heisserer, A.J. *Alexander the Great and the Greeks: The Epigraphic Evidence.* Norman, Oklahoma: University of Oklahoma Press, 1980.

Holland, Tom. *Persian Fire.* New York: Anchor Books, 2007.

Holt, Frank L. *Alexander the Great and Bactria.* New York: Brill, 1993.

———. *Alexander the Great and the Mystery of the Elephant Medallions.* Berkeley: University of California Press, 2003.

———. *Into the Land of Bones: Alexander the Great in Afghanistan.* Berkeley: University of California Press, 2005.

———. *Thundering Zeus: The Making of Hellenistic Bactria.* Berkeley: University of California Press, 1999.

Hyde, Walter Woodburn. *Ancient Greek Mariners.* New York: Oxford University Press, 1947.

Ivantchik, Askold, and Licheli, Vakhtang, eds. *Achaemenid Culture and Local Traditions in Anatolia, Southern Caucasus and Iran.* Leiden: Brill, 2007.

Kagan, Donald. *The Peloponnesian War.* New York: Penguin, 2004.

Kent, Roland G. *Old Persian.* New Haven: American Oriental Society, 1953.

Kovacs, Maureen. *The Epic of Gilgamesh.* Palo Alto, California: Stanford University Press, 1989.

Kuhrt, Amélie. *The Persian Empire: A Corpus of Sources from the Achaemenid Period,* 2 vols. New York: Routledge, 2007.

Mossé, Claude. *Alexander: Destiny and Myth.* Baltimore: Johns Hopkins University Press, 2004.

Olmstead, A. T. *History of the Persian Empire.* Chicago: University of Chicago Press, 1948.

Parker, Grant. *The Making of Roman India*. Cambridge: Cambridge University Press, 2008.

Pearson, Lionel. *The Lost Histories of Alexander the Great*. Philadelphia: American Philological Association, 1960.

Pollard, Justin, and Reid, Howard. *The Rise and Fall of Alexandria*. New York: Penguin, 2006.

Pritchard, James B., ed. *Ancient Near Eastern Texts Relating to the Old Testament*. Princeton: Princeton University Press, 1955.

Renault, Mary. *The Nature of Alexander*. New York: Pantheon Books, 1975.

Roisman, Joseph, ed. *Alexander the Great: Ancient and Modern Perspectives*. Lexington, Massachusetts: D. C. Heath and Company, 1995.

———. *Brill's Companion to Alexander the Great*. Leiden: Brill, 2003.

Romm, James S. *The Edges of the World in Ancient Thought*. Princeton: Princeton University Press, 1992.

Romm, James S., ed. *Alexander the Great: Selections from Arrian, Diodorus, Plutarch, and Quintus Curtius*. Indianapolis: Hackett Publishing, 2005.

Ross, David. *The Works of Aristotle: Volume XII Selected Fragments*. Oxford: Clarendon Press, 1952.

Sedlar, Jean. *India and the Greek World*. Totowa, New Jersey: Rowman and Littlefield, 1980.

Spencer, Diana. *The Roman Alexander*. Exeter: University of Exeter Press, 2002.

Stark, Freya. *Alexander's Path*. Woodstock, New York: The Overlook Press, 1988.

Stevenson, Rosemary B. *Persica: Greek Writing about Persia in the Fourth Century BC*. Edinburgh: Scottish Academic Press, 1997.

Stoneman, Richard. *Alexander the Great*. New York: Routledge, 1997.

———. *Alexander the Great: A Life in Legend*. New Haven: Yale University Press, 2008.

———. *The Greek Alexander Romance*. New York: Penguin, 1991.

Strassler, Robert B., ed. *The Landmark Herodotus*. New York: Pantheon Books, 2007.

———. *The Landmark Thucydides*. New York: Touchstone, 1998.

Talbert, Richard J. A., ed. *Barrington Atlas of the Greek and Roman World.*
     Princeton: Princeton University Press, 2000.
Tarn, W. W. *Alexander the Great: Volume II Sources and Studies.* Cam-
     bridge: Cambridge University Press, 1948.
———. *The Greeks in Bactria and India.* Chicago: Ares Publishers, 1984.
Thomas, Carol G. *Alexander the Great in His World.* Malden, Massachu-
     setts: Blackwell Publishing, 2007.
Tod, Marcus N. *Greek Historical Inscriptions From the Sixth Century B.C.*
     *to the Death of Alexander the Great in 323 B.C.* Chicago: Ares Pub-
     lishers, 1985.
Tuplin, Christopher, ed. *Persian Responses: Political and Cultural Interac-*
     *tion with(in) the Achaemenid Empire.* Swansea: The Classical Press of
     Wales, 2007.
Wheeler, Mortimer. *Flames Over Persepolis.* London: Weidenfeld and
     Nicolson, 1968.
Wood, Michael. *In the Footsteps of Alexander the Great.* Berkeley: Univer-
     sity of California Press, 1997.
Woodard, Roger D., ed. *The Ancient Languages of Asia Minor.* Cambridge:
     Cambridge University Press, 2008.
———. *The Ancient Languages of Mesopotamia, Egypt, and Aksum.* Cam-
     bridge: Cambridge University Press, 2008.
———. *The Cambridge Encyclopedia of the World's Ancient Languages.* Cam-
     bridge: Cambridge University Press, 2004.
Worthington, Ian, ed. *Alexander the Great: Man and God.* Harlow, En-
     gland: Pearson Education Limited, 2004.
———. *Alexander the Great: A Reader.* New York: Routledge, 2003.
———. *Philip II of Macedonia.* New Haven: Yale University Press, 2008.

# ILLUSTRATION CREDITS

1. Sarissa spear formation: Rob Shone/Getty Images
2. Mount Olympus: Philip Freeman
3. Acropolis of Athens: Alison Dwyer
4. Tomb of Philip: Philip Freeman
5. Ruins of Troy: Philip Freeman
6. Priene inscription: British Museum
7. Halicarnassus: Philip Freeman
8. Tyre: Frank and Helen Schreider/Getty Images
9. Alexander mosaic: Museo Archeologico Nazionale, Naples/Getty Images
10. Pyramids at Giza: Philip Freeman
11. Palace of Darius: DEA/W. BUSS/Getty Images
12. Tomb of Cyrus the Great: Dmitri Kessel/Getty Images
13. Hindu Kush mountains: Grant Dixon/Getty Images
14. Coin celebrating victory over Indian king Porus: British Museum
15. Coin minted by Lysimachus: British Museum

# INDEX